Warsaw in Exile

Warsaw in Exile

Stefan Korboński

Translated from the original Polish by
DAVID J. WELSH

FREDERICK A. PRAEGER, *Publishers*
NEW YORK · WASHINGTON

BOOKS THAT MATTER

Published in the United States of America in 1966
by
FREDERICK A. PRAEGER, INC., *Publishers*
111 Fourth Avenue, New York 3, N.Y.

© *George Allen & Unwin Limited, 1966*

Translated from
W. IMIGNIU POLSKI WALCZACE
© *B. Świderoki, London, 1963*

Library of Congress Catalog Card Number: 66-12476

Printed in Great Britain

INTRODUCTION

Stefan Korbonski was born at Praszka, in Poland, in the year 1903. Educated at a school in Czestochowa, he left in December 1918, volunteered for the Polish army, took part in the defence of Lwow against the Ukrainians, and then went back to school. In 1920, during the Polish-Russian war, he enlisted again, and in 1921 fought against the Germans in the Silesian uprising. On leaving the army he studied law at Poznan University, entered the ranks of the Polish Peasant Party in 1925, and in 1929 set up in practice as a lawyer in Warsaw. Continuing his political activities, he was elected in 1936 chairman of the Peasant Party in the Bialystok province, and member of the party court.

After the outbreak of war in 1939 he was taken prisoner of war by the invading Soviet forces, but managed to escape from the transport to Russia and returned to Warsaw, where he joined the anti-German underground. In 1940 he represented the underground Peasant Party on the Political Committee, which was at that time the supreme underground authority. In 1941 he was appointed chief of Civil Resistance, taking orders from the Delegate of the Government, the official title of the political head of the underground Polish state. The underground parliament was the Council of National Unity, and the fighting force the Armia Krajowa (Home Army), known as the AK, part of which were the Peasant battalions, 167,000 strong, recruited from the peasant youth.

As the chief of Civil Resistance, he established underground radio communication with the Polish government-in-exile, in London, informing it daily about all happenings in Poland, especially about the extermination of the Jewish people. He organized underground courts of justice which condemned about 200 Gestapo agents to death, and these sentences were also carried out. He organized the general resistance of the Polish nation, including sabotage in industry, transport and agriculture, and boycott of the laws and decrees issued by the German occupier.

In January 1942 the Russians, having decided that the communists should also have an underground movement in Poland, formed in Warsaw the Polish Workers' Party (PPR) and the People's Guard, later renamed the People's Army. Under the German occupation, the two undergrounds confined themselves to infiltrating and observing each other, the communists being few by comparison with the members of the national underground.

Following the death of General Sikorski in an aeroplane accident at Gibraltar in July 1943, Stanislaw Mikolajczyk, a prominent member of the Polish Peasant Party, became head of the government-in-exile. In November of that year Wladyslaw Gomulka became secretary-general of the Polish Workers' Party, and on December 31st Boleslaw Bierut, a Soviet-trained political exile in Moscow, assumed the presidency of the so-called National Council of the Homeland.

On August 1, 1944, the Poles in Warsaw rose against the Germans and, under General Tadeusz Komorowski (General Bor), commander-in-chief of the Home Army since General Rowecki's arrest by the Gestapo, carried on the heroic struggle until the rising was finally crushed on October 2nd. During this period the author assumed the additional duties of Director of the Department of the Interior in the underground government. On December 31st the provisional government of Poland was established in Lublin under the auspices of the Russians, with Bierut as president, the Socialist Osóbka-Morawski, another tool of the Soviets, as premier, and Gomulka as his deputy.

It was early in 1945 that the national underground came into conflict with the Polish Workers' Party and the Peoples' Army. On March 28th sixteen leaders of the underground were invited by the Russians to a talk, then abducted to Moscow and imprisoned in the Lubianka. They included Vice-Premier Jan Jankowski, Delegate of the Government, and General Niedzwiadek-Okulicki, who had succeeded General Bor as commander-in-chief of the Home Army. Colonel Jan Rzepecki replaced General Okulicki, with the title of Delegate for the Armed Forces in Poland, while the author was appointed acting Delegate of the Government in place of Vice-Premier Jankowski.

Great Britain and the United States having provisionally agreed to recognize the Lublin government on the understanding that, *inter alia*, it should be extended to include democratic as well as communist elements, Mikolajczyk, who had resigned from the premiership of the government-in-exile in November 1944 (the Peasant Party withdrawing at the same time), visited Moscow in June 1945. After discussions there with the Russians and members of the Lublin government, he became joint Vice-Premier with Gomulka of the Government of National Union, which was established in Warsaw on June 28, 1945.

Already the Lublin government had called upon members of all underground organizations and groups to report to the Ministry of Public Security. Both Colonel Jan Rzepecki and the author were among those who failed to report to the authorities. Rzepecki went free for the time being, but on June 28, 1945, the author and his wife Zosia were arrested in Cracow and imprisoned in Warsaw until released at the end of July by order of the Council of Ministers.

With this ends Korbonski's first book entitled *Fighting Warsaw*, which is actually the story of the Polish Underground State in the period 1939-45. This is where his second book *Warsaw in Chains* begins.

The day after leaving prison, Korbonski started overt activity within the ranks of the anti-communist Polish Peasant Party, in which he had successively held the posts of chairman of the district of Warsaw, member of the supreme council, and member of the chief executive committee. From that moment on, Korbonski had to live in a world of paradox. On the one hand, as the last head of the Polish Underground State, he had been subjected to constant surveillance, wire-tapping, and provocations on the part of the communist Security Police, which was under the orders of the Soviet NKVD. Incidentally, the NKVD had in the meantime managed to arrest Colonel Rzepecki. On the other hand, Colonel Smirnoff, the Soviet Judge-Advocate, calls Korbonski a leader of the Polish nation, and quotes testimony given by him before the Nuremberg tribunal. On the one hand, the remaining members of the Polish guerrilla units, who were being mopped up in the woods and given wholesale death sentences by the communist military courts, were turning to Korbonski for instructions. On the other hand, he was receiving visits from soldiers of the Polish underground who took advantage of the amnesty announced by the new Polish government and wanted to return to normal life. Though recently Korbonski had been a political prisoner held by the Security Police and, as such, had been interrogated by its high-ranking dignitaries, he was now visiting some of those dignitaries as an attorney and leader of the Polish Peasant Party, seeking release of its members who had been unjustly arrested as well as the release of former members of the Polish underground. The main area of Korbonski's activity was Warsaw, still a city of ruins and a cemetery of more than 200,000 people who perished there during the Uprising. Their bodies were now being exhumed in large numbers from every little

A*

backyard, park or public square, and a cadaverous odour hovered over the entire city. Korbonski describes the pilgrimages the entire Warsaw population made to the Cemetery of the Insurgents, in which the prime of Warsaw's youth had been buried. Later, he gives a colourful account of Warsaw slowly coming back to life; how on New Year's Eve the city became the site of boisterous parties in which he and his wife, Zosia, took active part.

As they toured the whole country they had an opportunity to see the gas chambers and piles of human ashes at Stutthoff, former Nazi concentration camp. They saw the glorious landscape of Poland's western Recovered Territories. One night, they would wander through a ruins of Wroclaw, a city transformed into a desert, and give alms to German beggars. Another day, they would bask in the sun on a Baltic beach, dividing their attention between the police agents who watched them, and the ships moving wondrously across the horizon towards the dream-like free West.

All these events and impressions Korbonski registers day after day, offering the reader a faithful picture of life in Poland at the turn of two epochs, separated by the Second World War. That life was being choked more and more by the iron tentacles of the communist octopus, and was changing right before his eyes into a nightmare of captivity. The daily threat of arrest hanging over Korbonski contrasted sharply with the normal, sometimes even gay, life, he and his wife were living. As a result, a somewhat grim humour pervades almost every story he tells. All this contributes to the atmosphere full of peculiar charm that emanates from the pages of his book.

With all the difficulties and risks surrounding him, Korbonski played a big part in the activities of his party in its fight against the communist dictatorship. Korbonski describes the so-called referendum in which 83% of the Polish people gave a negative answer to the questions put to them by the communist government. Korbonski also participated in the preliminary election campaign during which 118 leaders of his party were murdered by the Security Police and nearly 100,000 of its members were arrested. Among them were 162 candidates for Parliament. Even though on election day, January 19, 1947, 68% of the votes were cast in favour of the Polish Peasant Party, it won only twenty-eight seats in Parliament out of a total of 444, as a result of fraud committed by the communist-controlled election boards.

Korbonski, who was one of the twenty-eight, having been elected a deputy to represent the City of Warsaw, gives a shocking account of the farce into which the communists had turned the ceremony of the opening of Parliament and the 'election' of Boleslaw Bierut, a communist, to the office of President of Poland. Shortly thereafter, Korbonski took part in a debate on the new amnesty law aimed against the anti-communist underground of which Korbonski was the last head and which was still in existence. While seeking the release of all those arrested, Korbonski launched a vigorous campaign against the lawlessness and terror of communist rule. A speech he delivered at that time sealed his fate. Korbonski was found intransigent and the communists decided to strip him of parliamentary immunity and to arrest him in the Parliament building. A communist dignitary whose life Korbonski had saved during the Warsaw Uprising tipped him off.

The final chapters of *Warsaw in Chains* have the ring of a dramatic count-down. The communist notable told Korbonski the probable date of his arrest, so that he and his wife were able to make preparations accordingly. Finally, the tip-off man signalled the time for the escape and the Korbonski's disappeared from Warsaw without leaving a trace. Soon, they were able to reach the Baltic coast. Mikolajczyk's unexpected escape to England, undertaken some time earlier, had put the entire Security Police on the alert, and the coastal region had been placed under special watch. Nevertheless, the Korbonski's, using a disguise, managed to get aboard the *Drottning Victoria*, a Swedish ship, which took them to Trelleborg, Sweden.

Their escape became a front-page story in Sweden and a world sensation. During the few days of their stay in Stockholm, they successfully withstood an attempt to kidnap them by the agents of the Polish Security Service, who posed as officials of the Polish Embassy. The Swedish authorities hurriedly put the Korbonski's aboard an airliner bound for New York. An unidentified fellow passenger greeted them with these words. 'Welcome to the Free World. God bless you!'

This is the end of Korbonski's second book *Warsaw in Chains*, a faithful account of life in Poland, in the first three years after the establishment of communist rule. At this point his third book *Warsaw in Exile* begins.

CONTENTS

ILLUSTRATIONS

I

'ALL COLUMBUS'S FAULT'

We landed at New York's La Guardia airfield in the afternoon of November 26, 1947, in a group consisting of Mikolajczyk, the Baginskis, Zosia, myself and Zaleski, our secretary. When the door of the aircraft opened over a dozen people invaded the interior, and instead of making our way to the exit we found ourselves in a crowd of people, stretching out their hands to greet us. Amidst unknown faces I immediately recognized Arthur Bliss Lane, the former American Ambassador to Poland, who introduced us to Congressman Sadlak, Dimitrov, leader of the Bulgarian exiles, and others.

My first experience on American soil came on the platform of the steps drawn up to the plane, from which I looked down upon a battery of cameras pointed at us. Suddenly the entire human load of the aircraft wanted to leave with us, so as to appear before the cameras, and the stream pushed Zosia and me back into the interior as they rushed by. Thanks to the efforts of Bliss Lane, we were extricated and reached the bottom of the steps. The flashes of bulbs, the shouts and manoeuvring of photographers, the roar of aircraft engines converging from all directions and the sight of the vast hangars are still associated in my mind with my first glimpse of the New World. But the advice of one of the Polish contributors to our welcome has still more firmly stuck in my head : he said 'In America you must have strong elbows, otherwise you'll be pushed aside, as you were just now in the airplane'.

Thus, thanks to the discovery Columbus had made nearly 500 years earlier, we set foot on the free land of America, across which we still move, though nowadays by car rather than on foot. From the first day I noticed that there is a certain isolation between man and this earth—that formed by car tyres. Thousands of cars crowded the asphalt highways and streets along which we drove to the Lucerne Hotel on 79th Street, while thousands of others were reposing along the pavements, like horses asleep.

Hardly had we crossed the threshold of the hotel room than the telephone rang. I picked up the receiver, and we hardly stirred from it for several hours as Zosia and I took turns on duty. First a familiar voice called from Los Angeles : 'The radio has just announced your arrival! Welcome to the free land of George Washington!' After struggling with the creaking and intermittent post-insurrection telephone system of Warsaw, this voice from Los Angeles 2,000 miles away was my first encounter with the high standards of American technology. Friends and acquaintances gave notice of themselves from all parts of the American continent, sweetening our loneliness in this strange new land.

In the meantime the first knocks had come at the door, and within an hour the room was filled with people I had not seen since the outbreak of war. They were somehow the same, yet different. Their hair had either turned grey or grown thinner, their features sharpened or blunted by stoutness and age. Eight years is a long time. A bottle, ice and soda appeared from nowhere, and amidst the sound of revelry questions and answers flew. But the noise changed to silence, gladness into sorrow, when the unavoidable words had to be uttered : 'He was murdered ... missing without trace ... in prison ...' Gaps in knowledge caused by the war were soon filled in.

At dinner that evening, to which we were invited by Congressman Sadlak, a young man who spoke good Polish, I was served with half an ox and told that it was steak, the American national dish. I tackled it with knife as sharp as a lancet, though without the effect it deserved. The waiter took away at least half. The difference in the consumption of meat between poverty-stricken Poland and wealthy America was no longer a matter of statistics but was now one of the capacity of my stomach.

Late that evening Zosia and I—tired from a sleepless night in the plane and exhilarated by the excess of new impressions—went for a stroll down world-famous Broadway in order to relax a little. Scarcely had we gone a few dozen steps than a familiar face appeared in the crowd of passers-by. I stopped Zosia and looked around. The passer-by did likewise. I exclaimed, 'Schultz! What are you doing here?' 'Waiting for a tramcar,' cried my pre-war colleague, the lawyer Schultz, using a well-known Warsaw saying as he hastened towards me with hand outstretched. 'I've just flown in from Rio de Janeiro, where I live, and when I heard on the hotel radio that you'd arrived I was coming over to see you.'

Behind us was crippled, dark and poverty-stricken Warsaw while here, like a brilliant stage set, was Broadway, with its flood of lights and seething crowd, and there, a thousand miles away, was the legendary Rio de Janeiro which Schultz mentioned as people in Warsaw mention Radom. We had entered a world of different dimensions and would have to get used to it.

Next morning someone knocked and a bell-boy, whose smile betrayed his curiosity, brought us a pile of newspapers. On the front page of the *New York Herald-Tribune* and others was a photograph of our group, with Ambassador Bliss Lane shaking Mikolajczyk by the hand. Next to him was Zosia in all the elegance of a Warsaw hat and suit, described with a complimentary 'pretty', while beside her I had had my head cut off, as it would not fit into the picture. This was decidedly a bad omen. Headless in America!

We went to a Broadway cafeteria for breakfast and sat down at a table, calmly expecting a waiter and looking round in the meantime. The gleaming metal of the kitchen equipment, the counterhands in spotless uniform and, in particular, the enormous quantities of dishes and titbits behind huge sheets of plate-glass gave us a foretaste of the lavishness which would presently begin to depress us in comparison with Poland. The waiter did not appear, but one of the counter-hands came over and leaned down to say : 'Where are you from? What language do you speak?' When Zosia replied in English, she explained : 'There are no waiters in cafeterias. Take trays and point out what you want to eat at the counter.' I obediently took a tray and marched along the counter. When we had finished, several portions of untouched butter still lay on the table. Up came a little cart and the cleaner shovelled them with a single movement into the garbage basket. This really shocked us. Even in America it was wrong to throw untouched butter into the garbage. It was too much, it was sinful! I recalled my grandmother's threat that if I didn't eat my carrots, 'One day you may be glad of them'. And there had been such days.

We set off by bus into town, putting our fares into a machine beside the driver which acknowledged them with a discreet ring of its bell. This bus without a conductor was another new experience : in Warsaw the conductor watches his passengers as suspiciously as a public prosecutor lest anyone gets off without paying. This was also my first encounter with American mechanization.

The woman sitting next to Zosia began to examine her closely, first looking at her, then at the newspaper she was carrying. I peeped over and caught sight of the *Herald-Tribune* with the photograph of our group. The lady could not help thrusting the photograph under Zosia's nose, chattering away. My 'better half' turned pink and said something shyly, nodding in agreement. Other passengers joined in the conversation and put out their hands in welcoming grasps. Somewhat troubled by this human approach, of which we had lost the habit during the savage war years, we got out sooner than we should. I was projected on to the pavement as the result of a forceful friendly clap on the shoulder in farewell. This encouraged us greatly. These 'bloodsuckers of Americans', and 'exploiters of the workers', as Bierut, the communist President of Poland called them, seemed to have good hearts nevertheless.

As we walked along Fifth Avenue to the Empire State Building, I looked at the unbroken stream of magnificent cars driving soundlessly along the broad street while Zosia scrutinized the women who passed and was absorbed in the luxurious displays in the shops. She was stopped by a woman in furs and diamonds who asked her a question very flattering to Warsaw tailors. 'Where did you get that jacket?' On learning that it was from Warsaw, the woman's eyebrows went up in surprise and she asked, 'Where's that?' This elegant woman of Fifth Avenue would have been surprised had she learned that this jacket was the costume in which Zosia had escaped and that it was at this moment almost her only wardrobe.

In front of the Empire State Building I looked up and muttered the Biblical verse 'And they said, Go to, let us build us a city and a tower, whose top may reach unto Heaven' as I surveyed the American embodiment of the tower of Babel, the summit of which was lost in the clouds hanging low over the city as though to confirm that this blasphemous purpose had been attained. Though the sun was not shining, the tower gleamed like the gigantic figure of a knight in armour with the metal of ironwork and the chains of a thousand windows. It was beautiful in its simplicity of shape and proportion.

The elevator shot up like a rocket to the eightieth floor and I felt the pressure in my ears. We went out on to the balcony with its protective balustrade, mingling with the multilingual and multicoloured crowd of tourists ('and the Lord confounded their language, that they could not understand one another's speech'). The view was like that from the peak of the highest mountain, over the lesser peaks of skyscrapers, leaping up from the throng of parallel mountain chains of apartment houses, cut across by valleys of streets, with a river of people and automobiles flowing endlessly along the bottom of each valley. This massif of cement and steel lying at our feet was divided by two gleaming ribbons of water—the Hudson and the East river, crowded with ships, full of movement and smoke, fading away into the bay where the enormous Statue of Liberty looked from this distance and height like a porcelain statuette on a shelf. On arrival we had not passed by this statue, which is always greeted by the tears of immigrants on every ship entering New York harbour. My feelings at looking down on to the sea of houses covered by a film of fumes and smoke from one horizon to the other, concealing within it eight million people each in pursuit of their own eight million concerns, at the summit of the Rockefeller Center, rival of the Empire State building, at the dark rectangle of Central Park, at the bridges linking the Manhattan peninsula with Brooklyn and New Jersey, at the ships in the port and the transatlantic giants at rest in the docks—were not at all the tranquil emotions aroused by the sight of nature or a work of art. Amazement and admiration for size and power, admittedly—but at the same time the sight intimidated and overwhelmed, intensifying the feeling of one's own smallness and isolation.

I wanted to lean over the balustrade to find out how I would react to the height after so many years away from mountain-climbing, but my way was blocked by wire netting to prevent those who choose a leap from the Empire State Building as their way of leaving this vale of tears. However I understood the choice of location, since the threatening perspective from up there contains nothing to restore the desire for life to those who have lost it.

When we had seen the city from above we descended into its entrails at the subway station on 42nd Street. Cement corridors led off in all directions from a spacious hall under the surface of the earth surrounded by newspaper stalls, flower-shops, coffee shops and automatics : these passages, like the arms of an octopus, were streaming with crowds of people hurrying to various platforms, from which we could hear the rumbling of the trains. It was like the antechamber to Hell. The train was full of people going home from work, packed like sardines, and we were among them. At first it seemed like Warsaw—the crowd, the homely Warsaw tramway crowd—but no one swore at anyone else, and if someone stepped on his neighbour's foot, he would say 'Sorry' and the injured party would smile 'Never mind'. When Zosia asked where to get out, several people volunteered information. A mood of mutual understanding prevailed in the carriage. These people had not been turned savage by the war years and their nerves had not been shattered by enemy occupation. But all the same, they were handicapped by Fate in other ways. Throughout the journey we did not hear a single wisecrack intended for the whole compartment, nor a single apt remark of the kind at which the people of Warsaw, the wittiest people in the world, excel.

At our press conference in the hotel, attended by some fifty reporters, questions were mainly asked about relations inside Poland, the behaviour of the Russians and details of our flight and plans for the future. The reply to the last question has remained relevant to this day : 'We're going to carry on our fight in the free world for the restoration to Poland of her independence and a democratic system of government.' On this occasion we met representatives of the Polish-American press, including Felix Poplawski, the Polish-born newspaper editor who has been in America for several decades.

At the end of the conference I was invited by the representative of an American press agency to have a private talk with him, and he offered me what—in view of my empty purse—seemed a breath-taking sum in dollars for my account of our flight to Sweden—on condition that it should be one hundred per cent authentic. I re-fused very firmly and this produced from him a professional though not altogether unfriendly comment which was my first in-troduction to the secrets of the greatest journalism in the world, to the effect that 'This is the one and only chance you'll have to sell this story profitably. Today it's valuable, because it's a sensation. In a week's time it won't be worth five dollars.' I was soon to find out how true this comment was. Nothing ages so fast in America as a newspaper front-page story. Its life can be reckoned in terms of hours, or a week at the best.

Thus our life in America started, full of new impressions and stirring political activity. Within a few days Zosia and I had left the hotel and settled down in our new home on 113th Street, from which we made excursions into New York and got to know the world's largest city. This was the first time since 1939 that we had been able to go to bed at night without being afraid that the darkness would bring hammering at the door and the voices of Germans, Russians or, worst of all, Poles shouting 'Open up !' The tension began to decrease, though slowly, and for many nights to come the slightest movement on the stairs would arouse us. During the daytime we were in the United States but at night, in our dreams, we were still in Poland—in the streets of Warsaw, at Lesna Podkowa, in the Sejm or the offices of the PSL (Polish Peasant Party), watched or pursued by the security police agents, running along streets and up stairs, only to wake up as the police spy seized us and to mutter as we wiped away the cold sweat that 'it was only a dream'.

Many days had to pass before I could cease, quite unwittingly, eyeing passers-by in the street as the result of many years of habit : or before Zosia stopped warning me, with a significant touch of the hand. 'There's been someone following us for some time'. And it was not until a visitor remarked 'Why in heaven's name do you use such strong electric bulbs?' that we realized it was to appease our hunger for light, a hunger that had grown in the course of the years spent stumbling through dark streets, and in rooms sparsely lit by the flickering unsteady lights, due to German restrictions on the use of electricity.

We still carried on interminable conversations together about our flight, about the friends we had left behind in Poland and the arrests, examining meanwhile the policy of the PSL and trying to answer the question whether its policy had been right, inasmuch as it had led us into exile, or whether some other road of action should have been taken.

News reached us from Poland of the appointment by the Sejm of a special commission to inquire into the reasons and circumstances of our flight. This was under Zenon Kliszko, and the commission reported to the Sejm on November 15, 1947, as a result of which the Sejm deprived Mikolajczyk and myself of our seats as deputies. Mikolajczyk was simultaneously deprived of his Polish citizenship. The prime charge against Mikolajczyk was his alleged concealment of a letter from Alexander Cadogan, Permanent Under-Secretary of State for Foreign Affairs. The letter, dated November 2, 1944, was addressed to Tadeusz Romer, then the Polish Minister of Foreign Affairs, and expressed the readiness of the British government to guarantee with the Soviet Union the Polish frontier on the Oder and Neisse rivers. Mikolajczyk replied to this charge in New York and explained that upon relinquishing the premiership in London in November 1944 he had handed over the letter along with all other state documents to the new government of Tomasz Arciszewski, and that in addition he had had the opportunity while Vice-Premier in Poland of confirming that the contents of Cadogan's letter were known to the Warsaw government. Thus the attack missed fire.

The first days of our stay in New York gave us an impression of tremendous drive, wealth and technical and economic power, requiring every adjective used to describe size or quality to be in the superlative. In material matters it was a true paradise on earth, not merely the paradise promised in Marxist manifestos. Yet the question arose whether this immense material power concealed equal moral power. This could not be answered at once. A few days did not suffice.

II

THE CAPITAL OF AMERICAN POLONIA

Mikolajczyk, Baginski and I—the presidium of the PSL—met Karol Rozmarek, president of the Polish-American Congress (KPA) and his colleagues in a Chicago hotel on December 15, 1947, after an eighteen-hour express train journey from New York, during which we covered a distance more or less twice that from Poland's west to east frontiers. This helped me to understand the obvious fact that America is not a country but a continent. During the journey I was at the window day and night, gazing at this legendary America. What passed before my eyes confirmed the impression made by New York. Power and wealth sprang to the eye from the countless towns, factories and farms, the many-laned cement highways, the countless bridges, the pylons and criss-cross high-tension cables, the thousands of cars running level with the train on the parallel asphalt roads which never left our sight for a moment. This impression did not decrease in the evening, but merely took on another shape, as the express roared through the flood of electric lights which clustered round the cities and grew less frequent beyond, but which were always glittering somewhere in the darkness. It was as though the whole country were illuminated. This extravagance of light appalled me, a man who only a few weeks earlier had left Poland plunged in darkness.

Mikolajczyk was somewhat hesitant about meeting Karol Rozmarek. I insisted that a visit must be paid to the leading personality of American Polonia and co-operation with him developed, as well as with democratic Polish political parties in exile, since we ourselves were not able to provide much effective defence of Polish interests. Mikolajczyk's reaction was negative: 'We still have plenty of time for the Polish-American Congress. As for émigré political parties, we have a mandate directly from the Polish nation, given us at the elections only a few months ago. We shall weaken this mandate if we mix with people who have been in exile since 1939 and have lost physical and spiritual links with Poland. You were elected a deputy to the Sejm by the heroic people of the city of Warsaw. What better mandate could you have? Could co-operation with other parties add anything to it?' It was obvious that Mikolajczyk was still working on the principle, 'Poland is the peasants, the peasants are the PSL, the PSL is I—therefore I am Poland.'

Neither Baginski nor I agreed with this attitude and it was due to our pressure, and the initiative of the Polish-American Congress, that the Chicago meeting came about. Its mood was not happy, for ever since our meeting with Mikolajczyk after our flight, his relations with Baginski and myself had been tense, mainly because of the way in which he had organized his flight. However, I agreed with Baginski that in the interests of mutual action nothing of this was to go beyond the three of us, so that externally we gave the impression of a solid group, agreed between ourselves on action and policy.

The meeting with Rozmarek, who was accompanied by Judge B. Gunther, chairman of the Western Pennsylvania division of KPA, Edward Pluzdrak, president of the Illinois division of KPA, and Jan Stanek, its secretary, started off in a somewhat tense atmosphere. After a formal welcome, Rozmarek, who was a man in the prime of life, tall and with a strong, firm voice, asked Mikolajczyk a number of questions which placed him in the position of a defendant who must account for his acts, particularly for his share as Vice-Premier in the Warsaw government, which Rozmarek regarded as collabora-tion with the communists and implying approval of the Yalta agree-ment. It was clear from the start that the charges contained in Rozmarek's questions were directed only against Mikolajczyk, and did not refer to Baginski or myself. During the several hours of argu-ment, one of the KPA representatives explained to me in an aside : 'We've nothing against the people in Poland for adapting them-selves to the situation created by Yalta, since they'd no choice. But Mikolajczyk was in London, in the free world, and made his own choice without being subjected to the force used in Poland.' Aided by Baginski and me, Mikolajczyk was easily able to reject the first charge, by showing that his part in the Warsaw government, while apparently constituting co-operation, had in reality been a constant struggle against the communists, a struggle in which 118 PSL mem-bers died at the hands of the security police, while thousands more were jailed. Mikolajczyk condemned the Yalta agreement in prin-ciple, while endeavouring to show that its full implementation would guarantee Poland her independence, admittedly without her eastern territories though possessing frontiers on the Oder-Neisse.

After reaching agreement without difficulty in our views on the attitude to be adopted towards Communism and on the principle of mutual co-operation, a communiqué was drafted for issue next day, December 16th. This read:

> Prompted by our desire to serve the Polish cause and working on the assumption that the activities of the presidium of the Polish Peasant party, which has come to America to present the real state of affairs now existing in Poland to the American people, should be co-ordinated with those of the Polish-American Congress (KPA), the aim of which is a strong, free and independent Poland with its western frontiers on the Oder-Neisse and eastern frontiers as of 1939, a conference was held in Chicago on December 15, 1947, in which the following took part:

> Representatives of the Polish-American Congress: Karol Rozmarek, president; Jan Stanek, secretary; Judge B. Gunther, president of the state section of Western Pennsylvania and director of the executive committee, and Edward Pluzdrak, president of the state committee for Illinois and director of the executive committee.

> Representatives of the Polish Peasant party (PSL): Stanislaw Mikolajczyk, president; Kazimierz Baginski, vice-president and Stefan Korbonski, member of the supreme executive committee.

> During the three-hour conference, the following matters were discussed and agreed upon:

> I. Both the representatives of the KPA and the presidium of the PSL confirm that the subjection of Poland to blood-stained communist dictatorship demands the unification of all forces acting to regain Poland's independence.

> II. Both the representatives of the KPA and the presidium of the PSL declare that they will oppose Communism as the greatest danger threatening the world as a whole, and the United States and Poland in particular.

> III. Both the representatives of the KPA and the presidium of the PSL confirm that the Warsaw régime represents not the Polish nation but a foreign power, and was forced upon Poland by false elections.

> IV. Both the representatives of the KPA and the representatives of the PSL consider it necessary and essential to warn the American people of the threat from communist Russia.

> V. As regards the independence of Poland, both the representatives of the KPA and of the presidium of the PSL consider it necessary to co-operate in this action with all Polish elements working for the same aim.

> VI. The agreement signed at Yalta without the participation of Poland is regarded by the conference as the height of evil, particularly in that the failure to implement this agreement has deprived Poland of her independence, and therefore both the representatives of the KPA and the presidium of the PSL pledge themselves to action for correcting this evil.

VII. The conference considers that the defence of the western frontiers of Poland is the duty of all Poles, no matter what their political views, and also that both the KPA and the presidium of the PSL will act towards this end in the United States, emphasizing at the same time the threat to the United States, to Poland and to the entire world of the rebirth of German imperialism.

VIII. In order to avoid misunderstandings harmful both to the cause of Poland and to American Polonia and the United States, the conference has agreed that the activities of the presidium of the PSL among American Polonia shall take place in consultation with the KPA.

IX. The presidium of the PSL, aware of the importance of the action taken hitherto by the KPA on behalf of Poland, welcomes co-operation from this organization and wishes to express its conviction that the support of the KPA will facilitate the work of the presidium of the PSL and will contribute greatly to the cause of Poland.

X. The representatives of the KPA express their satisfaction at the fortunate escape of the presidium of the PSL from the clutches of the communists and extend a welcome to its members on American soil, believing that mutual efforts will bear good results to the cause of Poland.

I now sighed with relief. The error had been corrected.

During both days I met a number of the leaders of Polonia, including the close co-workers of president Rozmarek—Franciszek Dziob, a former captain in General Haller's army in World War I, and Karol Burke, a lieutenant in the same army, and a number of others. Just as on November 26th I had discovered America for myself, so on December 15th I came across a corner of Poland in Chicago. All these leaders of the KPA, which had been founded by Polish organizations at a congress in Buffalo in 1944 to defend the Polish cause over which dark clouds had already begun to loom, spoke to us in Polish—those born in the United States with a slight accent, but those of the older generation with no trace of one. During the conference in the hotel, I might have thought that the talks were taking place in Warsaw and that afterwards I would go out into Nowy Swiat or the Jerusalem Avenue for a breath of fresh air, were it not for the various appurtenances of American luxury surrounding us and the occasional exchange of phrases in English by representatives of the KPA. It was primarily the subject of the talks which caused this impressions : the worlds 'Poland' and 'home' occurred all the time. Mention was made of restoring her independence to Poland, of the frontiers of Poland, of the communist dictatorship forced upon Poland and of the unification of all Polish forces in exile for the struggle with Communism. Yet at the same time the representatives of the KPA were loyal American citizens and their concern for the United States was apparent in the final agreement in which it was stated that Communism is the greatest threat to the United States, against which the presidium of the PSL was to warn the American people, as well as drawing their attention to the threat of a resurrection of German imperialism. The concordance between the national interests of Poland and those of the United States facilitated the harmonious linking of Polish and American matters.

The agreement with the Polish-American Congress initiated a number of public appearances before American Poles and Americans. It began with a journey on January 14, 1948, to Buffalo, where we were welcomed at the railway station by Bernard J. Dowd, the mayor, and then proceeded to a reception arranged on our behalf by the Association of Polish Business and Professional Men at the Lafayette Hotel, attended by several hundred persons. On this occasion, I met Justyn Figas, a radio commentator who was very popular among Poles. That evening we were guests at an annual banquet given by the Buffalo chamber of commerce, where some 3,000 people gave us an ovation.

We arrived in Washington on January 19th to meet the central committee of the International Peasant Union, known as the 'Green Internationale'. Driving by car from the railway station to the meeting I had but a glimpse of the dome of the Capitol and of broad Pennsylvania Avenue, where stands the mounted statue of Pulaski in his Cossack cap with a feather in it.

Eminent leaders of peasant parties from other countries of Central and Eastern Europe, now émigrés in the United States, were waiting for us at the office of the union. In the forefront was Ferenc Nagy, former Hungarian Prime Minister and president of the Hungarian Smallholders' party, a dark-haired man in the prime of life, who had left Hungary for Switzerland for a rest-cure some months earlier and could not return home. Dr Vladko Macek, a small, grey-haired man, and president of the Croatian People's Party, gave the impression, thanks to his decisive manner, of a 'peasant Napoleon', the nickname he had been known by in Croatia; while Dr Georgi Dimitrov was a high-spirited and enthusiastic 'tribune of the people'. Finally, Milan Gavrilovic, representative of the Serbian Agrarian Union, was a highly typical Slav and Grigore Buzesti, representative of the Rumanian peasants, was a southern type, with sallow complexion.

The result of our talks was that we joined the International Peasant Union to fight in co-operation for the liberation of our countries and the peasant masses. The American press, of which some thirty representatives had been present at our press conference, gave this fact wide and sympathetic publicity.

On January 25th we spoke to 5,000 people in Chicago, at a large meeting in the Opera House, while a further 2,000 were turned away for lack of accommodation. On the platform were Polish and American banners held by former members of the Haller army in blue uniforms, which I had not seen for many years. The meeting was opened by president Rozmarek, after which he introduced each of us. We described the situation in Poland as it had developed from the outbreak of war. I described the underground battle, first against the German then the Soviet occupying forces, and poked fun in my introduction at communist leaflets being distributed outside the Opera House. The audience were most responsive.

On the following day a banquet was held in a very cordial atmosphere, given for us by the KPA at the Wonderland Ball Room and attended by several hundred persons. Once again the speeches of the hosts echoed with the words 'Poland', 'Poland's interests', 'the liberation of Poland'.

In the intervals between public appearances we paid visits to Polish-American organizations, such as the Polish National Alliance, the Polish Women's Alliance of America and others, as well as the editorial offices of the newspapers *Polish Daily Zgoda* (organ of the KPA) and the *Polish Daily News*. Nor did we fail to visit the Polish sector of Chicago and the famous Lenart restaurant. During these walks through streets where the Polish language was to be heard on every side and Polish names hung above stores, during our visits to the well-equipped offices of Polish-American organizations and the editorial offices of Polish newspapers in America, and finally while eating the excellent Polish dishes in the Lenart restaurant, where the menu differed little from that offered at the Bukiet restaurant in Warsaw, our first impression was that a section of Poland had been cut from the maternal soil and transferred to another continent, where it had taken root. I met dozens of people who, while different from the Poles in Poland because of their dress and way of life, spoke to us nevertheless in the same language as the Poles at home, and referred to the same problems that had stirred us during meetings in Warsaw. The predominant question was 'What can we do to help Poland?'

In Lenart's restaurant, now run by the founder's widow and children (who were born in America but educated in Poland) an elderly man approached our table and asked : 'Mr Korbonski, may

I ask what your father's first name was?' Upon hearing that it was
Stefan, he seized me by the hand and shook it vigorously, exclaim-
ing 'I went to school with him!' This was followed by questions
about my uncles and my father's native region of Kalisz. The elderly
man was deeply moved. Looking at me affectionately, he talked
about my father, and kept repeating 'Good heavens, Stefan's son
here in Chicago . . .' I shared his emotion. The feeling of blood relationship with the people all around us in Chicago intensified.

Two days later I was back in New York to take part in the 'Live
Newspaper' at the Polish National Home on the subject of the situation in Poland and the political struggle of the Polish Peasant Party.
The first casual exchange of greetings before the lecture showed
that the hall was full of the 'new emigration', with only a small
percentage of the older Poles in America. The audience provided a
typical cross-section of the many hundreds of thousands of people
whom the war had driven out of Poland. There were soldiers of the
underground Home Army, of General Anders's Second Corps, the
Polish army of September 1939, workmen, government officials and
white-collar workers. The older generation included a few Polish
Socialist Party members of 1905. I was told that they never missed
any Polish meetings, so they had come to this one too. I shook hands
with them, much moved by meeting the oldest living generation of
fighters for Poland. They gazed with eyes dimmed with age at Zosia
and me, smiling in a friendly way though with a tinge of pity for
these newest arrivals. Some, however, such as Stefan Sieradzki,
who had travelled specially from Philadelphia, were the personifica-
tion of vigour and energy and he is still today the leader of Polish
activities in that city.

When my speech ended and requests for further details began to
come from the audience, I at once realized I was in the presence
of people with highly developed political views. The questions asked
by the audience clearly reflected all the sore points, the conflicts and
passions of Polish reality. Yalta was the dominant subject, and the
participation of Mikolajczyk (who was not present) in the communist government, as well as our attitude towards the government
in exile in London. The same manifestations I had observed earlier
in Chicago, recurred here. No blame was cast upon the Poles in
Poland for adapting themselves to the conditions created by Yalta,
though Mikolajczyk was attacked for the fact that, while living in
the free world and not under pressure, he had nevertheless approved
this fourth partition of his country. After discussing our attitude to
the government in London, my argument that the PSL had continually fought against the 1935 constitution and was critically dis-

posed towards governments based upon it, was refuted by the argument that after all Mikolajczyk had recognized that constitution since he had become Prime Minister of the government in London precisely on the basis of it. It was impossible to find any retort to this argument.

During the course of the lively discussion, I noticed that when it became heated a tall, handsome man with greying hair would rise to make a conciliatory comment or put a helpful question. It was clear that he was steering the discussion with great experience and tact, ensuring that it did not go adrift on the rocks of problems which still aroused bad feeling and temper. After the meeting we shook hands and I learned that he was Ignacy Morawski. This was the start of my acquaintance with one of the leading publicists and activists of Polonia, who skilfully played the role of a catalyst between the old and new generations of exiles.

After New York it was the turn of Pittsburgh, where we held a meeting in the theatre attended by several thousand persons. Here one of the activists of Polonia, who was seated beside me on the stage, whispered, 'At least one-third of the people here tonight keep away from Polish meetings. But they have come today, since all the American newspapers are writing about your group and of Polish affairs, so this has revived their interest. The visit of your group has also contributed to the enlivening of our Polonia activities.'

While in Pittsburgh we visited the headquarters of the Falcon organization, full of various relics, and met the president, Dr Starzynski, who was already advanced in years. It was here that I heard a story revealing its popularity in American military circles : 'During a conflict between the United States and one of the southern republics, the president of the Falcons offered to the American army the entire organization, consisting of about 100,000 persons. The offer was not accepted, since there was no need, but this readiness to fight and shed blood for the United States has never been forgotten.'

Invitations succeeded one another rapidly. These included a banquet in connection with the jubilee of Smolenski, deputy to the New York State legislature. Another invitation was to Elizabethville, near New York, where we visited the local Falcon offices after the meeting.

When we reached the Lucerne Hotel, surrounded by wailing sirens and the red lights of police cars and motor-cycles, Mikolajczyk invited our escort of policemen of Polish descent in for a drink. As soon as they reached the hotel room, all formality left them. They threw their caps into a corner, opened their jackets, and one

lay down on the settee to rest after his labours. I got into conversation with one fair-haired young policeman and praised his command
of the Polish language. He was reluctant to believe me. 'Do I?
Honest? I'll tell Mother, she'll be pleased. I was born in New Jersey
and it was she who taught me to speak Polish.' Another, who spoke
much less well, confided a secret dream : 'I'd like to be an officer in
the Polish police force sometime.' An hour later the senior present
snapped his fingers, they all jumped up, straightened their uniforms and said good-bye in the most formal manner, expressing
their thanks to Mikolajczyk for the honour he had bestowed on
them. I was pleased by this American version of the Polish saying,
'A country squire, as poor as he may be, is equal to a palatine'.
Clearly, a policeman in this country was the equal of a premier, at
least off duty.

The development of political activity included my wife, who
made her début in a way I envied, at least as far as language was
concerned. For Zosia was invited to talk to a gathering of a charitable organization of American women, where she spoke in English
to several hundred women on the part of women in the Polish underground movement. Zosia was somewhat critical regarding this first
encounter with Anglo-Saxon women, and said. 'When we came to
questions, they were so naïve that I often didn't know how to
answer. In their view, a woman exposed every day to the danger
of arrest, torture and execution was not a woman. She was violating
her sex. A woman like this was to them an unreal figure out of some
fantastic novel or from another planet, not of this world.'

Shortly after this, Zosia also talked on the 'Live Newspaper' programme, which constituted a kind of forum for discussion and took
place once a month. It proved to be lively and interesting, particularly at the start, when laughter and cries of protest greeted the
chairman, an old Polish Socialist Party member clearly accustomed
to presenting persons of his own age, when he introduced Zosia with
the remark : 'She began her fight with the eternal Muscovite enemy
early, in the year 1905'. 'Just ten years before she was born,' I commented.

In April Mikolajczyk, Baginski and I were invited to Canada by
the Polish Canadian Congress, and on April 11th a meeting, attended by several thousands of Polish Canadians, was held in Toronto.
The Prime Minister of Ontario province, G. Drew, was present at
this meeting. Our reception and the atmosphere resembled those
we had encountered in the United States. The meeting was preceded by a surprise in the persons of a former colleague, Ostrowski,
a lawyer from Warsaw and now one of the leaders of the new emigra-

tion in Canada, and Mr From, also from Warsaw, owner of a well-known driving school, who visited my hotel. We plunged into the customary recollections, wondering at the fate which had thus, willy-nilly, cast natives of Warsaw across the globe.

We left Toronto that day for a meeting at Hamilton, from where Mikolajczyk returned to the United States, while Baginski and I toured a number of smaller places, speaking at them all on the subject of the struggle of the Polish people between 1939 and 1947. We were welcomed everywhere very warmly, just as we had been in the United States. Yet both the people we met and their language, also their reactions to what we had to say, differed somewhat from American Polonia. The reason for this was that the Poles in Canada were one or even two to three generations younger than those in America, and it sometimes happened that people spoke to us who had emigrated not during the period of the partitions before World War I, but during the period of independence. They referred to pre-war Polish matters with knowledge gained from first-hand observation, not from newspapers. Several times we met former members of the Peasant party, for whom Witos, Rataj and Stanislaw Thugutt were not legendary but living persons they had met and known. We passed two interesting days with one of them, a young peasant from the Lublin district.

He came to pick us up at Brandford in his new car, and we drove through the Canadian plain, talking by turns about rural matters in a Lublin village and in Canada. Our host had come to Canada at the age of just over twenty, and had worked from the first in agriculture. He had done well and married, and was now the owner of a tobacco farm worth a quarter of a million dollars.

On arrival at the small township where he lived we went to inspect the Polish National Home, where we were to speak that evening. Looking round the bright, clean new building, we found ourselves in a large theatre, where a play was being rehearsed on the stage in ... Italian. Surprised, we asked for an explanation. The reply was the tale of the emergence of this Polish outpost.

'Once there were only two Polish families in the township, my friend's and mine. The others were Italians, Hungarians and other nationalities. But there were over a dozen Polish farms in the area. When we two hit upon the idea of building a Polish national home, people used to joke, 'Who are you building it for? Two families?' We persisted and, partly with our own money and partly with a mortgage, we built the house. Now we rent out the theatre and offices to other nationalities for theatricals, marriages and banquets. What you see now on the stage is a rehearsal of an Italian produc-

B

tion, for which the theatre has been rented. What they pay goes towards our own debts and paying off the mortgage. Soon we'll have a Polish National Home built with Italian and Hungarian money. They're indifferent to these matters, so why shouldn't they pay.'

After the evening meeting, attended by Polish farmers from the neighbourhood, we went to the farm of our host, where we spent the night. Next day we inspected it thoroughly. Machines, machines and yet more machines, his own petrol station and greenhouses where tobacco plants were cultivated. The host and his wife gave the impression of wealth, and confidence in their own strength and future. The children spoke to us in Polish, but used English among themselves. Our host, seeing me listening with curiosity to this, remarked with a smile : 'My English is not very good, so I'm learning from them. They're my teachers.'

After lunch I had a talk with a former soldier of the Polish Second Corps, who had recently come to Canada and was working on the farm. He was pleased with the country and with his host. 'You know,' he said, 'before coming, I had to sign a contract to work for a specified time for my sponsor. I signed it, but the day after I got here my boss called me in and said that if I didn't like it on the farm, or could find a better job, he'd release me from my contract at once. He's a good man. I eat meals with them, the pay is good, the work is all right, though insufferably boring !'

I understood him perfectly. To cross Russia, Iran, Iraq and Palestine to Italy, and then, via Monte Cassino and Ancona and England, to finish up on a farm in Canada—hardly an exciting end to a stormy life full of adventures.

My most interesting experience at this first period in America was at the convention of the Polish-American Congress, held every four years. This took place in Philadelphia, from May 29 to 31, 1948, and we were invited to attend as guests of the Congress. A large hotel in the city centre was put at the disposal of 5,000 delegates and their families for three days, since the convention included not only meetings but banquets, balls and other diversions.

One of the first speakers was a lean, tall man with greying hair. When President Rozmarek introduced him, he was welcomed by an outburst of applause and everyone rose. I asked my neighbour who this eminent guest was. 'He's Tom Clark, member of the American government, U.S. Attorney-General,' he shouted in my ear. In his opening words Clark stated he had been delegated to the convention by President Truman. In his speech Clark praised the activities of the KPA and the attitude adopted by Americans of Polish descent towards the threat of Communism. By this time I knew enough

English, to the study of which I devoted all my spare time, to be able to understand some passages in his speech. One passage has stuck clearly in my mind : 'At the time when almost all the American people believed in the friendship of Stalin and the Soviet Union, you were the only ones not to be deluded, and as early as 1944 you founded this Congress for the defence of the interests and rights of the country of your forefathers—Poland—and the United States, before the threat of Communism. In this way you formed an advance guard for the American nation in their fight with aggression from the east.'

The political parts of the speeches, to which I listened attentively, were almost entirely concerned with Polish matters, primarily the action necessary for Poland to regain independence. The word 'Yalta' was uttered as though the worst of curses. The American government and the late President Roosevelt were thoroughly taken to task for not keeping the promises they had made to Poland. The freedom, sharpness and boldness with which these words of criticism were uttered startled me, unaccustomed as I was to it over the past years. It was evident that none of the speakers reckoned in any way that he might encounter difficulties or repressions for what he said. Thus yet another impression was added to what I was learning about America—its freedom. Polish matters predominated in the speeches to such an extent that I rubbed my eyes and wondered whether I really was in America. The illusion receded only when a speech was made in English by the representatives of the younger generation.

At the end of the political debate a number of resolutions were passed which defined the attitude and policy of the Congress on Polish matters. All in all, they led to a single one : 'All methods and means must be used to restore to Poland her independence'.

Behind the scenes I made many new acquaintances and revived earlier ones. I paid a visit to the central office of the convention where I met the hard-working chief of staff of the Congress, Captain Dziob, Karol Burke and others. People kept inviting me for a drink, for coffee or a sandwich, so that I finally reached my hotel late in the evening, more dead than alive. But here Mikolajczyk was peevishly waiting with the important news, 'Yolles, editor of *Nowy Swiat*, has been calling for the past two hours. He wants an interview with you for all the Polish press in America. He's waiting in room such and such.' When I reached the door of this hotel room I was struck by the noise of many voices within. When I went in, I found myself in a cloud of cigarette and cigar smoke, among over a dozen people without their jackets, collars unfastened and sleeves rolled up. A battery of bottles and silver bowls of ice were standing on the table. I was greeted by a loud cry and a glass was at once thrust into my hand. Yolles, flushed, came over and nudging me exclaimed, 'What have you been up to? I've been calling you for the last two hours in vain!' 'I'm ready for the interview,' I replied, 'and I'm sorry if my absence has inconvenienced you.' 'What interview?' Yolles laughed. 'We wanted to have a talk with you without Mikolajczyk, so I told him about the interview as a pretext.' Then they started to besiege me with questions, searching and aimed at clearing up the most complex matters. This day of the KPA convention did not end for me until five in the morning.

Everything I have written so far on the subject of my first encounter with Polonia in America and Canada looks very pious, standardized and patriotic. I can imagine certain of my readers grimacing with distaste and saying, 'How shallow! Everyone patriotic, the word "Poland" incessantly recurring, everyone pleased with himself and America—an idealized picture, devoid of life which is always so full of contradictions and struggle.' However, after coming from terrorized Poland, highly aware of the cause round which conflict was raging, I had found thousands of people in dozens of American and Canadian towns, disinterestedly spending their time, thoughts and hard-earned money on this cause—that was what had inspired so uncomplex an impression. In the first place, the mere fact that the KPA and the KPK (Polish-Canadian Congress) existed, and everyone had become accustomed to them and regarded them as a fact of everyday life, was in itself unusual. Thus, thousands of country folk, after emigrating to America because they were starving in their own country, did not turn away from Poland indifferently, but instead organized themselves to help her. The basis of all this was an organic link with their homeland, deeply rooted in their spirit and handed down from one generation to the next, giving birth to a special kind of Polish-American patriotism, which may well have appeared over-simplified to newcomers from Poland but which, most important of all, existed and had become a factor exerting influences over the political mood and views of all America, as had been proved in the speech made by Tom Clark, a member of the American government. This fundamental truth dominated all other observations and aroused in me the feeling of close kinship and gratitude with which I always think of Polonia in America.

III

'THIS IS RADIO FREE EUROPE!'

The hands of the clock were on the hour, a red light flashed and a man behind the glass screen brought down his upraised hand. The young man seated opposite me at the microphone began to speak in a level, clear voice: 'This is Radio Free Europe. The voice of free Poland. You are now going to hear a talk by Stefan Korbonski, former chief of the underground Directorate of Civil Resistance, who carried out the duties of the last delegate of the Polish government in exile in London during the war.'

The young man broke off and pointed his finger at me. I took a deep breath and leaned towards the microphone as I started to speak in a voice charged with emotion: 'Dear fellow-countrymen...'

It was thus that in 1950 I started my broadcasts to Poland which continue up to the present. Their main theme is international events affecting Polish matters, primarily American policy regarding Poland, and also various national anniversaries, celebrations and ceremonies. Zosia's voice reached Poland even before mine, since she was employed by the official 'Voice of America' in 1948 and broadcast daily. The parts we had played during the war were now reversed. Then we had spoken, sometimes in code, from underground broadcasting stations in occupied Poland to the government in exile and to fellow countrymen in the free world, whereas now we spoke from the free world to fellow countrymen in Poland under yet another occupation. In the underground we had listened to Western broadcasts at the risk of our lives. Now other people in Poland would be risking their freedom to listen to us.

This contact with Poland by radio was rendered possible by the establishment of the Free Europe Committee in the United States, the task of which was the mobilization and support of all efforts aimed at restoring independence and democratic government to the countries of Eastern and Central Europe. It started its activities on June 1, 1949, by the establishment of a broadcasting station to transmit programmes to the countries behind the Iron Curtain in the languages of those countries. The first broadcast was made on July 14, 1950, the anniversary of the fall of the Bastille. The Committee's main task was to provide these countries, deprived as they were of free press and radio, with factual news from the West, not falsified or suppressed by communist propaganda, and not restricted by the policy of the American government, to which the official 'Voice of America' had to conform. At the same time a 'Crusade for Freedom' was organized under the leadership of General Lucius D. Clay, to collect funds from the American people for the activities of the Free Europe Committee. This was inaugurated by a speech by General Eisenhower who was made a member of the Free Europe Committee council, in which he appealed for generosity to the cause. The then President of the United States, Harry Truman, gave this campaign his approval in a letter to General Clay, in which he emphasized the importance of private organizations and associations taking the initiative in this cause.

Over the years the Free Europe Committee and the Crusade for Freedom have developed into powerful organizations with such branches as Radio Free Europe, a Mid-European Study Centre, a Free Europe press, a section for co-operation with political refugees, and the Free Europe University, which included in its scope not only America but also had outposts in certain countries in Europe. Radio Free Europe, which started its activity with one small, short-wave broadcasting station, in the course of years developed into twenty-eight stations located in West Germany and Portugal; despite jamming it is so widely listened to behind the Iron Curtain that it has become a sort of everyday institution there, stubbornly attacked by the communist press and radio.

An important question was facing the Polish political émigrés in the United States. Should financial help from the Free Europe Committee be accepted? I had heard complaints on all sides about the lack of such assistance from the American government and people ever since I landed in the United States. When it was offered, criticism occurred mostly from those organizations and persons who had been left out. Those who accepted, including the entire presidium of the PSL and members of other political parties in the United States, acted on the assumption that without this assistance any kind of wider political action in conditions prevailing in America would not be possible. There were two alternatives : earning a living, or political activity. As far as daily, planned action was concerned, the one excluded the other. The émigrés in London were in a more favourable situation than for instance those who had fled from Poland since the war, often with only the clothes they stood up in.

The London exiles had large sums of money left over from the war period, houses they had bought and savings they had accumulated. The choice was decided by the fact that the assistance was granted under just one condition, which in reality was not a condition at all, i.e. that the money should be used in the fight to restore her independence and a democratic system to Poland. Admittedly, the receipt of money creates an unspoken and unwritten dependence between giver and recipient, but the identity of the political aims of both parties levelled this out in matters of greater importance while, in lesser, the significance of the whole matter boiled down to whether the recipient side would have the courage to say no should this be necessary. Consideration as to who had this courage and who had not would reduce the whole question to pieces.

The second problem was the character of Radio Free Europe. Was it to be an American broadcasting station or, in the relevant section, Polish? Several years of practical activity were to show that in fact it would be neither, but would have a mixed Polish-American character. Admittedly the main leadership was in American hands, but Polish political groups and over a hundred Polish writers, journalists, politicians, artists and scholars were, by the strength of their number, intellect and patriotism, to exert such an influence on the American management that whenever fundamental Polish interests were concerned, such as the defence of the Oder-Neisse frontier, still not recognized by the United States, Polish views won the day. Polish-American co-operation was facilitated by the unity of the main aim, i.e. the restoration to Poland of her independence and a democratic system of government. As regards the way to attain this aim, i.e. strategy and political tactics, differences existed between the American and Polish points of view. In matters of this kind, the policy of Radio Free Europe became the resultant of a conflict between American and Polish views.

My first encounter at close quarters with the purely American world came about within the framework of a campaign organized by the Free Europe Committee. By this time I had mastered enough English to set off in May 1950 on my first lecture tour, at the invitation of the powerful farmers 'Grange association', with a lecture on 'The situation of the Polish village under the communist system.' I was accompanied on this trip by a young American lawyer, Henry Kirsch, of the Free Europe Committee, as my guide and guardian. The tour, with breaks between one cycle of lectures and the second, included the states of New York, New Jersey, Maryland, Pennsylvania, Western Virginia, Wisconsin, Illinois, Vermont and Michigan, and it brought me into contact with the American 'village',

which does not in fact exist, inasmuch as the farmers either gather
in townships or live on individual farms at a distance from each
other. The landscape, though different in the great plains and in
the mountains of Vermont, where it is reminiscent of the Beskidy
Mountains, had one trait in common—the appeal of nature still not
yet fully dominated by man. The railroads and magnificent highways along which we travelled from one place to the next gave the
impression of domination. But it was enough to leave the highway
for a few yards into the forests to find oneself in a thicket of fallen
trunks, tangled roots, hanging bindweed and moss, and the thought
involuntarily came to mind that no human foot had ever stepped
here before. Every now and then along the roads notices warned
of deer crossing at this point, and in reply to questions as to what
animals were to be found in the forests the farmers driving us
would answer, 'bears and roebuck', as though they were referring
to hares and pheasants. This impression intensified when I came
across deserted farms in clearings in the forest which had surrounded them on all sides and were slowly being engulfed again by
the inroads of brushwood and undergrowth. All that was missing
was an Indian peering out of the undergrowth at the deserted wig-
wam of the palefaces. For 300 years man has not been able to har-
ness and smooth out this nature, as in overcrowded Europe. All in
all, the sight of the extensive green plains, sparsely dotted with
farms, the hillsides covered in woodland, the well-watered rivers
and lakes, contained something calm, majestic and a silence unbroken by the few cars that passed along the invariably asphalted
highways. To one accustomed to the crowded Polish villages, this
country seemed scarcely inhabited, and capable of accommodating
many more millions. When Henry Kirsch asked what sort of impression the American landscape made upon me, I replied without
thinking 'America is green and uninhabited.'

The trip followed a schedule laid down in advance. We travelled
from New York to our destination by train but, once there, farmers
would drive us by car from one lecture hall to the next, and as a
rule, after my evening lecture, which ended with questions from
the audience, we would spend the night at a farmer's house : next
day he would show us round the neighbourhood and in the afternoon pass us on to the next. The farmers drove to the lectures with
their entire families, wife, children, and food, and afterwards small
receptions were held. An observer from poverty-stricken Poland
could not help being impressed by the fact that they were all well-
nourished, the men big and muscular, the women and children glow-
ing with health, adequately though simply dressed and shabby

clothing was hardly ever seen. At the end, everyone would sit down at tables that had been brought in quickly, hot coffee would be served in paper cups, and sandwiches were unpacked and partaken of, while I was questioned on various matters.

The atmosphere of the lectures and the talks over coffee was pleasant and friendly. These people, like the countryside that surrounded them, were tranquil and without a trace of urban nerves, they spoke without excitement and ordinary human benevolence radiated from them to me. They asked questions in front of the crowded audiences without embarrassment, showing familiarity with speaking at public meetings. When I remarked admiringly on this to Henry, he gave a simple explanation: 'In American schools children get used to saying things in public from the earliest age.'

They knew little about Poland and for them I was an exotic newcomer from behind the Iron Curtain, from the other hemisphere, from a country over which the hammer and sickle banner flew. This was usually revealed by the way in which the local chairman introduced me, and they did not try to hide the fact. 'We have with us today a guest from Poland, and it is my task to introduce him to you. But I'm afraid I shan't be able to do it properly, since all I know about the country refers to Kosciuszko and Pulaski. But I also know that the Poles are a fighting people who opposed Hitler and that's why our boys had to fight in Europe and some from our neighbourhood didn't come home. Now the Poles are again having trouble, with the Russians, who have occupied their country.'

Elsewhere, the lady-chairman, who was musical, had obtained her knowledge of Poland from another sphere. 'I know that Chopin and Paderewski were Poles, but as for the rest of our information on Poland, I'll have to ask our guest.'

In yet another case, the chairman unwittingly touched upon a profound note: 'As I see from his biography, our guest speaker to-day took part in the Warsaw insurrection. I hope he will tell us some details of that heroic act by the Poles, which was often mentioned here during the war.'

These confessions were made in a frank and sympathetic way, with a smile which asked forgiveness, and I preferred them to bombastic compliments. Bearing them in mind, I used to say a few words at the beginning of my lecture on basic information about Polish events since the outbreak of war.

The audiences listened to the lectures with much interest and in complete silence, broken from time to time only by the children sitting on their mothers' laps who, naturally enough, were bored

B*

and made this plain. I mentioned not only the compulsory deliveries enforced upon villages and the urge towards collectivization, but also the lack of personal freedom, the terror of the security police, the press censorship, the lack of freedom of the spoken word, the threats and chicanery used against the Church, and finally the threat of Communism to the whole world, including America.

What the audience thought of this subject was best reflected in the questions asked after the lecture. 'What does a Polish village look like?' 'Why do you use the word "peasant", which has something contemptuous in it?' 'What kind of food do they eat in Polish villages?' 'What's the average size of a Polish farm?' 'What do Polish farmers produce?' 'What machinery do they use on their farms, are the farms electrified and do they have cars?'

They grasped the political and economic situation of the Polish village very well as information, but they did not understand or feel it. An invisible filter prevented the meaning of my words from reaching and penetrating the depths of their consciousness. The conditions these frank and open people had been born and grown up under rejected the idea that the State might take away someone's farm and force him into a collective farm. Such things might happen on the moon, but not in the United States. This want of understanding of a situation created by foreign occupation sometimes led to such naïve questions as 'If you don't like the communist government, why don't you drive these people out?'

As for the threat of Communism for the United States, they underestimated this entirely. They knew something of the activity of the Communist party in the United States from the newspapers and radio, but not by their own observation or experience. I, as a newcomer to America, was startled in several cases by questions such as 'Do you really think that there are people in the United States who want to overthrow our government and bring in a communist dictatorship?' When in my reply I mentioned the trial of the leaders of the American Communist party, which was going on in New York, this was not regarded as a sufficient proof. 'Yes, there may be such people in New York, which is a real Sodom and Gomorrah, but not in our state.'

The height of naïvety was a question I fortunately only heard once : 'Do you really think that there are communists in America? It seems to me that this is only an invention by the government for putting up the taxes.'

Two questions recurred at every lecture. The first was always asked by a woman : 'Are Polish children communistic?' and the second always occurred towards the end of the meeting: 'How can we help Poland?'

I was struck by the lack of political experience of these people as regards the question of Communism when compared, for instance, with that of the Polish peasant. But the explanation of this was clear enough. For the Polish peasant, Communism is there on the spot, in Poland, in his village; it is a fact which has become an element in his everyday life. Any steps the communist government took immediately affected his life, possessions, income and standard of living. He was forced to adopt an attitude towards government regulations preceded by a process of thought based on everyday experience and in this process he attained the high standard I had found so striking during the PSL congress in January, 1946.

Yet for these American farmers, Communism was a fairy tale about a bad wolf, which the lecturer said existed and might devour them. But if the worst came to the worst, the wolf was overseas, and in any case his American farm was protected by the foremost military power in the world, that of the United States. Hence their lack of any deeper concern with the danger, which to them was more or less theoretical. I am certain that if my lecture had been concerned with an American problem the standard both of questions and discussion would have been immeasurably higher.

When the lecture was over, we would go home with a farmer and sit down to a supper at which all the dishes were served simultaneously, including coffee. The hosts were hospitable, but without insistence. They urged us to eat and kept offering other dishes, but after one refusal the offer was not repeated. If they caught signs of tiredness in their guest, they would show him his room and retire discreetly. This atmosphere of benevolence and calm started to act upon me too. Despite the nervous effort of every lecture, I felt relaxed and refreshed.

Trips round the neighbourhood facilitated observations quite beyond my expectation. Apart from a sector of the state of Wisconsin, where the farms were reminiscent of wealthy peasant farms in the best cultivated area of Poland, the Poznan district, all the others were richer, more up-to-date and specialized. I could not help making a comment which the local newspaper caught: 'This isn't a farm, but an agricultural factory.' This occurred after inspecting a large, electrified farm with brick buildings, roofed with sheet-metal, where I did not see a single horse, but only machines, and where eighty cows were looked after by one man by means of mechanical devices providing pasture, removing manure and milking them: the cows were, moreover, artificially fertilized and fed according to a formula prepared by scientists. I saw many more of this type of farm. They had dwelling-houses, usually two-storeyed, well-furnished, with carpets of American manufacture in the sitting-room, a radio set, often television, with bathrooms, ice-boxes, and central heating. I need hardly add that all this separated them from any comparison with the Polish village. Specialization was apparent in the fact that in one district there would be nothing but chicken farms, in another fruit farms, while in a third region only cows were bred, etc. A farmer could produce and sell eggs, or fruit, or milk, whereas all the other products required for his family, including bread, would be bought in the local township, into which he would naturally drive by car. When I was asked my views on this specialization, I had only one criticism to offer : 'In the event of a war or other crisis which might paralyse your system of precise communications and supply for even a short while as the result, for instance, of a temporary shortage of petrol, you would starve. Our peasant is far more self-sufficient, since each produces his own grain, eggs, milk and fruit, as well as keeping pigs, and the only use he has for petrol is for his cigarette lighter, since he travels everywhere by horse and cart.'

Henry, my fellow-traveller, was the first American I got to know and he left his mark in my life by being the person with whom I held my first conversation in English without the assistance of an interpreter. This occurred at a cocktail party given by Waclaw Solski, a Polish émigré writer, who kindly proposed to act as interpreter. Henry politely dismissed this offer. 'Leave us alone, we'll manage somehow.' After an hour of conversation I rose as tired as though I had been working hard. But the iron curtain which divides a newcomer from the language of the natives had been lifted. After a few talks, I noticed that Henry had an unmistakable liking for Poles, and I asked him why. 'My grandmother came from Wilno and believed it was the most beautiful city in the world, and that Poles are good, reliable people,' Henry explained. I was not surprised by this admiration for Wilno, a really beautiful city, since I had already got used to hearing that the most beautiful town in the world for anyone coming from Poland is the town they were born in, no matter where it was. It appeared from further confidences that Henry was his grandmother's darling, that she was a great authority for him and that, when grandmother had one of her rare fits of anger, she would always swear in Polish, of which her young grandson remembered only the word *psiakrew*. In any case, what the grandmother had induced into the child still remained in the grown man and facilitated our acquaintance as well as rendering the journey more agreeable. Only in one respect did I disagree with grandmother, but Henry, who had a good knowledge of my war-time adventures, accepted this with indulgent tolerance. The most beautiful town in the world is not Wilno, but Warsaw.

IV

HAROLD MACMILLAN AMONG THE ÉMIGRÉS

I received a letter dated London, November 29, 1949, containing the following : 'As you know, the European Movement has formed an East European section to deal with the various problems of particular interest to the countries of Eastern Europe. I would like to ask you, as a former member of the Underground Government in Poland and representative therein of the Peasant Party, to become a member of the Polish group of the Eastern European section and participate in its work.' The letter was signed by Harold Macmillan, chairman of the East European section.

I examined the notepaper on which the letter had been written. The name of one of the honorary presidents brought up many thoughts : it was 'Winston Churchill'. How much this name had meant to us in the underground movement in the years 1940 to 1944, and how suddenly it had fallen from the pedestal on which it had been placed by Polish naïvety and lack of understanding of the motives behind the international policy of the Great Powers. It had been once a symbol of courage in battle and of genius in leadership, but today it is uttered by Poles with grief and resentment. He had been one of those who, at Teheran and Yalta, had left the 'inspiration of the free world' to its own devices, to take on the form of Soviet occupation. He and others had been responsible for our understanding of the bitter truth that no treaty is observed by any state merely for the principle of keeping an obligation once entered into, but only if it is required by the interests of the country concerned. This principle was clearly expressed by Churchill himself in a dramatic talk with Mikolajczyk, after the latter's return into exile in October 1947. Mikolajczyk, who made no secret of the fact that he admired Churchill, questioned the rightness of the advice given him in 1945 to come to terms with the Yalta agreement, go back to Poland and fight for its implementation. Churchill replied to this with brutal frankness : 'I was then the Prime Minister of Great Britain and what I advised you to do was dictated by the interests of Great Britain. You, on the other hand, were the Prime

Minister of Poland and it was up to you to reject my advice, if it did not agree with Poland's interests.'

Despite these discouraging recollections, the letter predicted some kind of action as regards the cause of Eastern Europe, so I accepted the invitation and on June 27, 1950, took part for the first time in a meeting of the European section in London, under the chairmanship of Harold Macmillan, Conservative MP and signatory of the letter. Apart from myself, the Polish representatives were Ambassador Edward Raczynski, president Tadeusz Bielecki, Franciszek Bialas, Professor Stefan Glaser, Rowmund Pilsudski, Jerzy Zdziechowski and Boleslaw Wierzbianski.

This was how I became acquainted with the European Movement, which had emerged on the principle that the nations of Europe needed more unity to be able to solve urgent problems of reconstruction and further existence. This movement gave birth to the Council of Europe and the Consultative Assembly in Strasbourg. Since the introductory talks showed that European unity would not be complete without the participation of countries behind the Iron Curtain, representatives in exile of these countries were invited to take part in the opening talks, which were held within the framework of the conference of the European Movement in 1948 at The Hague and in 1949 at Brussels. As a result of these talks, the Central and Eastern European section was formed at the end of 1948 under Macmillan's chairmanship, consisting of émigré leaders from Poland, Bulgaria, Czechoslovakia, Hungary, Rumania and Yugoslavia, who agreed with the view that after their countries, amounting to some hundred million people, had regained freedom, they would have to enter into some form of unification in order to play a full part in a wider European union. Representatives of Estonia, Lithuania, Latvia and Albania entered the section later.

From the very beginning of my membership of this body it became apparent to everyone that it was of a mixed character, since it was headed by a Scot, whereas its members were exiles : in this respect it differed from the similar body formed on American initiative, the Free Europe Committee, which was established to assist exiles but did not attempt to form any mixed organizations. A further observation was provided by the basic declaration of this section on December 6, 1949, from which it became clear that its approach to East European matters was—as it were—from the rear end, inasmuch as its programme referred exclusively to the principles on which the countries of East Europe would base their existence after regaining their independence, while it did not mention a single word as to how this independence was to be regained. The only reference to this most important problem was this :

> 7. When the countries of Eastern Europe are liberated from Communist domination, the Western World must generously give its financial and technical help in the economic reconstruction of these countries.

This aroused my scepticism, but as half a loaf is better than no bread, I remained in the organization, which eventually adopted the name of the Central and Eastern European Commission. Macmillan shortly afterwards left for Strasbourg, where he placed a resolution before the Consultative Assembly which was adopted by the Assembly on August 28, 1950. Its most important points were :

> The Assembly, recognizing that certain nations which are precluded from participating in the work of the Council of Europe, nevertheless form an integral part of Europe, decided to instruct the Standing Committee to constitute a special committee whose duty it would be to ensure that the interests of these nations shall be considered in every proposal which may be formulated by the Assembly or its committees.

In this way the special committee was formed to safeguard the interests of nations not represented in the Council of Europe; it is still in being and continually examines the situation in countries behind the Iron Curtain, submitting reports and relevant recommendations to the standing committee. Its first chairman was Harold Macmillan.

Visiting London again at the end of June 1951, I had the opportunity of direct contact with this leading actor in the East European campaign at a lunch for three at the home of his right-hand man in the Commission, Major Edward Beddington-Behrens.

Mr Macmillan betrayed a good knowledge of Polish matters and much sympathy with Polish aims. He was primarily interested in the activities of our political émigrés in the United States and our relations there with American political circles. He was impressed by the fact that Polonia in America, represented by their own congress, amounted to over six millions and that there were usually more than ten Congressmen of Polish origin in the United States House of Representatives. During our talk, I emphasized the need for closer co-operation between the Commission and the Central and Eastern European Conference recently established in the United States, which had come into being on Polish initiative and consisted of exiles from the countries of East and Central Europe. This met with full understanding from my two interlocutors.

Our host was an example of a special kind of political philan-thropist. He was not a professional politician as Macmillan was, but merely a person with political interests and of independent means and thus able to devote his time and energy to so unreward-ing a cause as the countries behind the Iron Curtain, while perhaps also serving his own country at the same time. Shortly after Mac-millan entered the government, Beddington-Behrens was appointed chairman of the Commission and remained in this post till Septem-ber 1952, when he was replaced by Richard Law, a Member of Parliament.

During this stay in England I also had the opportunity of visiting the Distinguished Visitors' Gallery for a lunch given in July 1951 by Beddington-Behrens in honour of the president of the Consulta-tive Assembly, Paul-Henrie Spaak. The list of guests, apart from the guest of honour and exiles, read like an extract from the register of the Houses of Parliament. But my attention was primarily drawn to two persons : one was Professor Salvador de Madariaga, a Spanish exile from the Franco government, who might well be named the world's leading emigrant, an inspired, fiery speaker, reminiscent of Skarga in Matejko's painting. The voice of this widely respected man and scholar resounded across the entire world when he spoke out in defence of people oppressed by Fascism and Communism. The other was a man of medium height, aged about fifty, who wore an irreproachable suit, and did not betray by his appearance the important though secret part he played in the war. When we were introduced, we looked at one another with the smile of people who know a little about each other and we at once entered into a talk, during which I forgot about the rest of those present. This was General Colin Gubbins, responsible during the war for the co-ordi-nation of European underground movements within the frame-work of Allied strategy. During our brief conversation I heard enough compliments from him about the Polish underground con-spiracy to last for several hours of talk. My new acquaintance ended by wishing success to our present activities as a prolongation of the earlier, underground ones. Thus, at a banquet in London's smart Claridge's Hotel, the echo of earlier matters and years returned once again : flights across Poland on clear moonlit nights, drop-ping arms and ammunition, blowing up bridges and munitions trains, salvoes of machine-gun fire, marching German units.

Macmillan, now a minister, took part in the conference called by the European Movement in London in January 1952. He said : 'I am here on behalf of and as a member of H.M. government to wel-come you to our capital city. In particular, the Foreign Secretary has asked me to do this on his behalf and to say how much he hopes the Conference may be successful and fruitful.'

Thus the work of the conference was given official approval by the British government, and this time it made the liberation of Eastern Europe a condition of lasting agreement with the Soviet Union, by stating : 'A lasting settlement with the Soviet Union will only be achieved when national independence with personal freedom has been established in the countries of Central and Eastern Europe and when, assured of the enjoyment of that independence, they can unite with the rest of the European family.'

But it was not until a resolution of the special committee of the Consultative Assembly was placed before the Assembly on September 29, 1952, that definite form was given to this political concept, which had evolved over a period of three years :

> The Assembly requests the Council of Ministers to discuss and initiate without delay any peaceful measures which will hasten the day when the peoples of all countries in Europe are free to choose their own governments, to develop their democratic institutions as part of the European community, and to work together with unity of purpose for the maintenance of peace, and the promotion of the well-being of all Europe.

This resolution was subsequently developed and confirmed in a resolution of the Consultative Assembly on May 28, 1954, in which the Assembly undertook to do everything within its power to create a political and diplomatic international situation which would enable the peoples behind the Iron Curtain to regain full independence and their democratic freedom.

The Assembly reverted on several occasions to this problem during its further work, and kept on the agenda the case of the peoples of Eastern and Central Europe not represented in this body, whereas events went otherwise in the Central and Eastern European Commission, which evolved negatively and ceased in practice to function after the end of 1952. Finally, after electing the French Senator de la Vallée Poussin its chairman in April 14, 1954, it transferred its secretariat from London to Brussels, and later to Paris, i.e. to countries with a different political atmosphere. This was equivalent to the withdrawal of British leadership and initiative in matters concerning the Iron Curtain countries, and was done with all the polite ceremony required on such occasions, in the form of the usual phrases and a smoke-screen of thanks and compliments. Macmillan and Beddington-Behrens were elected honorary presidents of the Commission. This came about despite the fact that on December

8, 1953, Prime Minister Churchill had signed the Bermuda declaration along with President Eisenhower and the French Premier, Laniel, in which a passage referring to the Iron Curtain countries said :

> We cannot accept as justified or permanent the present division of Europe. Our hope is that in due course peaceful means will be found to enable the countries of Eastern Europe again to play their parts as free nations in a free Europe.

The initiative for introducing this paragraph came from the American side and this may explain the apparent contradiction between the withdrawal of British leadership from the Central and Eastern European Commission and the principle expressed in the Bermuda agreement. In fact, this contradiction did not arise : what occurred was merely a withdrawal from political action in favour of platonic declarations, while in the later course of events American policy took over British initiative in matters concerning Eastern Europe, the first indication of which was the creation of the Free Europe Committee.

Why did this liquidation of political action come about, headed as it was at first by the man who was to become the Prime Minister of the United Kingdom? The reasons may well be various, but one was certainly the thrusting aside of Eastern and Central European matters into the second rank of problems concerning Soviet Russia, and the growing atomic power of the Soviet Union for which the British Isles form an excellent target. Another, more practical, cause was undoubtedly the fact that all the émigrés from the Iron Curtain countries, with the exception of the Polish Political Council and the August Zaleski group, created their own national representations in the United States, thus transferring the centre of gravity of their political activities to America.

I had no further contact with the work of the Central and Eastern European Commission except for some meetings with its general secretary, Dr Jozef Retinger, an old friend from the underground movement. After the icy shower he got in Poland in 1944, when a cart taking him to a secret airfield overturned and he fell into a ditch full of water, Retinger never really recovered his health, and now he walked with a stick, dragging his legs. I already knew that he was a controversial figure among the Polish emigration in London, who suspected him of being in close touch not so much with British politics as with certain of its discreet institutions. To me, however, he was still the emissary 'Salamander' who, despite the fact that he was no longer young, had risked a night parachute jump into Poland during the war, and had moved about Warsaw, with the Gestapo on his trail, with unshakable courage, or more precisely with unusual nonchalance. So I took every opportunity of meeting him, in restaurants and at his home where, as we recalled adventures in the underground movement, we surrendered to the grateful occupation of comparing the taste of Scotch and wartime 'hooch'. Salamander was the soul of the Commission, into which he put a great deal of effort and work, and he took its collapse rather hard.

V

THE BIRTH OF POLONIA

We left Washington by car early in the morning in order to arrive in good time. The day was fine and sunny, and my old Ford was in good order, so we drove fast along the highways of hilly Virginia enjoying the view of the motionless, deep blue woods, the green fields and meadows.

When we reached Jamestown I was able to see for the first time the spot where on October 1, 1608, five Poles had landed from the *Mary and Margaret* under her captain Christopher Newport, thus initiating the stream from Poland to America which is still going on today. I had the clear impression I had come to a place with which something linked me, although I had never seen it before. For Michal Lowicki (or Nowicki, as another source gives) from London, Zbigniew Stefanski from Wloclawek, Jan Mata from Cracow, Stanislaw Sadowski from Radom and Jan Bogdan from Kolomyja, who had landed here more than 350 years earlier, started the chain in which Zosia and I were also links. The successors to these first Polish settlers amounted in the United States census for 1950 to 5,332,115 people, and now number about seven millions. Their descendants in America, and they must have had some since in this respect the reputation of Poles is sufficient proof in itself, ought to be prouder than the best American families descended from the Pilgrim Fathers, who came to Plymouth in the *Mayflower* in 1620, for their American origin is twelve years older. These Polish wanderers started many things in America, and the first was the contorting of Polish names, which still goes on. In addition, it was they and not the Carnegies or Fords who laid the foundations of American industry by building the first glass-blowing factory in America, and started the first pitch foundry, sawmill, soap factory and potash industry. One of their first products were bottles, which gave me an idea and set me going through old chronicles. However I did not come upon the traces either in old chronicles or in Jamestown itself of the first distillery, but my search led to the idea that our émigré prototypes had, in establishing the first American factories become the first capitalists, from whom the bankers of Wall Street must be directly descended. Unfortunately, the latter do not admit to this relationship, as is evidenced by the cry which arises constantly among newcomers, 'no money!' A fact apparently in contrast to this idea is that in 1619 the Polish settlers organized the first strike in America, which might make them working-class. This came about because they were refused the right to vote in elections to the Legislative Assembly. According to one source, this was done on the allegation they had not paid for their journey from England to America, but according to another it was because they had not been born in England. This contradiction—capitalists or workers—is apparent in that strikes in a man's own factory are a well-known phenomenon, except that they are called lock-outs. In other words, the first Polish settlers organized the first capitalist lock-out in America which, by creating a shortage of products on the market at Jamestown, sought to exercise influence over a political decision. Their act can only be called the first strike in America in this sense had their factories passed into other hands in the interval between 1608 and 1619, of which there is no proof. However this may be, they behaved in a truly Polish manner and have gone down in history.

As for the pretext used for refusing these first settlers the right to vote, this is reminiscent of similar means applied by the communists in Poland in the falsification of the election in 1947, when under one pretext or another over a million people were refused the right to vote. When it came to my attention that the Polish communist ambassador in Washington, Spasowski, was planning to organize a celebration at Jamestown of the 350th anniversary, I realized that he did not plan to honour the first Poles in America, but Yardleye, the English governor of Virginia, who must be reckoned the first falsifier of elections in America if not in the world. It turned out however that I was mistaken, inasmuch as Ambassador Spasowski sought, under the pretext of honouring the settlers, to link them by blood or descent with the régime he served, so as to gain certain propaganda advantages. With this in mind, he arranged a date with the local authorities for the celebration, and sent out invitations to eminent Americans, including the governor of Virginia. When the Polish-American Congress intervened and unmasked the real intentions of the ambassador, the eminent Americans one after another began to withdraw from the affair, Spasowski gave up, the ceremony was called off and passed into the hands of the Polish-American Congress as the only body entitled to hold it.

These and similar thoughts passed through my head as Zosia and

I walked round the wide expanse of Jamestown, looking at the few remaining ruins and greeting fellow-countrymen, of whom several thousands had travelled here from all over America to celebrate the arrival 350 years earlier of their protoplasts. This crowd presently took their places in an amphitheatre to listen to Rozmarek, speaking in the name of the organizers of the ceremony, the Polish-American Congress, as well as Fred Seaton, Secretary of the Interior and a member of the government, delegated this day to Jamestown as personal representative of President Eisenhower, to pay tribute to the Poles in America.

As I sat among the guests on the platform, I was able to enjoy the beautiful view provided by the wall of trees surrounding the amphitheatre in the hot sunlight, and the carefully-kept flower-beds, against which a colourful group of halbardiers in mediaeval armour and helmets stood out brightly, giving splendour to the ceremony. I did not fail to observe a kind of 'playing at Indians' which started immediately after our arrival when a visitor from Poland, who had come from New York to Washington for a few days and accompanied us to Jamestown, suddenly jumped aside and concealed himself behind a tree. Accustomed through the years to various kinds of surprises, we did not even slow down, in the belief that sooner or later the reason would be explained. And this happened fifteen minutes later, in a secluded spot where not so much racial as sexual segregation prevailed. Here the visitor from Poland whispered to me : 'I caught sight of three officials from the embassy, whom I met when I reported there on arrival, and did not want them to see me here, and in your company too.'

My blood boiled, like an old cavalry charger when it hears the trumpet call to battle, and in my mouth I felt the bitter taste of conspiracy.

'Show me them,' I whispered in his ear, simultaneously pushing the pedal so that the noise of rushing water would drown any possible eavesdropping, in accordance with the principles of conspiracy.

We went out separately, and after a number of manoeuvres he indicated with his gaze three young men ceaselessly moving amidst the crowd. So Ambassador Spasowski, once his idea had gone for nothing, had sent his subordinates to report to him how it went off. And they were now fereting about, collecting material for their report and giving us the opportunity of watching their behaviour, which reminded me of the games of careless childhood. All that was lacking were bows and arrows. For when the agents of the embassy moved left, the visitor from Poland moved right. When the agents went forward, he would retire, and this went on for an hour, as the speeches were being made. The visitor came off best, since when the ceremony was over he reached our car without having been noticed, and with a deep sigh of relief fell back against his seat. That evening in Washington we let him get off, just in case, in a shady, empty, side street, and he disappeared from sight in a moment.

A year later, on September 3, 1959, in a deserted little church in Jamestown only rarely visited by tourists, three persons were standing at the altar : an elderly man in black, and a young couple in front of him. The man was holding a Bible in one hand and saying something in a low voice, as he turned from the slender girl to a tall, broad-shouldered young man. He finally raised his voice and said, 'I declare you man and wife.'

In this manner, one of the youngest soldiers of the Home Army, Julian Kulski, who had recently arrived in America, made a leap into the past and formed a link with his fellow-countrymen who had preceded him by 350 years. Having found his life's companion, he wondered how and where to hold the marriage ceremony. In his homeland the wedding was held either in one's own parish, or else a place associated with family history, or famous, such as Jasna Gora at Czestochowa. But how was he to find a similar place in foreign America, where he was moreover a newcomer? Learning by chance of the ceremony which had taken place a year earlier at Jamestown, he realized, 'This is the place I am looking for.'

The celebration of a marriage there was no easy matter. It required first of all permission from the Secretary of the Interior, within whose competence this kind of historical spot falls. Later it was necessary to find a clergyman of the appropriate rite and bring him to the spot. Two declined the proposal, but the third, struck by the originality of the idea, let himself be persuaded. Once he had got over these obstacles with the courage proper to a Home Army soldier, Kulski and his fiancée and the priest went to Jamestown by car, where on presentation of the letter from the Department of the Interior they were admitted by the guards, who saluted respectfully, into the first settlement, and the marriage with the past took place. The witnesses of the ceremony were the spirits of the first settlers. When the newspaper in nearby Williamsburg announced in the 'marriages' column that Kulski was the descendant of a 1610 settler, 'Bohun', confidence may be placed in the printed word that Kulski, who by the way is a son of the former Vice-President of Warsaw, was married in his own parish.

Each year, on the anniversary of the birth of Kosciuszko or the death of Pulaski, two delegations appear at intervals of an hour before their memorials in Washington. Both lay wreaths, and both make speeches in praise of the Polish-American heroes who fought for the freedom of both countries. A squad of American soldiers and a bugler attend both ceremonies. And the same representatives of the State Department are present at both. A chance observer would spot the first difference as soon as he compared the number of persons present at the ceremonies, and the atmosphere prevailing. Whereas the first is attended by a few nervous and embarrassed people, who do not feel well-adapted to their part and try to hurry through the ceremony as fast as possible, the second is attended by a large crowd who, with calm solemnity and self-confidence, listen to several speeches. And if the chance passer-by wishes to listen, he will also observe a marked difference between the contents of the speeches of both delegations. Whereas the first flounders in *clichés* and generalities, avoiding any reference to the armed fight of Kosciuszko and Pulaski against Russia or to the present rule of Russia over Poland, very similar to that against which Kosciuszko and Pulaski fought, the second delegation will devote attention primarily to this very subject.

These two ceremonies are a small fragment of the stubborn battle for the moral right to represent the Polish people which is going on in America between the old and new emigrations on the one hand and the communist embassy on the other. It goes on over the policy of using Kosciuszko's name for communist propaganda, starting from the use of the name 'Tadeusz Kosciuszko' for an infantry division organized in Russia under the command of General Berling and for a secret Soviet broadcasting station transmitting in Polish which hypocritically appealed to the population of Warsaw to rise in 1944. Its officials form the first delegation while the second consists of representatives of the political emigration and of Polonia in America, among whom as a rule one or more United States Congressmen of Polish descent are present, with the organizer of the ceremony, Karol Burke, representing the Polish-American Congress. This delegation always places the wreath after the communist régime's delegation and the transition from one ceremony to the other also has the nature of a ceremony repeated annually. One actor in it is always the same—a lady from the Polish Club in Washington. She rushes up amidst the sudden silence that falls upon the crowd of those taking part in the ceremony at the memorial, seizes the wreath from the Embassy and carries it round to the other side of the memorial, or in the case of Pulaski to the tail end of his horse, muttering, 'That's your place.' The atmosphere at once improves and the second ceremony in honour of the national heroes starts on the battlefield thus cleared for the moral right to honour the national heroes.

Both Kosciuszko and Pulaski, along with well-known Maurycy Beniowski, Jan Zielinski, Karol Litomski and others, belonged to the second wave of Polish immigrants which reached the United States after the collapse of the Confederacy of Bar in 1768 and the first partition of 1772. Kosciuszko landed in America in August 1776 and Pulaski in July 1777. Both became national heroes of the United States—Kosciuszko as 'father of the artillery', Pulaski as 'father of the American cavalry'. Every American child learns this in school. It is to these two that the Polish emigration owes its strong moral position in America, since in fighting for the independence of the United States they were included—and the Poles through them—among the founders of the United States. We have always shed blood needlessly, but rarely has the death of one man brought so many advantages to Poland as that of Pulaski. It constituted the cement which has united the Poles with the rest of the American nation, though it gave wider popularity to Pulaski than to Kosciuszko. He has more memorials than Kosciuszko, and his name has been given to more towns, highways, bridges and other objects to which the names of national heroes are given. He also has the advantage of Kosciuszko in that the name Pulaski is easier for an Anglo-Saxon to pronounce.

It so happened that I spoke several times at the annual Kosciuszko and Pulaski ceremonies at the invitation of the Polish-American Congress. Pulaski's monument is on Pennsylvania Avenue, the main street of Washington. He is galloping on a fiery steed in the direction of the White House, though for some unknown reason his head has been adorned with a peasant fur hat and feathers. Not wanting to make do merely with patriotic *clichés*, I read everything I could lay hands on about the stay of both heroes in America and I was struck by a totally different attitude towards Kosciuszko in the United States from that in Poland, also visible in the style of the monuments. To the Americans, Kosciuszko is primarily a level-headed professional engineer, officer and leader, who built excellent fortifications near Saratoga and at West Point and contributed towards forming a regular army, primarily artillery, out of farmers, hunters, merchants and tradesmen. Hence on every monument he appears in an officer's cloak, with a tricorne hat on and a sword by his side, dressed, as it were, according to American army regulations. All the average American knows about his later history is that he returned to Poland and headed an insurrection. In Poland, all the monuments I remember show him dressed in a peasant coat such as the one he wore at Raclawice, which emphasizes his role as a social reformer and the author of the Polaniecki Manifesto of May 7, 1794, in which he proclaimed the principle of liberating the peasants from serfdom and announced immediate freedom for those who, armed, would take part in a battle for Poland. This Kosciuszko, the political reformer and freethinker, is comparatively unknown in America, undoubtedly because his later history had no connection with the life of the United States. As for Pulaski, a much more colourful personality than Kosciuszko emerges from American books, full of unbridled temperament, bursting with energy and with a clearly adventurous turn. He made himself known in covering Washington's retreat at Brandywine when his counterattacks in the rear saved the American army from certain destruction. Four days after this battle, Congress appointed him a general. During the severe winter when Washington's army was starving at Valley Forge, Pulaski and his cavalry fought their way through the British lines and returned with food and other army supplies. He was an excellent cavalry leader, of the same type as Sienkiewicz's Wolodyjowski, and in addition an individualist who could not endure bonds, and found it difficult to submit to the command of anyone except Washington. The latter had a number of rows with Pulaski on these grounds, which he only disposed of by permitting him to organize a semi-independent brigade of cavalry. At the head of these rowdies of his, he was wounded by a bullet in the charge near Savannah, and died in the hospital ship *Wasp*.

Following the emigration of the time of Kosciuszko and Pulaski, a new wave arrived after the Napoleonic wars, after 1812, and Poles, including Dabrowski's legionnaires, once again fought with the United States against Britain, in 1812-1815. After the 1831 insurrection in Poland, scattered insurrectionists arrived, including two boat-loads of 235, exiled in 1834 by the Austrians. The revolutions of 1846 and 1848 brought new exiled wanderers to the shores of America, including Jan Tyssowski, leader of the insurrection in Cracow, and Wlodzimierz Krzyzanowski, Jozef Karge and Albin Schoepf, later brigade-generals in the army of the United States.

General of Brigade Albin Franciszek Schoepf, born at Podgorze near Cracow and educated at the Military Academy in Vienna, quit the Austrian army after the outbreak of the Hungarian insurrection in 1848 and joined the forces of Ludwig Kossuth as a private, where he rapidly rose to the rank of major. After the suppression of the insurrection, he went to Turkey and served there under General Bem. He came to the United States in 1851, and upon the outbreak of the Civil War ten years later he joined the Northern

army, in which he was appointed General of Brigade. He commanded in many battles, but made his mark in particular at Perry-
ville. He ended his military career as a member of the Supreme
Army Tribunal.

Polish-American historians, including the very worthy Mieczyslaw Haiman, had long since learned that General Schoepf was of
Polish descent and the course of his army career was known to
them from official documents of the Civil War; but as for his later
years, the traces led to Washington, then broke off. It was Wiktor
A. Wojciechowski who happened by chance upon a tomb-stone in
the Congressional cemetery on the outskirts of Washington bearing
the name Schoepf, and informed Congressman Tadeusz Machrowicz
of the fact. The latter visited the grave in 1957 and checked the
cemetery records, where he found the entry : 'Albin Schoepf, General of Brigade, born March 1, 1822, died May 10, 1886, at Hyattsville, Maryland, buried May 12, 1886.'

Hyattsville is part of Greater Washington, and Machrowicz was
able to confirm without doubt that General Schoepf and his family
had lived there and that he is buried with his wife and children
in a large tomb in the cemetery there.

This discovery had a certain significance in the life of Polonia as it
was yet another proof of their contribution to the development of
the United States, a country which suffers a little from a lack of
history and tradition, and is envious of the many centuries of
Europe's past and Europe's old monuments. Because of this, Americans surround with great piety everything connected with their brief
past and hundreds of thousands of motorized pilgrims annually visit
their historic places. Thus it is not surprising that, only a year
after the discovery, a ceremony was held at the grave of General
Schoepf similar to that which has for years taken place at the grave
of the other General of Brigade in the Northern army, Wlodzimierz
Krzyzanowski, in the National cemetery in Arlington, where the
eminent are buried. This makes of it something of an American
'Skalka'. This courageous leader of an infantry brigade unexpectedly
became the central figure of a sitting of the United States Senate
about a century ago. President Lincoln promoted him to the rank
of general for the courage he had shown in the battle of Bull Run,
and his nomination was placed before the Senate for approval in
accordance with procedure. When the official reading the decree
came to the name 'Krzyzanowski' he choked and uttered a series of
hissing sounds, supposed to render this fine-sounding Polish name,
but to the ears of the senators it was the voice of a man with something caught in his throat. Thereupon a voice was heard from the

Senate hall, saying, 'We cannot confirm the nomination of a man whose name no one can pronounce.' And the matter fell through. Krzyzanowski did not take the advice of friends to change his name, thus setting his descendants a good example. He soon obtained full satisfaction, however, since towards the end of the war his nomination went through Congress with no difficulty.

It is not far from Krzyzanowski's grave to the place where, close to the grave of the Unknown Soldier, lie the remains of a man whom Polonia still admires and whom all America remembers and respects—Ignacy Paderewski. His remains rest in a metal coffin, in a memorial chapel erected in honour of sailors who perished in an explosion in the American battleship *Maine*. And they will rest there, in accordance with the wish of Paderewski, which President Roosevelt confirmed, until such time as Poland regains complete independence. Another 'duel with wreaths' took place at this grave in 1960. On the centenary of Paderewski's birth, which was officially celebrated by the American Post Office with a stamp bearing his likeness and by ceremonies in front of his memorial, attended by the Postmaster General, Arthur Summerfield, agents of the embassy left their wreath in front of the chapel before the ceremony began, then disappeared. The wreath was noticed, placed inside the memorial and took no part in the ceremony.

This is not the end of this tour round the cemeteries of Washington, since in the third of them, Mount Olivet, are the remains of the former Polish ambassador, Lukasiewicz, who committed suicide in Washington, broken by the disasters which had come upon Poland; General Rudolf Dreszer; General Antoni Monter-Chrusciel, leader of the Home Army who fought during the Warsaw insurrection; Halina Omiecinska, for many years an official of the Ministry of War; and finally Ambassador Jozef Lipski. The death of the last-named affected me deeply, since during his several years' stay in Washington I had become very friendly with him, as well as greatly esteeming his devoted work as unofficial Polish ambassador. It so happened that I had been talking to him on the day of his death. He was in bed, though he felt well enough to plan to go to Newark near New York for a meeting on the following Sunday. I had some difficulty in dissuading him from this plan. Some hours later, notified by a call from his wife Anna, Zosia and I were standing by his corpse.

VI

LANCERS IN A BOAT

Polonia in America has undergone and is continually undergoing changes. Whereas the first group of settlers who landed in Jamestown must be reckoned as coming to earn a living, the later arrivals after the 1812 Napoleonic wars, the 1831 insurrection and the revolutions of 1846 and 1848 were political and military exiles. But later political refugees after the 1863 insurrection and the 1905 revolution were absorbed by the mass of wage-earning immigrants which started about 1850, and this gave its nature to the old Polish emigrations in the United States. Among them a political process took place in their relation to their new homeland—a normal phenomenon—but also in relation to their former homeland, a less usual phenomenon. The peasants comprising the main body of the working emigration, came to America from their decayed and poverty-stricken villages in search of bread, along with workers and craftsmen from the towns, and they occupied themselves with earning a living and growing richer. But at the same time they began to take an interest in the regaining of Poland's freedom. While they were still living in Poland this interest had been stifled by poverty and the partitioning governments of Russia, Germany and Austria. Now organizations arose, the statutes of which show that their aim was the liberation of Poland from the rule of the three powers. In 1887 the Polish 'Falcon' organization was formed, a kind of Polish army in exile, which was to constitute the main core of General Jozef Haller's army in 1918, together with various other associations of Polish armed forces. A typical example of such an association was the Society of the Fourth Regiment of Red Lancers, formed in 1901 in Brooklyn, four years before the 1905 revolution and seven years before the emergence in 1908, in that part of Poland which was occupied by Austria, of the Association of Active Struggle. According to its constitution, the aim of the society was : 'To serve the homeland (Poland) and exercise in the art of war so that in the case of need the Society will produce from its membership persons capable of training other brothers. Each member undertakes to equip himself with a lancer's uniform in the course of six months. He is required to present himself at every regimental summons for the purpose of exercise in military arts.' This was in principle an officers' school, preparing instructors for a future Polish army. Photographs of the period show grown men with flowing moustaches in colourful lancers' uniforms of the eighteenth century, with a slight error as far as their headgear is concerned, since they are wearing Prussian lancers' caps, with long swords at the side. This was a cavalry regiment *dismounted* from the very beginning, as they had no horses and galloped down the streets of Brooklyn on their own legs. But their enthusiasm must have been considerable, since a paragraph of the constitution states that 'for drawing the sword in a fight—$5 fine'. However this may be, under the conditions of unusual freedom existing in the United States, these people in whom poverty in Poland had killed all feelings except hunger, began to develop Polish patriotism. The phenomenon emerges of a more flourishing national Polish life in exile than in the Prussian and Russian sectors of Poland itself. And this life sought an opportunity to expand into a wider arena. This was obtained for instance during the ceremonies in New York in 1909, the 300th anniversary of the arrival of Henry Hudson in the Dutch sailing-boat *Halve Maan*, and the founding of the first settlement of white men on Manhattan. This ceremony coincided with the hundredth anniversary of the building of the first steamboat, the *Claremont* by Robert Fulton. An aquatic parade was therefore arranged on the Hudson river, headed by replicas of both boats, and these were followed by warships sent by various nations, including Russia and Germany. At this time Kornobis, a member of the Association of Polish Armed Forces in America, decided to show the world that 'Poland is not lost, while we still live,' and hastily hired a yacht, loaded it with a squadron of lancers armed with swords and, as some who recall the period claim, with scythe-bearers in white coats, and hoisting a Polish standard they sailed down the bay into which the Hudson flows. Since Poles are fond of symbolic gestures, they here performed a rite at sea, dipping the standard three times in the salt water, then sailed up the Hudson to join the parade. There are two versions of what followed. One says they succeeded in getting into the middle of the parade, where amidst warships from all over the world they aroused a great sensation, particularly by the costumes and weapons of the crew. Instead of gun barrels, drawn swords and scythe blades glittered in the sun. However, the commanders of the ships belonging to the partitioning powers realized what was happening and declared that unless the Polish frigate was at once removed, they would withdraw their ships. To avoid an international incident the dock police were called, and took Kornobis's yacht in tow into Brooklyn. The other version says that the police stopped Kornobis's vessel before it reached the parade, though the episode itself got into the newspapers and became well known. Both versions agree that after this first manifestation of Polish naval power since the time of King Wladyslaw IV, the boat returned to the Brooklyn dock whence it had come, after which the crew in their military attire, with lancers trotting ahead on their own feet, set off to a Polish saloon, where they celebrated till late at night the successful demonstration which had become a local sensation and contained the makings of an international one.

The Polish 'Falcon' and General Haller's army have a special place in the history of the armed deeds of the Poles in America.

I was once sitting at a Polish-American banquet between two members of the Haller army in their blue but already faded uniforms. One wore the Virtuti militari medal, the other the double Cross of Valour. Learning that both had been born in America, I wondered what had decided them to enter the army.

'It was through Sienkiewicz,' said one. 'When my father used to come back from the coal-mine, I had to read him the *Trilogy* aloud. This happened every day for an hour. When I'd finished *Pan Wolodyjowski* I would start *By Fire and Sword*, and so on. This made a Polish patriot of me.'

'My mother told me to,' said the other. 'When they began recruiting for Haller's army, I wanted to join because I'd heard so much about Poland at home that I wanted to see it. But I was young and was afraid to tell my mother, and put it off. Then one Sunday mother shut herself in a room with me and said, "Son, go and join the army to free Poland". So I went.'

In view of such feelings among the Poles in America it is not surprising that when a Polish consulate opened in New York after World War I, pilgrimages from all over America began to make their way there, merely to see the Polish flag and the White Eagle over the building. It reached such a point that the New York police had to close the street to traffic, since it was always crowded with pilgrims, sometimes kneeling to pray and weep.

Independently of the development of Polish patriotism, feelings of gratitude and attachment to the country which had given them unusual freedom and the opportunity to reach a standard unknown in Poland also developed and took root among the Polish immigrants of the first generation. American patriotism was born, and I frequently came into contact with it. I was speaking once in Cleve-

Pope Paul VI addressing Zosia and author in Polish. See *Epilogue*

Banquet in honour of the US Congressional Committee investigating the Katyn massacre. From left to right : Congressman Machrowicz, chairman of the Committee, Congressman Madden, Monsignor Lipinski, Dr Zlonczewski, the author and Ambassador Lipski. See chapter : *The Mystery of the Pentagon*

land, in a hall where two-thirds of the audience were elderly ladies. They listened with great attention, but did not applaud until I stated that American freedom and power have no equal in the world. But before the Poles in America stood on their own feet, life was not easy and every member of the older generation has tales to tell of difficult struggles in the beginning. The worst was homesickness.

'I came here with my husband after the revolution of 1905,' said the mother of Mrs. Yolles to Zosia and me. 'He belonged to the Polish Socialist party and had to flee. Everything you two have been saying is just like my own youth. I know it all by heart—the arrests, the gendarmes coming at night, ambushes, passing messages, breaking down prison gates. ... When we came to America, I felt so homesick for Poland that I couldn't sleep or eat and was fading away. At length my husband in despair suggested I should go back to Poland by myself, as I'd at least stay alive there. Or perhaps things would improve and he'd come back too. He began saving money for the journey, but he was earning little and it took a long time. In the meantime, she was born,' she indicated one of her daughters, 'so the journey had to be put off. Then she was born,' here she indicated another of the ladies present, 'and in the end I stayed here.'

I was once travelling through Pennsylvania by car from one meeting to another in the company of several American ladies of Polish descent. One was talking about her impressions of a Polish film. 'There was a scene when country girls were walking barefoot in a meadow with rakes over their shoulders. When I saw this I remembered my youth and wanted to join the girls so much that I almost burst into tears.'

An old socialist of the 1905 generation once confided, 'I've been living in this country forty years, but two or three times every week I dream I'm in Poland'.

A millionaire potato farmer on Long Island spoke thus of his start : 'By day I worked on the farm, and at night I'd cry with homesickness for Poland'.

As well as homesickness, almost everyone has known poverty and hard times. 'Other immigrants such as the Germans either arrived with a small capital or had their own organizations here who helped with loans,' my neighbour once told me at a Polish-American banquet. 'These things were handled best by local Jewish organizations. But all the Poles brought were strong arms. But at the beginning, before I got a steady job, I slept on park benches and under walls, and lived on dry bread.'

o

'I wasn't educated and didn't know the language, so everyone took advantage of me and paid me in pennies,' an elderly Polish-American worker recalled, 'but each of my four sons has graduated.'

Sooner or later everyone managed, and after years of hard work came their own farms, houses, bank accounts, cars, ice-boxes, washing machines, radio sets and TVs. Some however went back with the dollars they had earned, so as to acquire the only thing in the world which has any real value to a Polish peasant—land.

The beginnings of American patriotism, which did not conflict with Polish patriotism, extend far back into the past, since during the 1861 Civil War 4,000 Poles served in the Northern army, and 1,000, including General Kacper Tochman, were with the South, i.e. 16% of the Polish emigration of the time, whereas only 14% of the total population of the United States took part in the war. The contribution of the Polish emigration in both world wars was particularly outstanding. During the first, as soon as volunteers were called for, there were 40,000 Poles among the first 100,000 and, by the end of the war, their numbers had increased to 300,000. In World War II about 900,000 Poles served in the American forces, which is an extremely high percentage in comparison with other national groups. No war film in the United States on the last world war or the Korean campaign is without a Pole, his name ending in -ski. As a rule he is a good, experienced, brave soldier, often a sergeant, life and soul of the company, though never an officer of higher rank. The films are a true reflection of reality; Air Force General Alvin Paczynski, Colonel-Pilot Franciszek Gabreski, retired Colonel and Congressman Frank Kowalski, the late Colonel Henry Szymanski and a couple of dozen others are exceptions to the rule.

Probably the best career lies ahead for another regular officer of the American army, whose story I heard from his sister during lunch in a small town in Pennsylvania.

'My brother graduated from a military academy and served on Eisenhower's staff towards the end of the war in Germany. He spoke Polish fairly well, so although he knew no Russian they used him as a kind of interpreter in contacts with the staff of Marshal Zhukov. One day his commanding officer told him he was in a group of some dozen American officers to whom Marshal Zhukov wanted to present Soviet decorations. My brother declared he would not accept a Russian decoration, as he was of Polish descent and Russia had again seized the country of his ancestors, as it had done in the time of Kosciuszko and Pulaski. This caused great consternation in the American staff and they began to summon my brother to various superior officers, and each one tried to dissuade him from his decision, even using the argument that he was harming his career. But my brother insisted on refusing the decoration, and did not go to Zhukov's HQ. Just imagine that instead of harming his career, it is of great assistance to him today. He is considered a very far-sighted officer, who as early as 1945, when the highest heads were still full of illusions, recognized Russia for what it is.'

The politicalization of Polonia in relation to the United States is much clearer in the strictly political field. Here, the ever-increasing ranks of intellectuals of Polish descent born in America and representing the typical American of Polish origin, are reaching out boldly for influence and a part in the political life of the United States. They can be found in the administration, in the courts, in the State and Federal police, and, more important still, in Congress, where Senator Edmund Muskie-Marciszewski had a seat in the 87th Congress, while there were eleven Congressmen in the House of Representatives : Tadeusz M. Machrowicz, former officer of Haller's army; Clement J. Zablocki, member of the Foreign Affairs committee; Roman C. Pucinski; Jan C. Kluczynski; Alvin E. O'Konski, whose Polish name of Okonski was given its Irish flavour by the Registrar of births; Colonel Franciszek Kowalski, Daniel Rostenkowski, Edward J. Derwinski, Tadeusz J. Dulski, Jan Lesinski Jr. and Jan D. Dingell Jr. There were others before them and it was one of these, now no longer with us, who defined his attitude to the Polish cause, in a talk with me soon after my arrival in the United States. His last words, I think, are to this day the guiding principle of every Congressman of Polish origin.

'Don't forget I am primarily an American and am guided by the American *raison d'état*. But I have much sympathy for the country I originate from. Thus whenever Polish interests do not conflict with American I try my hardest to assist Poland.'

VII

NIXON IN POLONIA

Richard M. Nixon turned to General Jozef Haller at his side and said clearly : 'They look like good soldiers.'

His words spread rapidly along the tribune of honour which was applauding the briskly-marching unit of men and women in dark-blue berets, recklessly pulled down over the left ear, and red and white arm-bands. The banner they carried before them said 'Former Soldiers of the Home Army'. As one of those present on the dais on October 12, 1952, before which the 'Pulaski Parade' was marching down New York's Fifth Avenue, I felt doubly proud. First because a compliment from the candidate for the Vice-Presidency of the United States, even if a *cliché*, always appeals to national pride, and second because I had caught sight of Zosia in the parade and was able to look down upon her from the elevation of the dais, whereas at home it was usually the other way round.

In the procession, which was led by the marshal of the parade and several dozen gentlemen in tail-coats and top hats, the Home Army detachment was preceded and followed by groups from various districts of New York, civilian and army bands, living tableaux on floats, units of veterans and of the United States armed forces and finally rows of children in Cracow costumes, looking like flowers against the background of the street and the grey houses, who called forth a storm of applause and much running about of photographers. A sight such as this only to be seen in Lowicz, during the Corpus Christi procession. Far and wide through the procession waved Polish and American flags as well as those of various Polish organizations in America, and the sounds of martial music were audible. As always, about a hundred thousand people were taking part in the parade and it was being watched according to a New York police estimate, by half a million New Yorkers. This day New York belonged to the Poles in America. And this day was also a reward for a year's work on the part of Franciszek Wazeter, permanent president of the Pulaski parade committee.

For me, however, the Pulaski Parade was an object of interest not so much as a colourful and impressive spectacle, but as a political manifestation playing its part in American public life. It is possible for a New Yorker, which I had been for seven years, to see countless such parades. The lead is held by the Irish parade on St Patrick's Day, from which all others derive. The Irish national colour, green, prevails everywhere in it, both in costumes and banners, to such an extent that the white lines in the centre of the road, dividing the lines of traffic, is painted green on the day before the parade. While watching this parade one year, I asked a talkative bystander wearing a green paper hat the reason for this. He breathed bourbon at me and explained, 'We Irish get steamed up on St Patrick's Day from early morning. That line shows the way the procession goes. Otherwise the marchers would wander away into the nearest saloons and that would be an end of the parade.'

The Polish Pulaski parades are exceptionally sober and only coffee and sandwiches are served to the guests of honour at the Biltmore Hotel, which suffices to assure priority in this respect to the Irish parade. Thus nothing clouds the gaze of a spectator wishing to contemplate the parade as a manifestation of the political life of Polonia and seeking to reach political conclusions from it. First, therefore, a glance at the dais. If this is not a year for elections to Congress, the observer will see that the first row includes—apart from leaders of Polonia—an average group of local American officials such as the Mayor of New York and the Governor of the State of New York, who, since they depend partly upon Polish votes, usually both attend. If it is an election year, the quality and quantity of the American guests increase. If it is the year of a presidential election, which occurs every four years, one may expect to see even candidates for this supreme post on the stand. Then it will be overflowing with eminent names known all over the country. Their bearers not only applaud the little girls in Cracow costumes and lavish their compliments but also pay close attention to what Polonia is saying, and will take notice of this in formulating their policy or at least their pre-election speeches. And Polonia speaks to these men by the banners with slogans which are carried in the procession. This is how the political programme of Polonia is announced and how their demands are made known to government and Congress. Such appeals as the following are always found : 'We demand the restoration of freedom and independence to Poland !' 'Out with Soviet Armies from Poland.' 'The United States must recognize the Oder-Neisse frontier.' 'We demand UN investigates the Katyn massacre.' 'We demand liberalization of the immigration law !' These are supplemented annually by appeals and demands dictated by the present political situation or the latest international events, such as 'No fraternizing with Khrushchev, Stalin's fellow-murderer!' 'Long live Poznan!' and the like.

When he had studied these demands, the electoral candidate may decide his attitude towards them on the spot and make an appropriate statement to the radio commentators and the press. His statement will travel right round America, primarily through Polish-American papers and broadcasting stations. The late Piotr Yolles, the well-known editor, said this of the latter : 'If one knows their programme in New York, then by going from one wavelength to another, one can hear Polish transmissions all day long.'

Where is the political programme of Polonia, as expressed on the banners in the Pulaski and other parades, hammered out? Mainly in the kitchen of the average Polish home, where wife, mother and lady of the house in one person is cooking dinner with the radio turned on, listening to the news from all over the world and muttering her own commentary to it. She shares her opinions with her husband or children when they come in from work. They supplement it with news from Polish papers published in America or the local American newspaper, which the family usually reads in the evening. This news from all over the world provides the raw material, while the commentaries on it formed round the family hearth gives the 'grass-root feeling'. This voice coming from below is listened to attentively by the editors of the Polish newspapers in America, the radio commentators, and the politicians. They may be in complete disagreement with it, may try to influence it by what they say and write, but they never ignore it or pass over it in silence. In this way, mutual dependence and mutual interaction result. Next is the pulpit, which has always played and still plays an important role in the formation of the views of Polonia; similarly, the meetings of many organizations as they pass resolutions not only on their own matters but also on political matters concerning Polonia. The next factor is the National Home, where current events are discussed over a drink in the bar. The last factor is the mass parades on the national holiday of May 3rd, August 15th (Soldiers' Day) and other days, as well as the banquets held on these occasions. The next most important event after the Pulaski parade in New York is the celebration of May 3rd in Chicago, at the Kosciuszko memorial in Humboldt Park, where the average number of those attending is 100,000. This is organized by the Polish-American Congress and the host is its president, Rozmarek. At these mass meetings, these views become the expression of all local Poles, adopted as a resolution. Here the local Congressman and Senator will get to know their views, for they endeavour to be present and make speeches wherever the electors can hear them. They bring the views of Polonia into Congress. There they make use of them, speaking on specific matters concerning Polonia, and also participating as a rule in the several hours' debate which Congress devotes annually to Poland on May 3rd. This debate is a kind of tribute to the Polish nation, and at the same time a survey of Polish problems. Since 1945 it has been dominated by the demand that full independence and a democratic system be restored to Poland.

Another process develops parallel to this, in which the main part is played by the Polish-American Congress and its supreme council, which carefully listens to the voices emerging from Polonia and, during the several days of meetings attended by Congressmen of Polish descent, analyses and transforms them into a programme of political action. The culmination of this campaign is the visit of the KPA delegation, headed for many years by Rozmarek, to the President in the White House, the Secretary of State and the leaders of Congress and of the Democratic and Republican parties. The resolutions of Congress on matters concerning Eastern Europe, such as that in 1959 on the Captive Nations week, the passages devoted to Poland or the nations behind the Iron Curtain at what are called the 'electoral platforms' of both parties, even the proclamations and statements of the President himself, terminate this process which starts in a Polish kitchen in America where the voice from the radio is accompanied by the bubbling of potatoes on the gas.

VIII

DARKNESS AT NOON

The arrest of Wladyslaw Gomulka at Krynica in August 1951 was the climax of the period of the greatest terror in Poland since our escape. It began with the arrest of some 2,000 members of the Polish Peasant party, including nearly all its most eminent leaders. In this way the remains of the open, legal opposition were liquidated, and with them the last pretences of a democratic system. The 'i' was dotted when in November 1949 the Polish Peasant party was joined to the pro-communist Peasant party. Once again, the recently released officers of the underground Home Army, Colonels Radoslaw-Mazurkiewicz, Wolanski-Gorazdowski and Jan Rzepecki, found themselves back in jail, along with hundreds of former underground members. Maria Hulewicz, Wincenty Bryja and Mieczyslaw Dabrowski, who had already been in jail a long time after being caught at the end of 1947 in Czechoslovakia, where they had fled after Mikolajczyk's 'escape' and had been handed over to Poland, now received long terms of imprisonment. The same fate met Pawel Siudak and Witold Kulerski, arrested after the departure of Mikolajczyk—men utterly devoted to him and whom he had brought back with him from London. Kazimierz Puzak, an eminent Socialist, an unbreakable figure, died in prison, though he had survived the notorious trial before the Soviet military court of the 'sixteen'. Arrested again in Poland in 1948 he refused to make any statement before the court, not being prepared to admit the Secret Police officials on the judge's bench as an organ of justice. I co-operated closely with him from the start of the underground movement until the treacherous arrest of the 'sixteen' and I took the news of his death very hard. The same death came to Antoni Zdanowski, former general secretary of the trade unions' central committee, whom I had accompanied one dark evening to a secret meeting at the Polish Peasant party office. Before this however both of us had to experience the merger in December 1948 of the Polish Socialist party with the Polish Workers' party into a new 'party', the Polish United Workers' party, which was equivalent to the incorporation of the Polish Socialist party into the ranks of the communists, thus terminating several decades of praiseworthy work by this respected political party on behalf of Poland and the working class. Cardinal Stefan Wyszynski was likewise imprisoned, along with many bishops and hundreds of priests who refused to subject the Catholic Church to communist policies, especially by joining the pro-communist Association of Patriot Priests, controlled by the Soviet agent and pre-war Fascist, Boleslaw Piasecki, appointed to this post by the notorious Soviet NKVD General Serov. Poland had entered upon the period of the greatest efforts of communist activity, now carried on at a greater rate and by the use of all manner of means of terror. It covered all life in Poland—agriculture, the last vestiges of private trade, industry, the professions, science, education, literature, art, culture, sport—in a word, all fields of life. Hundreds of forced labour camps were established, in which tens of thousands of stubborn opponents were imprisoned. These included peasants resisting collectivization, workers late on the job, or idling, or being absent, city-dwellers for any activity which resembled private enterprise, and many others. The largest percentage among those arrested, however, were what were known as 'reactionaries', or those whom the local communist chieftains regarded according to their own ideas as dangerous to the ruling system.

During this time, my past activities and escape were referred to during a number of 'show trials'. Thus my old acquaintance Adam Obarski of the Polish Socialist party, who had been in jail for a long period, stated as a witness during one of these trials that I had been in constant contact with the commanding authority of the new underground, the consultative committee of the Democratic organizations of the Polish Underground, or even a member of it. During the trial of Kasznica and Leszek Neuman of the National Armed Forces, which started in February 1948, the latter, also an acquaintance from the Poznan period, revealed secret contacts with me. He was condemned to death in any case. A third to confess on this subject was Zygmunt Lachert, of the National party, brought from jail for the Karl Nillson trial in October 1948. According to the *Voice of the People* newspaper of October 4, 1948, Lachert told the judge that I had acted as a link between the legal Polish Peasant party and the underground organization known as 'The Centre', which was formed by members of the illegal Peasant party, the WRN (underground Polish Socialist party) and the WIN (the underground 'Freedom and Independence' organization). The witness added that during the period prior to my escape, 'The Centre'

c*

made preparations to develop activity abroad, particularly in America. Lachert was implying that my escape was connected with these plans.

Finally, mid-way through December 1951 a trial was held in Warsaw at which, had I not fled, I should undoubtedly have been in the dock. Kurczewski and Zborowski, brought from jail as witnesses, accused me of murdering people of the 'left wing' with the assistance of underground law-courts (*Zycie Warszawy*, December 14, 1951).

All these trials were directed by the all-powerful Security Police, which was in fact controlled by officers of the Soviet NKVD or MVD, with General Serov at the head. They were bent on the liquidation of 'right-wing nationalist deviation' in the Polish Communist party. In the framework of this purge, the closest friend of Gomulka, General Marian Spychalski, until then, in fact if not nominally, commander-in-chief of the Polish army, was arrested first of all. This former member of the communist student organization 'Life' had had nothing to do with the army before the war, but worked as an architect first in Poznan, then in Warsaw. During the war, however, it was he who organized the communist underground 'Peoples' Guard', later transformed into the 'Peoples' Army'. In time this brought him the rank of general and the chief post in the army. But even he had to pay for the crime of admitting to the army a number of pre-war (and therefore 'reactionary') Polish officers while dismissing Soviet officers. He was subjected in jail to such ingenious tortures that he broke down and accused his friend Gomulka, thus facilitating the latter's arrest. The same fate lay in store for the nominal commander-in-chief of the Polish forces, Marshal Michal Rola-Zymierski, who was converted into a master-spy, serving in turn in the pre-war Polish intelligence, then in the French service and in the Gestapo during the war. With them in jail was also a communist of the International Brigade of the Spanish Civil War, General Waclaw Komar, as well as the former head of military intelligence and the former leader of the communist partisans in the Lublin district, General Grzegorz Korczynski, and many others.

After the arrests in the army, it was the turn of the other people close to Gomulka and his political co-operators. Thus Zenon Kliszko, Wladyslaw Bienkowski, Ignacy Loga-Sowinski and dozens of others landed in jail. This purge included the entire Party machine from top to bottom. Its crowning act was the arrest of Gomulka himself. It was at this time that a joke emerged in Poland concerning the three prisoners in one cell, of whom the first had been arrested because he had shouted 'Down with Gomulka' in 1946; the second because he had shouted 'Long live Gomulka' in 1951, while the third was Gomulka himself. In this way the communist Chronos devours its own children. I shook my head over these events, quietly muttering to myself the well-known 'popular-democratic' maxim : 'There's no life without prison', and I pondered over Gomulka, going back in my mind to recent times.

I had seen him for the first time in August 1945. He was standing on the platform in the 'Rome' auditorium in Warsaw, making a speech to the Polish National Council, fulminating against 'reaction', the anti-communist underground and the small opposition within the council of the Polish Peasant party, threatening it with merciless destruction. I gazed at his face and tried to solve the riddle of what it concealed. Gomulka was already the number one communist, whose pseudonym during the conspiracy period ('Wieslaw') was now chanted in chorus by thousands at every political meeting or manifestation, and who was becoming the idol of the Polish Workers' party before my very eyes. His powerful jaw, broad as a shovel, harmonizing well with his almost Mongolian cheek-bones clearly showed his strong character, stubbornness and obstinacy. Proof of these qualities fell daily upon his political foes. His high, protruding forehead enlarged by baldness, bore evidence of some intelligence, but its one-sided training was revealed in every one of his speeches as well as that to which I was listening. As it was generally known that he had no sense of humour, it is not surprising that what he said was basic and strong but lacking in any lighter moments or wit. The look in his eyes was sharp and unpleasant. When he referred to the 'enemies of the people' and the struggle against them, his eyes behind the metal-rimmed spectacles gleamed, while his voice rang with hatred. I was in the presence of a fanatical communist and a strong and independent personality.

When I met Gomulka in the Sejm eighteen months later, after the elections of January 19, 1947, I knew rather more about him than in August 1945. I had already heard of certain differences between him and his Soviet masters. The first took place against the background of the looting by the Soviet army of machinery from the Cegielski factory in Poznan, which had been renamed the Stalin factory. Gomulka had demanded of the Soviet general Shatilov that the dismantling of the machines and their removal to Russia should stop. During a violent argument, Shatilov seized Gomulka by the lapels and threatened him. The misunderstandings increased in connection with the looting of the Recovered Territories by the Soviet army, stationed there in large numbers. For Gomulka, as Minister of the Recovered Territories, this area was the apple of his eye and he devoted much energy and time to it. From 1945 on, a powerful machine of Soviet exploitation had been operating in this area, seizing and removing to Russia the factory equipment, coal, raw materials, steel, furniture, horses, cows and in fact anything they could lay hands on. This paralysed Gomulka's attempts to reorganize the area's economy as fast as possible. But since the reactions of characters such as his are rapid and decisive, he gave the well-known order to the Polish army to shoot Soviet soldiers caught looting, of which he informed the Soviet military authorities. Thus the first crack appeared in his loyalty to Russia. Good note must have been taken of this order in the Kremlin.

He was certainly not helped in Soviet eyes by sayings which went round Warsaw such as 'Poland is not yet ripe for Communism and its introduction must last many years. Poland will become communist, but—alas—not in my lifetime. I shall not live to see it.'

Some months after my escape, an open campaign started against Gomulka. First, after the discussion of his 'right-wing nationalist deviation' in August 1948 at a plenary meeting of the central committee of the Polish Workers' party, he was deprived of his post as first secretary of the Communist party; in January 1949, he was removed from the post of Vice-Premier and Minister of the Recovered Territories and then came his arrest by Jozef Swiatlo on August 1, 1951. Power in Poland had now come into the hands of the most hated man in the country—the Soviet Field-Marshal Konstanty Rokossovsky, who had refused to help the Warsaw insurrection in 1944. Now he was parading in a Polish army uniform, the same uniform as had been worn by thousands of Warsaw insurrectionists for whose death he had been responsible.

All Poland froze in horror before an outburst of terror worse than anything known before. People did not sleep at nights, listening to the whining of car engines and the thud of gun butts against doors, and often shots and screams were heard. Hundreds of Poles fled across country under cover of darkness towards the western frontiers but only a few managed to cross the minefields, barbed wire and thickly distributed armed guards assisted by dogs. A long dark night, without sign of dawn, settled down over Poland, isolated as she was from the world behind the Iron Curtain.

IX

THE MYSTERY OF THE PENTAGON

One day in the spring of 1943 a temporary change of personnel was made in the New York Office of War Information. An official whose task it was to study German newspapers fell ill and someone with a good knowledge of German had to replace him.

As a result of this chance, an Austrian immigrant named Julius Epstein set about reading the *Voelkischer Beobachter* that day and found it contained a report compiled by an international committee which, at the invitation of the Nazi government, had gone to Katyn and examined the recently discovered mass graves of murdered Polish officers. On the basis of proof they gathered, the committee stated the officers had been murdered by Soviet forces. Epstein noticed that the report included a signature of Professor Naville of Geneva university, a scholar of international repute, and the anti-Nazi refugee decided that perhaps for the first time the *Voelkischer Beobachter* was not lying. When he mentioned this to his office colleagues he was shouted down. 'The whole incident is an invention of Nazi propaganda.'

Julius Epstein's interest in the Katyn case dates from this day. However, the violence of his colleagues' reaction and the atmosphere prevailing in the office persuaded him that further remarks on the subject could only lead to his being regarded as an agent of Goebbels, despite his anti-Nazi background. He therefore did nothing until 1948, when the mood favourable to the Soviet Union began to evaporate. Then he sent a questionnaire to all the members of the international committee, asking the following three questions : (1) Did the German government exert any pressure upon you either before, during or after the investigation? (2) Are you also of the opinion at the present time that the murdered Polish officers found in the Katyn forest were massacred by the Soviet Union? (3) Would you be prepared to travel to the United States to appear and make a statement in connection with this matter before a private or Congressional investigating committee?

Out of twelve scholars to whom these questions were sent, four

replied : Professor Hayek of Prague, Tramsen of Copenhagen, Palmieri of Naples and Naville of Geneva. Hayek stated that although
no pressure had been exerted upon him, he had nevertheless changed
his mind in the meantime and was no longer of the opinion that the
Soviet Union had perpetrated the crime. Epstein nodded his head
understandingly as he read this. The communist coup had already
taken place in Czechoslovakia, and Hayek was now under Soviet
rule. A difficult time lay ahead for him. The other three all agreed
that no pressure had been exerted upon them, that they were still
of the same view, and were prepared to travel to the United States,
even at their own expense if necessary, in order to proclaim this
publicly.

On the basis of these replies Epstein wrote two articles, which the
New York Herald-Tribune agreed to publish, on the Katyn crime.
The second article ended with an appeal for investigation of the
crime by an entirely independent body, preferably a committee
appointed by Congress. These articles were published on July 3,
and 4, 1949, and aroused public discussion at once.

On November 21, 1949, a press conference was held, attended by
Arthur Bliss Lane, former American ambassador in Warsaw, who
announced the establishment by private initiative of the American
Committee for Investigating the Katyn Murders, of which he became president, with Julius Epstein as secretary-general. The committee included such eminent personalities as the writer Max
Eastman and the journalist Dorothy Thompson as vice-presidents,
also General William Donovan, Mrs Claire Booth Luce, the journalist George Sokolsky, Constantine Brown and Sol M. Levitas,
former Postmaster General Jim Farley and many others. This
committee, which was financially backed by the Polish-American
Congress and the Free Europe Committee, collected evidence for
nearly two years regarding the Katyn murders and formed public
opinion for the creation by Congress of an official committee. Their
efforts were finally rewarded and the appropriate resolution was
passed unanimously by the House of Representatives on September
18, 1951. A decision without precedent in the history of the United
States had been taken, since Congress had never before appointed
a committee to investigate a crime perpetrated outside the United
States, the victims of which were not American citizens. Immediately after the resolution had been passed, the Chairman of the
House, Sam Rayburn, appointed a seven-person committee headed
by Ray J. Madden of Indiana, the other members being Tadeusz M.
Machrowicz of Michigan, Alvin E. O'Konski of Wisconsin, Daniel
J. Flood of Pennsylvania, Foster Furcolo of Massachusetts, George

A. Dondero of Michigan and Timothy P. Sheehan of Illinois.

The inquiry which had started unofficially in October 1949 revealed initial deep incredulity on the part of President Roosevelt and the United States government that the Katyn murders had been committed by the Soviet Union, fear that discussion of the crime might harm relations with the U.S.S.R., and also the great efforts of the better-oriented pro-communist fellow-travellers to prevent the truth coming to light. When a highly-placed official of the American diplomatic service, George Howard Earle, had tried in 1944 to convince the President that the murders had been committed by the Soviet Union, Roosevelt interrupted him : 'George, this is entirely German propaganda and a German plot. I am absolutely convinced the Russians did not do this'.

Following this line of thought, the Office of War Information and the Federal Communication Commission in May 1943 had exceeded their powers in placing restrictions on Polish radio transmissions in Buffalo and Detroit, particularly on the well-known commentator Jan Marian Kreutz, and had rendered it impossible for them to point to the real murderers.

Robert H. Jackson, a judge of the Supreme Court, who had represented the United States at the Nuremberg trial, also revealed that on February 13 and 14, 1946, the Russian prosecutor, Colonel Pokrovsky, who had included in the charges the murder by the Germans of 11,000 Polish Officers, had presented the tribunal with a report by the Soviet commission which had investigated the Katyn murders, and had placed responsibility for the crime upon Goering and the other defendants. Their defence counsel, Dr Stahmer, had immediately rejected this charge and asked to call witnesses to contradict this report. The Soviet side had rejected this request, and stated that the report referred to was a state document and absolute proof, which could not be overthrown by statements of witnesses. The tribunal did not agree with this view and admitted three witnesses on either side. They were heard on July 1 and 2, 1946, after which the Soviet prosecutor, while complaining that only three witnesses had been questioned out of the 120 he could call, stopped supporting the charge and in his final speech for the prosecution did not even refer to the Katyn murders. The acceptance of the principle that evidence offered by Goering and his fellow-prisoners was admissible was too dangerous for the Soviet Union, as it risked betraying the truth. Hence they withdrew the charge.

Judge Jackson concluded his evidence by stating that the way to solving the identity of the real murderers was still open since

'nothing that was decided by the Nuremberg tribunal or contended
for by the American prosecution will stand in your way.'

On this occasion it was revealed that Judge Jackson had received
a letter from the then American ambassador in Warsaw, Arthur
Bliss Lane, dated December 16, 1945, which might be understood
as a request not to let the Katyn affair be referred to by the accused
Germans, since this could intensify the anti-Polish attitude of the
Soviet government. Ambassador Lane, when asked the meaning
of this letter by the Congressional committee, stated that he had
been of the opposite opinion and explained the sending of the
letter thus : 'It is very possible someone else (in the American
embassy in Warsaw) might have sent it. It is quite possible I may
have been out of town (i.e. Warsaw).'

Here we may well suspect the hand of some 'fellow-traveller'.

However, the greatest sensation was caused when the committee
confirmed the disappearance from the Pentagon of the report submitted by the American Colonel John H. Van Fleet, a POW in a
Nazi camp, who along with the American Captain Donald Stewart
and other Allied officers and POWs, had been taken to Katyn to
inspect the graves, bodies and other evidence found with them. At
the end of the war, Colonel Van Fleet made a report in Washington
to the deputy chief of staff responsible for intelligence, General
Clayton Bissell; this report stated categorically that the murders
had been committed by the Soviet Union. The report was made in
one copy only, and classified by General Bissel as 'top secret'. This
report had disappeared without trace from intelligence archives and
despite all the efforts of the Congressional committee it has never
been found. An inquiry instigated by the General Inspector of the
Army revealed that despite General Bissel's claim that the report
had been sent to the State Department it had never left the offices
of the American Army Intelligence and must have disappeared
there.

In this connection, the Congressional committee made this announcement after questioning General Bissel and witnesses, including high officials of the State Department : 'The Van Fleet report
was either removed or purposely destroyed in Army Intelligence
(G2).'

This matter has still not been explained and will probably remain
a secret of one of the Pentagon offices to the last.

While considering the case of the Van Fleet report, the committee
confirmed, on the basis of statements made behind closed doors
by three high-ranking officers attached at this time to army intelligence, that a group of pro-Soviet civilian officials and certain

army personnel had existed at that time in army intelligence; they had found justification for nearly everything the Soviet Union did. These people had done their utmost to suppress anti-Soviet reports.

Finally, the committee decided to send copies of its investigation to the Department of Defence so that appropriate action could be taken against General Bissell, since 'had the Van Fleet report been made immediately available to the Department of State and to the American public, the course of our governmental policy toward Soviet Russia might have been more realistic, with more fortunate post-war results.' The committee also recommended a thorough investigation into army intelligence activities for the years 1944-45.

During the course of the investigation, an echo was heard before the committee of the case of Roman Martini, the Cracow prosecutor, to the effect that he was to undertake investigation of the Katyn case so as to place the guilt upon the Germans, but had in fact drawn up a report charging the Soviet Union. As a result he was murdered, and those responsible for his murder were later allowed to escape from prison.

Mikolajczyk also gave evidence of a talk in August 1945 in Poland with the prosecutor Sawicki, who informed him that he intended, with the approval of the Minister of Justice (Swiatkowski), to renew a public trial in Poland of those responsible for the Katyn murders. When however Swiatkowski and Sawicki applied to Moscow for permission, they were forbidden even to refer to the matter.

Finally, the witness Kazimierz Skarzynski appeared one day before the committee, and what he said brought before my eyes the picture of a bank office in Zgoda Street, Warsaw, on a memorable and terrible day nine years earlier, when I had heard from him the truth about Katyn. The following dialogue occurred between him and Congressman Flood, a member of the committee :

Mr Flood: Did you make a report to the Polish Underground?
M. Skarzynski: I did, the same day I did to the Germans. I met the chief of what was called the civilian service.
Mr Flood: I thought you told us this morning that only the President of the Polish Red Cross had a contact with the Underground. How did you get it?
Mr Skarzynski: I got it when a friend of mine who was manager of a Polish bank, phoned to me the same day after my return from Katyn, and told me, 'You are today going to meet the chief of the civilian fighting forces of the Polish Underground,' and that was Mr Stefan Korbonski, who is today in America. Stefan

Korbonski was the chief of the civilian defence, not in the passive meaning but the active meaning.

In this office room of the bank director, my friend, I met him and I gave him a verbal report about two and a half or three hours, about my visit to Katyn.

Mr Flood: What was the difference, if there was a difference, between the oral report you gave to the representative of the Underground that day in your friend's banking office, and the report that you officially gave the Germans in writing?

Mr Skarzynski: The Germans we gave only the laconic eight points: and to Korbonski I repeated what I told you today, perhaps in a little more detail, because I had three hours' time.

Mr Flood: What did you say to the chief of the Underground or the Underground representative with reference to that? Did you qualify it to him, or were you more decisive?

Mr Skarzynski: I was more decisive.

Mr Flood: What did you say?

Mr Skarzynski: My personal intimate conviction is that the Russians did it.

Mr Flood: Was that your conviction then?

Mr Skarzynski: It was.

Mr Flood: Did you so report to him then?

Mr Skarzynski: Yes.

Nine years earlier, immediately after this talk with Skarzynski, I had hurried to Delegate Jankowski, to whom I repeated the information, then from him to the secret radio station, from which I sent then and on the following days a number of messages about Katyn to the government in London.

On December 22, 1952, the Congressional committee ended its investigation, during which eighty-one witnesses had been examined and more than a hundred depositions by persons unable to attend were examined; in addition 183 exhibits were considered. The final result was that the committee resolved to place a report before the House of Representatives, including as a component part the interim report of July 2, 1952, which stated categorically that the murders of the 4,253 Polish officers, whose bodies were found in a mass grave in Katyn, had been committed by the Soviet NKVD, and expressed the belief that the other officers, over 10,000 from the Ostaszkov and Starobielsk camps, who disappeared inside Russia, had met the same fate.

Witnesses and evidence showed that the prisoners from the Ostaszkov camp had been loaded into rafts and drowned in the White Sea, while those from the Starobielsk camp had been deported to the Kharkov region and massacred there. The committee based its belief partly on the statements of twenty-six officers who had been imprisoned at one time in the Kozielsk, Starobielsk and Ostaszkov camps and were able to show the committee the deportation methods used by the NKVD on the Polish officers in the camps, and also on the statements of five non-Polish doctors and scientists, Dr Edward Miloslavich (of Croatia), Dr Helge Tramsen (Denmark), Dr Ferenc Orsos (Hungary), Dr François Naville (Switzerland) and Dr Vincenzo Palmieri (Italy), who had been asked by the Germans to Katyn, attended the exhumations, and had themselves carried out autopsies and examined letters and documents found on them. Two of the doctors, Tramsen and Naville, provided the committee with papers, army buttons and officers' badges found at Katyn. All five confirmed their agreement with the document they had signed in Katyn along with seven other doctors and scientists on April 30, 1943, which was based in part on the observation of changes which had occurred with the course of time to the bodies, and was to the effect that the murders had been committed in Spring 1940, when the Smolensk region, where Katyn is situated, was a part of the Soviet Union and under its domination. This was a year before the outbreak of the Soviet-German war of June 21, 1941. The guilt of the Soviet Union was also confirmed by the American officers taken to Katyn by the Germans (Van Fleet and Stewart), and witnesses brought to Katyn from occupied Poland, Major Jozef Czapski and others. There was no lack of evidence from the accused Soviet side. One of the witnesses, whose personal details were known to the committee but whose name was not revealed for fear of consequences to his family in Poland, stated that in answer to a question about the lost Polish officers he had heard the Minister of State Security, Merkulov, say : 'We have committed an error. These men are not available. We will give you others.'

Similarly, the notorious Beria, when asked the same question by Colonel Berling, had stated in the presence of Colonel Gorczynski, who had repeated it to the witness : 'We have committed a great blunder.'

An officer of the Soviet army, Boris Olshanski, who had fled to the West in 1946, stated he had had a talk on the Katyn case with N. N. Burdenko, chairman of the Soviet commission investigating the Katyn crime and appointed in 1944, which had laid all the blame on the Germans. Burdenko told him that the report of this commission was untrue and added : 'I was appointed by Stalin personally to go to the Katyn site. All the corpses were four years old. To me, as a medical man, the problem was quite clear. Our NKVD friends made a mistake.'

Finally, Stalin's son Jakub Djugashvili, a prisoner of war in a German camp, had stated frankly in a talk with another POW, Lieutenant Jerzy Lewszecki, that the execution of the Polish officers was carried out by the Soviet Union : 'Why, those were the intelligentsia, the most dangerous elements to us, and they had to be eliminated.'

The most dramatic piece of evidence was a diary found on the body of Major Adam Solski, who had noted on April 8, 1940 : 'April 8, 3.30 a.m. Departure from Kozielsk station to the west. 9.45 a.m. At Jelnia station. April 8, 1940 : From 12 noon we are standing at Smolensk on a railway siding. April 9, 1940 : A few minutes before five in the morning reveille in the prison cars and preparation for departure ... We are to go somewhere by car, and what then? April 9, 5 a.m. From the very dawn the day started somewhat peculiarly. Departure by prison van in little cells (terrible); they brought us somewhere into the woods—some kind of summer resort. Here a detailed search. They took the watch, on which the time was 6.30 a.m. (8.30), asked me for my wedding ring, which they took, roubles, my main belt and pocket knife ...'

Here the diary breaks off.

While urging the House of Representatives to approve the report submitted, the committee also advised the adoption of a resolution appealing to the President of the United States to place the Katyn case before the General Assembly of the United Nations, so that the Assembly might initiate a case against the USSR at the International Court of Justice.

In its final passages, the committee did not hesitate to reveal and condemn all the machinations aimed at covering up those who committed the crime from the American people. And it did so without hesitation or scruples, ignoring all taboos, calling everything by its name and urging the opening of proceedings against the guilty. If anyone is disturbed by the fact of communist influences penetrating so deeply during the war and the first post-war years, they may take comfort from the knowledge that this committee, obtaining its powers through Congress from the American people, placed these influences before the pillory of public opinion, which is the highest court in the United States.

However, not all these machinations were the work of fellow-travellers. Some were certainly dictated by considerations of which the final report of the committee spoke thus : 'In those fateful days near the end of the Second World War, there unfortunately existed in high governmental and military circles a strange psychosis that military necessity required the sacrifice of loyal allies and our own principles in order to keep Soviet Russia from making a separate peace with the Nazis.'

Thus this Soviet blackmail gagged the voice of free American opinion and delayed the uncovering of the crime for many years.

The work of the committee was not completed, since Congress had not yet adopted the resolution put forward by the committee; but even so the committee's establishment—with the authority of Congress—of the responsibility of the Soviet Union for Katyn made a resounding echo in the press and public opinion of the free world.

At a banquet to celebrate the occasion thanks were offered to the committee by the vice-president of the Polish-American Congress, Ignacy Nurkiewicz, and the president for the State of New York Franciszek Wazeter, on behalf of Polonia. Ambassador Jozef Lipski decorated the committee members with the order 'Polonia restituta'.

The House of Representatives soon appointed another committee, this time to investigate communist aggression in the countries of Eastern Europe. It was headed by Charles J. Kersten of Wisconsin, and included Tadeusz M. Machrowicz. This committee set off first to the capital of Polonia in Chicago, and began its investigation there on the Polish National Day, 1954, by questioning Karol Rozmarek, Ambassador Lipski, myself and others. My old friend in the underground movement, now professor at Georgetown University, Jan Karski, appeared at the inquiries in an advisory capacity : he had been one of the first emissaries of the government in exile to reach Poland under German occupation.

After many months of inquiry, the committee established beyond a shadow of doubt that the communists had seized power in Poland by force in the form of the Soviet army, and were holding it against the will of the Polish people, using terror and deceit. Throughout all the inquiries of the committee the Katyn case ran like a scarlet thread and it was regarded as an early step in the domination of Poland by the Soviet Union. The murder of some 15,000 officers, including 4,253 at Katyn, the flower of the Polish intelligentsia who had been professors, scholars, writers, artists, politicians, judges, lawyers, doctors and members of the other professions in civilian life, was intended to deprive the Polish nation of their leading class and to make the Poles more submissive to their conquerors. This mass-murder supplemented and harmonized very well with the campaign to destroy the Polish intelligentsia carried on during the occupation by the Germans, as the Russians very well knew. Hitler and Stalin clasped hands in their common aim for removing independent Poland from the map.

As for the behaviour of the Warsaw régime, no one was much surprised by their Note of March 31, 1952, refusing the request of the Congressional committee to produce evidence and documents relevant to the Katyn case or to refer to witnesses who might be heard. The régime had no evidence or witnesses able to show the guilt of Germany, and had neither the wish nor courage to assist in exposing the real criminals. Stalin was still alive and the reign of terror in Poland at its height. But the situation changed after the events of October 1956, during which crowds demonstrating in the streets of Warsaw shouted 'Katyn! Katyn!' and rumours came from Poland to the effect that the Warsaw government planned to publish a White Book claiming that the guilt for the Katyn murders was that of the now dead Stalin and Beria. The indefatigable Julius Epstein, who had also been decorated with the 'Polonia restituta' order for his work on the Katyn case, took the opportunity of a press conference in New York called on October 5, 1959 by the régime's Minister of Foreign Affairs and brought about the following dialogue :

> Epstein: During the events of October 1956, Gomulka ordered the publication of a White Book on Katyn, in which the guilt of Stalin's NKVD in the massacre of thousands of Polish officers at Katyn and elsewhere was to be stated. Why has this White Book never been published?
> Rapacki: Gomulka has never ordered the issuance of such a White Book on Katyn, and there was no need for it since the question of Katyn was cleared up long ago.
> Epstein: Do you mean to say that you and the Polish government still believe in the German guilt as far as Katyn is concerned, in spite of the great American Congressional investigation?
> Rapacki: The way in which the American investigation was carried out only strengthens my conviction of the German guilt.

This reply was the best proof that a great deal of water had flowed under the bridges in three years. It was hardly to be expected that Rapacki would risk his neck and admit that the Soviet Union was responsible. Yet a dozen *clichés* exist to facilitate the smooth refusal to answer a journalist's question, and all Foreign Ministers know these by heart and can use them. But rather than take refuge behind such a phrase, Rapacki preferred the Soviet version, thus making it his own.

X

THEY CHOSE FREEDOM

What the American press called the greatest diplomatic defeat in 1953 of the Soviet bloc in the United Nations occurred when Professor Marek Korowicz decided to quit the Polish communist delegation to the United Nations, where he had been made chairman of the legal commission, in order to protest against the Soviet occupation of his homeland. He defected with my assistance.

During the next few days the telephone in my apartment never seemed to stop ringing. Press agencies, broadcasting and TV stations, editorial offices, all wanted details of the 'flight'. The flood of calls increased when the Polish communist delegation to the UN issued a communiqué implying that Korowicz had been kidnapped. The newspapers published with undisguised satisfaction my correction to this along with news of the consternation prevailing in all the UN communist delegations.

After the fever of the first few days, there followed an interrogation of Professor Korowicz by the Congressional committee, in which I too took part, and which was broadcast throughout America on TV, then his series of articles in the European press, and in *Life Magazine* and the *Readers' Digest* in the United States, and finally the lectures he gave in the main American towns. As a result, tens of millions of people, primarily in America and then in the rest of the free world, learned yet again the truth about Poland.

During one of my visits with Professor Korowicz to Washington, I had the opportunity to learn how funds are collected for the Crusade of Freedom, and through it for the Free Europe Committee and their radio stations. We were both invited to be guests at a meeting of several hundred representatives of American social, scientific, industrial, commercial, financial and political organizations. Among the speakers was Henry Ford, together with members of the government, United States senators and others. They all appealed for sacrifices on behalf of this organization. The case was put with particular clarity by Charles E. Wilson, Secretary of the Department of Defence.

87

'I am at the head of a department which spends about $50 million every day. If it were the intention of the government to cover the cost of, for instance, Radio Free Europe, from its own funds or from the pocket of the American taxpayer, then it would not be difficult to find these few millions. But neither the President nor his Cabinet wish to do this, since we all hold that this money should be donated by the American people from voluntary contributions. This is aid given by the people, not by the government, to help the peoples behind the Iron Curtain.'

During this time numerous sheets of paper had been reaching the chairman, who now announced : 'I am glad to report that offers of contributions amounting to nearly two million dollars have come in.'

The incident involving Professor Korowicz was not isolated. Both before and after it celebrated flights took place, helping to open the eyes of the West to what was happening in Poland. In the forefront of them all was the insane landing on the Danish Island Bornholm on March 5, 1953, of one of the latest Soviet fighters, a MIG, from which there leaped the young lieutenant of the Polish Air Force, Franciszek Jarecki. He was soon followed by Lieutenant Zdzislaw Jazwinski. Once again the West gasped with amazement at the courage and determination of these two lads, brought up in communist schools, which had not been able to uproot their free spirit. Jazwinski's flight was the more risky, since the Soviet commanding officers of the Polish Air Force, alarmed by Jarecki's deed, had doubled their vigilance and control over their insubordinate Polish pupils. The descriptions these young men gave of the political training in military schools were repeated in the American press. Jarecki was self-assured, balanced, planning his flight long in advance and in cold blood, fighting for it by working to obtain the best reports at his training school and the confidence of his Soviet superiors. Finally he lived to see the day when notices were put up in Air Force schools bearing his likeness and an appeal to the other students, 'Follow the steps of Jarecki'. He recounted this incident with ironic wit when he spoke at meetings of Polonia, and aroused much laughter. Jazwinski, who obeyed this appeal despite the fact that the notices had already disappeared, was a shy young man who avoided public appearances and longed to join the American Air Force. Both were soon adopted : Jarecki by Congressman Alvin O'Konski and his wife, Jazwinski by Mr and Mrs Jarzebowski, who have their own radio programme in New York.

When, at the end of 1957, Lieutenant Bohdan Kozuchowski landed another MIG in Sweden, after Soviet aircraft had prevented him landing on Bornholm, the West received the news as something quite natural.

In November 1953, I met Jan Hajdukiewicz in New York; he had chosen freedom in Korea, where he was an interpreter on the Armistice commission, which consisted of representatives of 'neutral' states. He also contributed to the fame of Polish escapes in the other hemisphere, in the Far East, from whence the news of his defection to the American military authorities electrified America.

Some fame was also gained in America by Klimowicz and the 'seven from the *Puszczyk*', who chose freedom in England; the latter were sailors who left their fishing vessel at Whitby after overpowering the captain and the political officer on September 23, 1954. This incident, thanks to the initiative of the *Polish Daily* in London, brought about an unusual wave of contributions from the Polish exiles in England, who soon collected the sum of £6,000 to pay for the defence of their right to political asylum before an English court.

This brings to an end the chain of escapes, the echo of which resounded round the whole world. They all left Poland to seek in the West the freedom that was absent in their homeland.

No echoes accompanied the choice of freedom made legally by my old school friend who hung in the air, not so much between Heaven and earth as between Poland and Israel.

'I'd had enough of the nightmare in Poland, so that on account of my Jewish origin I applied with my wife and child to go to Israel,' he told me, 'and after overcoming numerous difficulties, the whole family of us landed in Haifa. Troubles began after a few months. The Israeli authorities summoned me and told me point-blank : Why did you come to Israel? You have been converted from the Jewish faith, your wife is Polish and a Catholic by birth, so is your child. So what is it you want here?' When I explained I had saved my life in this way during the German occupation, they did not give up. 'Tell that to the marines, not to us. We know that you considered yourself a Pole before the war, so go back there.' I refused categorically to do any such thing and threatened they would have to use force. Then they gave me an exit visa to a European country, and back, but indicated that the return visa was merely for show, so that I'd get an entry visa into the European country. They threatened that if I tried to get into Israel again with the return visa, they would not let me land from the ship. This was how, after many misadventures, I finished up in America.'

But there were other kinds of flights, of no less fame, and perhaps even more, followed however by total silence. Thus in December

1953 Lieutenant-Colonel Jozef Swiatlo of the Security Police and deputy director of the 10th Department of the Ministry of Public Security in Warsaw, crossed the frontier into West Berlin. He was to reveal secrets of the security police which made one's hair stand on end. No one before or after him ever revealed so much about the security police and Communist party. What he said made one shudder with disgust. His account, broadcast to Poland first by Radio Free Europe and later distributed in pamphlet form, sent over Poland by balloon, shook the foundations of the secret police and the Party and brought about the dismissal of the Minister of Security himself, Stanislaw Radkiewicz, and his closest collaborators. But after a brief moment of fame in America, silence suddenly descended on him. This occurred when public opinion realized that a safe refuge had been found in the United States by one of those responsible for the mass murder committed by the secret police against the Polish people. Swiatlo himself brought this about. Being devoid of elementary moral feelings, he did not understand that his confessions accused himself. This, for instance, was how he described the arrest of Spychalski : 'He greeted me, gave me his hand, and I caught his hand and did not let it go.' He did not feel that there was anything repulsive in using a friendly gesture as a trap. He spoke with the same moral indifference of his arrest of Gomulka, Zymierski, of the struggle against Cardinal Wyszynski and other things he had done. When it was realized what sort of person Swiatlo was, a curtain of silence descended upon him, and he found no takers among American publishers for his memoirs. At present Swiatlo is living somewhere in hiding, in fear of his life, since the arms of communist agents are long and can extend even to America.

Two years later, with the arrest and sentence of his collaborators in crime, General Romkowski and Colonel Rozanski, as well as of his immediate superior, Colonel Anatol Fejgin, it became clear that Swiatlo had fled in fear of arrest from the people he had himself imprisoned—such as Gomulka, Spychalski and Kliszko—who were coming back into power.

Other refugees of the Swiatlo type include Colonel Marian Muszkat, a judge of the Supreme Military Court in Warsaw, who, in far-off Israel, found not only a peaceful existence but even became a university professor. It was this court which in the final resort decided hundreds of death sentences passed at political trials. And while Muszkat was serving on it, it was regarded as a political crime to have belonged, for example, to the Home Army during the Nazi occupation. Young Jews in Israel deserve better educators.

An entirely different type to Swiatlo was Seweryn Bialer, who fled from Poland in January 1956. This young man, who went through the hell of Nazi occupation and the ghetto, had come to believe sincerely that Communism would do away with war, terror and persecution and would bring a better future to the world. Talented, hard-working, devoted to the Communist party, and ideologically unshakeable, he attained, despite his youth, to the highest ranks of the Party cells. But once he confronted theory with practice, he lost his faith, broke down and fled to the West to tell the world of his disappointments and disillusion. He was a type of ideological communist whose inborn honesty forced him to speak out and tell the truth, and he aroused sympathy to the same degree that Swiatlo aroused disgust.

On the whole, it is to these rejects of the communist family who chose freedom in Europe and found themselves transported like lightning to the United States, that we owe one of the most bitter truths of life in exile, repeated time and again by people fleeing from Poland and waiting for years for a visa to enter the United States in the various camps and homes in Germany and Austria :

'The quickest way to America is via collaboration with the communists. And the longest—is to have fought against them.'

XI

STONES AGAINST TANKS

In October 1953 I was asked to give a lecture to the Overseas Press Club of America on the prospects of liberating Poland through the underground. A few months earlier, disorder had unexpectedly broken out in East Berlin, where the desperate inhabitants had demonstrated in crowds in the streets, burning newspaper stands with communist publications, overturning government cars and destroying the equipment and documents of Party offices. Soviet tanks had come out against them and restored calm without firing. This event made a great impression in the West and brought hopes of revolt spreading to other countries. On the other hand it emerged from the moderate statement of the United States government that, while supporting the rebels morally, no assistance could be given them.

I began my lecture by outlining the political and moral conditions for the existence of any underground behind the Iron Curtain.

The first and most important requirement is the existence within an occupied country of a desire to regain the lost independence and a spirit of rebellion against the occupation. This fundamental condition has always existed in Poland. During World War II it was the foundation on which was erected the Polish underground state, which had its own government, parliament and courts. It also had an army 300,000 strong, which at the moment of entry of Soviet troops into Polish territory in 1944 launched its attack against the rear of the retreating German army. This operation, known under the code name of 'Tempest', culminated in the Warsaw uprising, through which I lived from start to finish. The uprising broke out on August 1, 1944, and lasted sixty-three days.

The prerequisite I have described also holds true today in Soviet-occupied Poland. In this respect there is no great difference between the situation which prevailed during the war and that which obtains today.

Another prerequisite for the existence of an underground is a realistic hope that independence will be regained. No one is going to risk his liberty and his life unless he believes in ultimate victory. The

Poles are like other nations in that they do not care for fighting for the sake of fighting. Like everybody else they want to live in peace, but they will take greater risks and make more sacrifices than others if they see that such an act makes sense and has a real chance of success.

This hope existed during the recent war. Not for a moment did we stop believing that the Allies would win, and that we would be liberated from the German occupation.

How is it at present under the Soviet occupation? Hope undoubtedly exists, but it is much weaker and no time limit has been set for the termination of the occupation. Poles know that the United States does not want war, because they are being told so—and rightly— by American radio broadcasts. As they also feel that Russia too is not eager for war at the moment, they envisage a long period of uneasy peace. Therefore, in regard to the second main condition, there are important differences between the war years and now. Instead of a wait of several years for victory and liberation, we now have an indefinite period of waiting.

A third factor, the current international situation, is totally different from that of World War II. Twelve years ago the Allies were fighting the common enemy on all the battle fronts of the world. So the Polish underground organized itself into an armed military movement, which engaged the Germans in actual battle, in addition to carrying out acts of sabotage, diversion and assassination, blowing up bridges and trains and disrupting the flow of food and manpower to Germany.

The fact that we now have peace and that the occupation may last years makes the very idea of a military, fighting underground utterly nonsensical. If the Poles were to take up arms alone and the Western world did not take part in the combat, they would only be committing suicide. The Soviet occupation forces would enjoy a crushing superiority over the rebels. The correctness of this reasoning is evidenced by the recent riots in Berlin, which are erroneously called an insurrection. Why erroneously? Because an insurrection is an armed attack against an occupant, and not a single shot was fired at the Russians in Berlin or in East Germany. What the Germans did was to demonstrate in the streets, a splendid anti-communist demonstration, deserving the greatest credit, but not an uprising. You may remember the picture of two teenage boys hurling stones at a Russian tank. It is a stirring photograph. Stones against tanks! To me it is also a symbol of impotence. It is the best illustration of what human beings behind the Iron Curtain can do when left to their own devices. They can throw stones at tanks. That's about all. After the Berlin riots, it was stated on the highest authority in this country that the Iron Curtain populations can count only on moral support. Such a declaration merits the highest respect for its honesty and frankness. But it also makes it crystal clear that any further armed movements behind the Iron Curtain would remain on their own.

A fourth factor is the degree of control exercised over a country by the occupying power. Here too there is a basic difference between war-time and now. At that time, the combined forces of the Gestapo, the police and the army were unable to control the country completely. Today the entire Polish population is controlled by a secret police force of many thousands, working in conjunction with the million-member Communist party.

Under these circumstances, it would be a dangerous delusion to think that the peoples behind the Iron Curtain want or are able to throw off the Soviet yoke by their own armed effort.

I then developed the problem of the conditions appropriate to resistance in peacetime to be able to survive and develop under Soviet occupation :

It cannot create any great organizations, but must on the contrary act under the greatest possible decentralization and dispersion. The ideal decentralization is an infinite number of one-member underground organizations. The best police in the world cannot gain access to them, because each is locked within the human soul. Its only member attentively follows the international situation, listens to Western radio broadcasts and he knows the truth about the world. He—or she—preserves within himself the spirit of the fight for independence, as well as the hope of liberation, and constantly resists Communism, but in such a way as to keep his personal liberty, which he must safeguard for many years to come. He regards it as his important duty to maintain contact with the West and with the Polish émigrés, who represent him in the free world. This explains why we have such accurate information about conditions in Poland.

I am afraid some of you may feel disappointed as you listen to me. Perhaps you expected me to give you names of underground organizations, or facts and figures about fighting or assassinations. What I have told you about the new underground may strike you as propaganda generalizations, but only such an underground can withstand the Soviet occupation. To organize any other kind would be a mistake and a mark of short-sightedness. This underground can last for years, provided Western policy does not destroy the second condition for its existence: the hope of liberation. This hope rose after the pronouncement by President Eisenhower of the doctrine of liberation, on April 16, 1953. Despite the fact that the Poles do not see how it can be implemented by peaceful means, they regard it as a solemn act of non-recognition by the United States of the present occupation of Poland. This provides a long-range basis for moderate hope.

Ladies and gentlemen, we émigrés are of the opinion that war will not break out as long as the Russians know that their atomic or hydrogen bomb attack will not destroy in one day the entire defence potential of this country, and so long as they are aware that the retaliatory attack would be two or three times heavier than their own. If war should come, it would most probably be through miscalculation, for this is usually the cause of war. Aside from this big risk, total war does not at the moment threaten the world. The Soviets are at present carrying on their plan of world domination. This plan consists of ideological warfare which, in addition to local wars, is supposed to give the Soviets control over countries that are under neither their own nor Western direct rule. Should they succeed in gaining domination over vast territories of Asia, Africa and perhaps also South America, they would hope to achieve ultimate victory without a total war. So if ideological warfare currently has priority over total war in Soviet plans, let us not—for the sake of doubtful advantages—sacrifice the one hundred million allies behind the Iron Curtain, who are already in this fight on the side of the Western world. As Talleyrand might have said : 'This would be more than a crime—it would be a mistake'.

When I concluded, I tried to estimate the reaction of the audience, who had listened to the speech in complete silence. When the applause died down, I was pleased to note that the audience had not been bored. Some came up to me in order to shake the speaker by the hand in the traditional way and they all confirmed what the first of them said : 'You were absolutely right. It is stupid to revolt for the sake of revolting. It is precisely the reaction of the West— or rather the lack of any reaction—to the incidents in Berlin that warn against imitating such things.'

This was not my first meeting with the world of the American Press. After our flight with Mikolajczyk in November 1947 we had had the occasion for several days to meet the best-known names of this world, including Sulzberger, publisher of the *Times* and his staff during a luncheon at the offices of this eminent newspaper which, along with the *New York Herald-Tribune*, was soon to become my teacher in American political life. When the sensation passed, regular contacts developed, since the large majority of the American press was interested in the cause of liberating Eastern Europe and gave it their support. This interest underwent intensification or diminishing at various periods of time, depending on the changes in the international situation which dictated the contents of the newspaper more than the editor did. In any case, the papers published from time to time statements by émigré organizations, had interviews with members, attended press conferences and published letters to the editor, of which several dozen by myself have appeared over the years in the *New York Times*, the *New York Herald-Tribune*, the

Chicago Herald-Tribune, the *Washington Post and Herald,* the *Evening Star,* and others.

Conscientious study of the leading American newspapers and contacts with journalists has given me great admiration for the American press as an institution of public life. Its mother is unlimited freedom of speech, and its father the most highly developed journalistic technique in the world. It is only thanks to the press, supplemented by the radio and TV, that public opinion has become the real ruler of the United States. With the greatest wealth and variety in the world, thanks to its links with hundreds of groupings, ideas, influences and interests, it is the real and fullest reflection of American life in all directions. Nothing is hidden from it and no power exists which can silence it. The incredible number of publications, serving various views and trends, is in fact the finest guarantee of the independence of this press as an institution which is one of the foundations of the system of the United States. Its influence upon life is so great that to the three authorities laid down in the United States constitution—legislative, justice and executive—a fourth should be added, i.e., the press.

In the conflict between the democratic West and the totalitarian East, this press is a weapon still more powerful than atom-head rockets. A political war for ideas and the souls of its own people is carried on primarily by the aid of newspapers, and American newspapers serve this purpose very well, first because they tell the truth to their own people, and the truth is the best ammunition in this fight. However, political war is a war like any other, except that it is carried on by arms which hurt the soul, not the body. In this war certain rules have to be observed, the most important is that, while serving its own people, it should not also serve the enemy. This includes for instance publication of news of every failure in firing a rocket at Cape Kennedy, which enables the Soviet Union to compile accurate statistics of successful and unsuccessful experiments, of great military significance. The American armed forces would certainly gladly surround all these experiments with secrecy, but if they did all the newspapers would sound an alarm throughout America, protesting that attempts were being made to conceal something from the American people. During the war, a successful attempt was made to keep what was called the Manhattan project secret : this was the making of the first atomic bomb. The political war now in progress is more dangerous in its risk and aims than World War II and requires application of the same method.

Unfortunately, the newspapers are a real gold-mine of military information for Soviet intelligence, whose agents can acquire it

The New York Times.

Entered as Second-Class Matter,
Post Office, New York, N. Y.

NEW YORK, SATURDAY, SEPTEMBER 19, 1953.

Times Square, New York 36, N. Y.
Telephone LAckawanna 4-1000

cker Bares
id for Race

A. HAGERTY

ters said yester-
still pondering"
uld run for re-
dependent candi-
he expected to
over the week-

filing independ-
etitions will ac-

hree indications
ill seriously con-
or re-election on
party ticket, on
elected in 1950.

wing, who was
Citizens Com-
les E. Keegan,
nomination for
the Impellitteri
ocratic primary,
to Mr. Keegan,
in for election as
age 12, Column 6

TO TRACK
ON AIDES

nt, Could Not
0,000 in Bets,
ere Is Told

SHEAFFER RESIGNS
AS COMMERCE AIDE;
REPUTED ASTIN FOE

**Dispute Over Battery Compound
Recalled as a Key Member
of Weeks' 'Team' Quits**

By CHARLES E. EGAN
Special to The New York Times.

WASHINGTON, Sept. 18.—Craig
R. Sheaffer, a key member of the
"business man's team" with which
Sinclair Weeks, Secretary of Commerce, has surrounded himself, has
resigned as Assistant Secretary in
charge of domestic affairs. Mr.
Sheaffer, a fountain pen manufac-
turer, is expected to become chairman of the board of the company
that bears his name.

Official confirmation of Mr.
Sheaffer's resignation was given
tonight by Secretary Weeks, who
said he had accepted the Assistant
Secretary's resignation "on the
authority of the President."

At the same time Mr. Weeks
made public an exchange of letters
in which Mr. Sheaffer said he had
expected to stay with the department into next year but had decided to return to his business interests because "I am completely
convinced that the change is better
made now so that my successor
may have the advantage of two or
three months indoctrination in the

New Polish Alternate at U. N. Asks Asylum Here

Law Professor Quits
Delegation—Dulles
to Consider Plea

By JOHN C. DEVLIN

Dr. Marek Stanislaw Korowicz,
who arrived in the United States
Monday as the first alternate
member of the Polish delegation
to the United Nations, yesterday
asked for political asylum in the
United States.

The defection of Dr. Korowicz,
a graying, gentle-mannered former
professor of international law at
Cracow University, is the fourth
since last March, when a Polish
pilot of an MIG-15 fighter plane
flew his aircraft to Denmark.

Secretary of State John Foster
Dulles said he had been informed
of Dr. Korowicz' case, but was
not yet familiar with the details.
He said American policy was in
favor of granting asylum, but
each case must be considered
separately and in conformity with
law.

Dr. Korowicz, in announcing his
decision to seek asylum here, said
that 95 per cent of the Poles were
opposed to their Communist rulers
and that "now, for the first time,"
his countrymen had decided that
Soviet power in their country could
be "disrupted from within."

Asked what help he would like
to see the United States provide,
he replied that the Polish people
needed "the true news from

The New York Times (by Neal Boenzi)

Dr. Marek Stanislaw Korowicz, left, first alternate member of the Polish delegation to the
United Nations, as he announced here yesterday that he was asking for political asylum in
the United States. With him are Joseph G. Grew, center, chairman of the board of the National Committee for Free Europe, and Stefan Korbonski, a leader of the Polish underground.

Front page of *The New York Times* with the news about Professor
Korowicz's choosing freedom. From left to right: Professor
Korowicz, Ambassador Grew, the author. See chapter: *They Chose
Freedom*

Delegation of the Assembly of Captive European Nations/ACEN
accompanied by Korean army officers visiting the front at Pan Mun
Jom. From left to right : Dr Masens, Dr Kovago, the author. See
chapter : ACEN : *A Trip round the World*

without any effort, as they loll in deck chairs, smoking a cigar and marking up items with their pencils.

This magnificent free press also gives the Soviet Union much propaganda gratis. Each move by each Soviet official in the United States, for instance members of delegations to UNO, is described, every word they utter calculated as propaganda, each smile and gesture registered. In this way, representatives of one of the most inhuman systems are made to resemble ordinary civilized people, and normal revulsion against these barbarians of the twentieth century is diminished.

In cases of major political failures in dealings with the Soviet Union, this press reacts so strongly as to be almost hysterical, and it takes a lively part in national lamentations and self-criticism. This mood is implanted in the readers, whose reflection recurs in the newspaper columns in the form of articles on the mood prevailing among the population, so that the citizen reads of his own reaction and that of other people, and becomes still more depressed. Eventually time liquidates this see-saw, or else some other event occurs to conceal the previous failure. A certain professional discipline, moderation and tact would easily enough prevent these manifestations, which are destructive to the national spirit.

Other appearances like that at the Overseas Press Club provided further opportunities for informing the American people of various manifestation in Polish life in Poland and in exile, as well as providing opportunities for meeting interesting organizations and people. I once made a speech to the Society of Former FBI Officials on the subject of what individuals provide recruits for the Polish secret police. I was surprised to find out that some of these officials were now lawyers, counsels and judges, as well as industrialists, scientists, Congressmen and Senators, and one was even Governor of a State (Frank Goad Clement, of Tennessee). It turned out that service in this department, which is well thought of by the public, is a good introduction to a career. I also spoke alongside Herbert A. Philbrick, author of the best-selling book, *I Lived Three Lives*, in which he described the dangerous work of an FBI agent who entered the Communist party. We spoke knowledgeably of the organization of the communist underground in America, where it possesses all the embryo cells from which authority would emerge in the event of a successful revolution in the country. On the occasion of a banquet arranged by the International Rescue Committee, I met a lean man of medium height in an empty hotel room, who mentioned that his name was Bedell Smith. I was electrified to realize that I was face to face with the former chief of staff of General Eisenhower

D

and to get the conversation under way I told him that I had first seen his photograph in occupied Poland in a copy of the *Berliner Illustrierte Zeitung*. General Bedell Smith replied by a question about the Polish wartime underground and from this an agreeable talk developed, since I have rarely heard so many compliments with regard to the Home Army and Second Corps. It was interrupted by our worried host who hurried in, breathing heavily and apologising for his lateness. Other guests followed him, including a hero of the American people, the famous Polar explorer Admiral Richard Byrd, and the head of American strategic intelligence during World War II, General William J. Donovan. I had the opportunity of meeting the latter again later on and discovered he had a fair knowledge of the organization and activities of our wartime underground movement. He once told me with evident emotion that during the war he had once been present when Polish parachutists took off at night by plane to jump over Poland. 'I have never forgotten this meeting with young, intent but also cheerful men, preparing for a dangerous trip that might end in death in their homeland.'

Yet again, at a banquet given on the occasion of a NATO conference in New York, I was introduced to General Alfred Gruenther, who was also chief of staff to General Eisenhower at one time. He at once started to expatiate on the great contribution our movement had made to the common victory and ended with praise for the fighting of Second Corps and a request to greet General Anders when I saw him.

After all, these things have taken deep root in the awareness of the American Leaders in World War II.

Appearances on TV also opened new fields for new impressions and observations. The black hole of the camera, behind which millions of eyes were concealed, was in itself a sensation and aroused nervousness. Furthermore, one is only given a general idea of the subject of the broadcast, since the producer wants the replies to seem spontaneous. One must therefore keep a cool head in order that all may go well. The final verdict does not come till I reach home where Zosia, that most demanding of viewers, tolerantly says 'Not bad', or more often, 'Why did you wear such a dull tie?'

Upon being invited in February 1954 by Duquesne University, Pittsburgh, to take part in a TV feature on the subject of communist rule behind the Iron Curtain, I found myself among others in front of the camera with a Negro, and former member of the central committee of the American Communist party, who had quit and was now unmasking its organization and methods. Over coffee after the broadcast in a large group, this former communist started to talk to me about Polish affairs and in quite an aggressive manner, accusing the pre-war governments of reaction, social backwardness and the like. Although there was some truth in this, I began countering his arguments, since I was revolted by this renegade communist interfering in Polish affairs, and a member of the central committee into the bargain. But my irritation gave way to surprise when he began talking with expert familiarity of the Kiev campaign of 1920. I asked him where he had obtained his one-sided knowledge. He smiled condescendingly and said : 'In Moscow. I studied at the Lenin academy for two years. They taught us a lot about you Poles, for the Poles are regarded as dangerous enemies.'

In another case I took part with several émigré leaders of other nationalities in a TV programme called 'Town meeting of the air', broadcast throughout the United States, during which an audience numbering over a thousand were able to ask us various questions. Over a dozen of them were placed in line, including whites and coloured, Indians, Chinese, and one, an Indian, asked me : 'How are the non-white Russians treated in the Soviet Union?'

I did not know what he meant, so admitted it, adding that everyone knows which Russians are 'white' and their opposites are 'red'. The Indian objected. 'That isn't what I mean, but the other, non-white Russians.'

I was embarrassed, not knowing what to say, but the moderator guessed : 'I expect you have in mind people of other non-white racial origins, who are Soviet citizens.'

'Yes,' said the student and everyone sighed with relief.

As an Asian he was so self-conscious about the colour of his skin that he wanted at any price to avoid using the phrase in front of a predominantly white audience.

For eighteen months I took part in a weekly discussion programme over the New York station WFDR, which is under the control of the Union of Ladies' Garment Industry Workers, headed by David Dubinski, a well-known leader of the trade union movement, who was born in Lodz. The atmosphere was more like a Polish socialist meeting in Warsaw than a broadcasting studio in New York.

All these appearances were interesting and increased my knowledge of American life, but they demanded concentration and were exhausting. In addition, it was necessary to overcome the difficulty of speaking in a foreign language. In the end, as time passed, everyone got bored with his own statements, repeated frequently at various places and times, and even the sound of his own voice sickened him. Unfortunately one cannot doze off while making a speech and only one person has succeeded, and he, alas, in a joke : 'I dreamed

I was making a speech in the House of Lords,' said an English
aristocrat, 'and when I woke up, I found I was.' But this miracle
does not happen in real life, so another solution must be found to
avoid falling into a routine and not being overcome by tedium.
One opportunity for this was given me by an invitation I received
in January 1953 by the Freedom House organization, whose president was the famous Sumner Welles, to give a lecture on communist
rule in Poland. I had spoken on this subject dozens of times, so,
finding out that the audience at the luncheon-meeting would be
mostly women, I decided for a change to reverse the situation and
talk about communist rule in the United States. 'We've had enough
of fear in Poland; let them have a taste of it now,' I said to myself,
eyeing the several hundred ladies sitting round in groups at beauti-
fully laid tables. The hall looked like a flower-bed, since it was
fashionable to decorate hats with flowers, and every other woman
seemed to have mink on her shoulders. Here and there, like a nut
in a cake, a solitary man was to be seen. The ladies set about their
lunch vigorously, and when the waiters had served cake and coffee,
they were ready to listen to me. Introduced by the well-known
columnist Elsa Maxwell, I adopted a serious expression and began.

Mr Chairman, ladies and gentlemen: a good many people in this
country are familiar with a variety of facts about life in the Iron
Curtain countries, but few persons born and raised in the climate
of American freedom and democracy have a real comprehension of
the reality of daily living based on these facts. Let me try to give
you some insight into that reality by asking you to follow me as
I sketch for you a typical day in the life of a Polish city-dweller,
as it would look against the background of New York.

Just imagine that the communist administration has compelled
several families to move into your apartment on the East or the
West side, assigning each family one room and granting them all the
use of your kitchen, hallway and so forth. Since these families are
complete strangers to you, you must be careful not to say anything
criticizing the communist system. You must shut the door tight
when you turn on your radio and must tune it down to a mere
whisper when you listen, say, to the Voice of Canada, which is still
free and to you the sole and priceless source of information about
the free world.

When you leave for work in the morning you greet the doorman
with respect, because you know he is an agent of the secret police,
who is obligated to make periodic reports about you and the other
tenants in the building. You are in a very great hurry to get to your
place of work, because if you are a few minutes late three times, you
may be sentenced, in routine fashion, without a trial, to anything up
to two years in a labour camp. Let us say that New York has as

many camps of this type as—for instance—Warsaw; a dozen or so. They are either barracks or former factory buildings, surrounded by barbed wire and guarded by sentries with sub-machine guns.

When you enter the subway you buy any odd paper. It makes no difference which one you get, because they all have the same kind of articles and features, and all sport a picture of Stalin and, say, Alger Hiss on the front page. The paper refers to Stalin as the 'sunshine of nations', and calls Hiss 'the father of American democracy and great architect of the United States'. The newspaper's contents bore you, but you have to read it to become orientated regarding official policy and, above all, to know why you should hate the Canadians and what kind of bacteria and flies are being dropped on some new Korea. As you ride to work you worry about your wife, who has been standing in line in front of a store since dawn in order to buy some bread and milk. You worry about your worn-out shoes, to replace which will cost you a month's salary—about your children, who are being demoralized by the communist school, and about the circumstance that when your day's work is over, hungry though you will be, you will have to attend a rally in tribute to the new President you elected in November. In that election he was the only candidate running for the highest office in the land, and the Communist party's ticket was the only one presented to the voters.

If, on this sample day, your factory, office or institution, should send you on official business to Atlantic City, for example, you must be sure you have the following documents before you leave: a civilian passport, without which you are not even a human being; an army passport, without which you are a deserter; a certificate of New York residence, issued by the mayor, without which you are a vagrant; a certificate from your employer stating the destination and purpose of your trip, otherwise you would be travelling for an unknown, hence suspicious, reason; and finally you would have to get permission to be at the sea-coast, which is under special control, for otherwise you would be suspected of a desire to escape across the Atlantic. If you are making the trip by car—not your private car, of course, for such are non-existent—but in your office of factory automobile—you would be stopped on the outskirts of the city, at that point on the highway where you usually pay your toll-fare, by a policeman holding a sub-machine gun, who would check all your documents, write down your car's licence plate number and upon your departure telephone his opposite number in Atlantic City, giving him your name and license plate number, so that the fact and time of your arrival there might be noted. If you fail to arrive at your destination, you may be subjected to an investigation, followed by a trial before a military tribunal, whose judges are officers of the secret police, wearing army uniforms.

If, however, you go to work as usual on this day, you may run into a drive for compulsory contributions to help 'North Korean orphans' to the tune of ten per cent of your monthly salary, or you may be ordered to contribute toward the peace offensive, or to alleviate the misery of 'starving Canadian workers'. That evening, at the rally, under the watchful eye of police agents, you obligate yourself 'joyfully, spontaneously and voluntarily', as the standard phrase goes, to work several hours on Sundays and holidays to honour the 'sunshine of nations, Stalin', and to acquit yourself well in the work competition. As you go home you give the right of way to a group of officers, wearing the uniform of the American armed forces, but speaking Russian, and your goodnight words to your doorman are something to the effect that life has only now become wonderful, and that only in a communist society can a body breathe easily, as a popular Soviet song has it. At home, your wife reports to you what she was unable to buy after standing in line for hours, and she tells you on which day this month she will run out of money for household expenses. Finally, exhausted from hard work and worry, you and your family go to bed in your single room. Now, at last, you are yourself, a human being whose thoughts are still free. Straining to catch the sound of police knocking at the door downstairs for a nocturnal search, you think about the Voice of Canada broadcasts and what they had to say, you wonder how long this will last and whether the Allies will ever liberate you. Sifting through the lies of communist propaganda, you try to form your own opinion about the facts printed in the newspapers.

This, ladies and gentlemen, is what your life would be like if a Soviet system ever prevailed here. Be thankful that it is not so, and do everything you can to assure that it never is. . . .

As I was speaking, silence began to prevail and the usual whispering of luncheon-lectures died away. Fewer and fewer flowery hats inclined to each other to confide comments on the appearance and dress of a neighbouring lady or the latest gossip, and clatter of cups and saucers and forks diminished. Half way through my speech you could have heard a pin drop. When I finished and the ladies began to leave hastily, a strange sight met my eyes. On the tables lay 400 portions of cake, almost untouched. My words had taken away the appetite of the ladies even for cake. This was my greatest success as an orator in the United States!

XII

ASSEMBLY OF CAPTIVE EUROPEAN NATIONS
(ACEN)

It never occurs to the crowds of New Yorkers passing daily along West 57th Street that here, in the heart of Manhattan, at No 29, there is an island in the American ocean, inhabited by foreigners using many foreign tongues which sound exotic to the American ear.

This mixture of people and languages, a Tower of Babel on a small scale, is the Assembly of Captive European Nations (ACEN), composed of nine national committees and councils in exile, each representing an Iron Curtain country. The people here are political leaders and former members of the governments of Albania, Bulgaria, Czechoslovakia, Estonia, Lithuania, Latvia, Poland, Rumania and Hungary, leaders of anti-Nazi and anti-Soviet underground movements, former members of parliaments, diplomats, army officers, writers, scholars, trade union activists, who left their countries not so much to escape death or imprisonment but rather to fight in the free world for the restoration of freedom to their own countries.

Among them may be met Monsignor Bela Varga, the last postwar Speaker of the Hungarian Parliament and the constitutional Deputy President of Hungary, as he talks to Bela Fabian, a member of the Hungarian parliament imprisoned for five years by the Germans in Auschwitz. Peter Zenkl, former Vice-Premier of the Czechoslovak government and mayor of the city of Prague, also a prisoner in Auschwitz, hurries past them to the phone. He is regarded by the Czech communist government as their main enemy. Beyond a partition is the former Rumanian Minister of Foreign Affairs, Constantin Visoianu, who held on in his country to the last minute alongside King Michael and is now discussing current affairs with his younger compatriot, chief of staff of ACEN, Brutus Coste, and his deputy, the Albanian Nuci Kotta. Here also it is possible to meet the president of the Lithuanian National Committee, Minister Vaclovas Sidzikauskas, who like Fabian and Zenkl spent five years in Auschwitz; Vilis Masens, the former Latvian diplomat; Leonhard Vahter, former member of the Estonian parliament; Vasyl Ger-

103

menji, the Albanian professor; Boleslaw Biega, former Polish diplomat; Feliks Gadomski, a district judge from Warsaw; Wladyslaw Michalak, once a trade union leader; and many others. Most of them speak of German and Soviet imprisonment with as much familiarity as a New Yorker speaks of Fifth Avenue. Often some will shift into the Russian language in order to present the Soviet attitude in some matter more clearly, and they use it like their mother-tongue. Against the background of the pulsating life of New York, these stateless people with names well-known behind the Iron Curtain give a somewhat sad impression. It was they who, again on Polish initiative, decided to organize a body more closely resembling in its structure the United Nations Organization.

With this aim in view, each of the nine committees or national councils appointed a delegation to ACEN of sixteen people; in addition five international émigré organizations (the Christian-Democratic Union of Central Europe, the International Centre of Free Trade Unions in Exile, the International Peasant Union, the Liberal-Democratic Union of East and Central Europe, and the Socialist Union of East and Central Europe) appointed delegations of six persons each. In this way, what the *New York Times* called a 'little UNO' was established in New York parallel to the United Nations Organization itself. It consists of over a hundred émigré leaders, who hold their plenary sessions at the same time as the UN General Assembly in the building of the Carnegie Endowment, adjacent to UN headquarters. This reminds the members of the UN that the communist delegations of nine countries are not genuine representatives, but are subject to the Soviet Union.

Anyone walking in that direction will see on the building opposite the UN building nine flags waving in the breeze, with a huge sign under them always drawing attention to some Soviet crime perpetrated against these nine nations. These flags and signs, which change according to circumstances, belong to ACEN. They are best seen from the windows of the UN building, and are a sore point with the communist delegations.

While acting at the same time and in the same area as the UN General Assembly, ACEN pays careful attention to what goes on during the sessions of the Assembly, and tries to counteract every move of the communist delegations from the Iron Curtain countries which might harm the interests of a member nation or falsify their aims and views. For this purpose, ACEN publishes or distributes to UN members statements, memoranda, protests and corrections, and current information about the present-day situation in the Iron Curtain countries. Individual members of ACEN also personally lobby UN delegations and authorities. Finally, on the opening day of a new session of the General Assembly and on other important occasions, ACEN arranges its own manifestations in front of the UN building, always reported by the press, radio and TV.

ACEN has also taken upon itself all the authority of its predecessor, the United Nations Committees and Councils in Exile, and carries on widely developed activity among the peoples, parliaments and governments of the free world. The headquarters staff of ACEN in New York, as well as branch representatives in London, Paris, Rome, Bonn (where the Poles play no part), Stockholm, The Hague, Brussels, Beirut, Rio de Janeiro, Buenos Aires, Santiago de Chile, Lima, Montevideo, Sydney and Tokio, who mobilize the émigré politicians in their respective countries, when necessary lobby governments, the press and international conferences. When a button is pressed in the central ACEN office in New York, the overseas branches take co-ordinated action. In the USA, representatives of ACEN are regularly received in the State Department and other government offices, where they are regarded as unofficial spokesmen of the nations behind the Iron Curtain. They are also frequent visitors to Congress, where ACEN enjoys the support of such eminent persons as Senators Douglas, Javits, Humphrey (now Vice-President), Dodd, Keating and members of the House of Representatives such as MacCormack, Pucinski, Zablocki, Reuss, Madden, Flood, and a great many more. A similar situation obtains in other countries where there are representatives of ACEN.

Some time after the establishment of ACEN, the attention of thousands of travellers moving daily through Grand Central Station in New York was caught by an unusual sight. Huge photographs hung in the station and waiting-room showed startled passers-by such pictures as Stalin signing the pact of friendship with Hitler which encouraged the latter to attack Poland, the mass-graves of the murdered Polish officers at Katyn, and many others. Several dozen photographs revealed the appalling story of forty years of international deceit, murders, terror and massacres committed by the Soviet Union. When the president of the AFL-CIO, George Meany, later opened this exhibition in Union Station, Washington, he was fiercely attacked for doing so by the Soviet trade union organ, *Trud*. As a result of the enormous success of this exhibition in the United States, where it toured the larger cities, copies were sent to Australia and Europe. In Sweden, Denmark and Italy the exhibition caused a real sensation.

ACEN is recognized and supported by the Council of Europe, which passed a resolution acknowledging the right to independent

D*

existence of the nine nations not represented in the Consultative Assembly and established a special commission to safeguard their interests, which is in constant contact with ACEN.

A special section of the work of ACEN is its publications, such as the monthly ACEN *News* and the half-yearly *Survey of the situation behind the Iron Curtain*, an exhaustive source of information about what is going on in Europe under Soviet occupation, as well as special issues such as, for instance, *Violation of human rights behind the Iron Curtain* or *A few facts on new colonialism*, and almost daily communiqués to the press.

News of the activities of ACEN is broadcast behind the Iron Curtain by Radio Free Europe, which also gives members the opportunity of directly addressing their compatriots.

ACEN propagates the idea of applying political pressure on the Soviet Union by the mobilization of public opinion in the Western world and in neutral countries against the occupation of these countries by Soviet Russia. In the view of ACEN, this aim can be served by, for instance, presenting the demand at every international conference in which the Soviet Union takes part, and at every UN session, that Russia withdraw her troops and agents from the countries behind the Iron Curtain, enabling them in this way to hold free elections under international control. Although the Soviet Union will undoubtedly reject this demand, nevertheless it will give expression each time to the fact that the Western world does not recognize Soviet domination behind the Iron Curtain, and also this rejection will set the opinion of the free world against Russia. In this way, political pressure is brought to bear upon Russia from this side of the Iron Curtain, which in turn will strengthen the internal pressure exerted on the far side of the Iron Curtain upon the communist governments by the people, and will force them to make concessions. Thus Russia will not be enabled to stabilize her rule in the subjugated countries; on the contrary it will be weakened. At the same time, some hope for future, though perhaps distant, liberation will be maintained in the subjugated nations. And as long as these nations resist Soviet rule, Russia will not be able to risk aggressive measures directed against Western Europe.

As the former colonies in Africa are liberated, ACEN has concentrated its attack against the rule of Russia in Eastern and Central Europe mainly on the fact that she is now the greatest colonial empire in the world, dominating not only nations of other races, religion and language in Asia, but also the nine nations which were free before the war.

XIII

A SILENT PROCESSION

The day after my arrival in London in April 1956 I was able to join the 20,000-strong procession protesting against the visit of Khruschchev and Bulganin which moved through the streets of London to the Cenotaph in Whitehall. A snake of people several kilometres long was moving along, no one speaking or smoking, in accordance with instructions. Many had brought out their wartime decorations and old uniforms for the occasion. This was a silent procession, dramatically demonstrating against the presence in England of Khrushchev and Bulganin, who were received that day by Queen Elizabeth II at Windsor Castle.

I joined the head of the procession. Familiar faces were all around. In the forefront were two members of the Council of Three, the main organ of the Council of National Unity, namely General Anders and Ambassador Raczynski. I looked round for the third member, General Bor, but in vain. Behind them came the executive committee of the Council of National Unity, with its chairman Adam Ciolkosz, and finally the entire Council, followed by thousands of Poles from London and all over England, carrying standards and banners.

I marched in the ranks with the rest and thought of the great changes that had occurred in the Kremlin of recent years. Stalin was dead, having attained the peak of madness and crime, Beria murdered shortly afterwards by his sincere friends in the Politburo; Molotov, Malenkov and Kaganovich were in disfavour and exiled, and there was a new ruler in the Kremlin, Nikita Khrushchev, who had thrown a bucket of dirty water over the head of his educator, and 'little sun of the nations, Stalin' at the twentieth Congress of the Communist party. He was now seeking a rapprochement with the West, of which his visit to England was clear proof—in a word, there had been a sort of revolution in the Kremlin family and a slight relaxation of the chains on the Russian people.

There had been changes in Poland too; Bierut had died and Ochab was ruling. Gomulka, Spychalski and Kliszko were already free, and for a change the Secret Police officials Romkowski, Rozan-

107

ski and Fejgin were in jail, with Radkiewicz out of favour. The Ministry of Security had been abolished, an amnesty proclaimed for political prisoners, while repatriation was offered to us émigrés in daily appeals from the 'Kraj' broadcasting station. In a word—it was a small copy of what had happened in Russia.

When the head of the procession reached the Cenotaph, and the crowd began to pour into the wide street, I noticed banners of other colours alongside the many Polish flags. I was told that Albanians, Bulgarians, Czechoslovaks, Estonians, Yugoslavs, Lithuanians, Latvians and Hungarians were also taking part in the demonstration. There was also a group of about 200 women, many with children. I stood on tiptoe and read the banner : 'The English wives of Polish soldiers.' They had come to manifest their solidarity with their husbands, their brothers and homeland. Among the ranks of the men British uniforms were also to be seen here and there, covered with medals. These were Englishmen who had fought with Poles on the battle fronts of the world, had got out their old uniforms and were taking part in the procession, also expressing their solidarity with their Polish comrades. Finally I saw Bor. He was marching with General Pelczynski at the head of a Home Army column. Here again I saw familiar though dearer faces. And I was suddenly dazzled by the similarity between the column now marching before me and one of many years ago, the picture of which, brought out of the archives of memory, was standing before my eyes. It was Sniadecka Street on October 5, 1944, and the same column, led then as now by Bor and Pelczynski, was marching, after the surrender of the Warsaw insurrection, into German captivity.[1] Time had left its mark on the faces, but they were the same Home Army soldiers whose march, started twelve years earlier, was leading them today past the Cenotaph and would perhaps in the future lead them past a similar monument in the heart of Warsaw.

When the last rank had marched down Whitehall, the shrill voice of a bugle sounded and a hush fell upon the square. There was something profoundly moving in this silence, uninterrupted by the slightest sound, of these 20,000 people standing motionless, shoulder to shoulder, enclosed by the walls of the old buildings. Standing side by side at attention were soldiers of the September 1939 campaign, insurrectionists from Warsaw, victors from Tobruk, Monte Cassino and Ancona, who, instead of returning 'from Italy to Poland', as the words of the Polish national anthem have it, had come to England; there were also pilots of the Battle of Britain, and sailors from countless sea-battles and convoys, and finally those whose fate

[1] See *Fighting Warsaw*, p. 399.

had been the hardest—the former prisoners of concentration camps, each with the indestructible, many-figured number tattooed on his arms. All were lost in their thoughts and recollections, aware of the new injustice and humiliation for them in the presence in free England of the Soviet tyrants who ruled Poland.

A metallic sound was heard, and General Anders at the head of a group approached the Cenotaph and laid a wreath with a red and white ribbon at its foot. At this moment the song 'Poland has not yet perished' burst out. Everyone sang their hardest, head up, eyes on fire and a flush on their faces. After the Polish anthem came the British, then the Czechoslovak, Yugoslav and others. This ended the greatest demonstration in the history of the Polish post-war exile and soon the street was empty.

In a few hours the BBC, and later the broadcasting stations of the free world, announced the news of the unusual procession, and stressed in particular the impression made by its silence and discipline. The British authorities had posted large numbers of police along the route of the procession, but seeing the discipline of those taking part, they had been withdrawn long before the end. On the next day, the British and Western newspapers reported the procession with friendly comments, and the TV stations broadcast excerpts. The whole matter reached the ears of Nikita, who when speaking in Birmingham gave vent to his bad temper on this account.

On the day after the ceremony, I started my usual round of talks and consultations, of which the first subject was our activities in America directed towards the withdrawal of Soviet troops from Poland and the recognition by the United States of the Oder-Neisse line. Other matters included the obtaining of American support for the demand that Russia liberate the thousands of Poles still held there, attempts to prevent the release by the American government of the German funds frozen during the war which amounted to some half milliard dollars, until such time as the Germans paid the damages they owed to former Polish prisoners of German concentration camps, also counteraction against the repatriation campaign started by the communist régime in 1955 which was aimed at liquidating the political emigration in the West, and finally the activities of the National Treasury in the United States, the existence of which is a matter of envy among the other emigrations, despite the fact that its income covers only a small part of exile needs.

XIV

REBELLION IN POZNAN

On June 28, 1956, at seven in the morning, a strange procession
started through the streets of the ancient Polish city of Poznan,
whose cathedral entombs the first kings of Poland, Mieszko and
Boleslaw the Brave. The procession moved along the streets, of
which I knew every stone, having spent ten years of my life in
Poznan as a student and practising lawyer. Thousands of young and
elderly men marched in military order in broad ranks, often holding each other's hands, all in grimy workers' overalls. From the
Gorna Wilda quarter they marched towards the centre of the city
in gloomy silence, without banners or posters, without songs or
words, their starved pale faces stubborn and determined, and indignation in their eyes. The only sound marking their progress in the
streets, usually deserted at that hour, was the disorderly trample
of several thousand nailed shoes and wooden sabots. Eight thousand workers of the Stalin Metal Works (zis) and five thousand
workers from the Railway Repair Shops had struck and went out
into the streets to demonstrate against starvation wages that failed
to secure even the barest sustenance for them and their families. A
few days earlier they had sent a delegation to the central authorities
in Warsaw, demanding a rise and threatening a strike, but the delegation had returned empty-handed. A second delegation had failed
to come back, and the workers concluded that it had been arrested.
This was the straw that broke the camel's back : that morning the
workers decided to go on strike and march through the city, which
incidentally was full of foreign visitors who had come to attend
the International Fair taking place at that time.

Strange things happened wherever the silent procession appeared.
Tram-cars and automobiles stopped; conductors and drivers joined
the marchers. The shutters of shops went clanking down; salesmen
and customers formed additional ranks in the swelling procession.
Everybody seemed to know what this was all about and wanted to
be a part of it. All along the trajectory of the march telephones
rang and people ran about warning their friends and families. The

news spread like wildfire all over the city with its 365,000 inhabitants, and crowds from other quarters converged towards the centre, near the castle and Freedom Square. Meanwhile the procession moved on, silent and gloomy. It radiated strength and fury. Excited women and running children appeared in the streets. The children alone now broke the solemn stillness with their loud inquisitive questions. Along the marchers' route offices were abandoned and thousands of functionaries from innumerable communist agencies joined the ranks of the strikers. All Poznan, which for years had secretly seethed with discontent and rebellion beneath its apparently calm surface, went out on the street. The city's normal existence was paralysed. Excitement grew more intense as new crowds joined the demonstration. Then the electrified atmosphere had to be discharged—and suddenly a loud cry arose at the front of the procession : 'Bread and freedom !'

The marching mass echoed its response : 'Bread and freedom !' The first voice resounded again : 'Down with the Russkis !' Again the cry was echoed, rolling thunderously down the mile-long procession. From that moment on, one cry followed another, repeated by the marching columns.

Near the Fair grounds the marchers met the first foreign visitors. Older workers cried in German :

'When you go home, tell everyone what you've seen and heard.'

Waving hands and smiles greeted the foreigners. The procession also encountered the first militiamen on duty there; taken by surprise, they anxiously watched the approaching crowds, wondering what to do. Cries resounded : 'The militia is with us, with the people ! Join us, you're just as poor as we !' The militiamen exchanged glances, and adopting the cry 'Down with the Russkis', plunged into the crowd, which began to applaud. The feeling of national solidarity had won over discipline and enemy indoctrination. Next, men in uniform were noticed on the sidewalk. It was an excursion of soldiers who had come to visit the Fair. A cry rose :

'Long live the Polish army ! Join us, brother soldiers !'

The uniformed men vanished from the pavements and re-emerged in the crowd. The soldiers were embraced and kissed. Someone intoned the ancient Polish anthem. The song was picked up by thousands. Caps disappeared from heads, faces became animated, eyes grew tearful. After the first stanza ending with the words

> Before Thy altars we bring this prayer,
> Lord, restore our homeland, our freedom,

there was not a dry eye in the crowd, and for a moment a reverent silence prevailed. It was interrupted by an enthusiastic cry : 'Long live Poland !' The people became frenzied. The cry 'Long live' shook the walls, and the startled pigeons darted like arrows, straight into the dazzling red sun.

When the procession, after crossing the University bridge, reached the building of the provincial militia office, the previous scene with the militiamen was repeated, and the number of uniformed marchers increased. The overjoyed strikers linked arms with the militiamen. By nine o'clock, when the procession entered the square where stands the castle formerly belonging to Wilhelm II and now containing the offices of the local National Council, thousands of people from other city districts—the Rybaki, the Old Town, the Srodka, etc.—met them. Many climbed on top of the deserted tram-cars for a better view. The crowd now numbered about 50,000; another 100,000 had gathered in the nearby streets. The first ranks of the demonstrators approached the castle, crying :

'We want the mayor !'

No one came out. The immense Gothic castle seemed dead; all its occupants had fled. The human tide flowed towards the luxurious building of the provincial Communist Party committee. When the crowds began to cry threateningly, 'Where are our delegates? We want our delegates !' Krasko, the secretary of the committee appeared. Having calmed the crowd by gestures, he cried out :

'Comrades ! Our party and government realize your situation and are doing their best to help you. Soon important decisions will be taken, which will satisfy you. Trust your leaders and wait patiently.'

The word 'wait' had the effect of a lighted fuse attached to a powder barrel. The immense crowd burst into a tremendous cry of protest. Krasko, having received several punches, vanished, thrown on the pavement. Amidst shouts, 'This is our revolution ! Down with the Commune ! Down with the Russkis ! Long live Poland !' two irrepressible streams of people broke into the party committee's building and the castle. Several young boys appeared on the round tower and began to tear down the red flag. When it dropped to the ground, a powerful triumphant roar arose. The hoisting of the Polish white and red flag was met with another deafening joyous roar, and several tens of thousands of people intoned in one voice the national anthem, 'Poland has not yet perished'.

Meanwhile window-panes in the party offices were smashed, and the building seemed to vomit all its contents from every window—typewriters, desks, chairs, filing cabinets, portraits of communist leaders and red flags. Each large article flung out was greeted with applause and joyous cries. Pages of torn documents fluttered through the air like flocks of birds. The red flags were grabbed in mid-air and torn to shreds. After a while a smiling young face appeared at one window, and its owner displayed there a sign with the chalked inscription, 'Bread and freedom'. Then came a sign inscribed 'Down with the Russkis!' When all movables had been flung out and the building was empty, the sign 'To Let' appeared, received with a loud burst of laughter by the crowd.

All this time, improvised orators addressed the crowd at the centre of the square. They were primarily old workers and trade union organizers who had seen and experienced a great deal in the course of their careers. The strike and procession had been their brain-children. They mercilessly criticized the régime, while the crowd, excited by the sight of the destruction, punctuated their speeches with cries of approval. When one of the speakers asked the rhetorical question : 'Where are our delegates now? Where can we find them?' he was interrupted by a furious voice crying : 'In the prison in Mlynska Street!'

This was enough. The rest of the speech was drowned in a mass of cries : 'To Mlynska Street! Let us free the delegates!'

A group of young men cut through the crowd like a ship cutting through the waves, and set out for the prison by way of Gwarna Street, Mielzynski Street and Nowomiejski Square. Hundreds of others followed them. Now the square before the castle witnessed a phenomenon characteristic of every revolution, namely, the birth of anonymous leaders who inspire the crowd to act, and who later disappear without a trace, even when the revolution is victorious. Someone shouted : 'Follow me to the jamming station!' Immediately, part of the crowd flowed back across the University bridge, to the Office of Social Security, on the roof of which the radio-jamming station was situated. Someone else, who had enough sense to foresee that tanks might be used to quell the riots, summoned the crowd to erect barricades. Less than half an hour later overthrown tram-cars and trucks shut off access to the centre of the city. A voice issuing orders through a loudspeaker in a radio car could be heard. Men with white and red armbands acting as self-appointed traffic police also appeared, to restore some order in the movement of the still-swelling crowds.

When one of these crowds reached the red-brick prison building, separated from the street by a high wall with a gate at the centre, it suddenly halted. Automatic rifles ready to fire were aimed at them from the black barred windows. The demonstrators hesitated, and drew back a few steps, consulting among themselves. Not a sound came from the prison. The tenseness and nervousness grew more unbearable each minute.

Suddenly there was a loud cry within the building, followed by a confused buzz of many voices. The line of automatic rifles broke, and the threatening barrels no longer were aimed at those who listened to the noise within the prison. A few minutes later the rifles vanished, replaced by triumphant young faces. A court official had led a group of demonstrators inside the prison by a secret passage leading from the adjoining court building. The prison guards defending the prison, taken by surprise from the rear, had surrendered their arms without resistance. The gate was opened, and several hundred men rushed in. Along the corridors and in the offices a stream of shouting men disarmed guards and grabbed weapons from the racks and stores. The guards at the point of guns tremblingly opened the doors of cells. Each cell contained a wretched ragged prisoner, with shaven skull, who at the words, 'There's a revolution in Poznan! You're free!' burst into tears or knelt to recite a prayer of thanks or kissed the hands of his liberators. A man with a recently acquired gun slung over his shoulder embraced his imprisoned son. A brother welcomed a brother amidst laughter and tears. Two hundred prisoners, most of them political, who had been brought for investigation from the Rawicz, Wronki and Sieradz prisons, changed hastily into civilian clothes found in the prison store, and ran out, vanishing in the city streets. To wipe out all traces of them, the insurrectionists made a bonfire with the prison files as well as the judicial files brought from the neighbouring court building.

The delegates, however, could not be found. The terrified prison guards and officials swore that the delegates were not in the prison and had never been there. When it became clear that they were telling the truth, the conquerors of the prison concluded that the delegates were in the security police cellars in Kochanowski Street.

At this point the uprising had a relatively organized centre, consisting of a few dozen insurrectionists armed with automatic rifles, ordinary rifles, and guns, which they had seized in the prison. They were mainly young boys, some wearing communist insignia in their lapels, proud of their weapons, displaying them to each other, and intoxicated with the idea of possessing them. Having been trained in the communist schools in preparation for the coming conflict with the capitalist world, they knew how to handle their weapons. The crowd filling the prison courtyard watched them, and from among them came the initiative to attack the security police. They were sure that the security police would not surrender as easily as the prison guards, and groups of armed men on confiscated trucks went to all the militia stations, military schools and factories in search of weapons. But most of the armed boys drove directly, shouting and singing, to the security police office in Kochanowski Street.

When, after crossing the Theatre Bridge, they reached Dabrowski Street, this street and the adjoining ones were jammed by thousands of people who had come from the Jezyce and Solacz quarters and had joined the original procession of the strikers. The crowds were milling on the pavement, drunk with the victory they had won over the hateful radio-jamming station. For while one group stormed the prison, another crowd had reached the Office of Social Security, shouting :

'Up with you, boys ! Run upstairs and smash that disgusting thing !'

Several dozen boys darted to the door and vanished in the lobby. The crowd outside waited listening as the steps on the stone stairs stamped higher and higher. Stooping figures of officials began to steal out of the building, hissed by the crowd and greeted with hostile cries, although they were allowed to pass. A moment later the scene before the party offices was repeated. The windows on the top floor opened, and parts of the costly jamming apparatus began to fall. Each part as it was flung down was greeted with a thousand-voiced 'Hurrah !'

The armed boys in trucks were welcomed with more shouting. The crowd made a passage through which the trucks slowly moved ahead. The boys, brandishing their newly captured weapons, cried :

'We took the prison ! The delegates weren't there ! There're at the security police office ! On to the security police !'

With shouts 'To the security police !' the human tide rolled towards Kochanowski Street. There were joyous shouts from the rear : the trucks sent for weapons were arriving one by one. They swarmed with young boys displaying to the crowd their automatic rifles and guns.

It was noon when the crowd entered Kochanowski Street from two sides. The alert, armed boys spread out across the street marching in the front ranks, mingling with men, women and children who ran impatiently ahead of the crowd. The security police building seemed like a fortress preparing to repel an attack. The doors and windows were shut, there was no sign of life anywhere, though everyone knew that men armed to the teeth were behind the walls.

The front ranks halted close to the building, and cries were heard :

'Hand over our delegates!'

The building remained silent.

'Our delegates!' they shouted angrily.

The building was still silent. The stillness now was disrupted only by the increasing uproar of the crowd behind. A few boys, their rifles ready to fire, began to move carefully towards the main entrance.

Then hell was let loose. The windows were pushed open violently, there was a noise of breaking glass, and in each window appeared gun barrels spitting fire directly into the crowd. The automatic rifles fired continuously while the crowd, writhing convulsively, retreated in a panic into the adjoining streets out of range of the bullets which showered a metal stream on every corner. Terrified people filled the doorways and staircases of houses close by, and the street was emptied, except for several figures lying motionless in twisted poses, and several dozen wounded screaming for help. Next to each there was a spreading pool of blood. In front of the main entrance lay the body of a teen-age boy whose dead pupils seemed to reproach the sky. The firing from the building stopped as suddenly as it had begun.

Women and old men rushed to the scene of slaughter, removing the wounded to adjoining streets. Boys ran to grab the weapons scattered around the dead. Soon ambulances and nurses appeared. The wounded for whom there was no room in the ambulances were loaded in trucks and taken to hospitals. Then the street was deserted again, but the adjoining streets continued to swarm with thousands of people angrily waiting.

Then the first shots of revenge were fired. The insurrectionists had set up machine-guns on the roof of the Office of Social Security and in some neighbouring houses. The besieged security police fired back. A pitched battle began, lasting several hours, with casualties on both sides. Now and then, groups of insurrectionists with hand grenades and petrol bottles in their hands, under cover of fire from their own guns and automatic rifles, tried to break through the main entrance. A small group made its way to the staircase but was wiped out by machine-gun fire from the second floor. The other attacks were repelled by salvoes from the windows, but the security police suffered casualties from the machine-guns of the insurrectionists firing at the same windows.

Meanwhile the city was seized with patriotic frenzy. Crowds marched along the streets, carrying national flags and singing the national anthem, including groups of children with small flags in their hands. A procession carrying a white and red flag dipped in the blood of the fallen insurrectionists arrived at the Fair grounds. It was led by a girl whose face will never be forgotten by those who saw it—the martial Furies that soared above embattled armies must have resembled her. The guests from Western Europe, moved by this spectacle, did not spare expressions of sympathy for the fighters. The churches were full of praying, weeping crowds. Ambulances continued to rush through the city transporting the wounded, whose number kept increasing before the security police building. Citizens broke into the apartments occupied by security police agents and demolished them. Two agents, Kujanek and Izdebny, recognized in the streets, died under the furious blows of the crowd. The news of the Poznan insurrection had spread to the provinces and in several towns the people began to disarm the militia. At Czempin several dozen men who had armed themselves in that way set out in trucks to the aid of the Poznan insurrectionists.

Suddenly a new sound began to mingle with the noise of the firing in Kochanowski Street. This was the roar of the mighty engines of approaching tanks. The steel monsters followed by a truck loaded with soldiers appeared at the end of the street, and stopped facing the human wall which had closed the street. Women came to the front of the crowd. In the open turrets worried young faces in cotton-padded Soviet caps appeared. Someone in the crowd asked : 'Soviets or Poles?'

A friendly young voice answered : 'We're Poles, from the Golencin Tank School'.

Then there were cries : 'Long live the Polish army! Brothers, you're with us! Fight the Russkis and the security police!'

The piercing voice of an old woman rose above the cries : 'Your mothers are our sisters! They didn't bring you into the world to fire on us! Join us!'

For a moment the young soldiers showed some hesitation on their faces, but then the crew from the first tank cried 'Long live Poland!' and jumped down, followed by the other. There was an explosion of joy. Women kissed the soldiers and stroked their laughing faces. For a while the steel monsters stood helpless in the middle of the milling crowd, then some men jumped into them, the engines began to roar again, and the tanks moved off in the direction of the security police building, proudly flying white-and-red flags that had been hoisted on their turrets. The crowd joyfully made way for them. Soon the machine-guns of the tanks began to fire at the security police; but the big guns were silent, for the tanks had been sent without heavy ammunition. The battle now raged with greater intensity, for the tanks had raised the spirit of the insurrectionists.

In the late afternoon alarming reports began to pour in from the city. They were brought by pale, sweating men on bicycles and motor-cycles. 'Troops and tanks are entering the city from all sides.' As though in confirmation of this a squadron of fighter planes roared low above the crowd, which watched, immobilized. But the building continued to be fired at.

Soon a column of tanks appeared at the end of the street, followed by deep ranks of infantrymen ready to fire. The soldiers of the élite Security corps had vicious faces, for they had been told that 'enemy parachutists had landed at Poznan'. An officer commanded : 'Fire!' One of the soldiers, seeing that he was faced not by foreign uniforms but by Poles, cried hysterically :

'I won't fire at my own brothers!'

The officer aimed his revolver at the soldier and fired. The soldier fell, his skull smashed. An automatic rifle rattled, and the officer, with an expression of incredible amazement on his face, dropped dead on the pavement.

A disorderly shooting began then, for the troops fired above the heads of the crowd which dispersed quickly, leaving the streets deserted. The tanks surrounded the security police building, and the troops proceeded to crush the groups of insurrectionists one by one. The battles lasted for the rest of the day and the following night. On June 29th and 30th the army liquidated the remaining insurrectionists hiding in parks and attics. On July 1st calm prevailed in the city, disturbed only by the roar of patrolling tanks, some of which had come from as far as Silesia and Opole, and the buzz of planes constantly circling overhead. At night one could hear the cars carrying hundreds of people to prisons.

Nevertheless, Poznan, despite the proclamation of a state of siege, did not yield to the terror, and people walked among the tanks talking to the troops—two divisions of them had arrived in Poznan—and teasing them about 'the enemy parachutists'. The population, although it returned to normal life, was digesting the events of the three great days, and no one worked seriously. The Russians living in Ostrorog Street and Grunwald Street now only ventured to show their noses from their fortified houses, their faces betraying uncertainty and fear. The hospitals alone worked uninterruptedly, the operating rooms brightly lit night and day. The surgeons operated on a twenty-four-hour basis, in a state of exhaustion. They had to treat about 1,000 wounded, for whom there were not enough beds, so that many lay in the corridors. About 300 (according to the official communiqué fifty-three) men had been buried, among them the

youngest insurrectionists who had sacrificed their lives for their
country. The tablets on their graves said :

Roman Strzalkowski	aged 13
Jerzy Jankowiak	aged 15
Leon Kloj	aged 15
Wieslaw Kuzmicki	aged 16
Janusz Sikora	aged 16
Zdzislaw Dutkiewicz	aged 17
Andrzej Hoppe	aged 18
Bohdan Nowak	aged 19

Such a picture of the Poznan events can be created with a little
imagination in the other hemisphere, on the basis of news which
flashed like lightning out of that city. It acted like a bomb on the
opinion of the Western world. By a fortunate chance Poznan was
full on June 28th of foreigners and correspondents of foreign
papers who had come to visit the International Fair and it was impossible to hide what was happening or to present it, as the Communist press tried to do, by saying it was caused by German agents
or the underground. The Western visitors faithfully carried out the
duty imposed on them by the marching workers who shouted 'Tell
the world what you have seen here,' and almost each one of them,
after returning home, saw it as a sacred duty to inform the press of
what he had witnessed. In this way, dozens of English, French and
West German newspapers published eye-witness accounts which supplemented the numerous reports sent by foreign press representatives,
among whom the first place, as far as the United States is concerned, was held by the correspondent of the *New York Times*,
Sydney Gruson. Every detail was accurately described, every fact
precisely reported. Even the New York communist *Daily Worker*
concerned itself with the revolt and in its evaluation came out on
the side of the Poznan workers, making grave charges against the
Warsaw government and accusing it primarily of despising their
grievances. I added my contribution in the form of a letter to the
Evening Star of July 19, 1956, where I presented the meaning of
the Poznan events and ended by stating : 'The Poznan drama demands more than platonic declarations from the free world. It
appears that the situation behind the Iron Curtain is so tense that
it endangers world peace and security (UN Charter, art. 34). That
gives a formal basis for putting the matter before the Security
Council of the United Nations. Poland and the heroic people of
Poznan, who have shed blood for our and your freedom, are waiting for it.'

Hundreds of newspapers published photographs of Poznan, particularly of the many thousands of people in a crowd before the Castle, with red and white flags waving over its towers, surrounded by a crowd of excited young people, and, best known of them all, the picture that showed a young girl called the Polish Joan of Arc, who with a look of fury in her eyes is marching at the head of a procession with a banner soaked in the blood of the fallen. It surpassed in fame the picture taken during the disorders in East Berlin of June 1953, showing two young men throwing stones at a Soviet tank. One only had to turn on the TV set to see shots of the incidents, or to hear radio commentators discussing the course of the revolt and its meaning for both communist and Western worlds. A great impression was made by the statement of eleven well-known writers, including Mauriac and Camus, and three former communists: Arthur Koestler, author of *Darkness at Noon*, the Italian Ignazio Silone and the English poet Stephen Spender. They expressed full solidarity with the workers of Poznan and called upon the working-class of the West to come to their aid.

These events were referred to in parliaments, in the US Congress, in the Council of Europe and finally in the UN, where the Cuban delegate, Dr Nuñez Portuondo, demanded that action be taken by the Security Council, stating that the tension in Poland, of which the Poznan events were the best proof, required this body to intervene. American trade unions made their voice heard, while the Socialist party in the United States issued a special appeal. During the American national holiday celebrations of July 4th, there were few speakers who did not refer to the Poznan incidents. For its part, the Polish Council of National Unity in the US and ACEN dispatched hundreds of telegrams and made dozens of interventions, demanding both an investigation of the situation in Poland by the Security Council of UN and that it should take the steps laid down in the UN Charter. In the meantime, Cyrankiewicz added fuel to the flames by stating that 'everyone who lifts a hand against the People's government can be sure it will be cut off'. This caused widespread indignation, as did the refusal of the American offer of help made through the Red Cross. And when the news soon came from Warsaw that Cyrankiewicz had received through the mail many parcels containing a plaster hand, a somewhat macabre humour was added.

Everything that was said and written about the Poznan events in the United States revolved round the fact that it was spontaneous and not prepared in advance, that it was caused by workers, i.e. the class allegedly ruling in countries with communist systems, that young people aged between fourteen and twenty had taken part in it *en masse*, which proves that communist schooling had not been able to bring them up as supporters of the system, that police and tank crews had joined the workers, which showed that the anti-communist attitude of the Polish people knows no barriers, and finally that although the direct cause of the revolt was the low standard of living of the workers, it had immediately become a political and anti-Soviet demonstration. This was shown by the cries and slogans such as 'We want freedom! Out with the Russians.' All in all, it was regarded as a heavy blow struck against Communism not only in Poland but throughout the world, as undermining Soviet domination in Eastern Europe, and finally as a source of encouragement and hope for the Western world. To us Polish political exiles, people kept saying: 'Of course we believed your assurance that the Polish people hate Communism, but now we have had concrete proof of it'.

Behind these views was hidden admiration for the unquenchable spirit, courage and determination of the Poles. People saw proof of this more in the demonstration itself, in the way thousands of workers had come into the streets aware that repression was awaiting them for doing so, rather than in the armed attacks in the later stages on the jamming station, prison and secret police offices. So communist terror had not broken the Poles or killed in them the characteristics for which they are famous. After all, the position of the working class in other Iron Curtain countries was just as bad if not worse, yet they had not dared to take such a firm stand. The Americans, to put it simply, were impressed by the Poles. The Polish David had ventured to attack the Soviet Goliath. Perhaps deep down, consciously or otherwise, they were asking themselves: 'How should we behave in a similar situation?' And perhaps the reply was not as convincing as the one given by the people of Poznan.

Editor Piotr Yolles of *New World* told me a typical incident of these exciting days. 'I happen to know a high official in a certain institution, who is of Polish origin but does not admit it, since that would not help in his career. Born and brought up in the United States, as well as being persistent, talented and ambitious, he is climbing higher and higher and may end up very high indeed. He called me one day and invited me to lunch, during which he began to question me about Polish affairs, the situation in Poland and Polonia, betraying as he did so complete ignorance of the subject. I furnished him with basic information, but finally, unable to conceal my curiosity, I asked why he had suddenly become so interested in matters of no concern to him. He then admitted with em-

barrassment that after the Poznan events, his office colleagues, who
knew after all what his origins were, began questioning him about
Polish matters, became much more friendly; even the boss had
invited him for a drink and could not say enough in praise of the
Polish people and told him he could be proud of his descent. In
these circumstances, he decided to become better acquainted with
Polish matters and might even join a Polonia organization. The
Polish spirit had been aroused in him.'

A second wave of interest in Poznan flooded America when the
trial of those arrested for taking part drew near. For years there
had not been such a mobilizing of American public opinion as now.
All newspapers sounded the alarm, showing examples of previous
trials behind the Iron Curtain, which had been cynical denigra-
tions of justice, and expressing fears for the fate of the 123 prisoners.
Dozens of legal associations demanded that their observers be
allowed to attend the trial. Commissions were formed of eminent
lawyers to study the problems connected with the trials. All the
institutions and people who had adopted an attitude towards the
Poznan incidents had something to say. The Polish Council of
National Unity in the United States and ACEN called for demonstration meetings on September 27, 1956, the day when the first
trial began in Poznan. Finally, after such American personalities as
John Foster Dulles, the Secretary of State, and Sherman Adams,
the President's right-hand man had stated their views, President
Eisenhower himself spoke on the day before the trial and expressed
his concern for the fate of the accused, adding that 'the Polish
situation cannot be finally solved until the Polish nation are given
the chance of a free choice of their own government in free and
genuine elections.'

During the trials I was in South America, where I heard their
echoes almost daily. It was not however until after my return to the
States that I was able to learn of their course and the reaction of
the American people. The press gave detailed accounts and showed
many pictures of the law-court. The trials revealed certain hitherto
unknown details of the events of June 28th, such as the fact that
when the girl carrying the red and white banner at the head of
those attacking the secret police headquarters fell from a bullet, a
thirteen-year-old lad, Roman Strzalkowski, had seized and carried it until he in turn fell. An awed hush prevailed in the court
as a lawyer exhibited the boy's bloodstained shirt. The sister of one
accused shouted from the public gallery to the judge: 'Our father
died for Poland in 1939, our mother was killed in 1942, but now
they are repressing us worse than ever.' The events in the court were

dramatic, but some had comic aspects. Some of the accused made a mockery of communist doctrine and the judges. One said : 'I joined in the workers' demonstration because they taught me in school that the working class should always fight to better its existence. As the judges have over 2,500 zloty a month wages and I, a worker only have 700, the rich are judging the poor.'

This same accused admitted that he did not know what the weapons brought by lorry were for, and when the judge inquired : 'Why didn't you ask the driver?' he cracked : 'The lorry which brought us from the agricultural school, where we got the weapons, was doing eighty kilometres an hour, and I didn't want to distract the driver's attention by asking questions.'

Another accused explained that he had shown where the weapons were kept in the school because 'he did not want the school to be turned upside down during a search for the weapons.'

The course of the trials was completely different from well-known models. The judge did not prevent the accused from withdrawing statements forced out of them by torture, and excluded them from the evidence. Defence counsel acted boldly, without being gagged, and the sentences passed were lighter than those usually imposed by communist courts. However, the defence was unable to prove the arrest of the workers' delegates. When they demanded that the delegates should be called as witnesses, the court rejected the demand, despite their importance in the case. No doubt under the influence of the indignation and ferment prevailing in Poland, and also thanks to the attention focused on the trials by Western opinion, the communist chiefs had arranged that the trials be carried out in an unprejudiced and ... Western manner. As a result, American public opinion itself, which had reacted so powerfully to the incidents in Poznan, responded calmly and in a matter of fact way to the trials themselves. Its final conclusion was brief : 'The arrested were sentenced, but the communist system was guilty'.

A yardstick of the long-lasting interest in the trials was the fact that the National Broadcasting Corporation, which is one of the largest TV networks, presented a feature programme called 'The Poznan Trials' as late as February 1957, with an American actor of Polish descent in the role of the main defendant. Invited to make a comment at the end of the programme, I said as a last word : 'We can only pray that what began in Poznan will end with freedom for millions'.

The revolt in Poznan already belongs to the past. Its last visible trace in America was perhaps the inscription POZNAN on the white wall of the Warsaw Embassy in Washington. Done in red and black paint, its first letter was reminiscent of the sign 'Poland fights' which decorated the walls of Warsaw during the bloody years of Nazi occupation. Maybe it was done by the same hand? It could not be erased and is apparent under the whitewash like an actor's face under make-up. And just as it has not been possible to erase it from the wall of a villa in Washington, so it will not be possible to erase it from the pages of Polish history.

As for the indirect causes of the revolt in Poznan, they must be sought for as far back as Stalin's death in 1953, and the execution of the head of the political police, Beria. These two events brought about restrictions in Poland on the powers of the secret police and a certain diminution of terror. The 'thaw' was already prevailing in Poland, and was characterized by a bold criticism of existing conditions, taken up primarily in the press by intellectuals and university students, as well as a growth in the mood of open discontent, caused by the economic catastrophe and widespread poverty. The demolition of the Stalin myth by Khrushchev in February 1956 added fuel to the flames and increased the temperature in Poland to the border of open rebellion. The culminating point in this period was the Poznan uprising, and the greatest anti-communist demonstration in history, of over a million people on August 26, 1956, at Czestochowa.

XV

VOWS OF JASNA GORA

On April 1, 1656, the beautiful Gothic cathedral in Lwow presented an unusually picturesque view. The day was cold and sunny. Crowds of kneeling burghers surrounded the building, which could not contain them all, and among them, like poppies in a field, shone the colourful uniforms of military units. Hundreds of burning candles illuminated the interior of the cathedral, playing among all the rainbow hues in the innumerable jewels and votive offerings attached to the miraculous Madonna. A mass of people, dressed in many colours, in which the red, yellow and blue of the national costumes of the Polish nobility mingled with the dark shades of the foreign ambassadors and the royal dignitaries, crowded within. The high mitres and silver chasubles of the bishops assisting the nuncio, Pietro Vidoni who officiated at the Mass, could be distinguished before the altar. The prayers whispered by the thousands of worshippers were accompanied only by the thunderous sounds of the organ and the nuncio's chanted invocations.

The worshippers, however, did not glance at the miraculous image on the main altar, or at the papal nuncio absorbed in the solemn rites. Their attention was diverted from the hallowed service by a black-clad figure prostrate on the church floor, at the foot of the altar, its arms spread in the form of a cross. It was observed with reverence and love. Towards the end of the Mass, when that figure rose and knelt at a stand beside it, the whisper of prayers stopped, and the cathedral was silent. Then the kneeling man said in a clear voice :

'Great Mother of God made man, Most Holy Virgin, I, Jan Casimir, King by the grace of the King of Kings Thy Son, and my Lord by Thy mercy, do this day, prostrate before Thee, choose Thee as Patron of myself and as Queen of all my States and do offer my Kingdom of Poland and my Duchies of Lithuania, Ruthenia, Prussia, Masovia, Samogitia, Livonia, Smolensk and Chernikhov, as also the armed forces of my united nations and all my peoples to Thy especial care and protection.'

The King of Poland, Jan Casimir, was entrusting his kingdom to the care of the Mother of God, recognizing her as the Queen of the Polish Crown for all time to come. He did it to thank her for a sudden change in the fortunes of Poland, which only Providence could have wrought. For only a few months earlier his country had been fully occupied by the Swedes, who under King Carolus Gustavus had invaded western and central Poland including the cities of Poznan, Warsaw and Cracow, while the Muscovites and Cossacks had seized the southern and eastern provinces with the cities of Vilno and Lublin. The King himself had been compelled to seek refuge in the territory of the Austrian Emperor. In Polish history this period is called the Deluge or the Flood—indeed at that time the enemy tide had flooded the entire country.

Then a miracle had happened. One section had resisted, repulsing the flood. This was a small fortified monastery, on the Jasna Gora hill near Czestochowa, which since 1382 had preserved within its walls the Polish holy of holies, the picture of the Czestochowa Madonna famous for its miracles. The crew of this small fortress, consisting of 160 soldiers, seventy monks, and five noble families, led by the Paulinian prior Augustyn Kordecki, had refused to surrender to the Swedish King. For several weeks they were besieged by an army of 4,000 men equipped with heavy artillery and commanded by the famous General Mueller, but they resisted so vigorously that the Swedes were forced to retreat. Meanwhile the news that the heretics had attacked the greatest Polish shrine had spread all over the country, causing an uprising of the nation whose most sacred sentiments had been offended. The King, wishing to lead this uprising, made his way to Lwow with a small army, and now, thanking the Mother of God for the miracle of Jasna Gora, he had chosen her as the Queen of Poland.

On the tercentenary of this historic event, which was celebrated on August 26, 1956, more than a million pilgrims surrounded the high walls of the Jasna Gora fortress, which had been preserved intact. These pilgrims had come to Czestochowa, summoned by the Polish episcopate to pray to the Mother of God that she repeat her ancient miracle and liberate Poland from the invader, this time the Soviet one. They were to repeat the vow of 300 years ago, for Poland was once more submerged by an enemy flood.

An unforgettable view extended from the high steeple and the fortress walls. As far as the eye could reach, the grounds around the monastery and the adjacent parks were filled with a human sea, with faces absorbed in prayer, behind them the city, and on the horizon rocky and wooded hills and the towers of the mediaeval

Olsztyn castle. The greater part of that human mass had spent the night in the open, on those grounds and in those parks. Now they stood close together, peasants beside workers, the uneducated near the educated. Side by side with the mountain folk of the Tatra, the Gorals, in their colourful costumes, stood a group of black-clad university professors. Next to city artisans were young men in student caps with Home Army insignia on their lapels. Here was a cross-section of Poland, for even communists, hiding from each other, were there. All of them had been brought to Czestochowa by the Polish cult of the Mother of God, which is perhaps unique. They waited reverently for the moment when Her miraculous image would be carried out of the interior chapel, and placed on the outdoor altar on the fortress walls, where everyone could see it. They had come here in crowded trains from the remotest corners, often travelling on the roofs and the buffers. Those trains had been stopped at railway stations by crowds standing on the tracks, afraid of not being admitted because of overcrowding. For several days all the roads leading to Czestochowa had been jammed with thousands of trucks driving through the summer heat in clouds of dust, packed with standing passengers, and next to them sped innumerable bicycles and motor-cycles. For weeks hundreds of peasant processions had walked to this city through golden fields, green meadows, and sun-warmed, fragrant pinewoods, in the order that had been the same for centuries—a cross and a priest in a white stole in front of them, behind him women in white linen kerchiefs, after the women men, bareheaded and in the rear a caravan of horse wagons with canvas tilts on wooden poles. And in the trains, on the trucks, and among the pilgrims walking on foot, national and religious songs were sung and everywhere one heard the refrain : 'Hail, Hail, Mary.'

Even so, only the chosen few, although they were more than a million, could be present at Czestochowa on that day. The rest of the nearly thirty-million nation, in line with the recommendations of the episcopate, had gathered in thousands of Polish churches to repeat the same Jasna Gora vow at the same hour. Through all the width and length of Poland, everyone visited the churches, participating in that solemnity. An atmosphere of prayer and religious exaltation pervaded the country. All thoughts were focused on Czestochowa. All radio sets were tuned to the broadcasts from that city.

Within the space enclosed by the wall there was a little more room than outside. Special monastery guards in light blue uniforms admitted only the clergy, delegations, the press and foreign visitors.

But before the monastery gates were closed, 160,000 pilgrims had been allowed to make their confessions and receive their communion. Since there were not enough confessionals, priests received the confessions on the grass, in window niches or on the walls. Several thousand priests had come, including thirty-eight bishops.

Suddenly the loudspeaker was heard. The prior had begun to tell the crowd in front of the monastery what was going on inside. The miraculous image, he announced, had been removed from the altar in the chapel; it had been taken by the bishops, and then handed over to the Lowicz delegation, dressed in gorgeous regional costumes. At each Station of the Cross the image was accepted by another delegation. The procession advanced slowly on the fortress walls surrounding the monastery, while a million voices sang 'Mary of Czestochowa, star beautiful and splendid', and 'We want God, we are the subjects, He is our King, He is our Lord'.

Finally the van of the procession appeared before the eyes of the immense crowd—two rows of priests in pontifical garb, followed by nuns who with their white coifs resembled a swarm of butterflies settling on the walls surrounding the monastery, and finally white-clad girls in veils, bearing baskets of petals, which they cast about them, kneeling at the feet of the bishops whose pointed mitres emerged from the shadow covering that portion of the walls.

There was a blast of trumpets and the crowd was dazzled by the glow of the hundreds of diamonds and gold ornaments decorating the miraculous image. A million people fell to their knees, a million voices cried out, 'Hail, Mary'. The immense crowd wept, tears streaming down every face, unashamedly. Voices were heard saying, 'Have pity on us. Do not abandon us'. With raised hands the pilgrims made the vow. Here and there people fainted and were carried away. Some hoped for a miracle.

Meanwhile the image had been placed on an altar covered with red cloth. The crowd calmed down, absorbed in ardent prayer. The sudden stillness, interrupted only by sighs, was more impressive than the preceding outburst. The bishops posted themselves near the altar and High Mass began. Everyone noticed an empty chair near the altar, a spray of white and red roses on it. This was the rightful place of Cardinal Stefan Wyszynski, Primate of Poland. It was common knowledge that Wyszynski was at that moment in prison. The empty chair was a reminder and a protest in which the millions who observed it were involved.

Following the reading of a telegram from the Pope, Bishop Michael Klepacz recited the text of the vow adapted to the new situation, which began with the words :

'Queen of Poland, I renew the vow of our forefathers and recognize Thee as our Patroness and Queen. I promise Thee to do everything in my power to make Poland Thine and Thy Son's True kingdom.'

The crowd repeated the solemn vow, word by word, sentence by sentence. Once again tears glistened as the crowd prayed for a repetition of the miracle of 300 years ago. As the ceremony concluded, a group of timid voices intoned the old religious national anthem. The song was echoed by all, sweeping Poland through fields, mountains and woods. Everyone threw himself completely into the song, imploring God to restore the freedom of the country.

The celebration of August 26, 1956, was externally purely religious, since it had been confined to a mass pilgrimage of the faithful to Czestochowa, on the day of the annual Feast of Mary. But the renewal of the vow, which implies a prayer for the restoration of Polish independence, and the comparison of the 'deluge' of 1656 from which Poland had emerged free, to the 'deluge' of 1956 in which Poland was still submerged, made this celebration the greatest anti-Soviet and anti-communist manifestation in history. And the empty chair of Cardinal Wyszynski, who had been imprisoned by order of the Kremlin, had given it the final touch.

Thus, less than two months after the Poznan uprising, Poland had advanced a step closer to that historic event which is today known as the Polish October revolution.

America had not yet cooled off from the impressions caused by the Poznan riots, when news came from Czestochowa, which enabled us, by the addition of a touch of imagination, to recreate the course of events and the mood of the Jasna Gora celebrations. The newspapers, still devoting much space every day to the predicted trials for the Poznan incidents, published this news on the front page and when photographs of the ocean of people in the huge square under the walls of the Jasna Gora fortress appeared as well, the impression was tremendous. Photographs covering a whole page were taken either from the Jasna Gora steeple or from before the Holy Virgin's altar (*Life Magazine*) which rises outside the monastery proper, dominating the fortified walls. It was crammed with a mass of human heads, as though someone had scattered poppy seeds over a vast floor, and closed in not by walls but by a green belt of trees in the town park. Others published pictures of the altar, surrounded by a circle of pointed episcopal mitres and the white surplices of priests, with the empty throne of the cardinal placed on a carpeted platform. These pictures reflected an atmosphere of profound prayer

E

and religious fervour, well known to me from my several years at the Czestochowa high school. The knowledge that all this was happening behind the Iron Curtain made thinking Americans wonder. To the still unextinguished impression made by Poznan, heightened by anxious awaiting for the trials, there was added admiration for Jasna Gora and interest in Poland was quadrupled. Poznan had revealed to the Americans one aspect of the relation of Poles to their own reality, and Jasna Gora revealed another. Apart from the unquenched courage and unbroken spirit, they now saw another characteristic—deep religious faith as a protest against atheistic ideology, and the Catholic church, able to gather together in the course of a single day and despite interference a million people in the same place, now grew in their eyes to the role of an institution doing more than merely governing souls. Poznan and Jasna Gora illumined like a flash of lightning the dark night which had been hanging over Poland for years, and revealed her true features.

A yardstick of the impression which the Jasna Gora vows made in America was provided by a leading journalist, Joseph Alsop, who visited Czestochowa a year later, to witness a similar ceremony. Fewer people participated this time (only a few hundred thousand), but for all that the Cardinal's throne was occupied by its rightful owner. In a moving article, published in several dozen American papers, Alsop described the defence of Jasna Gora from the Swedes 300 years ago, and attributed to the miracle performed by the picture of the Virgin Mary, and added on his own behalf : 'I too witnessed a miracle at Jasna Gora just the other day. It was not easy to define, being the peculiar combination of a theme, a ceremony, a crowd and a man. Yet it seemed to be decidedly miraculous.'

XVI

JOURNAL OF A TRIP TO SOUTH AMERICA

In September 1956 I went to South America as one of the three-member delegation of ACEN. My companions were the Latvian diplomat, Vilis Masens, and the former Rumanian Minister of Foreign Affairs, Constantin Visoianu. Our primary purpose was to inform the governments and peoples of these countries of the existence of our organization and its purposes, then to ask that delegations of South American states to the UN should support our demands that the UN pass a resolution requiring Russia to withdraw Soviet troops from our nine countries and enable them in this way to hold free elections under international control. We also wanted to organize co-operation with émigrés from these countries in the South American states. Admittedly, Russia would certainly not respond to any such UN resolution; however, if it was taken up by this great forum of the world it would have its eloquence and political value.

Our first port of call was Rio de Janeiro, where a cocktail party was given for us on our arrival at the home of the president of the Committee for aid to Refugees, and the ambassador of the Knights of Malta in the same person, Prince Olgierd Czartoryski. I arrived early and had time to notice the photograph on a side table of a young man in a Polish officer's uniform. When asked about this handsome Lancer, my host explained it was a photograph of the brother of the Hapsburg Princess Czartoryski, daughter of Archduke Stefan of Zywiec. I recalled the grim days of German occupation and an underground report which described the tortures inflicted by the Gestapo on this Hapsburg, then a colonel in the Polish army, because he refused to join the 'Volkslist'. I pondered over this rare example of loyalty to an adopted homeland, and learnt that after the torture he never regained his health and shortly died.

During the reception, carefully piloted by our host, I was able to put the Polish and ACEN problems to the ambassadors of Equador, Chile, Uruguay, Costa Rica and Guatemala, and also to the Canadian chargé d'affaires, Fulgence Charpentier, who suggested that our delegation should visit Canada; and to Senator Hamilton Nogueira and other Brazilian politicians and diplomats of South American countries. I had a particularly warm talk on our cause with the former Brazilian ambassador to Poland, de Barros Pimentel, who remembered Warsaw well and inquired about the city and people. Another kind of informative talk was with the dean of the Supreme Advocates Council, Carol Pereira de Almeida Raposa, who asked questions about the fate of advocates under a communist system. The crown to several hours of talks was a discussion with the editor of the *Journal do Brasil*, João MacDowell, and the editor of the *Diarios Associados*, Astrogesilo de Athayade. Both wished to continue the press campaign after our visit, popularizing the liberation of Eastern Europe from Soviet control. I was also able to thank Mme Zelja Washington de Souza and Lincoln Nodari for organizing help for our prisoners of war : during and after the war they were at the head of the relevant Brazilian organizations and according to my compatriots worked in them with great devotion.

Three observations struck me during these interesting talks. The first was the pleasure with which some of those present spoke of holding the Polonia Restituta Order, awarded them before the war. The second was the fact that my interlocutors know a great deal about communist infiltration into Brazil but did not realize its danger. The third was the continual references in talks to the Poznan incidents.

At noon the next day we set out for the residence of the President of Brazil, Dr Juscelino Kubitschek. Dr Masens spoke to him about our cause, and in reply the President promised support and also commented that, in view of his partly Czech origin, he had particular sympathy for our cause. I think that it is only in the melting pot from which the young American nations emerge that it can happen for a man with a typically Czech name to reach the head of a nation, whose roots must be sought in Portugal, among Indians from the Brazilian jungle and dark newcomers from far-off Africa.

From Brazil we went on to Uruguay. At Montevideo, on the way to the office of the Minister of Foreign Affairs, Francisco Gamarra, we were passed by a group of people speaking Polish. The chief of the minister's cabinet explained with a mischievous smile that this was a trade mission ... from Warsaw. The minister himself was very definite in his statements, since without the need of much argument he promised us the full support of the Uruguay delegation at the UN. The fact that we were received immediately after the Polish trade mission was commented upon as the wish to emphasize that the development of trade relations is not equivalent to approval for the system of government.

We lunched at the Jockey Club with Pardo Regules, the leader of the Christian Democratic party and former Minister of Internal Affairs, Professor Carbajal Victorica, a very agreeable and outspoken scholar who hardly left us, a young university professor, Edward Jimenez de Arechaga, and Count Jerzy Lasocki.

A few days later we arrived in Buenos Aires. We paid a visit to the Minister of Internal Affairs, Dr Laureano Landaburu, and went with him on foot to Casa Rosada, the near-by palace of the President.

President Aramburu was a tall handsome man with a serious mien. His deputy, Admiral Rojas, was smaller, and had the look of a bird of prey. I regarded him with interest, knowing that he and his marines played an important part in overthrowing Peron. We sat down at a huge table, and spent an hour expatiating on our cause, and the President and Vice-President asked me about the course and Polish evaluation of the Poznan rebellion. We left the conference with a promise of support from the Argentina delegation at the UN and with words of encouragement regarding the organization of a section of ACEN in the Argentina.

Immediately before leaving the Casa Rosada, someone made sure we should know that our reception had occurred immediately after the delivery of his credentials by the new ambassador of the Warsaw regime, Wlodarczyk. The situation resembled that in Uruguay.

In the afternoon, we addressed the temporary Argentine Parliament, known as the Junta Consultiva, during a regular session. We spoke in English, which official interpreters translated into Spanish. It was a fine though not a large hall, with a round table in the middle at which were sitting the several dozen members of the Junta, leaders of the old, anti-Peron opposition, i.e. the Democratic Christian party, the Democratic Progressive party, the Democratic National, Radical and Catholic parties—in a word, the political cream of Argentina. I spoke for about fifteen minutes on the situation in Poland and the significance of Poznan. Afterwards, members of the Junta fired questions at us regarding all sorts of things—forced labour camps, the role of trade unions, political police, the situation of the Catholic Church, rural conditions, the degree of Soviet control and so forth. This was one of the rather rare meetings at which foreigners were permitted to speak at an official meeting of a parliamentary body, and it ended with a speech by the chairman who assured us of the deep sympathy and liking of the

Argentina people for the enslaved countries of Eastern Europe and promised the Junta's support for our programme.

On the morning of our arrival in Chile we went to the presidential palace, which looks as if transported from France. Influences of European architecture are apparent everywhere in Santiago. We were conducted into a large drawing room and introduced to a tall, elderly man with short trimmed moustaches. This was the eighty-year-old President of Chile, General Carlos Ibanez. We sat in a half circle in huge arm-chairs and an interesting talk developed. Having enquired in detail about the organization of ACEN and the purpose of our visit, and promised support of the Chilean delegation to the UN, he began to advise us on the tactics we should use to achieve our purpose. He did this in a way reminiscent of a professor carrying on a seminary with selected students and discussing some complex problem with them. The practical advice he gave us was excellent. We gazed with respect at this old gentleman, who had so rapidly formed his opinion in what was undoubtedly a new subject to him.

We were next received by the Papal Nuncio, Archbishop Sebastian Baggio, well-informed, lively and friendly. I noticed a similarity of atmosphere in all the Nunciatories we visited, with their simple yet not at all severe equipment, church-like hush and absence of many servants, and a similarity in the views expressed by nuncios.

We left the Nuncial palace for the Primate's palace. As we stood before the ninety-year-old Cardinal Caro, it became clear that we should restrict the visit to a minimum so as not to fatigue the polite old man.

During lunch we met representatives of the Ministry of Foreign Affairs, among whom was the chairman of the Chilean delegation to the UN, Roberto L. Aldunate, and in the evening we attended a banquet given for us by the chairman of the Commission of Foreign Affairs in Parliament, Louis Valdes Larrain, attended by about thirty deputies.

The reception passed off without incident, in an atmosphere of great cordiality. Our Latin fellow-guests soon made personal contact with us, they were frank and charmingly sincere. After dinner we went into the next room, where a lively discussion started about our cause, which went on till late at night. For several hours we discussed the various ways in which we could put the cause of the liberation of our countries before the UN. I had to answer many questions regarding the wartime underground, my experiences in Poland in 1945-47, and of course Poznan. The discussion terminated with our host stating that we could count upon the support of the

Chilean delegation to the UN, and encouragement for establishing a section of ACEN in Chile.

In Havana we were received by the Minister of Foreign Affairs, Dr Gonzalo Guel. He began by stating that we probably knew Cuba had never recognized the annexation of Lithuania, Latvia or Estonia, or the communist governments forced upon Poland and other countries by Russia. Of course the Cuban government was prepared to support our cause at the UN through its delegation. In conclusion we were informed that on the following day we were to be received by General Batista, who had summoned back from New York the head of the Cuban delegation to the UN, Nunez Portuondo, very probably in connection with our visit.

In the evening a compatriot called for me at the hotel, with his wife. He was the industrialist M. and had come to take me out for dinner. He did so as the result of a recommendation of a mutual acquaintance in Cuba who is at present in New York, and who wanted me to see the brighter side of Havana, rather than government offices. We met in the hotel hall and went by car to the 'Tropicana', a restaurant, casino and night-club known throughout the Western hemisphere. When I looked round I had to admit that the fame it enjoys is fully deserved. In a virgin tropical forest full of palms, they have built a huge ultra-modern construction consisting as it were of several huge flat slices, forming an arch in such a way that there is a gap between them, through which can be seen the forest and palms, illuminated from the side by carefully concealed floodlights. This combination of untouched tropical forest and modernist architecture gave an unusual effect, capable of stirring the dead nerves of rich tourists from the United States, for whom the whole business is calculated. It was crowded with them all around at the close packed tables. What therefore was the effect of this multiplied Warsaw 'Adria' on an émigré who had last seen this kind of haunt in another epoch altogether, namely 1938? In addition there was a stage on which a parade of nakedness worthy of the Casino de Paris took place several times in the evening; then a side dance-floor under the open sky, surrounded by hundreds of tables set amidst palm trees, some bars with dimmed lights, luxurious gambling rooms and artificial pools covered with tropical vegetation—all able to accommodate several thousand persons in an area of nine acres.

Immediately at the start of the evening I noticed a badge in the lapel of Mr M., which intrigued me. Trying to shout down the band I asked what it was. Mr M. shouted back : 'Jaworski's Cavalry', then added, 'But you're too young to know what sort of cavalry that was.' 'Too young?' I protested. 'After all, in 1920 I left school to volunteer for the army and remember those days.' Thus in the Tropicana, in exotic Cuba, among the noise of the band and the parades of naked bodies, there began a tale of the 1920 war, of the raids carried out by the 'wild Jaworski riders' behind the Bolshevik lines, of the famous partisan leaders the brothers Bulak-Balachowicz and their deeds, of Dabrowski's cavalrymen, battles for Vilno and so on without end. I listened sadly to those recollections, in which my companion, the descendant of Lithuanian Tartars, sometimes could not find the appropriate Polish word, so I had to help him out. He asked how 'Woyevoda' Wladyslaw Raczkiewicz and many other people were getting on, people who belonged to those already misty times. M. had left Poland thirty years ago, so that he only knew it as then and as it lived on in his memory. Everything else was unreal, being merely news in the papers or the accounts of a compatriot passing through. We left a few hours later hoarse with shouting. M. was clearly depressed by what he had heard.

On the way to the presidential palace I recalled my former doubts. Should a convinced and practising democrat ask for the political support of a dictator such as General Batista? A positive reply was facilitated by the fact that all the Cuban governments preceding Batista had, like Batista, taken a positive attitude to the cause of restoring independence to the nations of Eastern Europe. In this case, Batista represented the views and policy of the Cuban people. Should not the efforts of the communist government in Poland to get the United States to recognize our western frontiers be supported merely because this government is also a dictatorship though of a different colour?

When we had been introduced and sat down in comfortable armchairs Mr Masens began the ritual speech I knew by heart. Batista spoke English correctly and placed every matter in a concrete light, without a smoke-screen of generalities or reticence. When it was my turn, he began by asking whether I knew that Cuba did not recognize the communist government in Warsaw, that she still recognized the last Polish ambassador accredited to Cuba as the representative of Poland? When I said I did, he added that this attitude was the alpha and omega of Cuban policy towards the countries Russia had dominated. I informed him that this policy was generally known both among the many post-war Polish exiles and in Poland itself. This last statement greatly interested Batista, since he asked with some incredulity : 'You say that people in Poland also know of this?' 'Certainly,' I replied, 'at least those who are interested in such matters. I lived about three years under communist rule in Poland and I knew about it from foreign broadcasts and talks with those few people who had the opportunity of communicating with the West or of travelling outside Poland.' Batista was pleased with this, and moved on next to the Poznan events, asked for details and revealed a great knowledge of their course. Finally, he said that the Cuban people had a better understanding of our position than others, since the memory of the fight with Spain for the independence of Cuba still belonged to the living tradition of thousands of Cuban families, handed down orally from father to son.

The moment now came for which I had been waiting, to check certain information. When General Batista concluded, I spoke again. 'We Poles, with our admiration for the Cuban people and their former fight for independence, are particularly proud of the fact that in this fight a prominent role was played by a Pole, General Karol Roloff-Mialowski, who, after the liberation of Cuba became the first Inspector-General of the Cuban army and first Minister of War in the first government of independent Cuba.' As I recited these details carefully prepared in advance, and provided by compatriots in Cuba, a broad smile appeared on the face of Batista and with a nod of the head he confirmed each phrase. When I ended, he added, 'He was a prominent leader and our great patriot.'

In this way I made use of newly acquired historical knowledge of a generally unknown Cuban national hero, who is for the population of Cuba what Pulaski or Kosciuszko is for the average American. This figure still awaits a Polish historian.

At the end of our talk, General Batista assured us that the Cuban delegation to the UN would support any action aimed at liberating our countries, and that its chairman, Nuñez Portuondo, who had already been involved very often in this cause, would continue this policy.

In the afternoon, representatives of the press, radio and cinema entertained us in the Reporters' Club. Once again we encountered good knowledge of the situation in the countries of Eastern Europe and understanding for our demands, to which we had become accustomed during the course of our journey. The way in which questions were put by several clearly revealed the uneasiness pervading the Cuban press, and time and again we heard critical allusions to the situation prevailing in Cuba. However, we managed to avoid the underwater rocks of talks on Cuban internal affairs, and in this way our journey round South America ended.

It had served its purpose; interest in our countries and the prob-

E*

lems of their regaining independence had been aroused, promises
of support or possible future action in the UN had been received
and finally we had made contacts with the émigrés of the nine
countries represented in ACEN, and organized co-operation between
them.

We visited five countries and capitals, and two more en route.
We were received by four presidents of states and ten ministers,
and put our cause to several dozen other officials, including over a
dozen ambassadors accredited to these states, among them three
Papal nuncios. Finally, we spoke to over a hundred members of legislative bodies, and addressed a parliament. We had had six press
conferences, three radio broadcasts and two TV appearances. I had
explained the problem of Poland and Eastern Europe in the light
of the international situation at ten public meetings, speaking to
compatriots and others, and at six receptions for our delegation.
The same had been done by my companions, who spoke at meetings organized by exiles from the Baltic countries and Rumania. On
the journey we had collected 117 articles and press cuttings about
the problem of the countries behind the Iron Curtain and our visit.

On the next day we flew to Miami, and thence to Washington.
On the day after our return the October revolution started in
Poland.

XVII

'POLISH OCTOBER'

In the modern, luxuriously furnished plane approaching the Warsaw airport, the silence was tense. The passengers—Nikita
Khrushchev, Molotov, Mikoyan and Kaganovich—had completed
their consultation and were preparing to land. The group of be-
medalled Soviet generals in the rear seats had also become silent,
in deference to their leaders. Outside the windows, through the
faint light of a rainy morning, they could see dilapidated suburbs.
The lofty skyscraper, the Palace of Culture, rose against the distant
background of old war ruins and the recently rebuilt centre of the
city. The wet chequer-board runways at Okecie glistened below
them.

The door of the cabin opened, admitting a uniformed pilot who
respectfully gave Khrushchev a note. After glancing through it, the
Soviet leader snorted angrily and passed it to Mikoyan, who read
it carefully and passed it on. When it finally reached the generals,
who bent over it together, the four men in mufti were again engaged in a lively discussion. The note brought the following message :

'Stay in the air until landing permit is issued.'

In compliance with the order the plane dipped its wing, turned
gently and sped on. After a quarter of an hour Khrushchev received
another note. With an angry flush he cried out :

'They're liars, those Polaks ! They want to gain time !'

Once again the note passed from hand to hand. The last of the
generals crumpled it and flung it to the floor. This time the message
was :

'The Politburo and the government wish to welcome their es-
teemed guests at the airport. Since this will take some time, they
ask them for patience, and the plane must remain in the air.'

This was an unprecedented situation : Khrushchev's subordinates
would not wait for him, he had to wait for them.

During that time two men walked nervously back and forth in
the spacious waiting room at the airport. The older, a tall man with

the face of one accustomed to command, had the stars of a Soviet marshal on his uniform; the other wore a general's epaulets. They glanced frequently at their wrist-watches. A group of cigarette-smoking Soviet officers in a corner exchanged remarks in an undertone, occasionally casting anxious glances at the two men. Before the airport building a long line of mud-caked limousines waited with chauffeurs at the wheels.

A young colonel in Polish uniform rushed out of the main office, and running up to the Soviet marshal stopped in front of him, clicking his heels, and reporting loudly :

'Comrade Ochab presents his apologies, but the plane cannot land before the government and the Politburo have reached the airport.'

Marshal Konev, commander of the Warsaw Pact forces, swore obscenely, and with his companion, General Alexey Antonov, resumed his nervous promenade through the waiting-room.

That morning, on October 19, 1956, the members of the Polish Communist Party's central committee had assembled in the building of the former Railway Ministry, at the corner of Nowy Swiat Street and Aleja Trzeciego Maja. They were tense and excited. Each knew that at the current eighth party congress a decisive battle would be fought between two enemy camps. One of these, which met at Natolin, a country house not far from Warsaw, was referred to as the Natolin group, whose leading members—Mazur, Klosiewicz, Zenon Nowak, Berman, Jozwiak and Zawadzki—championed orthodox Communism and complete submission to Moscow and Marshal Rokossovsky. Frightened by the 'thaw' and the growing rebelliousness of the Poles, manifested above all in the Poznan uprising and the mass demonstration at Czestochowa, they advocated a return to the previous strong line. But they could not ignore Gomulka and his friends, whose popularity was growing daily and who, after their release from prison, were regarded as national martyrs both by communists and anti-communists. For this reason they sought an understanding with Gomulka, reinstated as a party member on August 5th, and offered him a seat in the Politburo, which would, however, remain under their control. Gomulka and his friends, who had emerged as changed men from prison, favoured democratization of the régime and rejected the proposition of the Natolin group, hoping to eliminate the Stalinists altogether. Attempting to help the Natolin group, the Kremlin had invited Gomulka to Yalta for a seaside vacation and discussions. But Gomulka, remembering the fate of Bierut and the Bulgarian Dimitrov, who had died suddenly during their visits to Russia, politely refused the invitation, saying that the Polish resort of Ciechocinek would suffice. Then the Natolin people decided to stage a coup; they knew that if they did not, Gomulka, who was now supported by a majority of the central committee, would be elected secretary-general by the eighth congress and would resume control of the government. With the greatest secrecy they prepared a list of 700 prominent advocates of democratization and presented it to Rokossovsky, who controlled the Soviet troops stationed in Poland as well as the Polish army. He was to arrest those 700 persons in one night and have them deported to Russia, whereupon, after the army had quelled possible riots, the eighth congress would grant full powers to the Natolin group.

But the camp opposed to the Natolin group was not slumbering. Whether it had learned of the conspiracy, or was aware of the ruthlessness of the other camp, it responded with counter-conspiracy and acted immediately. The leading members of this camp were Edward Ochab, secretary-general, Gomulka, Premier Cyrankiewicz and a few others, but its guiding spirit was Stefan Staszewski, secretary of the Warsaw party organization. The fact that Ochab belonged to the partisans of democratization had come as a surprise; for Stalin had designated him successor to President Bierut, and after the latter's death in Moscow on March 12, 1956, Khrushchev had actually confirmed Stalin's decision. But apparently Ochab too had had enough of Soviet orders, and had joined Gomulka. In this he had undoubtedly been encouraged by Chou En-lai, who had declared at Peking early in October that if Poland chose her own path to socialism, China would support her. As for Cyrankiewicz, well known as an opportunist and careerist, he had joined the Gomulka camp simply because he anticipated its victory.

During the summer of 1956, Staszewski organized in private apartments a number of meetings which resulted in the appointment of the recently released prisoner, General Waclaw Komar, a friend of Gomulka's, a commander of the Security Corps, comprising several thousand well-trained *élite* troops armed with the most modern weapons. Komar's friend General Huebner, who like Komar had fought in the International Spanish Brigade, was to be his deputy. When Premier Cyrankiewicz announced these appointments, Rokossovsky rushed into Cyrankiewicz's office, shouting furiously:

'How did you dare to appoint Komar without my knowledge and consent?'

Cyrankiewicz, pale but calm, replied: 'The purpose of the

Security Corps is to preserve internal peace. As Premier I was entitled to appoint its commander.'

Rokossovsky ranted, threatening the Premier, but to no effect.
Komar proceeded to appoint his trusted officers to all the important
posts, and shortly afterwards large units of the Security Corps took
up quarters in the capital. The project of arresting 700 opponents
was dropped, particularly since the new head of the political police
was a partisan of Ochab and Gomulka. Instead, a few days before
the scheduled opening of the eighth congress on October 19th Rokossovsky ordered certain Soviet units to draw closer to Warsaw.
Simultaneously, a number of Soviet divisions stationed in East
Germany began to approach the Polish border, and Czech divisions
were moved close to the Polish-Czech border. Finally one Soviet
cruiser and three destroyers appeared in Polish territorial waters
on the Baltic.

Reports about all this, as well as about the movements of Soviet
reinforcements in the Bialystok region and of Polish units in the
neighbourhood of Siedlce, Sochaczew and Lodz, had reached Warsaw, which vibrated with excitement and fear. On October 19th
the population of the capital did not work as usual, but waited
anxiously for news from the country and from the central committee.

Gomulka replied to the new Russian plan with vigorous measures.
Komar ordered the Frontier Guard units to mine bridges and to
open fire on any troops attempting to cross the Polish border. A few
days later there were reports of a clash with Soviet infantry that
had tried to cross the border near Szczecin, and had been compelled
to retreat. Under the pretext of carrying out anti-aircraft defence
exercises, Komar ordered his units to occupy all the strategic points
in Warsaw, and on the day of the congress anti-aircraft artillery
and armed patrols were stationed in the squares. All roads to the
capital were closed.

In addition, Staszewski mobilized all the forces under his command, and on that day about 60,000 workers of the Zeran automobile plant, the Kasprzak radio works, the optical works, the
motor-cycle factory and others remained inside the factories in order
to resist, if necessary, Rokossovsky's troops marching on Warsaw.
Those most determined were the 8,000 workers of Zeran, whose
popular leaders were Gozdzik and Pechcin. Since the Poznan uprising a rebellious mood had pervaded this plant, as well as others.
The workers had spontaneously appointed a workers' council, and
the communist authorities did not dare oppose the move. From
among those workers, and university students as well, Staszewski
had begun to recruit his revolutionary militia, arming them with

weapons obtained from the military training centres for youth, from factory guards, and from General Komar's stores.

The meeting of the central committee opened simultaneously with a meeting of several thousand university students at the immense Polytechnic Institute auditorium. The purpose of this latter meeting was to mobilize the capital's youth against the armed *coup*. The students had held a preliminary meeting the day before, which had been forbidden by Rokossovsky but encouraged by Staszewski, who had triumphed. Special messengers on motor-cycles and cars ensured liaison between the students and the workers, who remained alert in the factories.

Several thousand workers and students were similarly mobilized at the industrial centre of Nowa Huta near Cracow and the university of Cracow. On that day they held joint meetings. Delegations from Nowa Huta and Cracow had reached Warsaw, and through them contact was maintained with Cracow. The workers were also organized at Lodz and Katowice.

When the members of the central committee gathered at 10 a.m. they knew all this, and the atmosphere of the meeting was tense. But the opening was delayed, and there were feverish consultations in the lobbies, in which Gomulka participated although he was not a member of the central committee. The excitement increased every minute. Finally Ochab appeared on the podium, and his first words had an explosive effect. With studied calm, he informed the gathering of the unexpected arrival of the guests from Moscow, and moved that the meeting be adjourned till 6 p.m. to give the leaders time to talk with the Russians. But he proposed that, before adjourning, comrades Gomulka, Spychalski, Kliszko and Loga-Sowinski be elected members of the central committee.

The communist leaders were stunned by the news. In a flash they realized that the march of the Soviet troops on Warsaw was a prelude to the visit whose purpose was obvious—to break resistance and reassert the power of the Kremlin over Poland. The idea behind Ochab's proposal was understood at once : it was necessary to confront the Russian guests with a *fait accompli*. The proposal was unanimously adopted; even the Natolin men did not dare vote against it. One member of the committee, a woman, Jaworska, foreseeing that the Russian guests would attempt to influence the elections to the Politburo, moved that these elections be held before the adjournment. She was seconded by Tatarkowna, but Ochab, who acted according to a plan hastily drawn up in collaboration with Gomulka and Cyrankiewicz, opposed it, and the motion was rejected. Thereupon Ochab, Gomulka, Cyrankiewicz, Zawadzki and a few others left for the airport. The conspirators were satisfied with their work. The postponement of the landing for more than an hour had enabled them to complete their preparations. Komar had occupied the radio station, the post office, the building of the Council of Ministers, and all other important government buildings. Staszewski had finished arming his revolutionary militia, and had stationed them wherever necessary. The workers in the factories had been alerted and would remain there for the night. Similarly the students at the Polytechnic Institute had been put on the alert, ready to answer any summons. The news of the Soviet march on Warsaw had spread through the city, and in conjunction with the preparations ordered by Komar and Staszewski had created a feverish atmosphere. Telephones rang everywhere, cafés were crammed and pedestrians, whose serious faces all mirrored the same thoughts, exchanged significant glances.

When the plane landed and the door opened, Khrushchev appeared purple with rage. Even before his feet touched the ground, he released a stream of abuse, punctuated by the words 'traitors' and 'ungrateful'. The hosts listened in surprise, not having expected such an outburst so soon. Cyrankiewicz was the first to come to himself. Pointing to the large retinue in uniform and mufti, he said calmly :

'Let's not discuss these matters here. Let's drive to the Belweder palace.'

Khrushchev, still shouting abusively, began to shake hands with each of the Polish delegates. On approaching Gomulka, whom he had never seen before, he asked contemptuously : 'Who's he?'

Before anyone else had had time to answer, Gomulka, looking straight into Khrushchev's eyes, retorted : 'A man whom you kept in prison for three years.'

Khrushchev, discomfited, turned and walked towards the exit, followed by the rest of the party.

In the historic little Belweder palace, situated at the opposite end of the street in which the central committee met, the talks began immediately. Khrushchev repeated the reproaches he had hurled at the Polish communists at the airport, spoke of the tens of thousands of Soviet soldiers who had died liberating Poland from the Nazis, said that Russia had given Poland considerable economic assistance, and accused his hosts of the most vicious ingratitude. He grew increasingly aroused while orating until his voice rose to a shout. At one point Ochab interrupted him in mid-sentence :

'If you exchange screams for speech, we refuse to discuss anything.'

After Mikoyan had interjected a few conciliatory remarks, Krushchev calmed down, announcing his ultimatum : the anti-Soviet mood in Poland must be eliminated by all available means, democratization must be arrested, and a new Politburo must be elected according to his approved list, not according to the list that Ochab had concealed from the Kremlin, and Rokossovsky must of course remain in the Politburo.

The first words spoken by the Poles made it clear that they would not yield. Calmly but resolutely they demanded that the central committee be given full freedom to elect the Politburo, and insisted on their right to follow a 'Polish path to Socialism'. For several hours heated discussion continued, without any apparent results. The Soviet group was angry and aggressive, while the Poles displayed remarkable self-control. At 6 p.m. the talks were adjourned, and the Poles drove to the building where the central committee met.

Its members had been waiting with impatience and anxiety. The corridors were filled with party officials and messengers from the factories and the Polytechnic Institute, under orders to return as soon as they learned the results of the talks with the Russians. Ochab opened the meeting, which lasted only a few minutes. According to the official stenographic records, this is what Ochab said :

'Comrades, I wish to inform you that our Politburo spoke with the Soviet delegation in a businesslike manner. The talks concerned basic principles underlying the relations between our nations and parties, and the development of the situation in Poland, which arouses the deepest anxiety in our Soviet comrades. Because our Soviet comrades have been compelled to fly to Poland rather unexpectedly, and because they wish to return as soon as possible, we should like to continue the talks tonight. The Politburo therefore moves that the meeting be adjourned till 10 a.m. tomorrow. Who wishes to take the floor in this matter? Comrade Cyrankiewicz proposes that the meeting be adjourned till 11 a.m., in order to give us some leeway. Very well then, 11 a.m. There are no objections. Therefore I consider that the proposal of the Politburo has been accepted, and I request you to be here tomorrow at eleven sharp. Thank you, comrades.'

After the Poles returned to the brightly illumined Belweder, the hosts, as before, occupied one side of the table, the Russians the other. The palace, which had been furnished by the communist

President Bierut with a splendour it had never known previously, swarmed with men belonging to the retinue and the bodyguard. The butlers moved noiselessly over the carpets, serving refreshments. In the Hunting Hall, with its doeskin-covered furniture and its glass cases containing precious arms, the Soviet generals commanded by Marshal Konev awaited orders. In the dining-room with its leather-covered walls and ebony furniture, the table had been set abundantly with food and drinks. Everyone listened intently to the raised voices behind the closed doors of the room where the talks were being held.

Suddenly, a storm was released there. Khrushchev, losing patience with the unyielding Poles, said he would use force. This time the roles changed, for it was not Khrushchev but Ochab who screamed :

'Unless you immediately order Rokossovsky to withdraw his troops to their bases, we shall terminate the talks !'

Gomulka, pale with anger, declared : 'If you continue to threaten us, I shall go to the radio and inform the Polish nation about your blackmail !'

Khrushchev retorted : 'Rokossovsky will bring you to your senses !'

'We shall summon 60,000 workers to resist his troops. Just try to shoot at them !'

According to several reports, the following incident then occurred. The door opened without a knock and an official hurried in. With a quick glance around him, he approached Cyrankiewicz and whispered into his ear. Cyrankiewicz jumped from his seat and ran out. A few minutes later he returned, excited, and walking up to Khrushchev said in a low voice : 'Comrade Chou En-lai is on the telephone.'

Khrushchev's face expressed complete amazement. Looking incredulously at Cyrankiewicz, he said :

'Please repeat; I haven't heard you well. Who wants to speak to me on the phone?'

'Comrade Chou En-lai,' Cyrankiewicz said tersely.

Khrushchev jumped up and left the meeting room. Half an hour later he returned, a changed man. This was no longer the screaming, brutal, abusive Khrushchev of a while back; the Khrushchev who re-entered the room was a smiling, kind-hearted plump man, with a round face and merry little eyes. Walking directly to Gomulka he said in his most cordial tone :

'Dear comrade Gomulka, of course we must reach an understanding. How can it be otherwise?'

From then on the atmosphere of the talks changed completely.

The Soviet leaders became conciliatory and promised the withdrawal of their troops before October 26th. Of course the election of a new Politburo was a matter concerning only Poland, and the central committee would be free to decide whether or not to keep Rokossovsky. Of course the Poles were free to follow their own path to Socialism, but it was hoped that this would not spoil the brotherly Soviet-Polish relations, etc., etc.

The guests left Warsaw unostentatiously at about 6 a.m. At the airport Gomulka revenged himself for Khrushchev's snub; shaking hands with everyone, he ignored Khrushchev. Only at the last moment, as though realizing his omission, did he hold out his hand.

'Goodbye, comrade Khrushchev,' he said. 'I'd almost forgotten to wish you *bon voyage.*'

What had determined the sudden change in the Soviet leaders' behaviour? It is said that they had been impressed by Chou En-lai's sharp warning against the use of the army to break the Poles' resistance, and his support of Gomulka and his policies. But the Russians no doubt were also impressed by reports, reaching them during the talks, that the Polish army would not obey Rokossovsky's orders, and would resist the Russian units. Ever more crucial was the consideration that the Poles would try to extend the conflict to East Germany, where the anti-Soviet mood was growing explosive; and an explosion in East Germany would have had incalculable consequences. But history alone will tell whether these were the real causes of the Russian capitulation.

On October 20, 1956, the central committee met at 11 a.m. Its members were joyful, although none had slept the previous night. Indeed, all Warsaw had stayed awake that night; every window had a light in it. Thousands of workers remaining in factories, and armed detachments of the students' and workers' militias, had been prepared to battle. The news of the victory over the Soviet delegation spread in a flash throughout the city. There were parades in the streets, songs and shouting everywhere. Anonymously published leaflets celebrating the victory flooded the capital.

After opening the meeting Ochab gave the floor to Zawadzki who reported on the results of the talks with the Soviet delegation. He said that the Russians had displayed interest in the composition of the new Politburo and the problems of democratization of the Polish régime, adding with a smile that the talks had occasionally been conducted with a bit of temper. But he was not allowed to disregard a question considered by everyone as the most important. One of the central committee members, Starewicz, took the floor to ask some questions.

'From statements made by several comrades whose task is maintaining order,' he said, 'several columns of tanks seem to have been approaching Warsaw, and there have been movements of certain Soviet units at our western borders and within Poland, in the region of Wroclaw. In connection with these reports, I should like to ask Marshal Rokossovsky, first, what was the purpose of those troop movements; and second, on the basis of whose decision have they been executed?'[1]

After he had been seconded by Wasilkowska and Putrament, Rokossovsky asked for the floor. He declared that the Polish troops had under his orders merely carried out tactical exercises. As for the movements of the Soviet troops, he said :

'It is true that Soviet units were on the move. They were going through autumn manoeuvres in the region where these units are stationed, and they were advancing towards Bydgoszcz and Lodz. At the request of the Politburo I asked Marshal Konev, who was in charge of these, to halt the eastward movements of the troops belonging to the northern group and to have them return to their bases. That is all I know.'

This explanation satisfied no one, least of all Ochab, whose motion that the matter be investigated and those responsible brought to account was adopted without opposition. This was a slap in the face for Rokossovsky.

Next, Gomulka delivered a long address in which he subjected the previous administration to crushing criticism, with particular emphasis on the six-year plan. He proclaimed the principle of full Polish sovereignty and equality with other communist countries, and announced a programme for a radical democratization of the régime. These statements were received with a storm of applause and cries of enthusiasm. One passage of his speech, however, reflected the spirit of the period between 1945 and 1947. He said, among other things :

'There was a time when the anti-Socialist forces ... disposed of a vast net of underground organizations. There was a time when the people's régime was attacked by armed bands and defended itself by force of arms, when members of our party, soldiers, and government officials, particularly those serving in the security forces, died by the hundreds and by the thousands.'

Later during the meeting this passage, at least regarding the

[1] According to the official stenographic records.

security police, was indirectly criticized by the communist Leon
Wudzki, who, admonishing Jakub Berman, said :

'People were seized in the streets and after seven days of investigations were released, incapable of normal life. They had to be taken
to insane asylums. People sought refuge in insane asylums to avoid
falling into the hands of the security police. Frightened, panicky
people, even decent people, fled abroad to avoid living under our
system. . . . The whole city knew that people were being murdered,
the whole city knew that there were prison cells in which people
were kept for three weeks standing in excrement up to their ankles,
the whole city knew that Rozanski personally tore off people's
fingernails, the whole city knew that people were drenched with
water and exposed to the cold—but comrade Berman, member of
the security committee, was unaware of all this.'

At the next day's meeting, Jakub Berman, replying to his critics,
revealed an important secret. He stated that the Russians Skul-
bashevsky and Voznesensky had been responsible for the arrests of
Gomulka, Spychalski and others. For the first time the leading part
played by the Russian MVD in the Polish security police was thus
officially admitted. As a result of the debates on the abuses of the
security police, the central committee appointed a committee to investigate it, particularly the case of General Komar who had been
imprisoned on a charge of espionage and subjected to tortures.

The meeting of October 21st culminated in the election by secret
ballot of a new Politburo. A few die-hards made a last attempt to
include Rokossovsky in the new body, but when the chairman of
the ballot committee mounted the podium and announced that
Rokossovsky had received only 23 out of 75 votes, and therefore
had not been re-elected, the announcement was received with
tumultuous applause. The election of Gomulka as the new secretary-
general was now only a formality, and the eighth congress was
closed with the singing of the 'Internationale'. The Polish October
revolution was now an accomplished fact.

On October 24, 1956, Gomulka spoke to 300,000 inhabitants of
Warsaw from the steps of the Palace of Culture. He was enthusiastically hailed by the people of the city, hostile to Communism
but, in the fight between Polish communists and the Kremlin, on
the side of the former. After his speech, those surrounding Gomulka
sang the 'Internationale'. Its melody died away against the voices
of hundreds of demonstrators, who started the Polish national
anthem. After the meeting there were anti-Russian demonstrations

in the streets of Warsaw, during which people shouted 'Down with the Soviets', 'Katyn, Katyn!', 'Send Rokossovsky back to Russia!'

On October 26th the Primate of Poland, Cardinal Wyszynski, was released from prison, and the arrested bishops and priests with him. All Poland offered up prayers of thanksgiving.

On October 29th Radio Warsaw announced that Marshal Rokossovsky had gone back to Russia on leave, a trip from which he was not to return. His place was taken by the recently tortured prisoner, General Marian Spychalski, appointed Minister of National Defence. This was the start of the events brought about by Polish October. The lead was however taken by the insurrection in Hungary.

XVIII

POLISH AND HUNGARIAN BROTHERHOOD

I looked at their faces and saw the likeness. These were the relatives of those who, thirteen years ago and in civilian clothing, with red and white arm-bands and rifles in their hands, had attacked German tanks and infantry in Warsaw, lain on the barricades under fire from Stukas and had crept along the sewers from one besieged district to another. These sitting before me in the hall in New York on April 4, 1957, no longer had weapons in their hands and there was no trace on their clothing of crawling through mud. But their faces, cleaned of grime, still bore traces of their recent experiences, and the look of amazement had not yet left their eyes, brought about by the unexpected change of fate which had driven them suddenly from the streets of their native Budapest to far-off New York. They were sitting in shabby garments so different from those I had been seeing for nearly ten years, foreign, solitary and lost in their new surroundings, and at their head were three people whose names had been mentioned in every communiqué issued from rebelling Budapest a few months ago : Anna Kethly, the only minister of Imre Nagy's government in the free world, whose journey to the Socialist International Congress in Vienna had saved her from arrest; a massive giant with a high forehead and bright open face, General Bela Kiraly, commandant of the rebel National Guard; and a slender dark man with nervous movements, Jozsef Kovago, mayor of Budapest during the first post-war years and during the insurrection. They constituted a part of the army of refugees, amounting to 200,000, who after the smashing of the insurrection by Soviet tanks had left Hungary and gone into exile. They were now eating the bitter bread of exile, full of frustration and disappointment, recalling the great times of past struggle and re-living each fragment of it, and, like the Warsaw insurrectionists, appealing to the free world for justice to their country.

But the world had treated them shabbily. Not only in that it had remained dead to the appeals and calls of the radio during the insurrection but also now, because it was closing its ears to appeals for action and help for the Hungarian nation confronted by a new, still greater reign of terror, the victims of which had already in their thousands been arrested and deported to Russia. The curse of the Hungarian insurrection was that it coincided with the Suez crisis with which there had appeared the spectre of a third world war. This had drawn attention away from the insurrection and brought about the inactivity of the Western world, though it did not justify it. There had been no response when Hungary left the Warsaw Pact or to her declaration of neutrality, either from the UN to which Nagy had appealed for support, or from the Western governments. On the contrary, some people had said that it had been a mistaken step, too impulsive, too far-reaching, which by creating a gap in the Soviet defence system had provoked the return of Russian troops into Hungary. The future was to add fuel to these speculations in the shape of a statement by Khrushchev that the second dispatch of troops into Hungary had been preceded by a stormy argument in the Kremlin, in which opinions had been divided. This was interpreted to imply that, had the declaration on the Warsaw Pact not been made, the opponents of armed intervention in the Kremlin might have prevailed.

Meanwhile, the Western world was not sparing in expressions of sympathy for Hungary and various kinds of help. Conscience-stricken by their political inactivity, people attempted to compensate for it by charity which developed on a vast scale. Every country, starting with little Austria and ending with the huge United States, had opened wide their gates to the refugees; and it was to this that I owed my presence at this meeting of Hungarian freedom fighters in New York, arranged a few months after the collapse of the insurrection.

We Poles were very sympathetic to the Hungarians, whose hospitality had been experienced during the war by thousands of our compatriots. We remembered their co-operation with Polish underground outposts in Hungary and the neutrality of the Hungarian troops stationed round Warsaw during the insurrection. But most sympathy was caused by the Hungarian version of the 'kidnapping of the sixteen'. The similarity was striking. In both cases the Russians had made conciliatory offers and assured them of their goodwill. The delegates had set out for the negotiations to Tököl as to Pruszkow, and had finished up in jail. In both cases the trap had been laid and sprung personally by General Ivan Serov. This had been confirmed as far as the Poles were concerned by Jozef Swiatlo of the Secret Police after he had 'chosen freedom'.

I told the Hungarians of this similarity during various kinds of meetings. 'We had never heard of the kidnapping of your under-ground leaders,' they replied. 'Had we known, we might have been more cautious.'

I was invited to this Hungarian meeting as representative of a country which, although under Soviet domination, had dared come out on the side of the insurrection, condemned Soviet intervention, spontaneously organized the collection of funds, medical aid and clothing for the rebels and had even offered care and hospitality for the orphans of those killed. In addition, 'Hungarian-Polish brotherhood' and the very fact that the Polish *coup d'état* had in-spired the Hungarians to rebel, were arousing increasing interest in the Western world.

As soon as news had come from Poland of the ferment among writers, it had begun to attract the attention of the West. Armed disturbances in Poznan had shaken public opinion as a bloody manifestation of the anti-Soviet and anti-communist feelings of the Polish people. The celebration of the anniversary of the Vows of King Kazimierz at Jasna Gora had been recognized as the greatest anti-communist demonstration ever to take place behind the Iron Curtain, while the revolt of October 19th-21st, which I have re-created from press reports, the official minutes of the session of the plenum of the central committee of the Polish United Workers Party of October 19th-21st, published in the communist magazine *New Roads*, and accounts of those who took part, was seen as a genuinely bloodless insurrection and the opposite of the bloody Hungarian one. Every detail of these few days was described in the Western press, every event commented on in all newspapers without excep-tion, beginning with the *New York Times*, whose excellent reporter in Warsaw, Sydney Gruson, had been sending alarming telegrams several days before the event took place. Dozens of newspapermen went to Warsaw and soon began to send back enthusiastic reports and dozens of photographs, praising the return of freedom of speech and press, the lively intellectual ferment among writers and artists and the magnificent attitude and spirit of the Polish people evident at every step. News began to come of the expulsion from the Party of the Minister of Security, Stanislaw Radkiewicz and his deputy, Mieczyslaw Mietkowski and of the former all-powerful Jakub Ber-man; and finally of the revision of prison sentences, amnesties, the liberation of thousands of political prisoners, primarily of the 154 Poznan rebels and former Home Army soldiers, of the increased repatriation of the remaining Poles held in Russia. Every newspaper printed on its front page the news that the Catholic Church had reached an understanding with Gomulka, and that the teaching of religion had been restored in schools, that General Spychalski had dismissed thirty-two Soviet generals from high posts in the Polish army and had started replacing Russians by Poles in the officers corps, finally that a Polish-Soviet agreement had placed a number of restrictions on the Soviet garrisons in Poland, putting an end to the lying legend about the Polish-Soviet brotherhood of arms. A furore had been roused by telegrams about such changes as the liquidation of the collective farms, which had given back their own farms to millions of peasants and permission for limited private trade and industry, also the practice of the professions and much else. And this had all been reported with the exaggeration typical of the American press. The see-saw had gone up.

On the other hand, the press and TV in the United States had been interested in the views of the Polish exiles on the events in Poland. I was asked about this on the TV in October 1956 by the commentator Mike Wallace, while a group of students from Fordham University had done the same in January 1957 on the radio. I warned them against exaggerated hopes and the idealization of Gomulka, and stated that he was a practising communist who would defend the system, but I estimated favourably the changes that had taken place and spoke up for American aid to Poland.

The echoes of October were heard in parliaments, at international conferences, and in the privacy of government and diplomatic offices, where it was regarded as proof of a serious ferment in the Soviet empire, the beginnings of which had to be sought in the condemnation of Stalin by Khrushchev at the Twentieth Congress of the Communist Party, while the end was hard to forecast. In Gomulka people saw a Polish Tito, and the dismissal of Rokossovsky and his replacement by Spychalski was seen as rendering the army more national; the liquidation of collectivization was understood as a return to private ownership, while the agreement with the Catholic Church represented by Cardinal Wyszynski was interpreted as a victory of the spirit over materialism. The idea was formed of a political communist commissar-Catholic cardinal axis, around which Polish matters would revolve in the future, and a powerful trend arose for giving Poland all manner of aid which might help her to grow gradually independent of Russia. Gomulka's clever strategy was admired—it was at his hands that Khrushchev met what was perhaps the first political defeat in his career; there was admiration for the determination and maturity of the Polish people, so prone to insane and often suicidal deeds. The phrase went from mouth to mouth : 'Now the Poles have behaved like Hungarians and the Hungarians like Poles.' In a word, the Polish nation had become for the second time the 'inspiration of the free world', which, while itself experiencing political defeat at the hands of the Soviets, was amazed at the success gained on the far side of the Iron Curtain by a people totally under Soviet domination, at a time when, on this side, indications of defeatism were apparent. The impossible had become possible and new prospects opened up.

And whereas in the first weeks after the Hungarian rebellion its drama seized the imagination more than the Polish October, yet as time passed the situation began to reverse. Comparisons began to be made, favourable for Poland. The Hungarians had rushed into the battle and had lost, the Poles had not fired one shot but had won. The Polish political rebellion brought success, the Hungarian armed uprising ended in defeat. The Poles were obtaining increasing freedom, while ever worse terror was prevailing in Hungary. The new Soviet troops had left Poland, and they were followed by Rokossovsky, whereas Hungary was in the power of doubled garrisons and Serov with his executioners. Cardinal Wyszynski, freed from prison, had made an agreement with Gomulka, while Cardinal Mindszenty, to avoid returning to prison, had taken refuge in the American embassy and the persecution of the Church was intensified. Most important however was the final result: Poland had prospects for the future while the Hungarian cause looked worse every day.

The Polish emigration reacted towards the 'Spring in October' with some reserve. All agreed that the new government of Gomulka was a continuation of the communist system, carried on by force by Russia, and that if the Polish people could give their own decision under conditions of complete freedom, Gomulka would be overthrown within twenty-four hours. Yet as far as the results of October were concerned, such as liberalization of the communist system, a great many differences of opinion prevailed, since some, though not many, circles of the emigration in London and Paris were carried away by enthusiasm. The hopes of certain persons in London went so far that they were ready to hasten to the aid of the inexperienced Gomulka in arranging new relations with Russia. Asked for my opinion I said, 'You are in England and should do what the fact implies. Watch British policy so that it is advantageous to the Polish people and leave the arrangement of relations with Russia to others.' On the other hand, the 'Komik' camp exaggerated in the opposite way, and declared that October had been carried out in close agreement with the Kremlin, that it had all been rehearsed and in accordance with communist tactics of 'two steps forward, one step back'; only tactical withdrawal had been brought about in October. The resultant of these evaluations was the belief, shared by the mass of the émigrés, that progress had been made in Poland towards greater internal freedom and a certain amount of autonomy regarding Russia, which should be seen as beneficial, and that help for further development should be provided by coming to the aid of Poland, primarily economically, only in such a way as would not strengthen the communist government, but strengthen the Polish people in their resistance to communization. The only exception was Mikolajczyk, who spoke out against economic aid in the belief that it would be exploited by the communist government to strengthen its own power. As a result of the campaign for aid, I was received on October 31, 1956, as chairman of the Polish delegation to ACEN, by the deputy Secretary of State, Robert Murphy, and the director of the office of East European affairs in the State Department, Jacob Beam. I told him that the delegation was for giving Poland far-reaching economic and other aid which might serve the interests of the Polish people but not the communist régime, and that this aid would draw the Polish people closer to the Western world, with which they had been out of contact since 1939. These arguments met with a favourable reception from both representatives of official American policy, though they did not conceal that the way to this aim would meet with many difficulties.

Next, the Council of National Unity in the United States passed a resolution in January 1957 calling for American help for Poland, and sent an appropriate telegram to Dulles, the Secretary of State. Finally, the Polish-American Congress in February 1957, passed a similar resolution.

However, there were voices opposing this in purely American circles. Among others, the Council for Economic and Industrial Research to the Senate Foreign Relations committee took a negative attitude in this matter, and this became the subject of press discussion. Opposing the views of the Council in a letter published on March 24, 1957, in the *Washington Post*, I stated: 'The anti-Communist Polish émigré circles support strongly the idea of economic aid to Poland in the firm belief that under the present circumstances in Poland this aid would be utilized to improve the lot of the Polish people, thus strengthening it in its struggle for a complete independence and a true democracy, a fight which the Polish nation is waging alone, supported only by the Poles living in the Free World.'

In further developing this campaign, I was received by the chairman of the Senate Foreign Relations committee, Senator Green; the chairman of the Committee of Foreign Affairs of the House of

Representatives, Congressman Thomas Gordon, who is of Polish descent; the leader of the Democratic majority in the Senate, Senator Lyndon Johnson; the leader of the Republican minority in the Senate, Senator William Knowland; the Speaker of the House, Sam Rayburn; the former Speaker, Joseph Martin; Senator Paul Douglas and others. With the exception of Senator Knowland, all were on the side of aid. Senator Knowland, however, while being a great friend to Poles, stated : 'As long as a communist government rules in any country, I have been, am, and will be opposed to giving it aid.'

This was how Polish and Hungarian affairs stood on the day when I sat down among the freedom fighters from Budapest. Although their revolt could not be compared with the Warsaw insurrection as regards the time it lasted, the intensity of fighting or the number of victims, yet the fact that it had broken out in time of peace and under worse political conditions offset the difference and facilitated the making of analogies, which I decided to express. I referred in two phrases to the King of Poland and Hungary, Warnenczyk, and the Polish King of Hungarian descent, Batory, to the hospitality extended to Polish refugees in Hungary during the war, to the correct behaviour of the Hungarian troops during the Warsaw insurrection, and having criticized the inactivity of the Western world and the UN, I concluded by discussing a certain external similarity between Warsaw in 1944 and Budapest in 1956.

'When we look at photos and films of the Hungarian insurrection, one and the same thought strikes us who took part in the Warsaw insurrection. This was how the streets of Warsaw looked in August and September 1944, this was how the Warsaw insurrectionists looked, starved with hunger and lack of sleep, in shabby civilian clothes but with the same fire and courage in their eyes. The same burnt-out tanks in the streets, and the same barricades. . . . And if, as the proverb says, "Poles and Hungarians are brothers", so Budapest of 1956 and Warsaw of 1944 are close relatives.'

As I left, bade farewell by leaders of the insurrection, I heard the bitter comment : 'The one thing we Hungarians can still count on is a minute's silence for those killed in action, and a few eulogies in the UN.'

XIX

TOWER OF BABEL ON EAST RIVER

I was listening to several such speeches in the magnificent UNO building of glass and steel, where on November 1st, at 10.26 a.m., the telegraph operator on duty heard an unknown station. 'I am calling the United Nations in New York . . .' The telegraph operator tapped the key of the apparatus and replied : 'This is the United Nations. Who is calling?' 'This is the Ministry of Foreign Affairs in Budapest . . .' he heard in reply, and immediately afterwards the dramatic words of Premier Imre Nagy's telegram began to appear on the tape, informing the UN that new Soviet troops had crossed into Hungary, that Hungary had quitted the Warsaw Pact and become neutral. The telegram asked the UN to defend this decision and to place the Hungarian problem on the agenda of the General Assembly. In this way, a matter penetrated the gates of the UN which was to become in time a reproach to the conscience of this most important international organization, from which it has not been freed to this day.

During the Hungarian debate I was quite often in the building on East River, either listening to speeches, or wandering about the passages and hall, in which most of the meetings take place between interested persons and delegates, in search of this or that delegate. In the building there was an atmosphere of excitement and fever, brought about by the collision of two events that had shaken the already tottering foundations of world peace, of which the UN seeks to be main sentry. Everywhere were groups of delegates talking to each other in a lively way and on all faces was uneasiness and alarm. Each group was of a different colour or shade of skin, and a different language. It was a real Tower of Babel, not only meta-phorically, but literally, since many delegates could not find a common language with the others as far as views and decisions were concerned. In the debating chambers, excited voices are heard and accusations hurled. Attention is mainly focused on two actors in the spectacle, seen daily on TV by millions of viewers. They are at the head of two conflicting groups, in their hands is the key to the situation and they direct moves on the chess board. The first is a tall man with projecting chin marking will and character, faultlessly dressed and speaking with hardly controlled passion and fire. He is the chairman of the American delegation, Henry Cabot Lodge, appearing in the role of prosecutor, whose task is to reach a verdict of guilty against the accused, the Soviet Union. The other is a type of bureaucratic diplomat, dry and cold, with a frozen face giving the impression that it has never seen the sunlight. This is Arkady Sobolev, head of the Soviet delegation, defending the accused in a way as old as the world itself but always effective—attack. In the galleries is an intent, concentrated crowd reacting merely by deep sighs or angry gestures to what is happening in the chamber, and among them are pathetic figures of the latest refugees, Hungarians. And wherever one goes there are the excited, hurrying figures of journalists, hunting round the information offices for news and running from the chamber to the telephone, or back.

Four hours after receiving Nagy's appeal, an extraordinary session of the General Assembly was held, not to consider the case of Hungary but the Suez crisis. Both problems, the Hungarian insurrection and Suez, began to compete with one another, and Suez won. 'Bad luck that the Suez crisis broke out simultaneously. Hungary had to give way, for Suez is in the Middle East and the Middle East is petroleum,' said Sam Rayburn, Speaker of the House of Representatives, sympathetically to the ACEN delegation, of which I was a member. He had been asked by us to put the Hungarian question on the agenda of the House of Representatives. Thus, on the days when Soviet tanks were crushing the resistance of the rebels, the General Assembly was debating Suez, and only passing comments were devoted to Hungary. Not until November 4th, when the insurrection in Budapest had been crushed, and Nagy taken refuge in the Yugoslav embassy, did the General Assembly pass a resolution demanding that the Soviet Union cease the attack and immediately withdraw its troops from Hungary. This resolution was complemented on November 9th by a decision demanding the holding of free elections in Hungary under the auspices of the UN. Other resolutions followed, and by December 12, 1958, there had been eighteen of them. None brought any result. In the voting on the Hungarian question, the Polish communist delegation also took part, voting hand in hand with the Soviet representatives.

Eleven years earlier, in 1945, at the inauguration of the United Nations Organization in San Francisco, the world-famous pianist Arthur Rubinstein, after playing the American national anthem, rose and stated : 'The places reserved for the representatives of my country are empty and no one will speak here today in the name of Poland. In order, however, to remind you of her struggle and rights, I will play the Polish national anthem.' The whole assembly, led by President Truman, rose and listened in silence to the Dabrowski Mazurka. This was not scheduled in the programme of the inaugural ceremonies and only Arthur Rubinstein could have permitted himself it, certainly unaware at that time that he was uttering prophetic words which are true to this day. The Polish people which spontaneously manifested their solidarity with the Hungarian insurrection were not represented at the UN, either in 1945, or when voting on the Hungarian question was held, or later. In the UN are seated representatives of a system which, no matter whether headed by Bierut or Gomulka, is holding on in Poland only thanks to Soviet protection. In order to remind the members of UN of this, the Polish delegation to the ACEN, the flags of which wave on the building opposite UNO Headquarters, state this annually in a memorandum sent at the beginning of every session to all members of this organization.

It became increasingly clear, against the background of the Hungarian affair, that the name 'United Nations Organization' had no backing in reality. In fact it is a body into which the nations have been organized but not united at all. A name nearer the truth would be the Divided Nations Organization. Russia did not pay heed to any of the resolutions passed against it in the Hungarian question, and no sanctions, provided for in the Charter of the United Nations, were imposed on it for not doing so. Nikita Khrushchev treated the UN as the legendary Mr Laszcz treated court orders, which, as a sign of contempt, he ordered to have sewn into his cloak as a lining. Admittedly the UN appointed a special committee to investigate the Hungarian problem, but it has never been allowed into Hungary and its activity has consisted merely in examining 111 witnesses on this side of the Iron Curtain and issuing a few reports condemning Soviet aggression in Hungary, the reign of terror there, the mass deportations to Russia and the ignoring of UN resolutions. Neither Dag Hammarskjöld, UN secretary-general, nor Prince Wan Waithayakon, nor Sir Leslie Munro were admitted on behalf of the United Nations, the last two after being appointed in turn when the commission had been wound up as officials in charge of the Hungarian question with instructions to inform the UN of events which might bear witness (Oh, irony!) that the decisions taken in the case of Hungary were being carried out. Not one step has been taken in Hungary which might show any concern with the UN resolutions, while on this side of the Iron Curtain the UN merely refused to accept the credentials of the Hungarian communist delegation, but admitted it all the same, by which the refusal of recognition was given merely the nature of moral sanction.

I was part of the ACEN delegation which was received at various times by Prince Wan, Sir L. Munro, Cabot Lodge and members of many other Western representatives in the UN. We demanded that sanctions laid down in articles 6, 41 and 42 of the Charter of the United Nations against any member who consistently infringes it be imposed against Russia and the communist Hungarian government. Their extent is very wide, ranging from partial or total breaking off of economic relations and communications etc., up to breaking off diplomatic relations, use of the international armed forces and expulsion from UNO. We met everywhere with complete understanding, while the Hungarian member of the delegation met profound sympathy and expressions of grief. As for the imposition of even the mildest sanction, however, arms were spread and the word 'impossible" uttered in every case.

This weakness of UNO was particularly shocking in comparison with the energetic steps taken against Britain, France and Israel in connection with the attack on Suez. The sight of Sobolev foaming at the mouth as he accused these states of armed aggression and shedding blood in Egypt, during the time when Soviet tanks were decimating Hungarian insurrectionists and massacring the people of Budapest, was unforgettable. All the resolutions against Britain, France and Israel were carried out. Their troops were stopped in the middle of a victorious campaign and forced to withdraw from the territories they had occupied, which were manned by an international army, provided by various members of the UN for the use of the organization. The campaign of the states of the free world against its own members, the action of allies against allies, was carried out fast, neatly and in an orderly way. But apart from resolutions no other step was taken against hostile Russia in connection with its aggression on Hungary. It became clear for the umpteenth time that under existing conditions only such UN resolutions as were agreed to by the Soviet Union could count on being carried out. In practice this meant the unanimity of the great powers, which is a fiction.

The epilogue to the Hungarian problem in UNO were two events. The first was the execution of Imre Nagy, Pal Maleter and others, announced by the Hungarian radio on June 16, 1958, and quickly condemned by the General Assembly, which took the opportunity once again of condemning the failure of Russia and the Hungarian communist government to carry out its previous resolutions. This reminded me of the death in a Soviet gaol of the heads of the underground government, Vice-Premier Stanislaw Jankowski and General Leopold Okulicki. The Hungarian 'kidnapping of the sixteen' had a similar epilogue and the same man carried it out—Serov. The second was the tragedy of the Danish diplomat, Povl Bang-Jensen, deputy secretary of a special commission of the UN, who had in his care the names of the 111 Hungarian witnesses it had examined. They made their statements on the condition that their names should remain a secret, since to reveal them would mean persecution of their families still in Hungary. When Bang-Jensen's superiors in UNO demanded that he give them the list of witnesses, at the end of 1957, he, wishing to keep his obligations and in fear of the Soviet citizens employed in the UN Secretariat, refused to do so, and was removed from his post as a disciplinary measure. On November 26, 1959, his body was found with a bullet in the head in a New York park, two miles from his home. The mystery of his death has never been explained to this day, and only the future may cast certain light on it. It matters not whether he died at the hand of a Soviet agent, or committed suicide from the depression which came upon him after his removal from his UNO post. In either case, this 'conservative', who still believed that a promise must be kept, was the last victim of the Hungarian insurrection, and the bullet which cut short his brief life was the last shot fired in that heroic fight.

Apart from the great disappointment which the UN caused in connection with the Soviet attack on Hungary, it created a precedent on this occasion which is of importance for the future. The basic demand of the ACEN, many times put to the UN in the name of the nine countries, was carried out in respect of one of them by the resolutions of November 4th and 9th demanding that Russia withdraw its troops from Hungary and thus enable the people of that country to hold free elections under UN control. What could be resolved regarding Hungary can be repeated with regard to other countries at the appropriate time and under conditions promising greater hope of their being carried out. Despite the ups and downs of this organization, despite the predominance of shadow over light in its activities, the number of UN members continues to rise and the significance and extent of its influence to grow. Each year new colonial peoples in Africa gain their independence and on the next day become members of UNO. Wilson's old doctrine respecting the rights of self-determination of every nation has come back to life. Ever more frequently the bitter comment is heard among political refugees from Eastern Europe : 'Too bad we are not black and our countries are not in Africa. We'd already be free.' Soon the colonies of the Western states will have disappeared from the face of the earth, and Soviet Russia will remain the one and only colonial state in the world. Maybe those rights will then be recognized for such nations as Poland, now celebrating the millennium of her national existence, which are not begrudged to the African nations (rightly so) which are merely on the threshold of development. Quite soon the small countries, including many former colonies, which have the tendency to keep themselves aloof from the disputes of the giants, will obtain a decided majority in UNO and the fate of the world may depend on which side this majority takes. It may at some stage turn against the last colonial state, the Soviet Union, who will find it increasingly difficult to maintain the great lie, the international 'stop thief' cry which accuses others of colonialism and makes a taboo of its own.

In a word, UNO can be regarded as a great disappointment for those who expected so much from it, or as a great hope for them and for all mankind : perhaps the latter.

XX

ACEN: A TRIP ROUND THE WORLD

On the occasion of my election as chairman of ACEN in September 1958, serious divergences of opinion were revealed among the various national representations forming this organization, the roots of which were in pre-war orientations governing the politics of Eastern and Central Europe, brought back to life by the attitude adopted by the Polish emigration to the events in Poland in October 1956. These were formulated briefly by the chairman of the Rumanian National Committee:

'We shall vote against the candidature of a Pole as chairman of ACEN for two reasons. Firstly because he represents a policy hostile to Western Germany, in which the question of German rearming and the frontier on the Oder-Neisse plays the main role. For this reason, the Poles boycott ACEN representation in Bonn, to which they have not delegated a representative. We Rumanians however see certain advantages for the future of our country in co-operation with a re-born Germany. Secondly, because the Polish candidate supports economic aid from the United States to Poland, as well as cultural and scientific exhanges with Poland, whereas we are of the opinion that as long as a country remains under Soviet domination it should not be assisted either economically or in any other way, since only the communist government profits by this.'

This attitude was fully supported by the chairman of the Bulgarian national committee. The Polish arguments were that the Polish nation does not want to be liberated from Soviet domination by a German army, as this would bring about new enslavement, and that all Poles will defend the western frontier on the Oder-Neisse, and in this respect there is no difference between the attitude of the Polish nation and emigration on one hand and the communist government on the other; finally, that economic aid and cultural and scientific exchanges are to the good of the Polish people but not of the communist government. These arguments failed to convince our opponents. Thus when a Pole was elected by a majority of votes, the Rumanian and Bulgarian withdrew as a mark of protest from the general committee of ACEN, only to return to it a few months later despite the fact that the Polish delegation had not altered their attitude by a jot or tittle. In any case, I started the year of Polish chairmanship with the general committee as a torso and in an atmosphere of crisis into the bargain. However with the support of the majority of members and with the fruitful aid of the secretary-general, a Rumanian, Brutus Coste, the activity of ACEN went on its normal course, starting with the plenary meetings laid down in the statute, visits to the Senate and the House of Representatives and to the State Department, and ending with the publication of two long pamphlets, of which one was a further survey of events in Hungary covering the period from September 1957 to July 1958 inclusive, and the second devoted to the violation of human rights in Eastern Europe. Both these publications were distributed primarily among UN delegations, while the chairman of the American delegation to the UN, Ambassador Henry Cabot Lodge, received 'The Survey of Events in Hungary' at a special meeting, which was sharply attacked in a press communiqué issued by the Hungarian communist delegation to the UN and on the Budapest radio. I made the acquaintance on this occasion of this man on whose shoulders has rested for many years the defence of the interests of the United States in the UN, and who is not afflicted with the inferiority complex regarding Soviet policy from which an increasing number of diplomats of the Western world are suffering. When the second pamphlet, written by the chairman of the Social Commission of ACEN, Boleslaw Biega, was sent to Mrs Eleanor Roosevelt, her reply gave a somewhat pessimistic forecast about putting into effect in Eastern Europe the UN General Declaration of Human Rights of ten years earlier. 'I hope that in the coming decade much more will be achieved under its [i.e. the Declaration's] influences.'

Ten years plus ten is somewhat slow progress!

As soon as I became chairman, the idea arose of sending an ACEN delegation round the world, firstly to the Far East and Australia, with the same purpose as the journey of its three members in 1956 round South America. A UN resolution calling on Russia to withdraw its troops from Eastern and Central Europe would have great moral and political meaning, since it would be an expression of world protest against the present status of this part of Europe and would keep its problems on the surface of international life as an open question continually awaiting solution. Such a resolution would permanently undermine Soviet domination in Eastern Europe, the countries of which have become basically Soviet colonies, exploited by Russia in every way, primarily economically. The stressing of this latter point, i.e. that Russia, now that the Western states are liquidating their colonies, is in fact the greatest colonial state in the world, would ensure better understanding of the problem of Eastern Europe in those countries of the Far East which were themselves colonies until recently.

It was finally decided to send a delegation consisting of the chairman, his deputy, the Hungarian Jozsef Kovago and the Latvian diplomat Vilis Masens.

The following pages consist of extracts from my diary of our journey round the world.

Tokyo, January 31, 1959. At lunch at the club of officials of the Ministry of Foreign Affairs, on Kayukai-kan, there was interesting talk about the problems of Eastern Europe. Masadika Kanayama, director of the European department in the Ministry of Foreign Affairs, asked me my views on the unification of Germany. He had been in Warsaw two months earlier, and made some comments which reflected his admiration for the attitude and vitality of the Polish people. The others present were—apart from Ambassador Miyazaki —Eiji Amau, vice-president of the United Nations Association, who had also visited Warsaw recently, Gunji Hosono, Dr Tetsuzo Watanabe, an expert on communist affairs and a militant democrat imprisoned under the government of General Tojo, Mitsu Watanabe of the United Nations department in the Ministry, and Professor Imaoka.

After lunch, Ambassador Miyazaki spoke, emphasizing that we have more friends in Japan than those gathered in the small dining room. In reply I began by giving thanks for the aid provided by the Japanese consuls to our compatriots stranded in Lithuania in 1939 and 1940, who supplied them with visas to reach the free world. I myself heard of cases when Japanese consuls had stamped any Polish identity papers with visas, and I know people who crossed right through Russia with such documents to Vladivostok and thence to Japan and to the rest of the world. At the same time, in neighbouring Polish eastern territories, Soviet secret police were loading my other compatriots into cattle cars and shipping them to Kazakhstan.

As soon as I began speaking, I noticed how the impassive faces of our Japanese hosts livened up and the beginnings of smiles appeared. When I concluded, a warmer atmosphere was prevailing. First I heard one neighbour remark : 'It was very kind of you to

mention this,' and from another, 'After all, you remember that!'
The conversation became livelier and from the visa question shifted
to pre-war Polish-Japanese relations. Such names were mentioned
by our hosts as Ambassador Michal Moscicki, Colonel Kowalew-
ski, who at one time revised the Japanese military coding system,
and others. They even recalled the stay in Japan during the 1905
revolution of Jozef Pilsudski, Tytus Filipowicz and Roman Dmow-
ski. I told our Japanese hosts how popular Japan had been in
partitioned Poland after the outbreak of war with Russia in 1905,
and that hundreds of Poles living in America to this day fled there
from the Russian occupation as they did not want to serve in the
Russian army against Japan. The talk now concentrated on Polish
affairs, and let me form three conclusions. The first was that the
Japanese are still as interested in Poland as before the war, as a
country lying at the opposite pole of the Soviet empire, and for this
it is of importance in Japanese-Soviet politics. The second was that
they are very interested in the further development of the Polish
experiment which began in October 1956. The third, that plain
courtesy reaches people better than learned argument.

February 4th. In the morning, a visit to Parliament. A huge overpowering building, in which we are received by the Speaker of
the Lower House, Dr Ryogoro Kato, member of the Liberal party
who, having listened to my brief explanation of the purpose of our
journey, assured us with emphasis of the interest of the Japanese
people in the liberation of the Iron Curtain countries and promised
support. In the Parliament building we had talks with, among others,
the secretary-general of the Liberal party, Takeo Fukuda, who has
organized a number of talks and meetings for us. It is hard to note
down all the names—some young MPs made a very good impression. They understood our problem and promised aid.

Later that afternoon we met a group of elder Japanese statesmen
at a club. They were led by Admiral Nomura, a massive tall man
by Japanese standards, who was the Japanese ambassador in
Washington when the attack on Pearl Harbour took place. Others
present were Dr Tetsuzo Watanabe, president of the Association of
Free Asia, Dr Komatsu, president of the American-Japanese society,
and Ambassador Yoshizawa. When we put our cause forward, all
were particularly interested in the idea of obtaining a UN resolution
on the liberation of our peoples. They saw deep into its political
value, particularly Ambassador Yoshizawa. They also devoted
much attention to what I have called the 'taboo' of the Western
world, i.e. its fear of making anything in the way of a Magna Carta

Libertatis for all the nations now constituting Soviet Russia. The latter does not hesitate to propagate world domination by Communism. Why does the Western world fear to reply by the propagation of ideas of the predominance of freedom and democracy in the whole world, including the Soviet Union?

Seoul, Korea, February 6th. Now the main attraction occurred— a visit to the front with an aide-de-camp of the Minister of Defence. Villages were poor but the inhabitants look well-fed, while rosy-cheeked children played in front of the houses. Half way we were joined by a jeep with four military police, armed with sub-machine guns. As we go through townships and villages, they turn on the siren and we drive through without being held up, saluted on each crossing by well-uniformed and well set-up sentries. Excitement gradually creeps up on me. I breathe in the familiar atmosphere of the zone close to the front line known from past experiences, passing military stores, tents pitched in a field, car parks and military trucks full of soldiers.

After some hours our vehicles turned aside sharply and we found ourselves on the edge of a parade ground, face to face with a band of several dozen and a guard of honour with banners. The car stopped in front of a stand full of civilians and military personnel, where we were greeted by the commanding officer of the first Korean division of marines, Brig.-General Kim Dong Ha, who introduced another Korean general, an American colonel and two rows of American and Korean officers. The band struck up the Korean national anthem, a voice of command rang out, the company presented arms and unfurled the banners. After this unexpected ceremony, which took us somewhat aback, a military display followed.

Lunch was then taken at the Army camp canteen, situated on the mountain slopes. The young officers were embarrassed, and I no less then they, at being given a reception accorded to VIPs.

After lunch came a report on the situation at the front. A young Korean officer, with a quiver in his voice, and peeping from time to time at notes concealed among papers on the desk, begins with a panegyric in honour of Poland and the Warsaw insurrection. Later, he shows on the map the position of the first division and the sites we are to visit. I liquidate the formal mood by stressing in my reply to his moving welcome that I was captain like him and in my life I have fought twice with the Bolsheviks and request them to treat us like older comrades in arms, not VIPs on an official trip. This setting of the matter appealed very much to the American officers, who had clearly had enough of this sort of gala.

Unexpectedly enough, a conversation was started by the Koreans on the prospects of unifying Germany. Surprised, I asked whence this interest in that distant land? In reply I heard : 'If the Great Powers find a method of linking the two parts of Germany, living under different political and economic systems, then that precedent may later be applied in Korea.'

On our return from the front we came late to the press conference at the Bando Hotel. About fifty reporters and photographers awaited us. They were interested, among other things, in the Rapacki plan, which I criticized, saying that although it appears to serve Polish interests, it is basically laid down by the Kremlin and is meant to start a withdrawal of American troops from Western Europe and in the longer view to lead to its domination by the Soviet Union without war.

Formosa, Taipei, February 9th. During an afternoon visit to Vice-President General Chen-Cheng, a 65-year-old, grey-haired, good-looking man, living in a modest little palace furnished in European style, I complimented him on his contribution to the land reform and measures I had seen earlier in the day and, to make the conversation less hackneyed, I informed him of our pre-war difficulties in this sphere in Poland. From this lively talk developed through an interpreter. Both General Chen-Cheng and the Minister of Foreign Affairs, Huang, to whom we went straight from the visit to the Vice-President, assured us that they would support us everywhere and at all times, and that they regarded us as natural allies. There was some merriment, since between the two visits we obtained a prophecy in a Buddhist temple. In front of the temple and inside was a noisy New Year crowd of indulgence-seekers, burning candles and setting off fireworks, to draw the attention of the deity to the penitent. I lit a candle and drew a prophecy. First our guide translated it, then the chief of the Information Office, present during the conversation with the Minister of Foreign Affairs, when I mentioned it jokingly. Both agreed that the prophecy recommends patience, but it forecast a return to Poland, which is what I dream of.

At five there was a reception at the government Guest House. About 300 guests attended, including all the government except General Cheng, foreign ambassadors, Parliamentary and political leaders, also those of the trade unions; in a word, as we were told, the whole political world of Taipei. Over the hall was a banner, 'Welcome to the ACEN delegation'. In occasional conversa-

F*

tions I was told that revolution in China is possible and that the army in Formosa, half a million strong, is burning with the desire to fight. All idea of recognizing Formosa as a separate state, i.e. the idea of two Chinese states, recognized by the United States and the rest of the world, is regarded as disastrous. It would suit communist policy, which is striving in the first stage for the recognition of the portions of national territories it has seized as independent separate states. This is apparent in Germany, Korea and Vietnam. In the second stage, the communists as a rule propose unification by way of negotiations between communist and democratic governments of the country concerned, holding that in the last resort this will lead to their dominating the whole country. In any case, recognition by the United States, in either situation, of the Chinese communist government would be the beginning of the end for Nationalist China, and among other things would lead to the switch of thirteen million Chinese, scattered throughout the countries of South Asia, to the support of the communist government.

Manila, February 11th. In the morning we paid a visit to the Minister of Foreign Affairs. Felixberto M. Serrano has already represented the Philippines in the UN, has heard of ACEN, and is well acquainted with the problems of Eastern Europe. He promised full support for our campaign from the Philippine delegation to UNO. After this visit we went for an audience with President Carlos Garcia, who resides in the fine Malaganang palace, with verandahs overlooking a river. We filed up one after the other to be introduced, and afterwards I explained to the President the aim of our visit and appealed for moral and political support. The President asked for the enumeration of the countries represented in ACEN, requested my view of the Rapacki plan, warmly assured us of the sympathy of himself and of the Philippine people, and promised full help. When we left the audience chamber by another door, the President was already shaking the hands of the next group of people.

February 12th. This morning we had a radio interview over nine stations. The well-known commentator who questioned us was fascinated by our talk of Eastern Europe and particularly by the fact that in nine countries behind the Iron Curtain about a hundred million people are opposing Soviet domination.

At ten o'clock we spoke in turn in the auditorium of the town hall to members of the town council and about 400 municipal officials. Seeing that Roces was chairman and being certain that many members of the Philippine underground were present in the audience, I jettisoned my political speech and improvised a talk on the magnificent struggle of the Philippine and Polish underground movements for the same aims and ideals. I was first interrupted by applause when I stressed that I was going to speak as a comrade in arms. The second came when I referred to the heroism of the Warsaw insurrection. When I ended with the cry of 'Long live the free Philippines,' the entire audience leapt to its feet and cheered.

In the evening a reception for a 100 people was held at Mayor Lackson's home.

Some guests, former members of the underground, asked me with curiosity about the Warsaw insurrection. We compared conditions under which both undergrounds had fought and agreed that they had had better terrain in the Philippines than we in Poland, because of the several thousands of islands and better communication—by sea—with the Allies. Also, in the second phase of the war, after the launching of the American offensive, they were better supplied by parachute drops.

Sydney, February 16th. At a crowded meeting at the Metalworkers Union, my hand was shaken by giants until my bones cracked. Clearly working hands from the workshop. An unforced atmosphere. The lively general secretary, L. Short, introduced me to the State Minister of Labour and Industry, J. J. Maloney, who informs me that he was Australian Ambassador in Moscow at the time when the Soviet Union broke off relations with the Polish government in exile and that he then took over the defence of Polish interests. In our talk he showed a very good knowledge of Polish wartime affairs, including the trial of the sixteen leaders of the Polish underground. When we recalled those events, I had the impression that Maloney was troubled by some thought and that he was eyeing me vigilantly. This was all explained when he asked : 'Where have I heard your name? Is it possible that we met during the war? What were you doing in those years?' When I began to explain my wartime activities he interrupted me in the middle : 'Was it perhaps you who wrote *Fighting Warsaw*?' I admitted it, and heard a few words as gratifying to any author as paradisical music. Maloney then asked for the floor, and spoke very warmly of the heroic fight of the Poles during the last war.

In the evening a magnificent reception was held at the home of the Krygiers, for several dozen persons, at which I met—among others—the former pre-war Polish Senator Haiman-Jarecki. Thus it had been necessary to come to Sydney to meet this figure, well-known in his time in Warsaw and Poland. As we reminisced I asked him if it were true that Vice-Premier Eugeniusz Kwiatkowski, after going home from a reception at the Senator's home, ordered that his tax return be revised, which resulted in additional taxation. I obtained a somewhat evasive answer, but there was opportunity for joking. Instead of flowers—a new income tax account.

Canberra, February 19th. We were received by the Minister for External Affairs, R. G. Casey, a typical Anglo-Saxon, to whom I expatiated on our plans and requests. He agreed that everything was well-equipped, promised to study the memorandum we leave at every visit to Ministers of Foreign Affairs, and to consider the way which might lead to our cause being taken up by UNO. Towards the end of our talk, he asked me, 'Do you know General Anders?' 'Of course,' said I, adding, 'I hope to see him towards the end of our journey.' 'Then give him my kindest regards. I often met him during the war and have much respect for him.'

Next we paid a visit to Prime Minister, Robert Menzies, an imposing, handsome, broad-shouldered man, who at once caught on to the idea of keeping alive the problem of Eastern Europe as an international problem waiting to be dealt with, promised help and stated that after reading our memorandum he would see Casey this same day in order to seek out practical means to bring the matter before UNO, perhaps first of all by way of appointing a commission like that on the Hungarian question.

During our talk, I repeated my thanks for the hospitality extended to my compatriots and emigrants from other Iron Curtain countries. The Prime Minister did not accept them with a cliché, but gave me a sharp look and asked, 'Are you sure your compatriots are satisfied?' 'I am certain of it, Mr Prime Minister,' I replied. 'I have already spoken to several dozen of them and they are all in general satisfied, though they add that it was hard to start with.' Menzies nodded with understanding. 'That's so. At first they didn't feel at home, because we Australians, living in a backwater of the world, had no idea what Eastern Europeans were like and we did not understand them. A long time was needed to get to know one another and fit in together. But today we all recognize that the newcomers have greatly enriched our life and raised the standard of Australian culture, not to mention cooking.' Here Menzies smiled broadly as if to show that he was not entirely indifferent to gastronomy, and added : 'Thank you for your kind words, which are an additional proof for me that a levelling-out of relations has occurred.'

Next on our time-table was the Minister for Immigration, A. R.

Downer, who made a pleasant impression. He spoke with liking of
the newcomers and believed that Australia should keep her gates
open. The one restriction is the necessity of keeping a balance
between the needs of labour and the influx of new manpower. He
invited us to coffee, and when I brought up the question of new
refugees who have chosen freedom in Austria, he showed a knowledge of the problem and assured me that he is at present dealing
with it.

After this meeting, the invaluable Wenthworth arranged a tea-
party with some high officials of the Ministry for External Affairs,
with whom we discussed various means of bringing our cause
before UNO. Towards the end of the meeting, two of them approached
me and, having explained that they had been observers from the
Australian Embassy in Moscow during the trial of the sixteen Polish
underground leaders, asked what had happened to Vice-Premier
Jankowski, General Okulicki, Kazimierz Puzak and the others, and
gave me details about the trial, which they had not left even for
fifteen minutes. They nodded sadly when after nearly every question
I replied : 'He died in the Lubianka jail ... arrested again ... he
died in gaol in Warsaw ... he is dead.' As I took my leave, I heard :
'That was the most cynical parody of justice it is possible to imagine.'

Saigon, February 26th. On the way to visit the mayor of the town,
Nguyen Phu Ha, at 8.30 a.m. we noticed a large banner on the town
hall, at the height of the first floor, across the façade, saying 'Welcome
to the ACEN delegation'. After the visit we were shown into a large
hall, in which a crowd of 3,000 persons awaited us. I was surprised
by this sight, since I had not for a moment credited the information
of Tran Tam, that several thousand people would turn up and listen
to us calmly for the scheduled three hours. Yet in the hall I saw a
sea of heads, and a crowd lining the walls. In the first rows I recognized familiar faces of ministers, and behind them the yellow splurge
of the khaki uniforms of generals. Waiting for the ceremony to begin,
I asked Tran Tam who these people were in the hall and how so
many of them had been able to gather. The reply was somewhat
unexpected. 'They are the intellectuals of Saigon and students. And
they have come because they are interested in the fate of white
races which are the colonies of another white race. In Asia, only
yellow races were subjected to the rule of the whites. Hence, in the
eyes of the Vietnamese, your situation is very unusual and intrigu-
ing.' For the first time I felt like a white Negro.

I started my speech, which was translated phrase by phrase into

Vietnamese, with expressions of recognition for the fight of the Vietnamese with the invasion from the North, which was received with warm applause. Later, after a short explanation of the aims and activities of AGEN, I jettisoned my prepared notes and improvised a lecture on Poland, a map of which was hanging behind me, about the Polish underground during the past war, the Warsaw insurrection, the arrest of the sixteen, the first years of Russian rule in Poland, the terror of the secret police, murders, and the elections of 1947. When I mentioned this or the other communist deception or act of violence, I was interrupted by exclamations. I leaned over to ask my interpreter what they meant. He replied, 'They are agreeing with you. They are saying that they know this from their own experiences.'

In the evening a supper was given by the Minister of Information. I used chopsticks to eat the Chinese food with as much skill as though I had never used anything else. The young, elegant Secretary-General of Parliament, seated next to me, wanted to know everything about Poland, noted down names and asked me to send him a list of books about Poland which he could put into the library. Over drinks, I met a young Englishman who had spent five years in a Chinese prison. He had already written one book on the subject and is writing another. What he briefly told me about it makes my stay in the Warsaw security police gaol sound like paradise.

March 2nd. Today we encountered the local opposition for the first time. We visited the Union of Victims of Communism, supposed to amount to a million and a half members, which publishes its own newspaper and gives help to refugees in the form of food, clothes and money. One of those present kept insisting that they are completely independent of the government. Two editors we met were also surely members of the opposition, as they smiled ironically when we praised the obvious progress, but they changed their manner when they also heard we had been struck by the great natural wealth of the country and the well-solved problem of the refugees who are housed in open settlements and their own little houses, not in barracks behind barbed wire.

At the headquarters of the Association for Cultural Freedom a meeting had been arranged for us with some young poets and writers, rebels by their looks, gestures and talk, though not the beatnik type. The conversation was mainly around Pasternak and Hlasko, whom they know and are going to translate from the French editions. This talk was very refreshing after the hackneyed political visits.

Calcutta, March 4th. Professor Banerjee introduced two interesting people in an interval between hurrying for the tickets : Bikash
Mazumder and Jnan Bhattacharjee. One had been in an English
gaol ten years and the other was ashamed he had only been inside
for four years. Both democrats through and through, they know our
problems and state that all Indian intellectuals know them also,
but no one knows how to help us. They show us a newspaper photograph of a Soviet delegation which arrived at the same time as we.
One cannot help seeing that the press describes their visit in identical
terms to ours elsewhere, i.e. as 'a mission of goodwill.' The devil has
dressed up in a surplice and is ringing the bell for Mass with his
tail. . . .

Professor Banerjee gave me genuine pleasure by presenting me
with a pamphlet with the picture on its cover of the Poznan uprising,
which has gone round the whole world, i.e. that of a group of lads
carrying a red and white banner stained with the blood of the fallen,
before whom a young girl is marching with determination in her face
and fire in her eyes.

In the evening we went along crowded streets to a meeting with
young socialists. We stopped in a dark yard, from which we were
guided to a poorly-lit room with portraits of Tagore, Gandhi and
others. The Spartan furnishings consisted of a table, chairs and
telephone. About twenty young people listened attentively to our
lecture and appeal for assistance. They reacted strongly to our
proof of Soviet colonialism in Eastern Europe. This is the argument
which proves most convincing in the Far East. It reminds the audience of the recent, familiar past. They are ready to help us to the
best of their ability and opportunities. On their side, they strongly
criticized the policy of Nehru towards communist China and prophesied that India would pay dearly for it some day.

The young socialists had lively faces, burning looks and enthusiasm in their voices. This same type of rebel, dissatisfied with the
existing order of things, is to be met with all over the world. They
were very anti-communist in their utterances, stressed the need for
action and struggle against this basically reactionary movement, not
merely wringing their hands. I parted from them under a strong
impression.

Karachi, March 7th. At 11 a.m. we paid a visit to the Ministry of
Foreign Affairs in the Mohatta Palace. The Secretary of Foreign
Affairs, M. S. A. Baig, entered into a long conversation with us. He
was interested in our evaluation of the situation in the Iron Curtain
countries, which he knows well. He regarded the question of possible

communization of young people in the countries of East Europe as the key. He asked me whom the Poles hate most—the Germans or the Russians? I said that the greater hatred for the Germans is fading gradually away into the past, while hatred for the Russians belongs to the present. But the situation may reverse under the influence of German arming and the making of revisionist claims to Poland's western territories. As to the communization of young people, I explained that in the events of Poznan and October, it was the young people who played the leading roles, which is the best proof that they have not undergone communization. Whereas the older generation betrays signs of resignation, the younger one, although educated in communist schools, rebels.

Our expatiations, connected with the main aim of the visit, were very affably received by Baig, and he promised to bring them to the attention of the President, General Mohammed Ayub Khan, who is at present making a tour of inspection of the country.

Istanbul, March 11th. I contacted former Polish Ambassador Sokolnicki from the Istanbul-Hilton hotel; he had already heard from the Ministry of Foreign Affairs that we were to be the guests during our visit of the Governor of the Ankara province who is also mayor of that city, Dielaver Argun. Three members of parliament, representatives of Turkey in the Council of Europe, who are also members of the Commission of this Council, appointed to safeguard the rights of Iron Curtain countries, Miss Nazli Tlabar, and Messrs Hamdi Bosbag and Basri Aktas will be expecting us in Ankara.

Ankara, March 13th. In the afternoon, accompanied by the MPs Bosbag and Aktas, we went to the Ministry of Foreign Affairs, where we were introduced to the Minister, Fatin Zorlu. As soon as we had exchanged the first courtesies, the Minister began to analyse the situation in Poland and Gomulka's policy, went on to discuss Hungary and expatiated his views on the tasks and activities of the emigrations from countries behind the Iron Curtain. We listened, pleasantly surprised by his knowledge of the subject, and the concord between the Minister's views and our own. During the talk the familiar note sounded of, 'We are not afraid for Poland and Poles,' said the Minister. 'You have been in worse situations and come out of them successfully. But other nations?' and he spread his arms in a gesture of helplessness. At the end we heard a concrete promise : 'I will do all in my power to have the cause of your countries brought up during possible negotiations with the Soviet Union, and in the way you suggest.'

In the evening there was a reception for some dozens of people in the apartment of the Ambassador and Mrs Sokolnicki, which is full of valuable relics. The ambassador showed me first of all, with the pride of a collector, a fine contemporary portrait of Kosciuszko, and among his books was a first edition of *Pan Tadeusz* and Kipling. Among those present were a number of eminent personalities, such as Tevfik Biuykoglu, former Turkish ambassador in Moscow, Georges Pesmazoglu, the Greek ambassador, Luis Norton de Mattos, the Portuguese ambassador, Vincent Coelho, the Indian *chargé d'affaires,* Count Gerard de la Batut, secretary of the French Embassy, Walter Harris Jr., secretary of the American embassy, Colonel Halford R. Greelee Jr., military attaché of the United States, Turkish MPs and a number of other personalities.

During the reception a man of medium height and greying hair approached me and started a conversation in Polish, asking about the course of our journey and the reception we received in various countries. I willingly provided my compatriot with the information, and he started to talk about current problems of Central and Eastern Europe, showing a profound knowledge of them. During the exchange of views, as is usual between exiled compatriots, I asked him when he left Poland. He looked at me with some surprise and replied : 'I have not lived in Poland for many years.' 'So you belong to the local old Polonia colony?' I then asked. My question apparently amused him, for he smiled and said : 'I see you take me for a Pole; yet I am a Norwegian.' It was now my turn to be surprised. 'A Norwegian speaking Polish like a born Pole? Where did you learn our language so well?' 'My mother was Polish and I graduated from the Rej Gymnasium in Warsaw.' I persisted with questions, as I wanted to get to the bottom of this. 'And what are you doing in Ankara?' The reply was somewhat unusual. 'My name is Ivar Lunde and I am the Norwegian ambassador in Ankara.' When after a time another guest spoke to me in Polish I was more careful, and rightly, as this time he was a Tartar, a university professor in Ankara Dr Akdes Nimet Kurat, who studied in Poland and speaks Polish fluently.

Towards the end of the reception a young man approached me, speaking in Turkish to Bosbag at his side, and again I heard Polish spoken. This time however I felt on safer ground and started talking with the enthusiastic claim that it is pleasant that so many Turks speak Polish. The young man looked at me and asked, 'How do you know I am a Turk?' My heart sank. This must be my evening for misunderstandings. But I had to get out of it somehow, so I said : 'I heard you talking to Bosbag in Turkish and as fluently as he does.'

The young man then politely explained : 'I was born in Turkey and am a Turkish citizen, but I come from the Turkish-Polish village of Adampol; my name is Erwin Ryzy and I broadcast from Radio Ankara to Poland in Polish. I must leave this reception now in order to broadcast a report to Poland on your visit to Ankara.'

For the rest of the evening I did not ask anyone where they came from, even the Hindu *chargé d'affaires*. I was afraid.

Ankara-Istanbul, March 14th. After returning to Istanbul, we attended a press conference in the Hilton Hotel; there were about a dozen reporters, including a celebrity in the person of Emin Ahmet Yalman of the *Vatan* newspaper. Before the conference began, he managed to tell us something of the vexing control of the press carried out not by special officials for the purpose, but basically by public prosecutors. This same complaint came from another reporter. When I opened the conference, the first question asked me started with the statement that on every other page of the history of Turkey, Poland is referred to and that in frequent battles together, the Turks acquired great respect for the Poles. This at once gave the conference a cordial tone and soon it changed into a friendly conversation.

We were joined by Kovago, who had spent about two weeks in New Delhi where he had had a number of interesting talks with Indian leaders, including Prime Minister Nehru, the Minister for External Affairs, S. Dutt, and the leaders of the socialist opposition. Both the Prime Minister and his Minister for External Affairs voiced the opinion that only a decrease in international tension and the liquidation of the cold war can bring an improvement in the fate of the nations of Eastern Europe. Expounding this theory to the extreme of logic, they were of the opinion that all discussions of the Hungarian question in UNO and the refusal to accept the credentials of the Hungarian communist delegation to this body are elements of the cold war and harm the Hungarian nation, which was provoked into rebellion by Western propaganda. Nehru explained the armed intervention of the Soviet Union in Hungary by its conviction that the Franco-British attack on Suez and the attack of the Israeli army on Egypt meant the start of the third world war, in view of which Russia could not permit a hostile state to emerge by its side. In Nehru's opinion, only Chou En-lai and China understood the unfavourable results which arose for Communism as a result of the Soviet intervention and they were very alarmed by it.

Neither Nehru nor Dutt were moved by Kovago's arguments that only the Soviet Union can liquidate the cold war by stopping its aggressive policy, including the withdrawal of troops from Hungary; that as one who took part in the uprising he could assure the Prime Minister that it broke out spontaneously; that the announcement of the neutrality of Hungary ensured against the country's joining the camp hostile to the Soviet Union; and that only constant references to the Hungarian cause in UNO would restrain the Soviet Union's application of terror. Despite all the sympathy both had for the difficult experiences of Hungary, Kovago left the audience in the Prime Minister's home empty-handed.

Athens, March 17th. In the morning I called Prince Pawel Sapieha, who is so like his late-lamented uncle that every time I see him I involuntarily look for the cardinal's ring on his finger. With his help our delegation managed to meet the secretary-general of the Ministry of Foreign Affairs, Economon Gouras. A lively elderly man with the habit of interrupting with questions directed at the heart of the matter, who devoted an hour of the time meant for welcoming the national hero Grivas, in order to receive us. He listened, like everyone hitherto, with much sympathy and understanding and promised to refer our views to the Minister of Foreign Affairs, who is busy with today's celebrations, and even mentioned the possibility of the Greek government taking the initiative; but he did not conceal his pessimism as to the results. 'I know the communists from close to. In 1944 I found myself in a part of Athens controlled by them and it was with great difficulty and danger that I got to the free districts. In 1947-49 we fought them along the northern frontier. Resolutions and protests will not wrest from the Communists what they have swallowed.'

On leaving we found ourselves at once in a dense, excited crowd. I left my companions, as I had decided not to let slip the chance of seeing the return of a national hero. After all, I was in the place where this very day the last act of the Greek tragedy entitled 'Revolt in Cyprus' was to be played out. The analogy with our underground fight was too close to pass by this event indifferently. The sympathies of a Pole who was also in the wartime underground, will always be on the side of people fighting in such a situation. The British may look at it differently but this world is so stupidly constructed that a man who is a hero to one nation may be a criminal to another, and often both sides are right.

Rome, March 19th. Today our activities began at 6 p.m. for it is a holiday, so it was one chance to go with Zahorski to Monte Cassino. As we drew nearer to Monte Cassino, the mountains come up to the railway line, and finally on one of them I recognized in the distance the memorial to the Border Division, familiar from illustrations.

Going on foot from the station to the town I had to stop several times to feed my gaze on the monastery, gleaming on the hillside with the white of its new walls. So it was here that a thousand Polish soldiers died on the way, as our national anthem says, 'from Italian land to Polish', which was for them the way to the grave and for the rest, the road to nowhere. So it was of the 'red poppies' on this hill that occupied Warsaw had sung in the countless bars, drinking hooch mixed with tears. It was of this hill that the young people of the Home Army had dreamed and sung as they prepared for the insurrection which a few months later was to change the capital into Monte Cassino ruins and bury these young people in the insurrectionists' cemetery. But the rebuilt monastery was smiling at the world with new walls, while Warsaw will for many years have to cure her mutilated limbs and bring up successors for those in the Home Army cemetery at Powazki.

In the brand-new little town, entirely rebuilt from the wartime ruins, we drank good coffee and after hiring a taxi drove up the winding road to the monastery.

In the cemetery near by I strolled from grave to grave, reading the names. On some were dry flowers and wreaths, proof of the memory of family or comrades in arms. Most of the names had a borderland sound, many were Byelorussian or Ukrainian of Orthodox faith, and eighteen were Jewish. The latter, as is known, might have stayed in Palestine like many others. However, they chose a different road, preserving to the end their loyalty to the country in which they were born and which they regarded as their homeland. I would send every Polish anti-semite to this cemetery. It might teach them something.

On leaving I noted a red and white flag, trampled in the mud. I picked it up and read the words 'To the heroes of Monte Cassino. Polish Peoples' Republic.' So here too is a duel with flags, not only at the Pulaski monument in Washington. I put the flag on the little wall. Despite all, it was not red but red and white.

We drove high up to the memorial of the Border Division, and here Zahorski, himself a former soldier of the Second Corps, gave me a review of the course of the battle. His hand pointed here and there as he spoke. 'The Americans attacked from that side, the British over there. There the Indians went and there the New Zealanders. Here the French fought and the Gurkhas. . . . Here two companies of Maoris perished, and there the Indian brigade was wiped out. . . .

Here the Gurkhas were cut down by machine-gun fire, and there a British battalion was hurled back. Here they decimated an American division from Texas and there a brigade of the Free French. . . .'

The litany of defeat and death went on without end and I eyed the steep stony unassailable hillsides, where thousands of Poles fought for several days and nights with indescribable heroism, in a storm of fire and steel, for every rock, shrub and foot of earth, and only one question came to me : 'Was it necessary? Was the capture of the monastery at the high cost of killing thousands of Poles necessary?' I was reminded of the tale of one who took part. When his commanding officer appealed to the soldiers, 'That monastery must be taken at any price,' a timid voice was heard in the silent ranks, 'Couldn't it be cheaper?' A grain of truth was concealed in this witticism. Why did they not attack from below, along the flat valley, which was as plain as a pikestaff? Perhaps it really could have proved cheaper?

Zahorski, excited, his hair tossed by the wind, looking tragic against the background of the huge memorial cross, went on : 'our tanks came that way, and the Carpathian division that way . . . here the Border Division attacked, here the Commandos. . . . This is called "Spectre" and over there is the Sappers' Road. . . . Here Colonel Kurek was killed, and there Major Rojek.' Suddenly before my eyes I saw Colonel Radoslaw, guiding me in 1945 round the cemetery of the insurrectionists in Powazki in Warsaw and showing the site where his soldiers were buried. The same gestures and words, though different names. Too many events have left cemeteries behind them, and too few living memorials.

Everything was as plain as a pikestaff, but did not supply an answer to the basic question. The Poles did not attack straight up the monastery hill, on which their many-tongues predecessors had burned their fingers, but had deeply flanked it. But why had they not attacked along the valley, on the Liva river? I put this question to Zahorski. 'Because,' he replied, 'as long as the monastery which dominates the valley was in German hands, well armed and firing, every attack in the valley was shattered by concentrated fire from the monastery and the neighbouring hills.'

And the Poles seized Monte Cassino, opening up the one road to Rome for the allies, as 100 years earlier Kozietulski, having with his cavalrymen captured the Samosierra ravine, opened up the one road into the depths of Spain for the army of Napoleon.

On the way back, the driver gabbled something fast in Italian, and called forth a smile on the face of my companion, who turned to me. 'He says he was captured by Poles near Tobruk. He says they are good people. They treated him decently, gave him food, water and cigarettes.'

In the little town we went to lunch with the president of the local Italian ex-combatants. He complained about the destruction of the cemetery. 'We'd gladly help, but we have no funds. Without money nothing can be done.'

In the evening we attended a dinner arranged by the representation of ACEN in Italy, with Ambassador Papée, the Czech Vanek, chairman of this representation, an officer of the Albanian army Frasheri, with a lancer's manners, and some others, also present. To judge by the mounds of macaroni with greenish cheese which was devoured by our hosts, they have undergone marked 'italianization'.

March 20th. We drove in the car of Ambassador Papée, who accompanied us, into the circle of the famous colonnade which surrounds with its two arms the square in front of the Basilica of St Peter. On the way I did not look at the city because my eye was attracted by something else. Rome had a dangerous rival, which drew my attention from the streets and passers-by from the moment we left the hotel. It was a small banner, red and white in colour, waving on the front of the car. A small thing, yet very significant. At this moment these two colours, waving during the fast ride like wings in the wind, said that after all the Polish embassy at the Vatican still exists as a symbol of the struggle of the many thousands of Polish exiles for the genuine freedom and independence of their homeland.

We drove into the first gate, saluted by the guards in their black uniforms, then we crossed a series of others, guarded by Swiss sentries in colourful, striped uniforms. When we stopped in a small yard, scarlet colours appeared at the top of the steps and I recognized the familiar figure of the former Papal Nuncio in Washington, Cicognani, among the cardinals moving towards their cars.

I was struck by the fact that all the Vatican officials we passed on the way greeted Ambassador Papée very cordially. When I asked him about it, he replied with a smile : 'During the whole war I lived on the neutral territory of the Vatican City and hence everyone here knows me.'

At last we found ourselves face to face with the Secretary of State, Cardinal Tardini, who accepted our statement with attention and assured us of the sympathy and support for the cause of the nine countries.

Then we were led into the audience chamber, where we did

not wait long. The side door opened softly and the figure of John XXIII all in white, appeared in it, accompanied by the chamberlain and papal secretary. I became all eyes, gazing with emotion at the figure who was the object of adoration of millions of people, for whom he is the earthly representative of heavenly powers.

When the chamberlain who introduced me placed stress on the words 'a Pole', the Holy Father raised his eyes and hands and began speaking about Poland with great emotion. He spoke warmly and with much feeling about the sufferings, courage and endurance of the Polish people and their attachment to religion. The words, 'You have God in your souls' fixed themselves in my mind. During the talk which started, the Holy Father named, among other things, some places he knew in Poland, such as Warsaw, Cracow and Czestochowa, and after a little thought also Poznan and Gniezno. The Holy Father terminated the audience by an appeal for endurance, patience and courage.

We left the audience chamber with the impression of the simplicity, warmth and goodness which shine in each glance and gesture of the Holy Father. When I later asked experts in Vatican affairs of the meaning of the audience granted us by the head of the Catholic Church, the reply was, 'It must be regarded as a Papal blessing upon your Association and its activity.'

On March 24th I took off from Rome on the return journey. I landed in New York next morning, finishing the journey round the world in fifty-seven days, not counting one day lost in the Pacific, in the place where I started it. I called Washington at once from Ildewild airport, to Zosia. When I heard her voice in the receiver I felt back at home.

Summing up of the Journey. During the train journey to Washington I had time to draw up the first balance of the journey and its results. It was advantageous as far as figures are concerned. We visited 12 capitals and countries (also 4 on the way), we were received by 1 president, 1 vice-president, 3 prime ministers, 10 ministers of foreign affairs and 10 other sorts of high state dignitaries, 3 speakers of parliament and 9 mayors. We had talks with a few hundred leaders of political parties, military leaders, writers, presidents and professors of universities. We held 16 press conferences, of which the results were exactly 140 articles and press notices devoted to the problem of liberating the 9 countries behind the Iron Curtain and the journey of the ACEN delegation, not counting the émigré press in these countries. We took part in 3 TV programmes and 12 on the radio. We spoke at 18 public meetings and were guests at 22 breakfasts, lunches and dinners, given in honour of the delegation. During all these events problems connected with Soviet rule in the 9 countries and activities of ACEN were discussed.

We were received very cordially everywhere, mainly on account of the understanding and sympathy which exists for the fate of the hundred million people living in what were independent countries before the war and are now subjugated by Russia, and a certain feeling of solidarity and community of fate of nations fighting with Communism. However, other factors entered into the account. In countries of the yellow races, the fact also contributed that the three white visitors had come from the United States not to investigate, control or offer anything, but to ask for political and moral support for the cause of liberating the white population of East and Central Europe. In the past, representatives of the yellow race from the previous colonies had appealed to the whites for justice. In this case, the roles had been reversed. It was often apparent that this flattered our interlocutors and raised the temperature of receptions. Apart from this, in countries which had been former French or British colonies, or which during the war had been in the hands of the Japanese, our problems were much better understood and felt than in some of the countries of 'fraternal' Europe. The cause of this paradox was explained in more or less the same way everywhere : 'We ourselves lived for many years under foreign occupation, so we know well what it means.' Furthermore, our countries, their causes and we ourselves were something as exotic for our hosts as for example a South Vietnamese and his problems for a Pole. Their attitude to Russia was much as ours to mainland China. For us, China was an ally of the main enemy, Russia; for a South Vietnamese the reverse applied—Russia was the ally of the main enemy, China. The change did not begin till Pakistan, which felt itself threatened by both China and Russia.

As far as the reactions to the main problem of the liberation of the nine countries is concerned, in general everyone who appreciated our arguments recognized as real and useful our idea of keeping alive the problem of the liberation of East and Central Europe as an international problem which awaits settlement. Reminding the public opinion of the world that this matter is still open will prevent it from becoming an internal issue of the Soviet imperium, as the Russians regard it when they use the argument of 'not interfering with the internal affairs of other states' and demand the recognition of the present *status quo*.

We also found agreement with our opinion that the problem of liberation ought to be raised by the representatives of the free world at every conference with the Soviets devoted to international affairs. If the Soviets refuse to discuss it, which is to be expected, then at any rate it will be a clear indication that the Western world does not agree with the present state of affairs in Eastern and Central Europe and will serve the first aim, which is keeping the cause alive as an international problem.

Also the idea of raising the matter at UNO meetings was regarded as appropriate despite the fact that scepticism was expressed as to whether the Soviets would conform, for example, to resolutions of the General Assembly calling upon them to withdraw Russian troops and agents from the nine countries to enable the populations to hold free elections under international control. However, discussion itself on this subject and the possible resolution would amount to condemnation by the most respectable and influential international organization of the rule of the Soviets over the nine countries and would have great political and moral meaning. We were promised support by the appropriate delegations to UNO when debates on the subject arise, while the opinion was generally expressed that the initiative for bringing our cause into UNO should be taken by the United States.

During the talks it was possible to note a difference in approaching the causes of Hungary and Poland. The first was regarded as lost and aroused more sympathy than interest. The Hungarians had entered upon an uprising in 1956 and lost, which finally buried all the possibilities of armed action against the Soviets behind the Iron Curtain, on account of the passive behaviour of the Western world. On the other hand, everyone was still interested in the Polish experiment and its further development. Poles took a different way from the Hungarians, since by means of political pressure, without the use of arms, they had won a certain amount of freedom. Admittedly, the situation had grown much worse since October 1956; however, of all the satellite states Poland preserved the greatest degree of independence and freedom. The stabilization of this gain at a certain level will, in the opinion of our interlocutors, give the reply to the important question whether within the framework of the Soviet imperium individual nations can fight to obtain by their own efforts a certain amount of independence and freedom.

As for the observations and conclusions concerning the situation in the countries we visited, then with the reservation dictated by the fact that we only spent a few days in each country, primarily we were struck by the fact that the determination to fight against Communism and fear of it are in inverse proportion to the distance of a given country from the frontiers of Russia and China. Examples of this paradoxical theory are Korea, South Vietnam and especially, Turkey. If one is to seek the causes of this attitude, it is to be found in the history of these countries. For a Korean or Vietnamese, resistance against the Chinese threat has been an element of everyday life for hundreds of years. He is born with it and dies with it. This theory seems even more apt in Turkey where there is no trace of fear of Russia. Turkey has been faced with Russian imperialism for centuries and the Turkish people have had time to become used to it and evolve the best policy, which is resistance without considera- tion of risk.

As far as the essence of the struggle which is being conducted in the countries which we visited is concerned, then the average man in the West reasons that the democracies in the Far East are threatened by autocratic communism. This view is the more errone- ous in that there is no genuine democracy in these states yet. Admittedly they have adopted a democratic system but it is still in swaddling-clothes there. Japan, which was autocratically ruled before the war, is no exception to this. The same applies to the countries which were colonies before the war, ruled with a firm hand by colonial states. In these former colonies, within the frame- work of accepted democratic systems people rule with a stronger hand than a democratic system normally permits, e.g. Syngman Rhee, Marshal Chiang Kai-shek, President Diem, General Ayub Khan or Nehru. This is perhaps a necessary evil during a transition period in nations which are only on the threshold of a State life, are not politically educated but drunk with freshly acquired freedom. This prevents anarchy but it is not democracy, or at most merely an introduction to it. Many years will have to pass before these countries, after going through various kinds of internal convulsions, become genuine democracies, having their own political and moral strength, capable of rejecting all kinds of assaults upon it. All this on condition that a cataclysm does not break out in Asia and that it does not yield in the merciless and political war which Communism is waging against it.

As to the so-called 'policy of neutrality' to which India, Indonesia and other states of the Far East are tending, then in general this is explained by the fact that the newly emerged states in Asia are too absorbed in their internal difficulties, especially by the question of raising their very low standard of living, to be able to afford the luxury of joining with one or other side of the cold war which is now in progress. To this and other reasons it is necessary also to join the supplementary motive in which appears a certain kind of Asian solidarity: the main partners in the struggle are at present the United States, Britain and France on the one side, with Russia on the other. This is therefore a struggle between white people, victors in the last war, including two formerly colonial powers not popular in Asia. So let them fight it out among themselves until they finish each other off, for the yellow races can only benefit by this. They do not therefore have any reason for becoming involved in this fight on one side or the other. This is a theory like that of the Soviets at the beginning of World War II: let the capitalist world finish itself fighting together, and then Communism will win.

Previous thinking is based on the assumption that communist China will respect the neutrality of these states. Were this assumption to prove wrong, Asian solidarity and the motive dictated by it will undoubtedly disappear.

As regards Russian-Chinese disputes, one would have thought that China was too dependent on Russian machinery supplies for heavy industry, aircraft, transport vehicles and arms to be able to permit itself this. However, these differences must appear with increasing power as China becomes independent of these supplies. Then a struggle will start for the domination of Russia in Asia over the peoples of the yellow race and she will then have to give way to China, which will be stronger than she is, and this regardless of China's future system. Understanding is already growing that Russia is the greatest colonial state in Asia.

The admission of communist China to UNO, or recognition of its government by the United States, would be the beginning of the end of the independence of the Far Eastern states. A collapse would occur of those factors on which the independence of the young states is based and an internal coup by communists would only be a question of time.

In South Korea and Vietnam much interest was shown in the question of the unification of Germany. If the Western states and Russia succeed by means of negotiation in finding a method of uniting Germans living under different systems into one state—then this method might be used with success in Korea and Vietnam. But if the partition of Germany is consolidated in some way or other, hopes will collapse in Korea and Vietnam.

Politicians of the Far East are reacting to the question of the so-called 'strong and decided leadership' of the United States with double nervousness in comparison to Western politicians. The main reason of this is the cult of power and authority, inborn for centuries in the yellow man through the conditions in which they grew up, and the Asian concept of 'preserving face' so foreign to the Western world. Observing this or that move by the United States from a great distance, they simplify the situation, and each concession in favour of Russia is considered as a symptom of weakness. The principle that a really powerful country can afford certain concessions, as known in the Western world, is completely foreign to them. To their minds, only he who feels weak can make concessions.

It is commonly held that the best ally of Communism in the Far East is the poverty there, which must be seen to be fully appreciated. It brings dividends to Communism for the simple reason that the countries of the Far East have been living for several years under a theoretically democratic system, so that this system can easily be accused of failure to raise the standard of living as rapidly and effectively as the communist system. In view of this, far-sighted and effective economic aid by the West for the nations of Asia is the most urgent necessity. Aid given by the Soviets provides Russia with great propaganda successes, but may in the future strike it like a boomerang, since an increase in the standard of living, even brought about by communist aid, as a rule gives birth to strivings to satisfy further needs appropriate to human nature, such as the desire for personal liberty, respect for the rights of the individual, in a word everything which the communist system contradicts.

The most effective anti-communist campaign hitherto is the agricultural reform started by General MacArthur in Japan, which then spread into almost all the countries of the Far East. The liquidation of the feudal agricultural system, in which the land-owners mainly lived in the towns, taking from 50 to 70% of his crops from the tenant, created thousands of self-dependent peasant farms. The former tenants are at present contented proprietors of the land and will fight to the last any system which might want to deprive them of their property and drive them into communes or collective farms. In this way each peasant farm has become and is becoming an anti-communist fortress. On the other hand, the humanitarian treatment of landowners, who as a rule are paid compensation in the form of bonds, as for instance in Formosa, instead of turning them into disinherited beggars, has assured them a means of support. In the duel between communist collectivization and democratic agricultural reform, the latter has decided chances of winning.

An effective factor in the struggle with Communism is the millions of refugees from communist rule : up to three million in South Korea, one million in Vietnam, a million in Hong Kong, a few million in Formosa, a constant though at present weaker stream of refugees from communist China making for the free countries by even such roundabout ways as Burma and Thailand. They are spreading the truth about Communism among populations who have not come into contact with it in practice. But the reverse side of the medal is the vast number of those refugees, their temperamental instability on account of the temporary and irregular nature of their position. If permanent conditions of existence are not created for them, then ferment in the opposite direction will not be prevented. A refugee, if he is not given even a small part of what he dreamed of under communist government, will first be disappointed, then dissatisfied, and finally likely to regret his decision.

A separate problem is created in Pakistan by the ten million refugees from Kashmir and those in India who opted for Pakistan. The poverty prevailing among them is creating favourable conditions for communist propaganda. A similar position obtains in India. On the whole the problem of refugees in the countries of the Far East is many times greater than in Europe and is crying out for action on a huge scale.

In conclusion, the countries of the Far East which we visited may be saved for democracy and freedom on condition that the Western world with the United States in the forefront leads a decisive, powerful and uncompromising policy towards China and Russia and comes to the aid of these countries with economic, political and moral assistance.

XXI

AT EUROPE'S CROSSROADS

I was sitting in the visitors' gallery and observing the hall, listening attentively to the words which flowed in an incessant stream at the ceremonial session in Strasbourg of the Consultative Assembly of the Council of Europe on April 20, 1959, devoted to the tenth anniversary of the establishment of this body. In the armchair of the chairman, under a sculpture representing naked persons lying under a tree, with a guard of honour of two resplendent functionaries in tails at the side, was to be seen the massive form of the president of the Assembly, a Belgian, Ferdinand Dehousse, while the speakers were in turn such personalities as Lodovico Benvenuti, the secretary-general of the Council of Europe, Lord McNair, the chairman of the European Court for Human Rights, the former French Premier Robert Schuman, the chairman of the European Parliamentary Assembly, the Minister of Foreign Affairs of Austria, Leopold Figl, and the French president of the Council of Ministers, Michel Debré, also the chairman himself, Dehousse. The hall was packed, in the amphitheatre downstairs by members of the Assembly; in the galleries by the press and visitors, with a large proportion of unemployed, overdressed ladies and young girls, looking like schoolgirls from a monastic establishment who had played truant and, tired of wandering about the town, come to rest in the comfortable red leather chairs. Against the dark, ceremonial attire of the members of the Assembly, the colourful figure of a prelate stood out, in purple with a golden cross on his breast, and a man in the uniform of an admiral, with golden stripes on his sleeves reaching almost to his elbows. Amidst those sitting downstairs I caught sight of the familiar faces, recalling pleasant memories, of the Turkish delegates, the MPs Tlabar, Bozbag and Aktas. I saw also the chairman of the Interparliamentary Union, the Italian Codacci Pisanelli, whom I had met during my recent journey round the world, which I had interrupted a few weeks before in Rome. But another face attracted all my attention. Prince Otto von Bismarck, a German delegate, occupied a place in the first row, in the centre of the amphitheatre.

In appearance he did not recall his great-grandfather, the Iron Chancellor, who always appeared in contemporary portraits in uniform and even in the helmet and armour of the imperial cuirassiers. A calm man in civilian dress, he was a sign of the new times, sitting in Strasbourg which Bismarck had seized for the Emperors of Germany, in friendly agreement with the present possessors of this town and approving, as it were, by his presence the return of Alsace and Lorraine to the bosom of their homeland. But he forced one to think of that father of modern German imperialism, whose ideas had been so easily seized upon by Adolf Hitler, who tried to realize them. Now, however, he and the entire German delegation were concerned with peace, agreement and unity in Europe, at a time when the ashes of Hitler had been blown by the wind into all four corners of the world from the ruins of the Chancery in Berlin.

In the meantime, one speech followed another from the platform, full of elevated thoughts and phrases, and the hall listened motionless, except for the putting on or taking off of earphones as the French language from the platform changed into English or German. It was a solemn, anniversary session.

When it was over, I felt disappointed. Many fine and right thoughts had come from the platform; the delegates had praised in an appropriate manner the idea of European unity and had paid one another deserved compliments for calling this Council to life ten years earlier, but no one had mentioned the real creator of the unity of Western Europe : a man who by his deeds and words had most effectively convinced the nations of Europe that there was no time for differences and disputes and that in unity and common action was their salvation from undoubted doom. No one had uttered a word of thanks to the 'great builder' of this new Europe, Joseph Stalin. How ungrateful!

I had come to Strasbourg this year as chairman of ACEN to watch over the cause of the nine countries of which the Council of Europe, a creation of the European movement, had stated with regret when it was established that, since they are not represented in the Council, the places due to them will remain unoccupied till they become members of it. In the meantime, the safeguard of the rights of these peoples was in the hands of a special committee established for the purpose, the chairmen of which, from the time when ACEN was established, were in turn a Swede, Senator Carl Wistrand; a member of the Danish Parliament, Karl Bogholm; and a member of the House of Commons, Peter Kirk. ACEN had started co-operation with this committee as soon as it was created. It had taken such

forms among others as plenary sessions of ACEN, taking place with
the participation of a hundred and more delegates from America
and Europe once a year in Strasbourg, at the same time as the
deliberations of the Consultative Assembly. It became a custom
that the eminent members of the Assembly, such as for instance its
chairman Dehousse, attended sessions of ACEN at the Château du
Pourtalaise, near Strasbourg, so as by their presence and speaking
to manifest solidarity with the exile representations of the people
not represented in the Council. The regular guests and speakers
included among others the Dutch MP and socialist Goedhart, expert
on relations in East Europe; the French senator Pezet, very pessimistic in his prophecies; and the chairman of the foreign affairs
commission of the West German Parliament, Kiesinger, who gave
conciliatory assurances of the good will of Germany in relation to
Poland, without however eliciting any response from the Polish
delegation. Words were not able to erase the recent past so easily.

In this way ACEN symbolically filled the gap existing in the Council
as a result of the absence of representatives of the nine countries;
just as by its plenary sessions in New York, called at the same time
as the General Assembly of the United Nations and held in the
building of the Carnegie Endowment which is in the vicinity of
the UNO building, it tried to fill the gap in UNO brought about by
the fact that the communist delegations of the nine countries represent only the communist governments in it. In these plenary
sessions in Strasbourg there took part at various times, apart from
the Polish delegate from the United States, representatives of the
Polish emigration in England and France, including Ambassador
Edward Raczynski, Adam Ciolkosz, Zygmunt Zaremba, Minister
Jan Starzewski and Ambassador Kajetan Morawski, the last uniting
eminent diplomatic talents with great literary gifts.

In the further course of events, co-operation between ACEN and the
Council of Europe was formally legalized by the Consultative
Assembly which, after hearing on May 3, 1958, a report of a special
committee on the aims and activities of ACEN, passed a formal resolution that the special committee should maintain relations with
ACEN; in addition it advised its social and cultural committees to
devote benevolent attention to the activities of ACEN in these two
fields.

Among the more important declarations of the Consultative Assembly in the cause of the nine nations the resolution of October
25, 1956, should be distinguished; it was made under the influence
of events in Poland and Hungary, and expressed 'admiration and
sympathy for all those who at this time are suffering and dying in

Audience of ACEN General Committee with Secretary of State, John Foster Dulles. From left to right : Bessenyey/Hungary, Coste—Secretary General/Rumania, the author/Poland, Dr Masens/Latvia, John Foster Dulles—Secretary of State, Dimitrov/Bulgaria, Sidzikauskas/Lithuania, Vahter/Estonia, Visoianu/Romania, Dosti/Albania, Slavik/Czechoslovakia. See chapter : *John Foster Dulles and the Policy of Liberation*

Zosia broadcasting to Poland over the *Voice of America*. See
chapter : *This is Radio Free Europe*

order that the torch of freedom shall not be extinguished'. It was an introduction to the recommendation of the same day, addressed to the Committee of Ministers, in which the Assembly stated that '... the Western powers have the right to ask that the freedom of decision by the people, guaranteed by free elections, should be restored to them. Any other policy will inevitably lead to further insurrections which Soviet Russia will not always be able to drown in a bloodbath. The Assembly is of the opinion that full self-determination for these people can alone ensure a lasting peace in Central and Eastern Europe, and it is therefore desirable for the governments of Member States to uphold firmly this principle and to raise it at the meetings of the United Nations.'

In the resolution of December 15, 1956, the Assembly stated that 'All peace-loving peoples should support the right of the nations of Eastern Europe, like all other peoples, to choose their own freely-elected governments', while a resolution adopted at sessions on January 14-17, 1958, said that 'Free Europe cannot give final recognition to the *status quo* in Europe which would mean, among other things, the continued partition of Germany.... The West must be faithful to the principle that all peoples, including the nations of Eastern Europe, have the right to choose their own régime.'

In a unanimous recommendation to the Committee of Ministers of October 17, 1958;

The Assembly,

Noting the reports of its Committee on non-represented nations:
Considering that the continued enslavement of peoples of Central and Eastern Europe is of great concern to the free nations of the world;
Considering that the situation in a number of countries in Central and Eastern Europe constitutes a threat to world peace;
Believing that it is necessary that the position of democratic Europe should be emphasized frequently and clearly so that there may be no misunderstanding;
Recommends to the Committee of Ministers,
That the Member Governments of the Council of Europe should forthwith make a solemn declaration that free Europe reiterates that it has no desire and never has had any desire to impose upon the peoples of Eastern and Central Europe any political, cultural or economic system;
the only concern of democratic Europe is that the peoples of Eastern and Central Europe, and they alone, should have the right to decide what system they desire to live under, and that no obstacles should be placed in the way of these peoples reaching such a decision;

that other governments throughout the free world should be invited to adhere to this declaration.

In a recommendation made on September 15, 1959, to the Committee of Ministers :

> The Assembly ... recalling also that nine states of Eastern and Central Europe are still kept under Soviet domination without their people being permitted any expression of opinion; reaffirming the right of these people to decide their own destiny; recommend to the Committee of Ministers: that in any Western negotiations with the Soviet Union the rights and the interests of these peoples shall be considered;
>
> that no settlement of the European problem shall be regarded as final until the peoples of Eastern and Central Europe have had an opportunity to decide on their future through free elections.

Previously, after the common session of the ACEN delegation with the special committee at the proposal of the latter, the Consultative Assembly on the tenth anniversary of its existence, on April 23, 1959, again confirmed in its political resolution that 'the West cannot renounce their support of the aspirations of all the nations of Europe to independence and freedom.'

In these resolutions and recommendations a full reflection was found of all the demands of ACEN, i.e. recognition of the right of the nine nations to independence and free existence, the realization of this right by means of free elections, refusal to recognize the present *status quo*, the necessity of considering the case of the nine nations by the UN or perhaps by its body, the Security Council, and finally the need to take into consideration the rights and interests of the nine nations during any negotiations with the Soviet Union, viz., taking matters practically, at summit conferences.

During my stay in Strasbourg, as chairman of ACEN I sent a telegram to the American Secretary of State, Christian Herter, in connection with the approaching conference with the Soviet Union in Geneva, demanding that at this conference the question of the restoration to Eastern and Central Europe of their freedom and independence be raised, and warning him against recognizing the present *status quo*. The Secretary of State replied in a letter dated April 30, 1959, containing among other statements the following passage : 'You may rest assured that in our forthcoming negotiations at Geneva I will have very much in mind the principles set forth in your message.'

What benefit derived from all these declarations? Everyone knows that freedom will not be restored to the countries behind the Iron Curtain by means of statements and resolutions. Despite this, however, the condemnations and protests contained in them against the domination of Russia in countries which were independent before World War II constitute a moral and political foundation under any kind of future action having liberation as its aim. Political approval of Soviet annexations in East and Central Europe, whether openly expressed or implied by silence, would be a threat to such action and a new Teheran or Yalta squared.

The background to the annual sessions of ACEN was beautiful old Strasbourg, with its famous cathedral, the destination of my pilgrimages in free times, dominating the town, surrounded by the narrow, winding little streets of the medieval quarter, full of real treasures—well-preserved, age-old houses with sculptured façades. The past spoke in this town at every step, and its very name brought to mind the turbulent history of Europe.

The way back led me every year from Strasbourg to Paris, via localities with names familiar from World War I communiqués, with the immortal and so innocent-looking river Marne, winding in mild turns along the railroad track in the framework of green meadows.

In Polish Paris, there was a pleasant rite of meetings with Jerzy Giedroyc. I once visited the offices of the monthly journal *Kultura* at Maisons Lafitte. The villa in a backwater, a flood of books on shelves and tables, the tranquil hard-working figures of the editorial staff, all made the impression of a scholar's study rather than an editorial office, which for me must always be full of noise and running to and fro. Perhaps I hit upon a calm day, just after the issuing of a number.

Another time, Count Stefan Zamoyski conducted me round the Hotel Lambert and, viewing the venerable walls and interior, I gulped in something of the atmosphere left in this headquarters of the Great Emigration by eminent predecessors. It was a comfort to think that we were not the first to eat the bitter bread of exile, but perhaps we shall be the last.

The temperature of the impressions caused by the Hotel Lambert went up when, leaving the Seine Hotel in the rue de la Seine next day, I glanced at the wall opposite and discovered a tablet informing passers-by : 'In this house Adam Mickiewicz wrote *Pan Tadeusz*.' So it was along this same street and this same pavement that once the great Adam had paced, selecting rhymes most appropriately representing the charms of Lithuania, his homeland.

Each stay in Paris ended as a rule with more earthly meetings such as, for instance, that with Zygmunt Zaremba somewhere in the suburbs, in a little old house lost in a wild neglected garden, where underground times were remembered, mingled with émigré talk of politics. In addition, Mass in a Polish church with a pre-war friend, the painter Edmund Ernest-Kosmoski, whose wife Halina died as a courier in the underground; a hasty visit to the Soldiers' Home or Polish bookshop; an occasional lecture, and always a stroll round Saint Germain and vicinity. Nothing can be compared with the charm of nocturnal walks round Notre-Dame. Unless perhaps a stroll by moonlight round the Warsaw Old City.

XXII

JOHN FOSTER DULLES AND
THE POLICY OF LIBERATION

On January 9, 1956, the building of the State Department looked as usual. The same line of black limousines with the letters DPL at the rear, driving up under the outstretched canopy of the entry, from which emerged diplomats with various coloured skins, brief-cases in their hands, hurrying to a conference; the same polite, carefully dressed lady behind the little desk, giving precise information with a smile; the same shelves with publications of the department, which anyone may take home; and the same marble commemorative plate with the names of officials who died in carrying out their duties. We gathered in the hall, nine of us, each the representative of a country behind the Iron Curtain, and a few minutes later we were led into a huge office with the star-spangled banner in the corner behind a large desk and with portraits of severe-looking men on the walls, and were introduced by the official accompanying us to a tall, broad-shouldered man standing not far from the door, with a face known so well to each of us from photographs which appeared almost every day in the press.

The man led us to a long table, at the head of which he seated himself, and the conference of the ACEN delegation with John Foster Dulles started without any unnecessary delay.

The subjects had been divided between the nine of us, so while awaiting my turn I subjected the Secretary of State to precise observation. He aroused interest not so much by his dry face with the sharp, clear profile, from which calm attentive eyes looked out from behind glasses, or by the strong voice in which he asked for explanations, as by what he represented in American policy. After the so-called 'appeasement' period in relation to Russia, which did not however appease her; after the policy of containment of Communism represented in the government of President Truman by the Secretary of State Dean Acheson—which did not however contain it, since under its rule the communists seized China and in 1948 perpetrated a *coup d'état* in Czechoslovakia—Dulles in 1952 initiated a policy of defensive alliances, NATO, and the liberation of

197

the Iron Curtain countries by the use of peaceful means. This con-stitutes the most far-reaching American declaration, since it included the principle of not recognizing the *status quo* in Eastern Europe and brought back to life the right of self-determination of peoples, the father of which was President Wilson and his Fourteen Points. A certain branch of this policy of Dulles was the principle of 'massive retaliation', total revenge for a communist attack, announced in a speech before the National Security Council on January 12, 1954. I had in my pocket, just in case, a note with Dulles's statements on the subject of Eastern Europe, in which he had defined his new policy and in case of need I was ready to argue. These were the most important extracts from his statements :

In a speech before the Foreign Relations committee of the House of Representatives on February 26, 1953 :

> One, the United States does not countenance the violations by which Soviet leadership has perverted past agreements and under-standings into chains of bondage. That is a result which the American people never intended, and which they will never accept.
>
> Two, the United States will never be a party to any international 'deal' or 'trade' confirming the rule of Soviet despotism over the alien peoples it dominates in Europe and Asia.
>
> Three, the United States seeks, as one of its peaceful goals, that these enslaved national groups of Europe and Asia shall recover genuine independence.

In a speech of October 11, 1955 :

> There are some sceptics who seem to doubt that change can be brought about peacefully. History does not justify that conclusion. The recent liberation of Austria came about primarily because world opinion insistently demanded it as a step which represented elemental justice. In the same way world opinion will act as a compulsion of the Soviet Union to relax its grip upon East Germany and to permit the unification of Germany. And I also believe that world opinion will compel the restoration of national independence to the captive states of Eastern Europe.

His statement of December 31, 1955, said :

> The peaceful liberation of the captive peoples has been, is and until success is achieved will continue to be a major goal of United States foreign policy.

Each of us had in mind these declarations when by turn we pre-sented to the Secretary of State our views as to the realization of the policy of liberation. We put forward a few ideas of international action in this direction, as well as indicating ways of mobilizing world opinion to exert pressure on the Soviet Union. For my part, I additionally brought up the need for liberalizing the immigration law and admitting refugees from behind the Iron Curtain into the United States as fast as possible, particularly those in camps in Germany and Austria.

During a very sincere discussion which developed, the Secretary of State showed first of all a thorough knowledge of conditions in the Iron Curtain countries, the communist repatriation campaign and émigré problems. He spoke with feeling, like a man profoundly convinced of the rightness of views, and promised consideration and benevolent treatment of the views and proposals we put forward. The conference terminated with a photograph being taken of all and an official communiqué, issued by the head of the information service of the State Department, Lincoln White, confirming yet again the principles of American policy towards the countries of Eastern Europe in the following terms :

> At 3 p.m. today the Secretary received the General Committee of the Assembly of Captive European Nations for an informal exchange of views on the situation in Eastern Europe. The Secretary reiterated the White House statement of December 30th, that the peaceful liberation of the captive peoples is and, until success is achieved, continues to be a major goal of United States foreign policy. Secretary Dulles emphasized that the United States will accept no compromise with the Soviet Union which implies acquiescence in the subjugation of the satellites.

We left the conference with mixed feelings. On one hand we had received authoritative confirmation of the policy of Liberation, which had political as well as moral value and rejected all Soviet ruses aimed at the recognition by the United States that the problem of the Iron Curtain countries is settled and had become an internal issue of the Soviet empire. On the other hand, we had not obtained a promise that any international concrete action having as its aim the realization of the policy of liberation would be undertaken.

The visit to the Secretary of State obtained much publicity. The *New York Times* of January 11th devoted its editorial to it, expressing the positive character of the policy of liberation, and not only the negative refusal to recognize the *status quo*, and it was followed by the European press, such as *Figaro, Franc Tireur, Le Monde, Neue Zürcher Zeitung* and others. *Izvestia* of January 12th also reacted and showered us with compliments such as 'footmen, scum of the countries of people's democracy, traitors' and the like. 'Having heard his master's voice,' whined Zbigniew Mitzner in

Warsaw Life of January 29/30, 1956. I did not recall him very well, but Zosia helped :

'We were at a party in his house in Komorow. He played up to you a great deal then.'

Well, times have changed, so has the direction of playing up. After these statements came others. In a speech to the Council of World Affairs on October 27, 1956, Dulles stated :

> And let me make this clear, beyond a possibility of doubt. The United States has no ulterior purpose in desiring the indepence of the satellite countries. Our unadulterated wish is that these people, from whom so much of our own national life derives, should have sovereignty restored to them and that they should have governments of their own free choosing. We see them as friends and as part of a new and friendly and no longer divided Europe. We are confident that their independence, if promptly accorded, will contribute immensely to stabilize peace throughout all Europe, East and West.

During a press conference on December 2, 1956, the Secretary of State replied to a question by a reporter :

> Nations both in Asia and Europe remain forcibly divided; many peoples are subjected to a ruthless external rule which they deeply resent, and many live in fear under the shadow of a similar fate.
>
> Those nations and peoples, we believe, should be allowed their own free choice of government with no servitude to any other.
>
> The President and I feel that this situation ought increasingly to engage the attention of the United Nations in the discharge of its Charter mission to promote peace with justice.
>
> A particular responsibility, we believe, lies upon those members of the United Nations which, by adhering to the Atlantic Charter, pledged themselves to the principles of self-government for those who had been forcibly deprived of it.
>
> If you will go back to the events of 1952 that you allude to, I think that you will find that in all of the statements that were made on the subject of so-called liberation by President Eisenhower and by me, we constantly emphasized that liberation would have to be brought about as an evolutionary process, and we did not see how violent revolution would prevail. And I think it has been United States policy since this administration has been in office to adhere to that point of view, and the broadcasts and the like which have been made by the Voice of America have all adhered to that basic philosophy of an evolutionary process.
>
> Q : Mr Secretary, would it be correct to label the policy towards the possible liberation of communist satellites as one of containment?
>
> A : I wouldn't describe it so, no. In fact, the contrary. Containment implies that you accept Soviet rule over the satellites. We believe that that rule can and must be ended. But we believe that

the processes must be evolutionary primary processes and not violent revolution.

Secretary Dulles also made statements on the subject of the nine countries either directly or indirectly in the following declarations and speeches :

In the final communiqué of the Conference of NATO Foreign Ministers, in Paris, December 11-14, 1956, in which Dulles took part :

> The peoples of Eastern Europe should have the right to choose their own governments freely, unaffected by external pressure and the use or threat of force, and to decide for themselves the political and social order they prefer.

In a speech at the annual dinner given by the Associated Press on April 22, 1957, he said :

> Let us also make apparent to the Soviet rulers our real purpose. We condemn and oppose their imperialism. We seek the liberation of the captive nations. We seek this, however, not in order to en-circle Russia with hostile forces, but because peace is in jeopardy and freedom a word of mockery until the divided nations are re-united and captive nations are set free.

At a press conference of the Secretary of State on April 23, 1957 :

> We have constantly emphasized our view about the liberation of the satellites for a long time, and in any general review of our basic foreign policy consideration I think that would have to be included. You may recall that we have never, out of deference to Soviet feelings, hidden our views about that subject. President Eisenhower brought it up at the Summit Conference. That was a conference which was supposed to lead to the improvement of our relations. But we made it perfectly clear there—President Eisen-hower made it clear—that freedom of these captive nations was in our opinion essential, both from the standpoint of better relations between our two countries and from the standpoint of peace. And that theme has been repeated again and again. I don't think that the President has made any major speech on foreign policy since then when he hasn't brought the subject up. And, indeed, to make a review of our basic policy considerations and not to bring that up would itself be a significant step backwards.

In a memorandum of the three powers—the United States, Britain and France—on May 28, 1958 :

> The Western powers believe that a serious discussion of the problem posed by the existence of tensions in Eastern Europe should be held with the aim of eliminating interference in the internal affairs

G*

of the countries of that region and the use of force in the settlement of disputes there.

All these statements can be divided into three groups. The first, with the nature of declaration, contained condemnation of the infringement of treaties guaranteeing independence to the countries of Eastern Europe, promises not to enter into agreements recognizing the *status quo*, a negative attitude to the policy of containment and a pledge of liberating the countries behind the Iron Curtain by peaceful means. The second group spoke of means of obtaining the basic aim, i.e. liberation, stressing the duty of UNO to concern itself with this matter and the same duty of NATO, the need of influencing world opinion and the necessity of serious discussion on this matter between the powers. The third group of statements, made after the Poznan rebellion, 'Polish October' and the Hungarian insurrection, contained for the first time the insistence that liberation ought to come by means of peaceful evolution, not violent revolution, or in other words by means of self-liberation, and even suggested rendering neutral the countries liberated by renouncing alliances with them and the assurance that they would not surround Russia with hostile forces.

This was how the political declarations looked. However, they were not accompanied by any of the planned actions, since neither UNO nor NATO, nor any of the conferences between the great powers, officially brought upon the agenda of their meetings the problem of liberation; and if in general there was any mention of the countries behind the Iron Curtain, then it was only in the form of a declaration, as in February 1955 at Geneva, without placing before Russia the demand which was itself obvious, viz. the withdrawal of her troops and agents from the countries of Eastern Europe, in this way enabling them to hold free elections, possibly under international or UN control. Hungary was an exception, since towards the end of the Hungarian insurrection the UN passed two resolutions on November 4 and 9, 1956, consisting in sum of such demands. However, no definite action was then taken with the purpose of realizing these resolutions, nor were they extended to other countries of Eastern Europe.

From competent information obtained by the political emigrations concerning the reasons for which the attempts to execute the policy of liberation had not been undertaken, despite many statements of Secretary Dulles, it was possible to determine that this was due to the significant changes which had come about in international relations on almost the day after the proclamation of this doctrine. The growing atomic power of Russia, which carried out the first explosion of a hydrogen bomb on August 12, 1953, the communist victory in Indochina, the progress of neutralization in the world and the defeat of the European allies at Suez, changed the relation of forces and created new problems, which pushed the cause of Eastern Europe into the background and brought forward the Asian question. To this was added the reluctance of the allies of the United States to engage in the policy of liberation and the new symptoms of the policy of appeasement which appeared among them, long since abandoned by the United States. In the altered balance of power, dramatically stressed by the Soviet Union's launching on October 4, 1957, of the first satellite, and in view of the growing arrogance of the Soviet Union on the one hand and on the other of increased propaganda for peaceful co-existence, the chances of success for any action were too small to begin it. This also related to UNO, where the obtaining of the required majority of votes seemed, in spite of the speedy action in the Hungarian problem, more than doubtful.

At the same time, there could be no question of the renunciation of the policy of liberation because of the impossibility of carrying it out, since this would bring with it catastrophic moral and political effects for the countries behind the Iron Curtain. There was therefore no other way out but to stick to this doctrine and wait for possible changes in the world which would facilitate its realization.

The émigré representations organized in ACEN, and primarily Polish, did not agree with these views and evaluations, as they considered that even every rejection by the Soviet Union of Western initiative aimed at realizing the policy of liberation would serve to mobilize public opinion and organize moral pressure on the Soviet Union. Members of ACEN, including myself, also held that even in the event of not obtaining a majority in UNO, despite the many promises known to the State Department of support obtained during the journey of the ACEN delegations to South America and round the world, the fact that several dozen states would speak out in support of the Western demands would serve the same purpose, i.e. the mobilization of world public opinion. On this point American and émigré views diverged, and even the future will not be able to reply to the question as to which side was right. Undoubtedly, however, a side-product of this political situation is the fact of the categorical refusal by the United States to recognize the *status quo* in Eastern Europe, which is equivalent to rejecting the Soviet claims that all problems of countries behind the Iron Curtain are the internal issue of the communist empire, and that any mention of them is interference in the internal affairs of another country.

I re-digested these problems, sitting on May 27, 1959, on a church bench in the huge Washington Cathedral at a service for John Foster Dulles who had died three days earlier and whose coffin, on the catafalque in front of the altar covered with a star-spangled banner and surrounded by a guard of honour of all three armed services, drew to itself the looks and thoughts of those who had gathered at this sad ceremony. He died of cancer after a relatively short illness, during which he did not stop work, introducing into office with persistence worthy of admiration and self-sacrifice his successor, Christian A. Herter. Invited by the State Department to take part in the funeral ceremonies as chairman of ACEN, I found myself in the cathedral in unique surroundings. In an area of a few square metres of the severe Gothic nave were gathered the cream of the people ruling the Western world. Looking round at the faces known from hundreds of photographs, I could not resist the insistent thought that one small bomb could bring about a pretty good chaos in this world. Such things have happened, to recall only the explosion of a communist bomb in the Orthodox church in Sofia, at the solemn service in which the king and government took part, which killed several dozen persons.

In the row in front I caught sight of the round head and thin hair of General Eisenhower and the thick hair of Vice-President Nixon, sitting with their wives next to the widow in deep mourning and her children. To the right were visible the set features covered with wrinkles of Chancellor Adenauer, and next to him the sorrowful, thoughtful face of Mme Chiang Kai-shek. Round about was a pleiad of known names and figures. The massive Australian Prime Minister, Robert Menzies, who a few weeks earlier had received the ACEN delegation in Canberra, the new Secretary of State Herter, Ministers of Foreign Affairs of Great Britain, Selwyn Lloyd, of France, Maurice Couve de Murville, of West Germany, Heinrich von Brentano, of Austria, Leopold Figl, of Turkey, Fatin Rustu Zorlu, with whom I had spoken about Poland in Ankara, of Italy, Giuseppe Pella and many others. And as well as these the Secretary-General of UNO, Dag Hammarskjöld, the Secretary-General of NATO, Paul-Henri Spaak, judges of the supreme court, chiefs of staff of the army, navy and air force and the entire American government, the Department of State and foreign ambassadors en masse. Seeing amidst them one figure I sighed with relief. The bomb would not explode. A few dozen metres from me was sitting the Soviet Minister of Foreign Affairs, with a frozen motionless face, Andrei Gromyko, looking straight ahead, indifferent to what was happening around him; and behind him Ambassador Menshikov surrounded by his officials.

'Smiling Michael' was this time a precise copy of his superior Gromyko.

As I sat there looking round at those present, I listened to the prayers and tried to sing Protestant hymns announced loudly by a clergyman, following their text in a prayerbook found on the bench. They had an easy and melodious sound and surely my Catholic execution did not spoil the choir of harmonious voices, resounding from the arches of the cathedral. However I soon stopped. One can only pray in one's native tongue. Primarily however I thought about the dead man and whether the policy of liberation had not finally gone to the grave with him and what would the future of the world be like, ruled by the people sitting around, to whom even in this cathedral the cold and hostile face of Gromyko uttered a challenge. They seemed to have been turned out by one lathe in well-cut dark clothes, with the same inerasable stamp of the West on their intent serious faces. They were certainly thinking, as I was of the fate of a man who had led them for so many years and was suddenly absent.

I could not help glancing in the direction of the Soviet diplomats and making comparisons. Their calm faces, so different to my Slavic eye from the Western ones and also so familiar, even close, said nothing, but it was possible to make out that they felt not at home in this huge cathedral amidst people praying and the church hymns, at the funeral of this man, burdened a few days ago by them with the most serious charges and insults. In their clothes they did not differ in any way from their Western colleagues, but there was something indefinable in their appearance which gave the impression that every suit had been borrowed.

But the hymns sounded on. . . . The harmonious voices implored God for mercy and forgiveness for the soul of the dead man, for fraternity and love among people all over the world, for peace on earth and salvation in heaven. The song flowed in waves round the huge cathedral, rose up into the high arches and was reflected back to the praying people, among whom a group of silent Soviet diplomats attracted all looks, standing as if in a pillory, accused by every word and sound of the sung prayer.

After the service the funeral *cortège* drove to the cemetery in Arlington, where the remains of John Foster Dulles were placed to rest for ever on the hill with a view of the Potomac and of the Lincoln memorial on the other side of the river.

A few days later it appeared that one of my fears was half right. Nikita Khrushchev took advantage of the fact that the dead cannot defend themselves and announced *urbi et orbi* that in the last period of his life the late Secretary of State had resigned from his policy of liberation, and had informed Anastas Mikoyan, who was then in the United States, of this. This forced the State Department to issue a denial, which came from the Under-Secretary of State Andrew Berding, among others, speaking at the celebration of Freedom Day, July 1, 1959, before the Statue of Liberty in New York Bay. He then stated with great emphasis : 'In recent speeches Soviet Premier Khrushchev has taken advantage of the death of John Foster Dulles to claim that Mr Dulles had changed his policies in the last period of his life. . . . I categorically deny that John Foster Dulles had changed his thinking on these basic issues. He was as stalwart just before he died as he was in the full vigour of his career in maintaining . . . that the United States does not recognize the permanence of Soviet-imposed rule in Eastern Europe and instead will use all legitimate means to promote the independence of these peoples.'

Apart from the above, the term 'policy of liberation' slowly began to disappear from the political vocabulary, and is no longer in use. It was replaced by the non-recognition of the *status quo*, and putting double stress on the Wilson doctrine of self-determination, complemented by belief in gradual, evolutional liberation of the nations behind the Iron Curtain by their own efforts. In practice no difference arose, since the unrealized policy of liberation led in fact from the very beginning only to the non-recognition of the *status quo*, but left the rest to the subjugated nations themselves. Such was and is the 'real reality'.

Where are the causes of this passivity to be found? To penetrate to the very depths of the problem, it is found in the passive attitude to these matters adopted by the American people. In a system so profoundly democratic as the American, the policy is what the nation is, and the nation is what the citizens are. In the latter's character, way of thinking and psychology—in a word, his soul—is the answer to this question.

XXIII

WHERE THE HEART OF AMERICA BEATS

The international policy of the United States in general and in relation to Eastern Europe and Poland in particular is mainly shaped by the President with the help of the State Department, Congress and finally the American citizen. Between these factors close mutual interdependence and interaction exist. The staff of the White House carefully study the thousands of letters which arrive there daily, since the American citizen, if something moves him in the activity of the President, does not hesitate a moment but seizes a pen and writes directly to him without any formality. For a citizen to address a head of state in Europe is a rarity and as a rule it is a humble petition; while here it is an everyday practice, dictated by satisfaction or dissatisfaction with the President's policy. Between the American citizen and the President, who addresses him a dozen or so times a year directly through TV and radio, and indirectly almost every week through the press, with which periodical conferences take place in the White House, the distance is markedly less than that between the head of state and a citizen in Europe. After every such appearance by the President, the White House is flooded with letters, up to 5,000 daily, in which citizens adopt a position with regard to what the President said. With their voices each inhabitant of the White House reckons, and the opinion of a citizen exerts an influence on his policy. And press communiqués from the White House quite often state that in a given matter so many letters to the President were for and so many against. Similarly the American citizen practises writing letters on political matters to the Senator and Congressman of his State or electoral area, who place so much importance on them that either they reply personally or in their own, stencilled, periodical publications, the so-called 'News Letters'. The saying 'Write to your Senator or Congressman' is a common one and is heard at every step. On the other hand, the Senator's and Congressman's checking of the 'grass-root feeling' in their districts belongs to the daily duties of the American legislators. And the influence of the citizens, or more precisely of the voter, on his representatives in Congress is still greater than that on the President, who does not approach his post, in contrast to the politicians, as a profession but as a historic mission. The voter has in his hand a stick for each of them in the shape of a vote in the elections every two years to the House of Representatives, every six years to the Senate, and every four years for the President—not to mention the State elections for local authorities, the results of which are a forecast for the federal elections and are important to the parties to which these persons belong.

On the other hand what the President or Congress says and does, communicated to the citizen every half-hour by radio, a few times daily by TV and at least once a day by the press, acts upon the political outlook of the voter, informing him of political events, with the addition of a commentary, usually on a higher standard than his own logic. In this is the strength of this influence, despite the fact that in principle the American citizen does not have too high an opinion of politics and politicians and accepts sceptically what 'people up there in Washington' say. He tries to form his own judgement, which does not necessarily stand on a high level, but with which everyone must reckon. As far as concerns the influence of the churches, Wall Street, trade union, social and veterans' organizations, ethnic groups, and industrial, commercial or farmers' interests, these are only additional forms of shaping the judgement of the citizen, exercised by the groupings of people connected by mutual bonds of interest. In view of the absence of an official Government press the same applies to newspapers, TV and radio, which are in private hands, and which in addition play an intermediary role when they inform or as a catalyser when they comment on events and views of the three main factors creating American policy. The answer to the question of which influence dominates cannot be expressed in a definite formula. It depends on the time and conditions in which the country is. During a war the influence of the President and Congress may prevail, in peacetime it is certainly the citizen. In any case the United States with its system, liberty and political philosophy is without doubt the country in the world in which the citizen has the greatest influence on politics.

Who, therefore, is this citizen politically and how under these conditions of mutual interaction do his views look and on what are they founded?

First it is worth repeating the common cliché that the average European knows only the caricature of an American. He makes up this idea of him from what he reads in his homeland, as he sees him in the movies, or in the best case observing him in a European milieu which is foreign to an American, under special conditions, since he comes as a tourist, dressed with bad taste according to European standards, hung around with cameras and scattering dollars right and left. In order to know the American through and through he must be seen in his own country and at home. Here alone may an answer be found to the questions mentioned and then only if, when in search of it, history is also taken into consideration, such as the reasons which persuaded the first settlers in Jamestown in Virginia and the Pilgrim Fathers of the *Mayflower* to leave Europe and settle in America. All their declarations led to one conclusion : they sought in America better conditions for creating a materially high standard of living and a life free from the political, religious and economic oppression they had suffered in Europe. And when the rigours of British rule stood in the way to these aims, they rebelled against this obstacle and overturned it. And perhaps this was symbolic of the trend in which America was to go, that the spark which caused the outbreak was the setting by England of a higher tax on tea, a purely economic measure, not political. These two canons—prosperity and liberty—stood henceforth as the foundations on which the development of America and the philosophy of her citizens stands and this simple truth prevails to this day. They gave the United States wealth and liberty unknown to any other country.

The second canon on which the United States is based is the delightful freedom in every direction, primarily personal, of the citizen, the manifestations of which even shocked me in the first years of my stay. Three weeks after my flight from Poland I suddenly found myself in a country where millions of people from birth to death have no personal documents or passports, where there is no obligation to report on changing address, where no document is shown in a hotel and it is possible to rent a room under one's own or an adopted name and where, in case of special need, a driver's permit is enough for identification. Delight filled me to see that in this country people do not fear the police merely because they are police, while the FBI is surrounded by universal respect, and considered as something of a knightly order, fighting with crime and lawlessness. The head of this institution, Edgar Hoover, is the hero of young Americans, and the adventures of an FBI agent are the object of his dreams. The pen draws back before making a comparison with the Secret Police or NKVD. Here the President is spoken and written of by his first name, and the word 'constitution' is in common use by every man, who has such a relation to it as the Christian to the Ten Commandments. For the average American this is not a document which is operated only by politicians in Washington, since along with learning to read and write in school he obtains the knowledge that it is a collection of principles on which all his future life will depend. Between him and the constitution there is no distance and reference to the constitutional rights of a citizen belongs to the arsenal of arguments of which he knows and which he is accustomed to use in time of need. Here no one would understand the joking saying put by Wiech into the mouth of a merchant from Nalewki Street : 'Constitution? We don't keep that merchandise in the store. You'd better ask in the police commissariat.'

The exercise of justice based on the jury, and procedure weighed down by formality which defends the accused, make the profession of prosecutor the most ungrateful in the world and cause litigation, but the citizen does not come out of it badly. If one reads the reports of the sessions of the Supreme Court, then the predominant note of the cases and judgements is the defence of the constitutional rights of the individual. I had never been able to find justification in my own mind for the division of American armed forces into Army, Navy and Air Force, the result of which is internal rivalry unknown elsewhere in the world and the doubling of armaments and expenditure. Then an argument heard by chance enlightened me somewhat : it defends the citizen from a military dictatorship, whereas one general staff, and the institution of a supreme commander who is not also president, facilitate its establishment. The same aim is served by the religiously observed principle of the supremacy of civilian over military authority; the Secretaries of the Department of Defence and subordinate secretariats of the Army, Navy and Air Force are as a rule civilians. There is no place for military dictators in the United States.

The other side of this coin are the overgrowths of freedom that cause me in moments of irritation to ask myself whether the United States is organized anarchy or anarchized democracy. The names of eminent gangsters are no less well known than eminent senators, yet by the aid of fine lawyers and on the basis of liberal law they mock the administration of justice for whole years. Soon after I came to the United States there started in New York, under the presidency of Judge Harold Medina, the trial of eleven members of the central committee of the American Communist Party. Despite so grave a charge as trying to overthrow the system, they all attended court, coming and going in their cars accompanied by lawyers. During the trial they had unlimited opportunities of conspiring against the administration of justice, while they transformed the dock into a tribune for speeches. Judge Medina conducted the case with unusual control and calm, observing the rules of procedure strictly, and avoiding the traps and ambushes set by the lawyers allied with the defendants. Only on account of the frequent abuse of the Court by the defendants did he commit them on the spot to the punishment of imprisonment, but this happened outside the framework of the trial itself. It is not hard to imagine the effect this must have had on me, a man who only a few months earlier had been in a country where people were seized in the street and disappeared without trace, where not only the defendants but the witnesses were held in prison, which was in most cases the place where the communist court held its secret sessions and measured out punishment. I considered that this freedom was going too far and would become its own enemy. I wrung my hands and prophesied defeat for America. I also personally experienced the trial for espionage for the girl clerk of the Department of Justice, Judith Coplon, caught as she was handing a copy of a secret document of the Department of Justice to an official of the Soviet delegation to UNO, Valentin Gubichev. Because however they searched her handbag without obtaining a warrant to do so, Coplon, although the espionage was proved and sentence passed by the lower court, was freed from punishment in the Court of Appeals, married her lawyer, and still benefits in the United States from that unusual freedom for the destruction of which she worked so hard. Such de facto tolerance seemed suicide to me, in the period of a fight with Communism in which the very existence of the United States is engaged.

However, the climax is the abuses committed in connection with the fifth amendment to the Constitution of the United States. It entitles anyone to refuse to answer a question by the court if telling the truth might constitute evidence against the person questioned in the case which is going on. The use made outside court, and tolerated, of this basically correct principle—one known to the law and legal proceedings of Western European states—leads to cynical mockery, as of the inquiries of the Congressional committees. Cases have occurred of a person being asked by such a committee whether he belonged to the Communist Party, and refusing to answer, shielding himself by a formula based on the fifth amendment, despite the fact that a positive answer, in view of the legality of the Communist Party, does not bring with it punitive measures. The committee is powerless and the witness smiles triumphantly. He is acting within the interpretation of the Supreme Court of his constitutional rights. Coming out of such a session I admitted in a state of irritation that the famous columnist Joseph Alsop was right when he wrote in his column : 'God looks after children, drunkards and the United States'.

Otherwise it would be hard to explain the fact that this country not only exists but is developing wonderfully and the end of this development is not in sight.

To these conditions of high prosperity and freedom in which the American grew up must be added the complete security which the territory of the United States enjoyed in practice until the explosion of the first Soviet atomic bomb in September 1949. Up to that moment the American could afford life in comparative isolation from the disputes and anxieties of the rest of the world, thus confirming the correctness of the principle that one's own security always gives birth to the desire to isolate oneself from dangers threatening others. If he joined World Wars I and II, this was not because of an immediate threat to his territory but merely on account of interests or at most the possible future threat to his territory. And an existent and possible threat are two different things. Occupied with taking advantage of material goods and increasing them, also enjoying a free democratic system and peace in his country for a hundred years, he admired isolationism basically. The Monroe doctrine 'America for Americans' had its counterpart in the refusal to enter Wilson's creation, the League of Nations, since that meant permanently taking part in solving other people's problems. Recognition of this isolationism dictated to President Roosevelt after the outbreak of World War II the assurance given to American mothers that their sons would never be used to fight outside the territory of the United States, to which however he was unable to adhere. Towards the end of the war, the American government broke completely with the policy of isolationism and became the main promoter of the United Nations Organization, on which it has based its policies ever since. But the average American has not broken with isolationism in his thoughts and reactions, and to this must be imputed the violent, almost anarchistical demobilization of the American armed forces after the end of World War II in 1945, despite the fact that the first signs of the communist threat had already appeared on the horizon. The Army simply went on strike. 'The war is over and we want to go home to our families and own business.' And isolationism translated into the language of international politics means a lack of interest and indifferece. Its existence is confirmed by eminent American politicians such as Senator Kenneth B. Keating, who commented jokingly that 'an isolationist is a man who holds that most of our worries come from the fact that America was discovered by a foreigner'. And in every good joke there is a grain of truth.

Russia's failure to withdraw from the countries of Eastern Europe, the *coup d'état* in Czechoslovakia in 1948, the Berlin blockade, the refusal to unify Germany, the seizure of China by the communists, the Korean war, the production by Russia of hydrogen and atom bombs and inter-continental rockets directly threatening the security of the terriroty of the United States, finally the launching of the Sputnik—all this has happened over a period of barely fifteen years, which is more than enough for changing the orientation of the political summits or Congress, the Cabinet and President, but is still too short a time to change the ways of a nation of about two hundred millions. Anyhow, even on the summits voices have been heard for the defence of the American continent and leaving the rest of the world to its fate, which is a sort of neo-isolationism. All these events have already aroused the American people, who are beginning to rub their eyes and wake from the sleep into which a hundred years' feelings of complete security had lulled them. The process of re-orientation has already started but, unless some shock of the dimensions of Pearl Harbor occurs, it may yet last many years. For the first time the American has felt threatened in his own country and this feeling aroused in him a new direction of thought, which however is still in swaddling-clothes. Despite all, Soviet troops are not yet on the frontier of the United States as they are on the Turkish, Swedish or West German borders, and there are rockets for rockets. For an inhabitant of a country behind the Iron Curtain, relations with Soviet Russia decide his everyday life and every fluctuation of them is felt on his own skin and at every step. Political understanding does not replace this for the inhabitant of the United States. It is emerging only slowly from out-of-date ideas of distance and time. In view of this, the threat of Russia and Communism seem to him, despite all he knows, quite far off from his house. To know something from newspapers, radio and TV, and to feel it on one's own skin, are two different things, causing different human reactions. The atom bomb has one eloquence for the Japanese and another for countries which have not known its effects. In a word, the American has not yet become accustomed to and familiarized himself with the new situation caused by the immediate threat to America, and much water will flow under the bridges before he matures to this. Possibly not till the next generation? He has passed through only the first shock, to which he reacted so nervously as to be almost hysterical.

All this acts as a brake on American policy and is responsible for its defensive attitude, securing the United States against danger but not liquidating it. For the government can only afford a political offensive accompanied by a certain risk when the population have matured to it. Under the American political system, this policy cannot be imposed upon the nation; it can only be advocated. In consequence people have been talking about an offensive policy for years, but no one has initiated it.

On the way to this maturity the American must still overcome an additional resistence, which is the side-product of isolationism. It is a reluctance to interfere in the matters of other nations, even if their policy arouses condemnation. Thus there is no sign in the United States of a desire for a crusade against Communism as such; and, if Russia had not tried to export it and force it on the rest of the world, she would have been left alone. The transfer to offensive thinking is still rendered difficult by the fact that from childhood the American is brought up to the doctrine of peaceful co-existence with others, whereas for example the Russian is brought up to the doctrine of essential and unavoidable showdown with the capitalist world. Khrushchev can talk about peaceful co-existence but in the communist schools they still teach Communism according to Lenin, not Khrushchev. Anyway, as he himself explained, his peaceful co-existence policy is only a masked form of this merciless struggle.

The process of re-orientation will also be delayed by the fact that the American people, apart from preserving peace, do not have any other international ambitions. The leadership of the free world was forced on them, and roles forced on one are not played well. They have no territorial ambitions, the realization of which from the very nature of things would demand an offensive and aggressive policy. Apart from this, prosperity and security make the strongest feelings sterile, although they facilitate humanitarian ones. A hungry nation desires and hates more strongly than a well-fed one. In the latter, wealth develops purely human feelings, a proof of which is the confidence with which in principle an American approaches another man, the politeness, kindness and simplicity in human relations and the directness, devoid of stiffness and formality. One of the commonest questions is 'What can I do for you?' and use of the first name is a common thing and need not be preceded by the ceremonious drinking of *Brüderschaft* and the exchange of embraces. This also encourages generous contributions for charitable purposes even on an international scale, but does not constitute a basis for offensive policies. From the time when the Civil War ended, the American people have not been through any hardships on a national scale, caused by defeats in their own country. The economic depression of the thirties must not be counted to this category. The losses in people in World Wars I and II and the Korean war caused suffering to American mothers, but only to one in a thousand. America herself did not feel any of the blows which afflicted bombarded England or France, not to mention Poland. The lack of this kind of experience has softened the national spirit and not deepened either patriotism or general understanding of such questions as war and danger. The vast majority of the American nation knows war only by hearsay, from theory, not from its own experiences. In view of this, America is worse prepared psychologically for war in their own country than e.g. the British and Russians. Perhaps the only consolation is that by not knowing war in their own country, they fear it less than those nations who have experienced its horrors. An American considers his service in the army as a job and duty, though they fight very bravely when necessary, and the army is neither the object of a cult nor an élite organization of the pre-war Polish type. Two world wars were required to change the attitude to military service from the contemptuous to a positive one.

In this blend of various factors, not everything that comes from Washington through the newspapers, TV and radio can be regarded as a confession of faith by the average American, who some decades ago still considered the government as a necessary evil, the leaders in Washington as jugglers, and the paying of taxes as his sole obligation towards the State, the carrying out of which frees him from others. His patriotism has no trace of such exaltation as the Polish. Its one easily visible sign is the calm emotion with which the American sings his national anthem and the cult of the Star-Spangled Banner hanging almost everywhere and on every occasion. Is he in the depths of his soul a nationalist? Yes and no, since like the Jews he considers himself on one side as the first nation in the world and on the other he suffers from an inferiority complex towards refined Europeans. The percentage of interest which he devotes to matters of international politics is minimal. The Joint Commission for Investigating Mental Illness and Health (*sic*) announced the results of its inquiries in 1960 and according to them only 13% of the Americans were worried by the international situation : those who enjoyed it were not found by the commission, fortunately. The rest—87%—were a sort of 'inner emigration', on the re-orientation and greater engagement of whom in the fight for the existence of America its leaders are working. But until the re-orientation is completed, American policy will not be able to take the offensive on a world scale, connected as a rule with greater risk than a defensive policy. Much is said and written about the fact that the spending of only 10% of the national income on the defence of America is too small. This must be agreed to without reservation. But the essence of the problem lies in increasing the nation's interest and devotion, not its expenditure. However, the question is whether Russia will leave the United States enough time to carry all this out? This is where the heart of the matter lies.

In a period when profound changes are taking place in the relation to the rest of the world and in the limits of interest which is only just growing, the question of Eastern Europe does not occupy the main place in the views of an American. Events on a larger scale veil it, having more importance for the security and future of America. Whereas the defence lines in Europe are more or less stabilized, today his uneasy eye turns towards Asia and Africa, where the communist victory in China and universally prevailing neutralism are creating gaps in the defence line. Interest in Eastern Europe and Germany is less than fifteen years old, and leads in the thoughts of the average citizen to sympathy for the occupied nations and a wish to assist them, but without any risk. So he willingly protests on every occasion against the Soviet occupation in the Iron Curtain countries, manifesting his compassion for them, and is sincerely indignant at the cynical lawlessness perpetrated on them by the Soviet Union. However, he does not believe in the possibility of liberating them without war and for him the cause of restoring freedom to the nations of Eastern Europe is more a moral question —the infringement of basic human rights—than political.

Exceptions to this rule are created by the Americans of the first or second generations from countries of Eastern and Central Europe, also from the non-Russian countries in the Soviet Union, with the numerous and active Ukrainian emigration in the forefront. These groups are much more mature politically and have amidst them many supporters of a global offensive policy, despite the fact that their interests are primarily concentrated on the countries they come from, and not Asia or Africa. They represent a programme of liberating these countries from Soviet rule by means of concrete action, which in the case of nations incorporated by the Soviet Union leads to a policy of dismembering the Soviet empire and recognizing the right of each member of it to self-determination of its fate and full independence. This is opposed by the anti-communist Russian emigration of the post-Revolutionary period, who put forward instead a programme of federating these nations after liquidating the communist system. These proposals are rejected primarily by the Ukrainian emigration and I was myself witness of an incident which occurred at a meeting of several thousand in New York, when former Premier Kerensky referred to such a federation. A crowd of Ukrainians present in the hall created a din and cries were heard : 'We do not want any federation with Russia! We know how this federation would look! We demand completely independent Ukraine!'

Kerensky did not have a lucky day, for when he came to describe the methods the Bolsheviks used to overthrow his government, a tall man in the front row got up and shouted in Russian : 'And you are responsible for their winning because you did not oppose them properly!'

At the head of the political action intended to liberate the countries of Eastern Europe and Poland in the first place, are the American citizens of Polish origin, dominating in number and activity. All in all, however, fifteen millions or so of so-called American ethnic groups, mostly living in their own communities and constituting a comparatively fresh position in national life, are not in a position to inject their views in the whole society; although it is much more than a drop in the American ocean, it is not enough to change the course of national thinking.

Having formed for myself such a picture of an American, I decided to penetrate to the very essence of the matter and survey the earthly embodiment of these freedoms, which had made him what he is. The journey did not last long, since it was only from home on Tunlaw Road to the building of the State Archives on Constitution Avenue. There, along with a crowd of suddenly quiet and serious tourists, I stood in the marble, circular sanctuary-hall in front of something like an altar where, illuminated by the discreet light of invisible lamps, are exposed to public view three original documents which constitute the foundation on which the United States are built. They are : the Declaration of Independence, the Constitution of the United States and the Bill of Rights. To the side of the 'altar' stand two armed guards, who did not let us out of their sight. They guard the documents for twenty-four hours a day. In the case of the slightest suspicion that something may threaten them, either from the tourists or elsewhere, the guard presses a button and the glass cases with the documents disappear like lightning into a cellar of cement and steel, situated twenty feet under the 'altar'. The distance between it and the cellar is filled by a steel-cement plate which even a hydrogen bomb is not able to destroy. The pressing of the button also closes the two bronze doors to the building, each weighing $6\frac{1}{2}$ tons and 11 inches thick.

The mood among the tourists was like that of a church. They

fastened their eyes as if hypnotized on the national relics, yellowing pages written in a fancy but already faded handwriting and only in a tense whisper do they read out the sacred texts. I followed their example and as my eyes went over the written pages, I recalled the familiar words quoted here at every step. They left nothing to be wished, either when they were born, or at present in the atomic age. Not a line has gone out of date, not one idea lost its relevance. They were not written by rulers for their subjects, or by tyrants for slaves, but by people for people, and written not for a year or for ten years, but for hundreds. In this place and at this time, I found a reply to the question where the heart of the United States beats.

In every country it beats in the place which is a synthesis of the national being, where the hidden note is most strongly and loudly heard in its citizens. In Poland it beat for me before the war at the grave of the Unknown Soldier, that symbol of the thousand years' history of bloody battles in defence of the national existence, and after the war it beat in the underground, an invisible pulse in every stone and brick of the Warsaw ruins. Here in this happy country which has not known war on its own territory for a hundred years, it began to beat in Philadelphia, in Independence Hall, on July 4, 1776, but at present it does not beat in that place nor on any grave or battlefield. It beats with a strong regular beat amidst the columns and banners of the national sanctuary in the centre of the capital and resounds with a hundred-fold echo in the nearby Capitol, the earthly embodiment of the commandments enclosed in the national relics reposing there.

When I left the marble hall, it occurred to me to wonder where is the manuscript of Karl Marx's *Capital,* for in the last resort the fight is going on between his manifesto and the profession of faith contained in the documents on Constitution Avenue. I was unable to find an answer, but it was replaced by the picture of the mausoleum on Red Square in Moscow, where not the work of Marx but the embalmed body of his 'apostle' symbolizes the world hostile to that which is personified by the documents on show in Washington. And as in the Basilica of St Peter, the question came to me : Who will win? If truth and justice ensured victory, the reply would be easy. As however it is not always so, the solution must be waited for. The relics in the treasury, well guarded against accidents and time on Constitution Avenue, will live to see it, but not I and my generation. I shall not complain of this, since my attitude to life is modelled on the British general who encouraged his soldiers to attack shouting : 'Go on, lads. Do you want to live for ever?'

XXIV

FIVE TO FOUR

The earthly symbols of American liberties are guarded in the sanctuary of Constitution Avenue by armed sentries, while their content and spirit is watched over by nine men, dressed in black togas on the Capitol Hill in the building known by the metaphorical name 'Temple of Temida', and in official and everyday language as the Supreme Court of the United States.

I climbed the stairs guarded at the sides by two stone seated figures, looked up at the allegorical figures crowding over the Grecian portico with its Corinthian columns, and wondered whom they represented. Having passed the giant, bronze sculptured door I found myself in the dusk of a huge hall, in silence and coolness, despite the fact that outdoors the unbearable Washington heat and humidity prevailed, and began a stroll along the marble corridors, the severity of which was modified by the gleaming brass of the doors to the lifts, meeting only a few human forms with documents or brief-cases in their hands. From the marble interior, decorated with a few statues and portraits of stern men in togas looking down on the intruder, from the library shelves full of books, from the purple curtains and cherry carpets lining the waiting rooms and offices, and finally from the heavy desks and leather chairs seen through half-open doors, came the familiar atmosphere of law-courts, in which I had lived in Poland for many years.

At the end of the corridor, a janitor in dark clothes discreetly opened the door and let me in. I hurried on tip-toe to the nearest empty seat and having sunk into the deep, polished bench, I raised my eyes.

All nine were sitting behind a long table covered with a cloth on a platform, their white faces standing out against the huge leather armchairs, the backs of which rose above their heads, somehow far-off and inhuman against the background of the slender Grecian columns of the huge hall and the purple draperies hanging in folds from ceiling to floor. Dressed in dark togas, apparently uniform, but in fact each a different and eminent individuality, all

219

these judges of the Supreme Court, with names known and respected throughout the country, were authorities in their profession, as I knew well; nonetheless I could not resist the temptation to look at them as a prosecutor at the defendant : guilty or not guilty of these excesses which are the sickness of American life?

From the memorable moment in 1803 when the president of the Supreme Court, Marshal, announced in the case of *Marbury v. Madison* the first verdict setting aside the law passed by Congress as violating the constitution of the United States, dates the overwhelming influence of the Supreme Court on American life. During the next 150 years, giving a meaning for the various provisions of the Constitution and interpreting in the light emanating from the basic source the countless laws passed by over eighty Congresses, the Supreme Court has become a decisive factor in the fight which is going on in every country between the individual and the State, and the regulator of their mutual relationship. This fight in the country of the greatest freedom of the citizen opposing the ever-increasing interference of the State in his life, dictated by the growing demands of modern, complicated, collective life, was and is particularly apparent. From this fight the citizen has so far emerged victorious and his personal rights dominate over the rights of the State, ensuring its most efficient functioning. This is the way the interpretation of the constitution and American legislation have gone through the Supreme Court, in which for decades the doctrine of the defence of civil rights guaranteed to the citizen by the constitution has indivisibly ruled, this constitution being to this day the best collection of principles effectively serving man in his pursuit of happiness. The Supreme Court, at times when the American nation and the United States was not threatened from outside by any serious danger, used to give superiority in its verdicts to the citizen over the State, and that was the main cause for the excesses, primarily in the sphere of personal freedom. This school of thought or trend in the Supreme Court outlived the conditions in which it was born and formed, which found its expression in judgements even when the United States was in a political war with communism threatening its very existence. This luxury, which the United States could permit itself up to 1945, taking this date as the start of the open conflict with Communism, was extended beyond this date, proof of which is the adjudication of the Supreme Court in relation to the basic problem of defence against subversive activity by communists. Congress provided legal weapons for this defence in the shape of the Smith Act of June 28, 1940, which, though aimed primarily against Nazism and Fascism, by recognizing as a crime the formation of any organization aimed at overthrowing the system, provided legal grounds for action also against subversive communist activity. It was supplemented by the Internal Security Act of 1950, which placed upon the subversive organizations the obligation of registering with the Subversive Activities Control Board. This brought with it the automatic necessity of submitting a list of members, marking correspondence as communist, and loss of the rights of members to passports for travel abroad. Congress did not make the Communist Party as such illegal, and did not regard membership of it as a crime, but created legal bases for counteracting its underground activity, aimed against the system of the United States. Further action rested primarily with the Supreme Court as a competent interpreter of the laws, and only at a later stage with the government as their executor. But alas, these men sitting on the Capitol Hill, people standing in relation to Communism beyond even a shadow of suspicion, and moved by a noble conviction of the absolute value of citizens' freedoms which must never be restricted or limited, in a series of verdicts weakened and even paralysed the effectiveness of the laws passed by Congress and of the steps undertaken by government organs, particularly the FBI.

And so the Supreme Court in the case against *Yates* by a majority of five votes to four, although they confirmed that the Smith Act was in agreement with the constitution, restricted its effectiveness to activities after June 28, 1940, i.e. after the date it was passed. Thus persons responsible for organizing the Communist Party before this date (it had existed in the United States since 1919) could not be held responsible for that, although their organisational activities continue to this day. The Supreme Court furthermore stated that propagation by word or writing of the idea of overthrowing the system is not in general punishable and is within the limits of the freedom of speech and belief guaranteed in the Constitution. It only becomes a crime when linked with physical action in that direction, consisting in the use of force and power. Finally, the Supreme Court laid down such difficult conditions to which the proofs of organizing a subversive party must respond that in practice it acted as a brake on all prosecuting investigations.

Also the Supreme Court upheld the constitutionality of the Internal Security Act, but when the Communist Party challenged the duty of registering, referring to the right guaranteed by the constitution of freedom of association, and did not submit lists of members, the same court, in the case of *Cole v. Young*, ruled by a majority of five votes to four that a State official who is not carrying out responsible functions has no obligation to reveal his membership of the Communist Party and cannot be dismissed for that reason. In addition, in the case against *Jenks*, the organizer of the trade union of electrical industry workers, members of which take part in such secret production as satellites and rockets, the Supreme Court expressed the opinion that testimony under oath by an FBI agent that a given person is a member of the Communist Party is not enough to establish this fact; they ruled that it is necessary to deposit in court the relevant FBI fiiles. These would then become available to the accused and his defence, despite the fact that they might include for instance the names of informers and reveal the method and technique of investigation. Finally in the case against *Briehl* the Supreme Court, again by a majority of five votes to four, found that until the obligation of the Communist Party to register had been confirmed, the Secretary of State could not refuse a foreign passport to a communist even to attend an international communist congress, since this would infringe the provision of the constitution regarding freedom of travel.

As to investigations by Congressional committees, the Supreme Court held in the case of *Watkins* that these committees can ask the witness only such questions as have some connection with the legislative tasks of the committees, which is the preparation of material for future legislation in a certain sphere; they cannot ask questions intended to reveal other circumstances merely for the sake of revealing them. In other words, the witness must not be asked questions regarding his membership of the Communist Party merely to explain his relation to this organization.

The Communication Act of 1934 permitted telephone-tapping only with the consent of the person overheard, i.e. in practice it forbade it. In 1940 President Roosevelt authorized the FBI to tap telephones provided that in each case prior permission had been obtained from the Attorney-General or Minister of Justice. This is still the practice; but as it is based on an administrative decree not in agreement with the law, the result of tapping cannot be submitted in any court action as evidence, and can only be used for internal orientation by the police. For instance, conversations overheard by the FBI between the Soviet spy Valentyn Gubichev and his woman agent Judith Coplon could not be used in court as evidence.

Reading and hearing about these decisions, I wrung my hands and asked myself : can it be that the communists in the United States enjoy special protection, and how in such conditions can this country win the political war which is in progress with Soviet Russia? They sufficed to show how the noble ideal of the defence of the constitutional rights of individuals is at variance with the demands set by a

fight against subversive activity. It seemed to me that the defenders
of the constitution were closing their eyes to what was going on
round them and, in blindly defending the citizen against the interference of his own state, were forgetting to defend him from the
external enemy, which is threatening his freedom more than his
own government since it wants to destroy it altogether. After all,
it emerges from the essence and spirit of the constitution that its
first requirement is the defence of citizens' freedom before an external enemy, and its agents inside the country, and only in the
second degree from the government, which in any case this citizen
himself chooses in free elections. Without the slightest change of any
provision of the best constitution in the world, and without infringing its principles, it would have been possible to adapt the decisions
of the Supreme Court to the demands of the battle between two
worlds, to quit the era of the musket or Indian bow and arrow and
enter boldly into the atomic age. The creative role of the Supreme
Court depends precisely on interpreting these rigorous rules in the
light of new times, of progress and public interest. The administration of justice is not an abstract idea, but a function of community
and State life, which ensures and cannot be indifferent to what
is dictated by the national *raison d'état*. In accordance with its
comprehension, this same Supreme Court, which a few dozen years
ago recognized segregation in schools based on racial appurtenance
as in accordance with the constitution, has in recent years, under
the influence of the idea of progress, changed its attitude and
pronounced that this same constitution requires integration in
schools. The same court decided during the war that the deportation of thousands of American citizens of Japanese origin from the
Pacific coast to special camps was in agreement with the constitution, despite the fact that this might look like violation of their
constitutional rights. Today it is possible to doubt the need of this
deportation, yet it was legalized by the highest instance, and this
principle entered into the verdicts of the Supreme Court. Meanwhile, these same American citizens, communists, who are notorious
agents of Soviet Russia, are treated with kid gloves in the political
war which is in progress, despite the fact that it is more dangerous
to the existence of the United States than World War II.

Between the excess of personal freedom, this luxury which the
United States at the present critical phase ought not to afford itself,
and police rule or a new MacCarthyism there exists a wide margin,
in which it is possible to find a balance between the two opposing
trends. The constitution, thanks to the verdicts of the Supreme
Court, ought to be a living law, which constantly develops, keep-

ing step with progress and the demands of the new era, not a dead parchment.

At the same time, the division of votes in the cases referred to here into five against four showed the existence in the Supreme Court of a deep internal crisis. Deciding the problems which have meaning for the very existence of the State by a majority of one vote had a profound, almost alarming, eloquence. So much depended on so little. The voice of one man might weight upon the fate of a hundred and eighty million people. And there is widespread discussion in the United States of the fact that when the verdicts referred to were announced, the majority was on the side of the five-person group of liberals or libertines in the nine-person judicial body and that the four members of the opposition group did not agree with such a lavish interpretation of the provisions of the constitution connected with civil rights.

In the end, that happened which had to happen under the influence of the new situation in which the United States found itself, and perhaps more through the national instinct for self-preservation. The transfer of one vote from the first group to the second occurred, and verdicts were issued which constituted a defence of the threatened existence of the State before the exuberant rights of the citizen. The excesses had begun to be restricted. Following a new way, the Supreme Court deprived of the right to repayments from Social Security all foreigners sentenced to deportation on account of subversive activity and placed the burden of proof on such a foreigner, if he claimed that conditions arose for suspending his deportation. The Supreme Court stated that if he refuses to testify on the subject of his relation to the Communist Party, then he cannot obtain such a suspension. A verdict was also issued explaining that the State can dismiss an official for disobedience, if he refuses to reply to a question from a Congressional committee regarding subversive activity.

Sitting in the session hall of the Supreme Court, I had before me a group of its judges, divided by a new line of demarcation which rarely underwent change in specific cases. The former five to four had changed in the most recent verdicts to four to five, and there are signs in the sky and on the earth that the present majority of five will increase in proportion to the increase of communist threats.

Finally the moment came which had brought me to the marble building of the Supreme Court. A voice announced the verdict of the Supreme Court confirming the sentence of the Court of Appeals, which had condemned the defendant to many years in prison for spying on behalf of a foreign power, and this despite the fact that

Vice-President of the United States Richard Nixon welcomed by the
population of Warsaw. See chapter : *Nixon on the Vistula*

Former President of the United States Harry Truman visiting AGEN exhibition. From left to right : President Truman, the author, Judge R. W. Hansen. See chapter : *The Tenant of the White House*

the action leading to the obtaining of evidence and catching the guilty party did not fulfil the conditions laid down by the Supreme Court in previous rulings. The defendant however was the head of Soviet espionage in the United States, Colonel Rudolf Ivanovich Abel, a star of the first magnitude in the espionage firmament.

I left the building of the court in a good temper, humming and jumping down two steps at a time. I knew now that on the list of the court there were several cases against trusts, in which as the past has shown the verdicts will obtain a greater proportion of votes than five to four. Following on the levelling of excesses of economic freedom which started years ago, the Supreme Court has finally entered upon the way of liquidating the excesses of personal freedom of the citizens, including its own previous verdicts. The awakening had included also the high priests of Themida, which constituted marked progress on the way to the re-orientation of the American people. Shortly afterwards, the Supreme Court in the case against *Braden* and *Wilkinson* decided that a person refusing to reply to a question about belonging to the Communist Party must bear the consequences provided by law. In another case against *Pugach*, it confirmed that the wire tapping forbidden by the Federal Communication Act can nevertheless be used as evidence before State courts, if the State law permits it. The United States has finally ceased to be an oasis of peace for communists enjoying in this country far greater security than in Soviet Russia, where during the time of the Stalinist purges thousands of heads fell. Apart from the communist couple Rosenberg, condemned to death for espionage, a separate crime in itself, no communist in the United States has lost his head. The most is a hair from the head.

H

XXV

REPUBLICANS AND DEMOCRATS

On entering the buildings on Capitol Hill that accommodate the offices of Congressmen and Senators, one stops in front of a tablet on which are visible their names, and next to each is the mysterious letter 'R' or 'D'. In this way is introduced into the Capitol the division between Republican and Democratic parties, but all differences between parties for the European end in this formal classification. What both parties say about each other, particularly during the elections, does not sound convincing to a newcomer from the other side of the Atlantic. In the view of the Democrats, the Republican party is a party of orthodox conservatives, isolationists, great interests, unlimited free competition and private enterprise, limited interference by the government, and economies in the budget at the expense of public needs such as education, social security and the like. In the view of the Republicans, the Democrats are a party of immigrants, Catholics, Jews and trade unions, all tending towards the welfare state and socialization, the squanderers of the public funds and political newsmongers. In reality, the differences not only do not look so extreme, but in the last resort they are so blurred that sometimes it is hard to distinguish them.

Anyone who consults the programmes of both parties will not find any fundamental differences in them. If he starts to compare the foreign policies of the Republican and Democratic governments of the post-war era—they are the same. During elections, both parties criticize each other's policy, but after the elections the victors unceremoniously adopt and continue the programme of their predecessor. If anyone begins to investigate the register of voting, then the discovery will be made that in practice party solidarity does not exist, since in the case of many a Bill both Republicans and Democrats vote 'for' while both Republicans and Democrats also vote 'against'. If the widely known fact is further taken into consideration that Democrats from the South are closer in their activity to 'old guard Republicans' than to Democrats from the North, and the so-called 'young Republicans' closer to Democrats from New

England than to the 'old guard Republicans', the picture becomes still more cloudy. Nor is it made clearer by the fact that often Republicans and Democrats from the agricultural states form temporary blocks to defend the interests of the farmers, and from the industrial states to defend workers' interests. In addition, in the present dangerous period, the number of causes in relation to which both parties are conducting a common or 'bipartisan' policy is also growing. Finally, although the opposition may for instance have a majority in Congress, the government does not resign and the President, who is the head of the party in power, has to look for and find compromise with the opposition; otherwise his budget will not be passed or the legislative programme adopted. As a result, in the eyes of a European politician, the American parties—compared for example to the British Conservative and Labour parties —look rather like two wings of the same party, based on the same programme, with members differing only in secondary matters; or, when political opponents join in forming temporary blocks, like a multi-party system with a face that changes on every occasion. Taking the existing division into parties as a vertical cross-section, it might be more realistic to divide their members into horizontal cross-sections, of liberals and conservatives, young and old, according to their outlook on the world, mentality or even temperament. Trade unions operate, but there is no workers' party of the type of the British Labour party. The Socialist party under the leadership of the widely respected Norman Thomas is not a real force and consists primarily of intellectuals, not workers. The same must be said of the well organized Communist party, amounting according to Congressman Walter to 25,000 members. The cause of this is the fact that the workers are not striving to make the country socialist and do not feel the need to form their own party, working on the assumption that the existing two-party system serves their interests sufficiently. On the other hand, great capital is not represented exclusively by one party, which would in the end create a marked difference, but by the appropriate centres within each. The real difference between the Republican and Democratic parties lies in the somewhat different type of man which each attracts and in the different atmosphere that prevails within them. The Democrats are less isolationist and more internationalist, more sensitive to new political trends, more prepared to experiment, whereas the Republicans are more cautious, keep to trodden paths and proved methods and more of them are supporters of isolationism. An example of this was the Republican idea of the 'American fortress', isolated from the troubles of the outside world and forming a defence against communist attacks from within. But although the Democrats are more progressive, the Republicans more conservative, this does not mean that amidst the Democrats there are no conservative elements or isolationists at all, since there are such people in the southern states; and there are likewise some progressive and internationalist Republicans. The difference lies in the 'more', which suffices for the Democratic party to have a greater attraction for the ethnic groups, farmers and workers. In the eighty-seventh Congress, out of eleven Congressmen of Polish origin, nine were Democrats and only two Republicans. The sectors referred to do not however vote for the Democratic party en masse, but also give a large number of votes for the Republicans. When the candidate for the presidency is a person who is generally popular, as was Republican General Eisenhower in 1952, the results of the voting give the lie even to this differentiation.

This lack of division between the parties into black and white, the non-existence of serious radical movements and the fluidity of the party ranks ('in the last election I was a Republican, in this I am a Democrat') are due to the satisfaction to a large extent of the desires and ambitions of the citizens. A hungry man will fight with a well-fed one, and a poor man with a rich one, but wealthy and well-fed men do not fight with wealthier men but only try to catch up with them. Theoretically and logically speaking, this process of levelling out the still existing differences ought to intensify in proportion as prosperity increases, and the democratic system improves. Will the United States, in the course of this democratic process, attain to a monoparty, of course of another type than that imposed and maintained by terror in communist dictatorships? Certainly not, since the basic trait of human nature is variety in views and reactions, sufficient in conditions of complete freedom for people to group under different banners. But these will no longer be the red banners of revolution nor the white ones of social reaction.

More important however is that this process of levelling out differences in internal American relations is accompanied by a process of deepening differences in international relations, caused by the fight of Communism with democracy. Almost every day new international problems arise, resulting in different reactions to them amidst the American people and creating new differences of views, not so much as to the aims of American policy but as to the strategy and tactics which should be used. This acts as a brake on the levelling-out of internal differences, and perhaps even counterbalances them. In a word, the existence of both parties—Democratic and Republican—is not threatened by anything.

Once every four years, on the occasion of the election of a new President, both parties manifest their existence at conventions the course and descriptions of which have long since become hackneyed. Some describe such a convention as the greatest spectacle in the world, some as a cross between a circus and the ancient Greek theatre, others as a carnival ball. To borrow a comparison from Polish terrain, it is a combination of a May 3rd meeting with a holiday procession in Lowicz. Bands play, not firemen admittedly, but yet in colourful uniforms; and grown-up children with coloured balloons in their hands, paper or straw hats on their heads bearing the name of the presidential candidate, and huge buttons with the same name in the lapels, shout, blow trumpets and in general create uproar; they also from time to time give each other black eyes. In the aisles between the rows of chairs a crowd constantly moves, greeting old acquaintances with loud shouts and back slapping. After speeches introducing a candidate, a procession moves along these gangways demonstrating in his honour, the duration of which is in principle the same for each candidate. Church banners and likenesses of saints carried on poles by girls in white are here replaced by flags and posters bearing the likenesses of candidates or the names of states, carried by sweating delegates, and the band, instead of hymns, plays lively tunes. Even the counterpart of the girls in white is not missing, in the pretty girls chosen as guides. This crowd surges round the huge hall, not much smaller than the market place in Lowicz, shrieking at the tops of their voices the names of their candidate and waving placards with his profile or full-face. And anyone who grows tired may drink and refresh himself in the lobby in an appropriate kiosk, no worse than in the wooden fair booths. In the meanwhile, someone amidst the fair-like hullaballoo is talking on the main platform, describing the virtues of his candidate to the accompaniment of patriotic phrases, while powerful loudspeakers help him dominate the noise in the hall.

The powerful beams of searchlights fall now and then on the platform, magnesium lamps flash and countless cameras click, while people with 'walkie-talkies' move around, keeping contact with the headquarters of the candidates, while others have portable TV cameras placed on the platform opposite the central tribune. And above all dominates calmly the face of the party symbol, a donkey if it is a Democratic convention, an elephant if Republican.

Behind this extraordinary picture, arousing mixed feelings, which again the whole country sees on the TV screens, is however hidden a serious political process, on which may depend the fate of not only the United States. At the pre-conventional meetings and in the smoky offices of the leaders, the proceedings are carefully prepared, but in the end the last word belongs to the convention, and surprises must be reckoned with. It alone approves the political programme of the party and elects a presidential candidate, who with the support of this programme moves on into the electoral campaign. This electoral platform, prepared with the aid of experts by special party commissions, which consult eminent personalities from the whole country, among them the president of the Polish-American Congress, always, during my stay in the United States, included a passage in which the party concerned defined its policy in relation to Poland and other Iron Curtain countries.

Not going further back than 1956, in the programme of the Democratic party adopted before the Polish 'October' and the Hungarian insurrection, the following was to be found on this subject :

> We declare our deepest concern for the plight of the freedom loving peoples of Central and Eastern Europe and of Asia, now under the yoke of Soviet dictatorship. The United States, under Democratic leaders, has never recognized the forcible annexation of Lithuania, Latvia and Estonia, or condoned the extension of the Kremlin's tyranny over Poland, Bulgaria, Rumania, Czechoslovakia, Hungary, Albania and other countries.
>
> We look forward to the day when the liberties of all captive nations will be restored to them and they can again take their rightful place in the community of free nations.
>
> We shall press before the United Nations the principle that Soviet Russia withdraw its troops from the captive countries, so as to permit free, fair and unfettered elections in the subjugated areas in compliance with the Atlantic Charter and other commitments.
>
> We rededicate ourselves to the high principle of national self-determination, as enunciated by Woodrow Wilson, whose leadership brought freedom and independence to uncounted millions.
>
> It is the policy of the Democratic Party, therefore, to encourage and assist small nations and all peoples behind the Iron Curtain and outside, in the peaceful and orderly achievement of their legitimate aspirations toward political, geographical and ethnic integrity, so that they may dwell in the family of sovereign nations with freedom and dignity. We are opposed to colonialism and Communist imperialism.

At the same time, the Republican party adopted the following attitude for its electoral platform :

> We shall continue to seek the reunification of Germany in freedom, and the liberation of the satellite states—Poland, Czechoslovakia, Hungary, Rumania, Bulgaria, Latvia, Lithuania, Estonia

and other once-free countries behind the Iron Curtain. The Republican Party stands firmly with the peoples of these countries in their just quest for freedom. We are confident that our peaceful policies, resolutely pursued, will finally restore freedom and national independence to oppressed peoples and nations.

As is evident from these texts, both the Democratic and Republican parties propagated liberation by the use of peaceful means, with the only difference that the Republican party expressed this attitude in a clearer manner than the Democratic party, which however indicated the way which ought to lead to liberation (the United Nations), and in addition referred in its statement to the Wilsonian doctrine of self-determination. Both declarations aroused certain hopes among the emigrations from Iron Curtain countries and great disapproval in the communist embassies in Washington, which reacted to them with the spiteful comment : 'The United States are liberating the satellite countries once every four years, during the presidential election, in order to obtain the votes of the so-called ethnic groups, but they forget about this the day after the elections'.

In 1960 the Republican party defined its position in a few words :

> The Republican Party reaffirms its determination to use every peaceful means to help the captive nations towards their independence and thus their freedom to live and worship according to conscience. We do not condone the subjugation of the peoples of Hungary, Poland, East Germany, Czechoslovakia, Rumania, Albania, Bulgaria, Latvia, Lithuania, Estonia and other once-free nations. We are not shaken in our hope and belief that once again they will rule themselves as nations.

In 1960 the Democratic party formulated its attitude at considerable length :

> However, we will never surrender positions which are essential to the defence of freedom, nor will we abandon peoples who are now behind the Iron Curtain through any formal approval of the *status quo*.
>
> To the people who live in the Communist world and its captive nations: we proclaim an enduring friendship which goes beyond governments and ideologies to our common interest in a better world.
>
> Through exchanges of persons, cultural contacts, trade in non-strategic areas, and other non-governmental activities, we will endeavour to preserve and improve opportunities for human relationships which no Iron Curtain can permanently sever.
>
> No political platform promise in history was more cruelly cynical than the Republican effort to buy votes in 1952 with false promises of painless liberation for the captive nations.

The blood of heroic freedom fighters in Hungary tragically proved this promise a fraud. We Democrats will never be party to such cruel cultivation of false hopes.

We look forward to the day when the men and women of Albania, Bulgaria, Czechoslovakia, East Germany, Estonia, Hungary, Latvia, Lithuania, Poland, Rumania and the other captive nations will stand again in freedom and justice. We will hasten by every honourable and responsible means the arrival of the day.

We shall never accept any deal or arrangement which acquiesces in the present subjugation of these peoples.

Comparison of both texts shows a weakening of the doctrine of liberation by the Republican party, which in 1960 no longer mentions liberation by political action from without, but only helping the enslaved nations to liberate themselves. As far as the Democratic party is concerned, it not only rejects this doctrine, but condemns it sharply.

Are political programmes contained in electoral platforms later carried out? Opinions as to this among ordinary citizens are divided. The Gallup poll in 1960 showed that as regards the Democratic platform, 44% of those asked their opinion believed it would be carried out, 22% were not sure, and 34% simply did not believe it. The same figures for Republican platform were 47, 21 and 32%. In any case, as far as the policy of liberation is concerned, its proclamation in 1952 was not put into deeds.

Senator Dodd adopted a totally decided attitude in this cause in his public utterance. He stated that the programmes contained in the electoral platform can only have an advisory significance, and the future four-year activities of the President and Congress must not be subordinated to what was prepared in the course of four days by experts who were not even delegates at the conventions.

During my several years' stay in the United States I have myself hundreds of times taken the measure, either as an individual or as a member of various delegations, of the mile-long corridors of the Congress buildings and have had the opportunity of talking on the subject of Polish and East European matters with several dozen Senators and over a hundred members of the House, with some of them on several occasions. They included Speakers of the House of Representatives at various periods of time, Sam Rayburn and Joseph W. Martin; the chairman of the Foreign Relations committee of the Senate, Francis Green; the chairmen of the Foreign Affairs committee of the House, Thomas Gordon and Thomas Morgan; leaders of minorities and majorities of the Democratic or Republican parties as the case may be, e.g. Congressman John W. McCormack or Senator Everett McKinley Dirksen; and in addition those Senators and members of the House who showed the most interest in and understanding of the problems of Poland and other countries of Eastern Europe, in most cases elected in states or electoral districts with a large percentage of people of East European origin, reckoned in the whole United States as fifteen million. To mention only the most important names, there were Senator Paul Douglas of Illinois, on whose territory is to be found the largest Polish centre in Chicago, well acquainted with Polish matters and a great friend of Poles; Senators Thomas Dodd, Kenneth B. Keating, Jacob Javits, Hubert Humphrey and (before his election to the presidency) John F. Kennedy; former Senator William F. Knowland; Congressmen of Polish origin, led by Tadeusz Machrowicz, and beside him Clement Zablocki, for many years a member of the Foreign Affairs committee, Alvin E. O'Konski, Roman C. Pucinski, John C. Kluczynski and others. Of Congressmen of Anglo-Saxon origin, particular interest in matters concerning Eastern Europe was shown by Walter Judd of Minnesota, Alvin M. Bentley of Michigan, Henry S. Reuss of Wisconsin, Francis Walter of Pennsylvania, Daniel Flood of Pennsylvania, Chester Bowles of Connecticut, Ray J. Madden of Indiana. The list does not end here.

And however often I strolled round the buildings in which are found their offices, I always looked in at the office of the Judiciary Committee of the House, to shake the hand of Counsel Wladyslaw Besterman, the journalist known in pre-war Poland and its Sejm, who knows political life in the Capitol like the back of his hand and is always ready with advice and help.

It is not a grateful occupation to knock at ever new doors for a cause in which each Senator and member of the House is full of goodwill and would like to assist somehow, but when it comes to considering concrete opportunities, his hands fall and he sinks into pessimism which only doubles his sympathy and feeling for the political emigrant, who represents such a serious problem as liberating the countries of Eastern Europe from Soviet domination, but there is not much consolation in that. Nevertheless, he is always ready to assist and always finds time for the talk which follows, despite heavy business, particularly in electoral periods, which occur every second year for members of the House. With the exaggerated intention of assuring the American people that their actual voice will always be heard in the House, and not that of a few years ago, the cadence of the House amounts to only two years, which in practice tears away a member of the House every second year from his legislative

H*

work, forcing him to devote main attention and effort to another re-election.

The cause of such an émigré visit is almost always the same : to convince the member of Congress that despite the difficulties of attaining the main end it is necessary to undertake certain action in the cause of the nations behind the Iron Curtain, whether in the shape of a speech which he ought to make on the subject, or in exerting influence in a certain matter on the State Department or even the President, or introducing into Congress a certain resolution. The aim of all these steps is to stress yet again that the United States does not agree with the domination of the Soviets in Poland and other countries behind the Iron Curtain, that it still recognizes their right to free and independent existence, and that all peaceful means must be used to liberate them.

None of the Iron Curtain emigrations propagates war as a method of liberation, only all possible kinds of action and pressure, both political, moral and propaganda.

A talk with persons familiar with the problems of the nine countries is factual and brief, without the need to start everything from the beginning. Most have a positive result. However, the first meetings with people from the Southern states, where there are no large ethnic groups, or those bordering on the Pacific Ocean, where not only are there not many ethnic groups but attention is directed more to Asia than to Europe, usually follow a different course. As a rule, the member of Congress from these parts of the United States is intrigued by the person of his guest, who looks like an American but whose foreign accent makes him listen intently. His interest increases when he learns that the person sitting before him knows not only from his personal experience what Soviet occupation is, but has more than once felt on his skin communist investigation and imprisonment. He therefore asks many questions on this subject, since he wants to learn something more from an eyewitness. Informed of the purpose of the visit, he is always full of sympathy for the Iron Curtain countries, the fate and situation of which is quite well known to him, and having learned that the initiative will be taken by colleagues more closely concerned and more familiar with the subject, gladly joins the campaign. Sometimes rather unexpected remarks are made during such first visits : 'I understand you better than anyone else. I come from the South which not so many years ago was defeated by the North and occupied for many years. We Southerners know from our parents what foreign domination is.'

On another occasion a Republican exclaimed : 'It was not us but the Democrats who sold you at Yalta ! You can't expect anything good from them, as they are too conciliatory towards Communism.'

On the other hand, more than one Democrat has taken advantage of the opportunity to find fault with the Republicans : 'This policy of liberation of theirs is only propaganda. They haven't done anything for you and never will.'

But the record for originality was beaten by a venerable elderly gentleman who, having listened with attention to my request, promised support, then unexpectedly asked : 'Do you know Poznan ?'

I hastily answered that I had spent ten years there studying at the University and at my practice in the court and know every stone in its pavements.

'I visited that town perhaps a quarter of a century back,' he began, 'and on one occasion I went by tram. And just imagine, right next to me such a pretty girl was sitting that I couldn't tear my eyes away from her. She noticed this and smiled at me very sweetly. As I was wondering how to get into conversation with her, the tram stopped, the girl stood up and as she left, rubbed so close by me with a charming smile that a shiver went up my spine. But before I could make up my mind to get out at this encouragement, the tram went on and it was only then that I noticed ... my gold watch had gone. But what a pretty girl she was ! I can see her still. . . .'

I expressed profound commiseration at the unfortunate incident which had happened to the eminent member of Congress in the town of my younger days, which in any case was not famed for its talented pickpockets as was, for instance, Warsaw, but he quickly interrupted : 'Please be quiet. She made such an impression on me that I didn't even report it to the police.' Then, winking one eye in a rather mischievous way, and putting out his hand in a gesture of farewell, he merrily added : 'I will not draw back the promise I have given you on account of that loss. You can count on me.'

The result of these countless interventions was speeches and resolutions passed in Congress, following the line of the demands of the Polish and other emigrations, creating a political trend favourable to liberation and an appropriate pressure on the government. However, they were also accompanied by one piece of advice : 'Because the President assisted by the Secretary of State and not Congress conducts foreign policy, don't forget to intervene at the State Department, and better still at the White House.'

XXVI

THE TENANT OF THE WHITE HOUSE

Former President Harry Truman came into the hall surrounded by the reception committee, greeted by an ovation of applause, stamping, whistling and shouting of several thousand people. The audience rose, and the smiling guest of honour moved down the centre aisle in the direction of the platform, giving handshakes right and left. When in the midst of redoubled cheers, noise, the flash of magnesium and the click of cameras, he appeared on the platform, three dull bangs of a gavel were heard and after a flowery introduction by the chairman, President Truman began speaking.

I was sitting in the hall in the aisle, invited to the convention of the Fraternal Order of Eagles in the Sherman Hotel, Chicago. On the previous evening, August 5, 1958, I had performed the opening of an ACEN exhibition in the lobby in front of the session hall, representing the 'blessings' which had fallen on the Iron Curtain countries from the hands of the Soviet 'benefactors'. Immediately it was opened a stream of 'Eagles' and their families began to flow amidst the stands on which photographs were hanging; they were looking with undisguised horror and alarm at the photographs of Katyn, the Poznan rebellion, the Hungarian revolt and others. And this always noisy American crowd suddenly quietened down and moved in intense silence from picture to picture, reading out the captions, explaining what they represented, and exchanging comments in whispers.

I stayed for the next day and, before President Truman arrived in the huge meeting hall, I listened to several other speeches, in which almost every speaker referred to the exhibition, either condemning the Soviet crimes committed against the peoples of Eastern Europe, or warning against the risk of their being repeated in America. The convention of the Fraternal Order of Eagles, which has as its aim social rather than political activity, did not diverge from the known order of clichés, and it progressed in the usual circle of speeches, resolutions, parades, receptions, dances, visits to the town and other sorts of events in which the families of the delegates also took part.

In his speech President Truman developed the idea that the Soviet threat demanded the mobilizing of the forces of all America and he warned his audience against putting any confidence in the agreements entered into by Russia. The packed hall listened to him with great attention, interrupting now and then with applause. But a deep silence, full of profound eloquence, fell when he very solemnly stated : 'I myself entered into and signed over a dozen agreements with the Soviets. And no one knows better than I do that not one of them has been adhered to.'

As President Truman was leaving the hall amidst applause, the chairman of the convention, Judge Robert W. Hansen, who was accompanying him, stopped at my seat and introduced me, referring as explanation to my last function in the underground. President Truman put out his hand and said, 'You people did a splendid job!'

I joined in his suite and led the President to the exhibition, since this was the main reason I had stayed on in Chicago. The very well-preserved elderly man started strolling from stand to stand, carefully looking at the photographs and reading the captions, and in the meantime I thought of the telegram I had sent to him in 1945 as head of the underground, with condolences at the death of President Franklin Roosevelt, and assurances 'that the Polish nation transfers to his successor all the trust and hope they had placed in the late President.' This hope led Poland through Teheran and Yalta, into the grip of Russia : and me into exile.

As he inspected the exhibits, the face of President Truman became increasingly angry and depressed. He muttered something under his breath, which sounded like an oath, but the only word I understood was 'Hell'. Most probably he was thinking of the present whereabouts of Stalin and his past collaborators. Finally he was photographed with Judge Hansen and me against a street scene of the Hungarian revolt, bade farewell and left.

In the plane for Washington I had time to sum up my impressions. This man, selected by fate, not necessarily happy fate, was thanks to the constitution : head of state, commander-in-chief and prime minister of the government, in one and the same person, had his existence guaranteed for four years and was in addition the head of his party.

This linking of four functions in one person apparently creates of the President a democratic autocrat, or if you prefer it, an autocratic democrat. In fact it is not so, but precisely the reverse, since one function limits the other. For what he can do as President or

Prime Minister is not allowed to him as party head; in that capacity, he must reckon with hundreds of leaders of his party, which is responsible for his policy, and if it is bad, will pay for it by defeat at the next elections. On the other hand, what he would like to do as head of the party is limited by the fact that he is President and Prime Minister, forced to take account of opposition in Congress, particularly when it has a majority (which happens quite often), not to mention all-powerful public opinion. The linking of the institution of President with that of the head of the party does not permit him, after elections carried out by all efforts of his own party, to retract from it, standing above the heads of both parties and representing exclusively the state and people as such, which is a rule in European systems. Such a concept of the role of President would not, for instance, permit him an attack on the opposition party, which is not a rare phenomenon in the United States. Under conditions such as these it should rather be accepted that it is not the President of the United States who is simultaneously Prime Minister but vice versa. The functions of the Prime Minister dominate over the functions of the President, the more so in that treaties entered into by the latter and the more important nominations require the confirmation of the Senate and are not merely privileges of his office. In this conception, the linking of the function of Prime Minister and the post of chairman of the party seems more healthy and natural from the point of view of European customs than linking President and head of party. This logic is not weakened by the fact that the President is also the commander-in-chief. This had great practical significance in the time of the presidency of the former commander-in-chief of Allied Forces and professional soldier, General Eisenhower, but with a civilian president in office it is more a title than an actual post. In any case, war is declared by Congress and it is carried on by the President as head of government. In peacetime it is in this character and not as commander-in-chief that he prepares the military budget, forms alliances, and directs the policy of the armed forces.

However, the argument that the prime minister performs the functions of the President and not vice versa gains support from the way Americans treat their head of state. At first, accustomed as I was to the distance which divides a Polish citizen from the highest person in the country and the ceremony which surrounds him, I was offended by the use of his first name to describe the man who not only represents but also symbolizes the United States, and in such diminutive forms as 'Harry' or 'Ike'. But this was nothing in comparison with the impression made upon me by the fact that the

Americans curse their President in word and press, and how! I found the explanation of this in the very circumstance that the President of the United States is primarily the Prime Minister, whose policy every citizen has the right to criticize. And if in doing so he crosses the bounds, that is a question of taste and discretion. In any case, I was pleased to find that the United States does not have trials for insulting the head of state, so frequent in independent Poland.

Three episodes provided me with the best lesson in the relation of the American citizen to the President and were at the same time a good demonstration of the unusual freedom which the American citizen enjoys. During the Korean war President Truman dismissed General MacArthur on account of misunderstandings which arose between them against the background of carrying on the war. At the time, one of the big film companies arranged a poll, in which a newsreel reporter stopped passers-by in the street and asked : 'Who was right—Truman or MacArthur?' In the resultant film I saw the reporter approach a policeman, directing traffic at a street crossing and, after asking him the ritual questions as to his name, address, weight and height, wife and children, ended with the sacramental 'Who was right?' The policeman, without interrupting his activities, grunted angrily into the microphone : 'Harry should be impeached.' I tremble to think what would have happened in pre-war Poland to a policeman who dared to say anything similar of his president.

The second incident occurred in San Francisco, during one of the early morning walks of President Truman, for which he is famous. It is said that as a young boy he worked on a farm and there became accustomed to rising early and walking, a habit that remained with him the rest of his life. He strode quickly along the empty streets accompanied by secret service agents, and after him came a crowd of reporters, hunting for news. He noted a young sailor deep in a dispute with a taxi-driver, stopped and asked the reason. The driver explained that he had driven the sailor all night from bar to bar, and when it came to paying for the ride, it seemed too high to him. In President Truman there awoke the artillery captain of World War I, who knows how a young warrior spends his leave, so in a fatherly way he advised the sailor to settle his bill, and passed on. The reporters surrounded the sailor and after asking his name inquired what he thought of the Presidents' interference. The sailor burst out : 'He ought to mind his own business.' He did not for a moment fear that such a comment on his commander-in-chief, published in the press, might not be good for him. As a citizen he was within his rights.

The third incident occurred in Chicago, where President Truman was stopping at a hotel (in the United States, when presidents travel to other cities, they stay like ordinary mortals in a hotel and do not have castles or palaces at their disposal); after the traditional walk, he returned to his hotel with a good appetite, and at once sat down to breakfast. What he ate was described in the press in great detail, not to mention that he gave the waiter a dollar tip, on which he wrote his autograph. And again reporters surrounded the waiter and, after taking down his personal details, asked what he thought of the President and his original tip. The waiter shrugged : 'What a guy ! I don't like him, I never voted for him and never will.' And the waiter was not fired.

President Eisenhower also enriched this collection of observations. During a parade that was going along the streets of Washington after the President had taken the oath in the Capitol in 1953, a cowboy from Hollywood, Monty Montana, rode up on a fine horse to the President's stand and asked his permission to lasso him. The President nodded with a sour smile, since a refusal would have clouded the joyful mood of the parade, and then the cowboy, having wound up the rope, cast it neatly over the President's shoulders. Fortunately he did not pull the noose, or then the treatment of the President of the United States as a cow at pasture would have been complete. And no one was to be found to teach the cowboy a lesson.

In addition to this familiar treatment, the President does not really have any private life and everything he does, even within four walls, is mercilessly brought out and revealed by the ubiquitous press which first prints the news, then eagerly reports how the public reacted to it. President Truman, who does not play golf, was reproached because in the evenings he plays poker with friends, and Eisenhower, who does not play poker, because he wasted time at golf. One was bad and the other not good. Even the golf, prescribed to Eisenhower by doctors, obtained international fame and became the tool of the 'cold war', since the time when Khrushchev rebuked him for it. It also played a role in internal policy : a poster during the Democratic Party convention in Los Angeles in July 1960, praised the virtues of Adlai Stevenson, candidate for President, in the following words : 'Adlai is a lousy golfer.'

The discretion which surrounds the private life of a European head of state and his family is unknown in the United States. President Truman, in order to be by himself from time to time on his morning walks, had to ask reporters specially not to come with him. Their whole crew, also photographers, reside constantly in the White House describing and photographing everything and everyone. In addition, crowds of tourists surge round the seat of the President five days in the week and the guards have to watch out to see they do not yield to the irrepressible desire to invade the part closed to the public. As for when the President leaves the White House for official functions or on holiday—then every step and word of his is repeated by the press and commented on. In the last resort, he is an actor who ceases to act before a crowded audience only when he is asleep, and when he is in the closest family circle, but even then not always.

Every week or two, the President is submitted to several hours' interrogation, at which the prosecution is changing all the time, surprising him with unexpected questions. He is the only citizen in the United States who does not dare refer to the fifth amendment to the constitution which entitles him to refuse to reply if that would harm him. This all happens at the press conferences, when the President stands before two or three hundred reporters and blinded by the light of floodlights, in the roar of radio and television apparatus, he replies for about an hour to the most testing questions. Admittedly, the press office of the President foresees most of these in advance, since as a rule their content is dictated by the current internal and international situation, and he is prepared for them, but for an unexpected question, the reply has to be improvised so as not to fall into a trap. These questions and answers are then published word for word by all the larger newspapers, and abridged in the smaller ones, and of course every word is commented upon. And it may happen that the President, led out of patience and balance by some question, bursts out for a moment but later controls himself and the conference goes smoothly on. The prosecuting attorneys of the press are in a better position than the man under questioning and it is not worthwhile offending them.

Such are the shadows in the profession of President, which the lighter side certainly does not counterbalance. Putting aside the undoubted fact that the presidency of the United States is in these times a historical vocation, and always brings the person in this post into the pages of history, which may in itself level out all the difficulties and disagreeable aspects of his position, these same Americans who have no mercy on their President may have many warm feelings for the man in this position, and for his family. They complained along with President Truman when the artistic performance of his daughter was severely criticized, and when the President railed against a critic of the latter by letter, most came out on his side and said : 'In any case, our Harry is a good father.' When President Eisenhower had a heart attack, one hundred and eighty million Americans held their breath as they listened to news from the hospital. And when he recovered, general rejoicing prevailed and the White House was flooded with thousands of letters and telegrams. Whole volumes were then written in the newspapers on the subject of every detail of this illness and its cure.

The present President, and his living predecessors such as Herbert Hoover and Harry Truman, are very popular figures and generally respected; President Eisenhower, as the commander-in-chief of the World War is undoubtedly a national hero. Wherever they appear, they are the objects of warm ovations. When in July 1960 President Eisenhower arrived at the Republican convention in Chicago, a million people lined the streets to bid farewell to a man who was to step down from his office within a few months. And there were people weeping in the cheering crowd. I saw him several times going along the streets of Washington and New York among cheering thousands and had to admit that his person and particularly his smile very much appeal to people. For me however, feeling for the President more sympathy than admiration, his famous uplifted hands looked like the prelude to crucifixion.

Each of these living presidents played his part in Polish matters and those of Eastern Europe. The name of Hoover will never be forgotten in Poland in connection with the assistance he organized for Poland, starving and destroyed by World War I. This was many years before he was elected President. The grateful people of Warsaw named one of the squares by his name. President Truman did not, of course, take part in the conference at Yalta, but as Vice-President he was partly responsible for the decisions taken at it, which led to the fourth partition of Poland. However, these same decisions, rightly considered as unjust by the Poles, were positively estimated by other emigrations from Eastern Europe, particularly countries allied with Germany during the war such as Bulgaria, Rumania and Hungary, which take them as a basis for demands for Soviet troops quitting these countries and free elections under international control. In this respect a fundamental difference exists between them and the Polish emigration. On the other hand, President Truman, as a member of the Potsdam conference, contributed to handing over what are called the 'western territories' into Polish possession, which must with time lead to the recognition of the Polish western frontiers by the United States. As for the policy of President Eisenhower towards Poland and East Europe, its best spokesman was his Secretary of State, John Foster Dulles, whose statements were the reflection of the President's attitude. Regardless of this, President Eisenhower himself spoke on these matters, under circumstances different from those under which Dulles spoke, and it was he and not Dulles who was the main person at international conferences which considered them. In view of this, the relevant texts are supplemented by the statements of Dulles or vice versa. These are the main ones :

Declaration in the State of the Union Message of February 2, 1953 : 'We shall never acquiesce in the enslavement of any people in order to purchase fancied gain for ourselves. I shall ask the Congress at a later date to join in an appropriate resolution making clear that this Government recognizes no kind of commitment contained in secret understandings of the past with foreign governments which permit this kind of enslavement.'

The relevant proposal of President Eisenhower of February 20, 1953, sent to the Senate and the House of Representatives, came to a halt in the Foreign Affairs committee of the House without going any further.

A communiqué issued jointly by President Eisenhower, Prime Minister Winston Churchill and the French Premier Laniel after the Bermuda conference, December 4-7, 1953 : 'We cannot accept as justified or permanent the present division of Europe. Our hope is that in due course, peaceful means will be found to enable the countries of Eastern Europe again to play their parts as free nations in a free Europe.'

A declaration known as the Potomac declaration, issued on June 29, 1954, by President Eisenhower and Prime Minister Churchill : 'As regards formerly sovereign states now in bondage, we will not be a party to any arrangement or treaty which would confirm or prolong their unwilling subordination.'

President Eisenhower's speech at the Summit Conference in Geneva, July 18, 1955 : 'On a broader plane, there is the problem of respecting the right of peoples to choose the form of government under which they will live : and of restoring sovereign rights and self-government to those who have been deprived of them. The American people feel strongly that certain peoples of Eastern Europe, many with a long and proud record of national existence, have not yet been given the benefit of this pledge of our United Nations wartime declarations, reinforced by other wartime agreements.'

The White House confirmed the text of this statement on December 31, 1955, adding : 'The peaceful liberation of the captive peoples has been, is and until success is achieved will continue to be a major goal of United States foreign policy.'

The 'Washington declaration' of February 1, 1956, issued by President Eisenhower and the British Prime Minister, Anthony Eden : 'Because of our belief that the state should exist for the benefit of the individual and not the individual for the benefit of the state, we uphold the basic rights of peoples to governments of their own choice.'

A communiqué of March 24, 1957, issued by President Eisenhower and British Prime Minister Harold Macmillan, after the conference in the Bermudas, contains in its first appendix, para. 7, the following statement : 'Sympathy for the people of Hungary, condemnation of repressive Soviet policies towards the peoples of Eastern Europe and of Soviet defiance of relevant United Nations resolutions.'

The American-British communiqué issued after the press conference of President Eisenhower and British Prime Minister Macmillan on October 25, 1957, in Washington : '... continued suppression of freedom in Eastern Europe undermines international confidence and perpetuates an injustice, a folly and a danger.'

The letter of President Eisenhower to Premier Bulganin on January 13, 1958 : 'Surely the Hungarian developments and the virtually unanimous action of the United Nations General Assembly in relation thereto show that conditions in Eastern Europe are regarded throughout the world as much more than a matter of purely domestic scope.

'I propose that we should now discuss this matter.

'There is an intrinsic need of this in the interest of peace and justice, which seems to me compelling.'

President Eisenhower's letter to Premier Bulganin on February 15, 1958 : 'I noted that Mr Khrushchev devoted a considerable part of his Minsk speech to a discussion of conditions in Hungary, Poland and East Germany. Does the Soviet Union claim such a proprietary interest in these lands and people that to discuss them is solely a matter of Soviet domestic concern? If not, and if these lands and peoples can be discussed by Soviet leaders as an international problem, why cannot we both discuss them?'

Apart from the statements which were in agreement with the utterances of Dulles, such as emphasizing the principles of liberation by the use of peaceful means, not entering into agreements approving of the *status quo*, of the right of self-determination of the peoples and choice of system of government, President Eisenhower also condemned the secret agreements which had enabled the Soviet Union to dominate Eastern Europe. He undoubtedly had in mind the Teheran agreement, recognizing Eastern Europe as an area of Soviet influences.

As for the declarations issued jointly with the Prime Ministers of Britain and France, they were maintained within the limits of the four principles referred to, though their tone is feebler than the one-sided American statements. The explanation of this must be sought in the fact that at the international conferences they were the result of a compromise between the far-reaching proposals of the American side, on the initiative of which the question of Eastern Europe was considered, and the more moderate position adopted by the European partners. It is immediately apparent that Churchill was more concerned with these questions than Macmillan, perhaps influenced by the situation of the Western states which had deteriorated in the meantime.

As for the statement of President Eisenhower made at the opening of the conference in Geneva and in his subsequent letters to Bulganin, it is clear from them that attempts were made to enter into a discussion with the Soviet Union on the basis of the principles of American policy referred to above, but they met with the unshakeable resistance of the Soviet Union.

However this may be, all the declarations quoted and attempts to take action, like all Dulles's enterprises, gave no positive result. In practice, the policy of liberation by peaceful means was transformed to a policy of not recognizing the *status quo* and keeping the question of Eastern Europe an open international problem awaiting solution and better times.

This situation cannot satisfy either the political emigration from the countries of Eastern Europe, primarily Poland, or—which is far more important—the peoples themselves behind the Iron Curtain, which in addition formed the idea that the President of the United States is a sort of Archangel Gabriel, who with a fiery sword in his hand at the head of the heavenly host of Americans will strike at Anti-Christ and his cohorts, destroy them and introduce peace, justice and prosperity throughout the world. This is correct only inasmuch as the political conflict between the United States and the Soviet Union is really reminiscent of the conflict between good and evil, or Ormuzd and Ahriman. But the contemporary sword of fire—the atom bomb—hits blindly and may endanger not only the forces of evil but of good also. In view of this, in the day of the atom bomb, the Archangel Gabriel holds the sword in its sheath and does not fight but persuades and negotiates, counting on time and changes which the world has always undergone, undergoes and will undergo. Above all, Anti-Christ and his armies are only rebellious angels, which in the course of time, as in proportion with the violent evolution of the whole world, may repent and knock at the heavenly portals.

XXVII

NIKITA KHRUSHCHEV'S ACHILLES HEEL

The ceremony of handing over to the ACEN delegation President Eisenhower's proclamation of July 17, 1959, concerning the celebration of Captive Nations week (July 17th-23rd), was brief and devoid of unnecessary pomp. Our delegation consisted of the chairman, his deputy, the Hungarian Kovago, member of the general committee, the Lithuanian Sidzikauskas, and the secretary-general, the Rumanian Coste. Under-Secretary of State Douglas Dillon, whose parents came from Poland, rose from behind his desk in the State Department and handed me a document which read :

> Whereas many nations throughout the world have been made captive by the imperialistic and aggressive policies of Soviet Communism; and
>
> Whereas the citizens of the United States are linked by bonds of family and principle to those who love freedom and justice on every continent; and
>
> Whereas it is appropriate and proper to manifest to the peoples of the captive nations the support of the government and people of the United States of America for their just aspirations for freedom and national independence; and
>
> Whereas by a joint resolution approved July 17, 1959, the Congress has authorized and requested the President of the United States of America to issue a Proclamation designating the 3rd week in July 1959 as 'Captive Nations Week' and to issue a similar proclamation each year until such time as freedom and independence shall have been achieved for all the captive nations of the world :
>
> Now, therefore, I, Dwight D. Eisenhower, President of the United States of America, do hereby designate the week beginning July 17th, 1959, as Captive Nations Week
>
> I invite the people of the United States of America to observe such week with appropriate ceremonies and activities and I urge them to study the plight of the Soviet-dominated nations and to commit themselves to the support of the just aspirations of the peoples of those captive nations.
>
> In witness whereof I have hereunto set my hand and caused the seal of the United States of America to be affixed.

Done at the City of Washington this 17th day of July in the year of Our Lord, 1959, and of the Independence of the United States of America the 184th.

I asked Under-Secretary Dillon to convey our thanks to President Eisenhower for arranging the celebration of Captive Nations week, and I expressed the hope that the next step would be concrete political action such as bringing up the question of the liberation of Eastern Europe on the agenda of all international conferences devoted to settling European affairs, and in the UN.

Douglas Dillon, who was encountering representatives of ACEN for the first time, emphasized that the attitude of the American government, which refuses to recognize the domination of the Soviet Union over the subjugated peoples, is clear and decisive, and that this government has always supported the right of these peoples to independence and choice of a government according to their own beliefs, and also their right to participate in the privileges and freedoms of the individual. He ended his statement by declaring that the concern of the American government and people in the question of our countries was deep and lasting.

The visit to the State Department was only one of the political events of the Captive Nations week, which came into being thanks to the untiring efforts of such friends of the cause of liberation as Senator Paul H. Douglas, of Illinois, Senator Jacob K. Javits of New York, and the leader of the Democratic majority in the House of Representatives, Congressman John W. McCormack, who were joined by several dozen other members of Congress. On their initiative, both these bodies passed resolutions stating that since 1918 the imperialist policy of communist Russia had led by direct or indirect aggression to enslaving Poland, Hungary, Lithuania, the Ukraine, Czechoslovakia, Latvia, Estonia, Belo-Russia, Rumania, East Germany, Bulgaria, mainland China, Armenia, Azerbaijan, Georgia, North Korea, Albania, Idel-Ural, Tibet, the Caucasus, Turkestan, North Vietnam and other regions, and also requesting the President, to proclaim a Captive Nations week.

A novelty in the Congressional resolution was the breaking down of the taboo which the pre-war frontiers of Soviet Russia had hitherto created for American policy. Whereas this policy did not hesitate to support the cause of the nine nations of Eastern Europe which were independent before the war, it had never aimed at independence for the nations constituting pre-war Russia, with the Ukraine in the forefront—equivalent to the idea of splitting up the Soviet empire. American initiative had never gone this far, since it would have excluded the possibility of coming to a lasting agreement with Russia, which this policy sought; it would have led to the mobilization around the communist Kremlin of all Russians without exception, together with the enemies of Communism; and a Russia broken down into a number of states would not have been able to create in Europe a counterbalance to a powerful Germany in the future. The Congressional resolution made a breach in this attitude, the importance of which should not however be overestimated; the distance between declarations and actions is a long one, and in addition the American foreign policy is run by the President with the aid of the State Department, not Congress. Meanwhile, the President's proclamation spoke only generally of many nations subjugated by Russia, without enumerating them as the Congressional resolution had done.

The Congressional resolution aroused certain misgivings because of the uniform treatment of the cause of the nine nations, independent before the war, with the problem of the Caucasus and Idel-Ural, which were revolutionary ephemera of 1918. These nations support their right to obtain independence not only on historical reasons or the right to self-determination, but essentially on the fact that before World War II they formed sovereign states and were deprived of this sovereignty by Soviet aggression, with the infringement of many treaties and international agreements. The rest of the nations referred to in the resolution had not created independent states before the war and constituted, as they still do, an integral part of Soviet Russia. Thus, apart from their right to a free and independent existence, this failure to differentiate between the nine nations and the other nations in the resolution, was equivalent to a sort of de-classifying of the main argument, which could not but be regarded as a minus from the point of view of the nine nations.

In connection with the Week, I was received in audience by Cardinal Spellman in New York, a result of which was a ceremonial mass for the captive nations in the Cathedral of St Patrick and all churches of the New York diocese, and others followed this example. The Cardinal received me very civilly and cordially. He was familiar with our problem and there was no need of long expositions.

Next in the celebration of the Week the ceremony of raising the flags of the nine nations opposite the UNO building took place on July 20th. The nine national anthems were played and the main speaker was Senator Jacob K. Javits from New York, who discussed the political aims of the Week.

Then an ACEN delegation went to Washington where they laid

a wreath on the tomb of the late Secretary of State, Foster Dulles. During our stay in the capital, we were received by the president of the American trade union organization AFL-CIO, George F. Meany, a large man with authority written on his face who had already issued a statement calling upon some dozen million workers in this organization to observe the Week. Finally the delegation set off to Capitol Hill where during a special ceremony they presented the initiators of the Week (Senators Douglas, Javits and Congressman McCormack) with scrolls expressing thanks for their action. The course of the visit and the speeches made were included by one of them in the Congressional record.

The dimensions which the observance of the Captive Nations week took on were impressive. After the President's proclamation some dozen State Governors and dozens of mayors of larger cities issued their own proclamations during the Week, arranging ceremonies in the States and cities concerned, while the press, radio and TV also seized upon the subject, the fruit of which was a hundred and more editorial articles and a number of TV and radio broadcasts in which ACEN members took part, devoted to the problem of the captive nations, some of which were broadcast throughout the whole country. Several newspapers also published my letter, containing facts and dates of the subjugation of each of the nine countries by Russia.

However, the Week owed its greatest publicity not to ACEN activity or to those of its friends, but to . . . Nikita Khrushchev. He learned of the observance of the Week during a ten-day stay in Poland and there, on July 21st, at a press conference in the palatial Soviet embassy in Warsaw, angry and excited, he violently attacked the United States on this account, stating that 'Only in capitalist countries are there captive peoples, not in the free land of the Soviet.' And since Vice-President Nixon was due to arrive in Moscow in two days' time, to open the American Exhibition there, Nikita cast a doubt on the value of this visit, saying that it was at variance with the intentions of the United States as laid down in the proclamation of the Week. He was echoed on the next day by Moscow *Pravda*, in a three-column editorial devoted to the Week, accusing the United States of undertaking a provocative campaign against the Soviet Union which was at striking variance with American assurances of their friendly intentions and with the opening of the exhibition which was, after all, intended to bring the two peoples closer together. The article warned that the Soviet people would be vigilant during Nixon's visit and ended with the statement that one could only laugh at the American attempts to find captive peoples in the genuinely free Socialist states. It was in the United States that paradise existed for capitalists, and enslavement for the working people. It was only the United States which by the threat of bayonets and what was called 'aid' were enslaving other nations. This article was followed by others, and all the Soviet press and radio set out after them to attack.

When on July 23rd Vice-President Nixon and his wife landed in Moscow, Khrushchev, who had arrived two hours earlier from Warsaw, was already addressing a crowd, brought to the Sports Palace, angrily attacking the Captive Nations week.

'On the one hand they send eminent people including governors to our country and open an exhibition and send the Vice-President to us, and on the other hand they do a thing like Captive Nations week.'

He called the observance of the Week 'direct interference in the Soviet Union's internal affairs, and an anti-Soviet campaign, dictated by the hysteria of panic-stricken monopolists, at the very time when Vice-President Nixon is visiting a captive nation. I hope that the Vice-President who has just landed will come and see these captive people, who are present here.'

On the same day Radio Moscow re-affirmed these charges, adding that the United States was trying to bring back the poisoned atmosphere of the cold war, that the provocative anti-Soviet campaign had been officially initiated, and that the President's proclamation was a cold war document and denial of the principles of peaceful co-existence.

The next day, July 24th, during Nixon's courtesy call in the Kremlin, in the course of which he handed over to Khrushchev a personal letter of greeting from President Eisenhower, Khrushchev abruptly ordered newspapermen recording this ceremony to leave his office. Then he motioned Nixon to the conference table and looking him up and down with obvious anger began to attack Captive Nations week, calling it a provocation, and threatening war in the event of any effort on the part of the United States aimed at the execution of the Congressional resolution. Nixon's conciliatory explanations failed and Khrushchev, lashing himself into a fury with his own words and pounding the table with his fist, exclaimed : 'This resolution stinks!'—and then added some very indecent four-letter words, which made translator Troyanovsky blush bright red, and it took some time before he decided to translate them.

Later on the same day while Nixon was conducting Khrushchev round the exhibition, acquainting him with the equipment of an American kitchen, he was brutally attacked in the presence of the retinue of both dignitaries and a whole crowd of reporters. 'If you had not taken such a decision ... your trip would be excellent,' shouted Khrushchev, his face red with rage, shaking his finger in front of Nixon's nose, 'but you have churned up the water yourselves! Why this was necessary, God only knows! What happened? What black cat crossed your path and confused you? But that is your affair, we do not interfere with your problems.'

Then he put his arm round a bystander and added : 'Does this man look like a slave?'

More charges followed these and the whole incident, unprecedented in the annals of diplomacy, called the 'kitchen debate' in America, gained world fame mainly because of the utter lack of account by the Soviet Premier of international custom accepted throughout the world and thanks to the fact that it was filmed for TV and appeared in newsreels all over the world.

Next, on July 25th, Vice-President Nixon visited the Soviet agricultural and industrial exhibition and found himself in the Uzbek pavilion, where a man approached him and asked : 'Why do you say that we are enslaved people. You can see that the Uzbek people are not enslaved. We consider this a provocation.'

Another man accosted Nixon near the pavilion of heavy industry : 'You said yesterday that we should come together but how can we do so in view of a recent statement regarding the enslaved nations which rudely violates the internal affairs of other countries?'

All Western pressmen present at these scenes were of the opinion that both men gave the impression of being planted, and their questions carefully prepared in advance. Their addressing Nixon had no traits of the spontaneous.

Finally, on July 26th, Nixon was taken to a *dacha* near Moscow, formerly the property of Orlov, a favourite of Catherine the Great; it is in such luxurious surroundings that the 'working-class' leaders of the Kremlin spend the summer. Khrushchev came to Nixon with the following proposition : 'First let us have pictures taken in front of the house, then a boat trip on the Moscow river, so you can see how our slaves live.'

After the photograph, all the company, including the President's brother, Milton Eisenhower, and the American ambassador, Llewellyn Thompson Jr., set off in the directon of the river. When they passed a group of bathers, and the latter started to applaud them, Khrushchev said to Nixon : 'You see, they are not captives.'

During the trip on the river in three motor-boats, they stopped eight times by the shore to exchange hand clasps with bathers. Each time Khrushchev asked them ironically : 'Are you captives?' and the bathers responded in a compliant chorus : 'No, no! Peace and friendship!'

Pleased with the good performance of this carefully rehearsed 'spectacle on the water' Khrushchev nudged Nixon in a friendly way in the ribs 'See how our slaves live.'

This was the end of Khrushchev's performances during Nixon's visit, connected with the Captive Nations week. The press and radio reported them down to the minutest detail, and thanks to this the moderate fame which the Week had enjoyed in the United States gained world status. Not in vain did the émigré circles make popular the sarcastic saying : 'If we can rely on someone for certain help, then it is the Kremlin only.' Not only the European press but that of other parts of the world also began to write on the subject of the Week. At a sign given by the Kremlin, a Red press and radio offensive also began in Albania, Bulgaria, Hungary, the Baltic countries and finally in mainland China and Poland. I also caught it, as that year's chairman of ACEN.

Why did Khrushchev react so violently to the Captive Nations week? After all, various kinds of American declarations in support of the right of the nations conquered by Russia during World War II or after it to freedom and independence could be reckoned by the dozen, and they had never brought forth any reaction in such a violent form. The Soviets had had time to get used to them. An undoubted cause of this was the fact that for the first time an official resolution of the Congress of the United States had enumerated the nations subjugated by Russia as early as under Tsarist rule, not merely the latest Soviet conquests. It is therefore not to be wondered at that the White Russian emigration came to the aid of Khrushchev, as well as their press, which attacked the Week not less violently. The chairman of the Central Representation of the Russian Emigration in the United States, Prince Beloselskii, and Professor Chebotarev, called the Congressional resolution an appeal to dismember Russia and this body sent a memorandum of protest to Secretary of State Herter. In the same way it was attacked by A. Nikolajevskii, chairman of the Russian committee of the Republican party, which consists of American citizens of Russian origin, who stated that the Ukraine, Georgia and Armenia are in Russian territory. The Russian émigré press in Europe began writing about the anti-Russian policy of the United States, about the partition of Russia, Russophobia, and the like. The Week even served the magazine *Voice of Russia*, issued in Munich, for an attack on the Central Representation of the Russian Emigration in the United States, and for a declaration that such a representation should have its headquarters in Europe, not in a country following a policy of partitioning Russia.

On the other hand, the powerful and influential Ukrainian organizations in the United States, various Cossack associations and their press organ *The Cossack,* not to mention organizations of Tartars, Turkistanis and various Caucasian nations, received the Week enthusiastically and took a very lively part in it, particularly the Ukrainians.

The Soviet sensitivity to the Week, shared by the White Russians, and to the nine captive nations grew in proportion as ever more subjugated nations transformed into colonies gained freedom and independence on the basis of the principle of self-determination. The knowledge that Russia is gradually becoming the last great colonial power in the world began not only to penetrate to public opinion throughout the globe, but also to unnerve the people ruling in the Kremlin. This fact is gradually becoming a real Achilles heel of the Soviet empire, and its present steersman, Nikita Khrushchev.

The confirmation of the rightness of this opinion was found by ACEN in the information from a reliable source to the effect that Nikita, obviously so as to put an end to these tendencies unfavourable to Russia, started confidential talks with Vice-President Nixon on the question of the United States recognizing the present *status quo* in the nine countries of East and Central Europe. 'This demand was formulated in a brutal manner,' said the informant, 'but Nixon rejected it out of hand.'

A year later, the Soviet counteraction to an identical proclamation by President Eisenhower on July 18, 1960, and the observance in the United States of the Captive Nations week on a still greater scale than the previous year, had already been planned in advance and carried out by leading figures in the Kremlin. It developed in the first place in the Baltic countries, and took the form of the joyful celebration of the twentieth anniversary of their integration into the Soviet Union. Wilno, the present capital of Soviet Lithuania, was visited by none other than Mikhail Suslov and he took part in huge public gatherings, attacking the United States and the Week. The same was done by a Finnish member of the Kremlin presidium, Otto Kuusinen, in Tallin, Estonia, and by M. Shvernik in Riga, Latvia. Of course, the crowds gathered at the meetings passed resolutions expressing joy at the liberation of the Lithuanian, Estonian or Latvian peoples from the Fascist-bourgeois yoke. As a year earlier, *Pravda* attacked the second Captive Nations week and

President Eisenhower, and was followed by the Soviet and satellite radio and press machinery.

These declarations of American policy are a good deal, as far as declarations go, yet not much in respect of action. The basic demand expressed to Dillon, the Under-Secretary of State, to the effect that we expect the declaration to be a prelude to definite action, still awaits fulfilment.

XXVIII

NIXON ON THE VISTULA

The reception prepared for Vice-President Nixon at the airport did not give any hint of what it was to become a few minutes later. On leaving the aircraft, he was greeted at the bottom of the steps by the American ambassador, Jacob D. Beam, and the former American citizen Oskar Lange, who reverted to being a Pole after the war. After the playing of the national anthems, both American and Polish, Nixon walked along the front of a guard of honour, commanded by an elegant officer with a drawn sabre in his hand and, unfamiliar with Polish military ceremony, he shuddered when the soldiers greeted him with a loud 'We salute you, Mr President'. After a colourless speech of welcome by Lange, devoid of any cordiality, the Vice-President stepped up to the microphone and made a short speech in which he reminded his listeners that the Poles were among the first group of settlers to land in America in 1608, and founded a colony in Jamestown, and that the names of Kosciuszko and Pulaski are known to every American. Next however his words referred to an event much closer in time, and was not necessarily agreeable to the ears of the communist journalists present at the airport.

'Yesterday you celebrated the fifteenth anniversary of the Warsaw insurrection. We Americans have not forgotten this heroic battle, which once again showed the unconquerable spirit and courage of the Polish nation.'

I heard this speech by Nixon as I was travelling by car in the streets of Washington. When they announced the broadcast of his address from Warsaw, Zosia and I glanced at each other. Would he say something or not? When Nixon began to speak about the insurrection, I sighed with relief and pleasure. After the news had been given in the papers that Nixon would travel to Warsaw on August 2nd, I had seized the telephone and pointed out to a certain person that Nixon would reach the capital of Poland on the day after the anniversary of the outbreak of the insurrection, and that that suggested certain ideas. The voice at the other end thanked me warmly.

255

'We are very grateful to be reminded, since it is hard for us Americans to remember such anniversaries as well as you Poles. I assure you that the attention of the Vice-President will be drawn to this.'

Nixon then, with the intention of stressing how close are the bonds between the American and Polish nation, introduced to his hosts a sort of American national hero, 'the father of the atom-driven submarine,' Vice-Admiral Hyman G. Rickover, saying he had been born in Poland near Warsaw. Until now everything had proceeded within the framework of the correct protocol reception of an eminent visitor from a country with which those welcoming him are not in very close and friendly relations.

This formal, official ceremony ceased outside the airport's gate when Warsaw began to welcome Nixon. Along the entire twenty-kilometre road leading from the military airport at Babice to the palace in the Lazienki where Nixon was to stay, a crowd of 300,000 Warsavians packed the sidewalks and roadway, leaving only a narrow passage for the procession of cars, with Nixon standing in the first. The crowd went mad. Shouts of 'Long live America! Long live Nixon! Long live Eisenhower!' and cheers uttered at the tops of their lungs poured into one huge uproar, which did not stop during the entire journey. A shower of bouquets fell upon Nixon and his wife, and the car was stopped on the way eight times to relieve it of the flowers. The crowd pushed up to Nixon, in order to touch his outstretched hand. The women threw him kisses, and on many faces tears poured down. In one place, the crowd greeted him with singing 'May he live a hundred years', and in another they sang 'Poland is not yet lost'. Amidst the flushed, feverish faces of the weeping and laughing populace, often holding children up so that they too might see the guest from legendary America, were also soldiers and policemen. All Independent Fighting Warsaw, unafraid and rebellious, had come into the streets this August day : nothing had been able to frighten them from manifesting their friendship with the United States, which was personified for them in a still young, unknown man who, exceedingly surprised and moved by the unusual enthusiasm of his reception—himself feeling moisture in his eyes—could only show his gratitude with an expression of the face, smile and gesture of the hand and repay this wave of cordiality which was coming to him from so many thousands. Yet this greeting was not restricted to Nixon only and to his wife, who was fighting back tears all the time. In the same way the next cars in the procession of the Vice-President and the buses with journalists were greeted. The latter, old stagers, rendered indifferent by the long exhausting

President of the Polish-American Congress Karol Rozmarek addressing the President Dwight D. Eisenhower at the Convention of the
Polish-American Congress in Chicago. From right to left : President
Rozmarek, President Eisenhower. First from left the author. See
chapter : *Le roi est mort, vive le roi*

Senator John F. Kennedy receiving the delegation of ACEN. From left
to right : Michalak/Poland, Kotta/Albania, Sidzikauskas/Lithuania,
Senator Kennedy, Zenkl/Czechoslovakia, Petkov/Bulgaria. Visible
on the table, author's book 'Fighting Warsaw'. See chapter : *Le roi
est mort, vive le roi*

journey, were prepared for anything except for what began to happen outside the airport gates. A sudden electric current ran through their group when they realized that they had unexpectedly become not only witnesses of an unusual event, but, for the first time during this journey, actors in it. So their quickly drawn-out notebooks and fountain pens disappeared and a hundred no longer journalists but Americans began to reply to the crowd with smiles and waves.

When Nixon was asked in the evening for his impression he could only raise his hands and reply : 'Words fail me in describing it. I have never known such a reception from foreigners in my life.'

A similar crowd and the same atmosphere accompanied Nixon wherever he went during the next two days. Whether these were trips to talks and receptions or a trip to the cemetery at Palmiry, which made a terrible impression on Nixon, where he visited the grave of Mieczyslaw Niedzialkowski, or to the ceremony of laying a wreath on the grave of the unknown soldier, he was everywhere surrounded by friendly, smiling, tearful and excited faces, everywhere flowers were handed to him and his wife, handclasps were exchanged, children were handed over to be kissed, people shouted : 'Long live America! Long live Nixon! Long live Eisenhower!', and 'A Hundred Years' was sung. A wave of sympathy accompanied them everywhere they encountered Warsaw, with a wave of cold and reserve at meetings with official circles. The cordiality and emotion of the welcome extended by the population exceeded the bounds known to Nixon, so it is not surprising that against this background a misunderstanding occurred when, after laying the wreath on the tomb of the Unknown Soldier, a grown man ran after Nixon and having caught him by both hands below the knees, tried to lift him into the air. Nixon, startled, made some resistance, and before the man succeeded in carrying out his intention, he was dragged from his victim by the bodyguard, after which it was explained to Nixon that this was a certain form of expressing liking. 'He wanted to raise you and with the aid of others to toss you several times in the air....' Thus Nixon's knowledge of Polish customs was enriched.

Such a picture of Nixon's reception was given by several persons who accompanied him with whom I talked. The same picture was given by the American reporters accompanying Nixon during all his journey in Russia and Poland, who let themselves be elevated by the mood of the Warsaw reception. All the American press, led by the *New York Times* and the *New York Herald Tribune*, gave descriptions of the visit of the Vice-President to Warsaw in the smallest detail and with pictures, struck primarily by the fact that this en-

i

thusiastic reception which was a manifestation of friendship for the
United States and an expression of faith in its mission, in which
Nixon played an incidental part, took place in a country behind
the Iron Curtain which was in Soviet domination. It was compared
to the reception which Nixon had in friendly Venezuela, where he
found himself in personal danger when his car had stones thrown
at it during his drive and then it was stopped, and Nixon was
very nearly dragged out to be victim of a furious, hostile crowd,
stirred up by communists. The welcome prepared for him was
compared with the official gala arranged in Warsaw for Khrushchev
a week earlier, stressing that Khrushchev was greeted by people
brought in trucks from factories and offices, who were strictly forbidden to leave the route until Khrushchev had passed. Flowers
were distributed to these people, paid for by the State, whereas at
the welcome of Nixon—which occurred on a Sunday—no one was
brought, but everyone came of their own free will and fetched their
own flowers bought with hard-earned money, sometimes perhaps at
the cost of other needs. The whole press emphasized that none of
the Warsaw papers gave the time of Nixon's arrival, nor the airport
at which he was to land, and merely mentioned that he was to arrive
on the Sunday afternoon. However, thanks to Radio Free Europe
broadcasting uninterrupted news of the arrival of Nixon, and the
stationing of police along the streets and roads leading to Babice,
the population of Warsaw knew where to go and some stood on the
route for several hours.

In connection with this action of Radio Free Europe I broadcast
a speech to the population of the city of Warsaw as its last Deputy
to the Sejm elected by genuine and not falsified votes in 1947. I
mentioned in it the recently ended Captive Nations week as an expression of protest against the domination of the Soviets over Poland
and I repeated the assurance given to the ACEN delegation by acting
Secretary of State Dillon. I defined the purpose of the coming visit
of Nixon as a proof of the sincere and deep feelings of the United
States towards Poland and its respect for the unfailing values of
the Polish people who were resisting so consistently communist
dictatorship and Soviet rule. I terminated by the appeal : 'People
of Warsaw ! The Vice-President of the United States is coming to
you on the fifteenth anniversary of the insurrection, the most heroic
event of the past war. He will be able to feel the deep grief but also
pride which characterizes the observation of this anniversary by
Warsaw. As a resident of the capital for many years and her Deputy
in the year 1947, I know the moods of Warsaw. I know that the
welcome she is preparing for Vice-President Nixon will be more

enthusiastic than any other given to him outside the United States. All of us here in exile share your deep satisfaction on account of the visit of the Vice-President of the United States to Poland. In greeting him, you are greeting a man who symbolizes those values which America wishes to ensure to the whole world—freedom and democracy, and to Poland, the recognition of her rights to genuine independence.'

The essential aim of the speech was to inform listeners in Poland that the emigration was positive in its attitude to the visit of Nixon to Warsaw, considering it as expressing the wish to bring about a rapprochement to the Polish people but not to the communist government.

Before this appeal to Warsaw was recorded, doubts were expressed as to whether the risk was not too great. 'What will happen if the people do not react to Nixon's arrival as you expect?'

'No fear of that,' said I, with unshakeable certainty, 'if only they are informed of the time and place of his arrival.'

This was already being dealt with by Radio Free Europe, and primarily by the chiefs of the Polish section, Jan Nowak in Munich and Karol Wagner in New York, with a result which surpassed all expectations. I spoke out in a similar way on the subject of the intended visit in an interview with the NBC on July 28th.

In saying these words to Poland I was not yet aware of the fact that I was giving Nixon's visit a significance diametrically opposed to that which the Warsaw press was attributing to it, as a cancellation of Captive Nations week. First *Slowo powszechne*, the organ of PAX, or the pre-war fascist Boleslaw Piasecki, hastened on the day before the visit to state that it would constitute absolute recognition by the United States of the Polish social system, that in the light of this the Captive Nations week was worthless and a tasteless political propaganda show and that Nixon's gesture was a wise concession to political realism. Similarly, the main organ of the Communist party, *Trybuna ludu*, in an editorial devoted to the visit, called Captive Nations week 'a rotten log in the stove of the cold war'. In this respect, the Warsaw press prophesied the event, since according to reliable information Gomulka complained during the long talks with Nixon of the observance of the Week as an act hostile to the Polish People's Republic which was, after all, an independent state and totally sovereign. 'A certain flavour was given these complaints by the fact, known to both sides, that at the head of the Assembly of Captive Nations that year stood a Pole, whose person was not unknown to Gomulka,' said, with a smile, my informer who had accompanied Nixon on the journey.

The fact will surely not arouse surprise that the American press gave a completely different interpretation to the reception which the population of Warsaw prepared for Nixon from the Polish communist press. The *New York Times* in an editorial article on August 3rd stated that the population of Warsaw gave 'the most effective answer possible to Premier Khrushchev's gibes at our celebration of Captive Nations week.' Stressing that Nixon was greeted in Warsaw as no leader of America ever was in a foreign country, the article stated that 'by their welcome the people of Warsaw destroyed the propaganda campaign which has sought so hard to prove that Communist totalitarianism has won over the people of Eastern Europe so there can be no more talk of captive nations. In one hour of truth, as the Nixon caravan rode from the airport to the city, the friends of freedom and democracy gained new courage and new heart, which cannot but affect profoundly the world political scene.'

In connection with this editorial I sent the *New York Times* a letter published on August 12th, and later inserted by Senator Keating in the Congressional record. In this letter, sharing the attitude adopted by the *New York Times*, I also added that the welcome prepared for Nixon 'was in effect the biggest anti-Communist demonstration ever to take place in the streets of Warsaw. It was actually a form of election where the Poles showed that, although they are still physically controlled by the Soviets, they are spiritually on the side of the free world. When they shouted 'Long live Eisenhower' they really meant 'Down with Communist domination'. Their unprecedented demonstration showed their deep longing for freedom and independence because they believe, against all odds, that the United States is the only power in the world that can help them regain their independence.'

XXIX

INTER-PARLIAMENTARY SQUABBLES
IN WARSAW

Such was the response of Warsaw to Captive Nations week. It was not only heard in the United States, but was reflected back to Warsaw during the conference of the Inter-Parliamentary Union which took place in the capital of Poland on August 25–September 2, 1959. Before the representatives of the United States Congress set out for Warsaw I was invited by the chairman of the American delegation, Congressman Harold D. Cooley, to a meeting in the Capitol on August 14th and I appealed to the members of the delegation to express at this conference the convictions and views which they had shown by passing the resolution regarding Captive Nations week. If they regarded it as possible to sit in one association with deputies from parliaments behind the Iron Curtain, where voting is done only on one list, then they had the holy duty, travelling for the first time to a country with a communist system, to condemn that system, particularly if they did not want their presence to be made to imply to the Polish nation recognition for the rule now prevailing in Poland.

The solemn assembly listened in calm silence with evident sympathy on their faces for the arguments of the speaker. But the calm suddenly changed into emotion when I drew out of my brief-case the Warsaw newspaper *Zycie Warszawy* of July 23rd, and on the basis of an interview published in it with Wende, who was chairman of the Polish communist delegation to the conference of the Union, I started to inform the senators and congressmen what matters he intended to bring up at the conference. For Wende had announced in advance that he was very worried by the parliamentary crisis in Burma and Pakistan and would bring up this matter at a session on the agenda. When commenting on this concern of Wende, I compared it with the indescribable falsities perpetrated during the elections in Poland in 1947, when during the electoral campaign the secret police murdered 118 Peasant Party activists. When I mocked at his concern for the legality of new parliaments in Burma and Pakistan when in Poland in 1952 and 1957 voting was done only

on one list, laughter mingled with cries of indignation. Next I
came to Wende's statement that he intended to familiarize those
taking part in the conference with Polish parliamentary traditions,
which had hundreds of years behind them. After my statement that
the people who had destroyed the parliamentary system in Poland
now wished to pose as the heirs of the former parliamentary institutions, the hall reacted as before. Hands reached out towards me for
the copy of the *Zycie Warszawy*, but as it was the only copy I handed
it to Congressman Cooley and everyone got only an English translation of the interview. Finally, those present were interested in
the passage in which Wende said that parliamentary delegations
often differ with the governments of their own countries, in which
is to be found the hidden hope that, for instance, it would be possible to obtain from the American delegation that which it was not
possible to obtain from the government. In a word, Wende's interview was very timely.

I ended my speech by reminding the audience that they would
reach Warsaw on the fifteenth anniversary of the insurrection which
broke out on August 1, 1944. Then the chairman called on the deputy
Under-Secretary of State, Foy Kohler, who had accompanied
Vice-President Nixon both on his journey to Russia and his visit to
Warsaw. Three days later, Senator Keating inserted in the Congressional record the ACEN memorandum devoted to the conference
which I had distributed to the delegates.

The first sensation at the session of the Inter-Parliamentary Union
in Warsaw was a speech by congressman Tadeusz Machrowicz. This
gentleman, born in Poland and later an officer in General Haller's
army, did not require either my or anyone else's information to say
what the situation required. On August 27th he began his speech
in Polish with expressions of gratitude to the Polish hosts for reminding him that this year's session of the Union was meeting on the
twentieth anniversary of the outbreak of World War II, which
started with a German attack on Poland. Next he came to discussing
the events preceding the outbreak and quoted . . . extracts from the
Soviet-German agreement of August 23, 1939, along with the secret
protocol to the agreement, also dated August 23rd and signed by
Molotov and Ribbentrop, which fell into the hands of the American
army after the defeat of Germany. This protocol introduced a division line between the German and Soviet zones, in the as yet un-
invaded territory of Poland, along the line of the Narew, Vistula
and San rivers. As to the very existence of the Polish state, the
protocol stated that 'the question whether the interests of both sides
would show the need for preserving an independent Polish state . . .

can be decided only during the course of further political negotiations'. Next Congressman Machrowicz quoted the contents of Ribbentrop's telegram of September 3rd, proposing that the Russian army move against the Polish army in the Soviet zone. As a result of this telegram, the German-Soviet agreement came into effect, determining September 17th as the day for the crossing of Soviet forces into Polish territory. Finally, discussing the Soviet-German treaty of September 28, 1939, which settled the division of Polish territory after it had been seized by Soviet-German forces, he quoted a secret protocol of that same day, in which both sides promised to stifle hostile agitation towards the other side in their territory and to exchange information in this sphere with this intention.

The effect of Machrowicz' speech was thunderous, particularly on the members of the Polish communist delegation and on other Poles present. They heard this speech first-hand, not translated like the rest through earphones. Thus, in the city where only a month earlier Khrushchev had stated that Stalin acted rightly in signing a pact with Hitler, since it was intended to prevent the mutual destruction of Germany and Russia, someone was daring to refer to the Soviet-German conspiracy, in which moreover the possibility of the complete liquidation of the Polish state was foreseen. For the ears of the Polish communists and Iron Curtain delegations this was really sacrilege. But the content of the speech was a surprise, it startled everyone, hence there was no immediate reaction.

The next fly in the eye of the organizers was a protest by the Dutch delegate, the Socialist J. W. A. Burger, who objected to calling Poland a socialist country, rightly stating that countries with a communist system are not socialist.

Encouraged by this example, the head of the Australian delegation, W. A. Haworth, and the Austrian delegate attacked Chinese communist aggression in Tibet, and the communist bloc motion to admit delegations from North Vietnam and North Korea were rejected. This was manfully contributed to by a Congressman of Polish origin, Edward J. Derwinski, who spoke against the motion.

Next day the organizers were already better prepared for surprises. That day Ostap Dluski took the chair, paying vigilant attention to what happened all around. Thus when Congressman W. R. Poage of Texas accused the Russians, after having reached the Vistula during the 1944 Warsaw insurrection, of having deliberately halted their offensive so as not to come to the aid of the fighting population of the city, Dluski seized the chairman's gavel and banging his pulpit with it, refused to let Poage go on speaking. To support this act by words, he added with incredible cynicism that if the people of Warsaw heard what the speaker had said they would not understand what he was referring to.

During the conference, the wife of Congressman Machrowicz, Zofia, a Polish lady by origin who spoke Polish fluently and because of this played the part of translator for the wives of other congressmen and senators, visited with them various institutions in the capital. During one such visit, someone whispered to her : 'Please thank your husband for his excellent and daring speech at the conference.' 'And how do you in Warsaw know about it?' Mrs Machrowicz inquired. 'We heard it from Radio Free Europe and the news spread all over the city. Everyone is talking about it and is very grateful. Pray do not forget my request.'

In this way the people of Warsaw through the mouth of one inhabitant expressed their gratitude at hearing words which should have been uttered in this city's official celebrations of the twentieth anniversary of the war and the fifteenth anniversary of the Insurrection.

XXX

NIKITA IN THE 'CAPITALIST HELL'

Before his visit with his family to the United States, Khrushchev
first sent patrols to survey the hostile territory. The first was
Anastas Mikoyan who arrived in January 1959, a dark man with an
eagle's broken nose and Chaplinesque moustache, who would not
require any characterization to play Mephisto in *Faust*. This con-
summate veteran of struggles for power and Kremlin purges was
greeted by a crowd of about 500 Americans, since this was the
number of Yew York policemen surrounding the spot where he
landed at the Idlewild airport; and also by émigré pickets, prin-
cipally Hungarians, who had special accounts to settle with him since
the insurrection in Budapest, and carried placards demanding freedom for the countries behind the Iron Curtain. At a press conference summoned in the headquarters of ACEN on January 13th, I
defined the purpose of his visit as the start of an offensive intended
morally to disarm the American people so as to make them more
susceptible to any kind of concession in the settling of disputed
problems. Some dozens of American papers, led by the *New York
Times* and *New York Herald Tribune,* repeated this warning. A
prominent place in the press was given to the former President,
Harry Truman, who criticized the enthusiasm with which some
eminent industrialists and financiers were inviting Mikoyan to
meetings and receptions. This attitude of his did not, however, prevent Eric Johnston, president of the Motion Picture Association
of America, from arranging a dinner in honour of Mikoyan, which,
however, was boycotted by a part of those invited, including Congressman Walter Judd and Mrs Judd. 'We will not be present (at
the dinner) for the same reasons that we would not attend a social
function honouring Hitler, Himmler, Nero or Genghis Khan,' was
the telegram of reply sent by Congressman Judd to Johnston's invitation. Those who attended this dinner in Washington were
greeted by pickets in which members of the Association of Polish
Ex-Combatants took part. Similar pickets greeted Mikoyan wherever he appeared.

He was several times asked about the Hungarian question and at a press conference, without blinking an eye he gave a classical example of the Great Lie : 'There is order in Hungary, there is culture, production and happiness. Recently, elections took place. I recently spoke with leaders in Hungary and with Hungarian people. They are happy. Relations are excellent. The situation is normal. It would be rather nice if the situation were as normal in many other countries as it is in Hungary.'

Asked about the intervention in Hungary at a TV interview with the well-known commentator Spivak, he replied : 'As for the decision of the United Nations on Hungary, it was adopted through the voting machine, the majority of which is at the disposal of the United States. And now Hungary is making very good progress, the atmosphere there is very good. There is a great consolidation throughout the country, all without your assistance and in spite of any decisions by the United Nations. And our troops in Hungary are stationed under the agreements, under the Warsaw pact and certain other agreements. They (Soviet troops) are friends. They do not interfere in the country's internal affairs and have very good relations.'

More sensitivity than Mikoyan displayed was shown towards everything connected with the countries of Eastern Europe by Khrushchev's next emissary, Vice-Premier Frol R. Kozlov. A thick-set, strongly built, fair-haired man with wavy hair, he sought on the model of 'smiling Michael', Ambassador Menshikov, to charm Americans by his broad smile, friendly behaviour and hand out-stretched to greet anyone within reach. But this smile went when the Governor of the state of Michigan, G. Mennon Williams, started to refer to the case of the nine countries of Eastern and Central Europe. Governor Williams himself told me what happened when I visited him with the general-secretary of ACEN, Brutus Coste, less than three weeks later in the state capital, Lansing :

'I first asked Kozlov when, in accordance with the statements of the Soviets regarding the right of every nation to self-determination, would the nations of Eastern and Central Europe be able to obtain independence by means of free and secret elections. The expression on the face of Kozlov underwent an instantaneous change. His smile disappeared without trace, he became gloomy and stated excitedly that these countries have governments which they themselves chose and if I had heard anything to the contrary it was only propaganda. I then started to analyse the present situation in each country behind the Iron Curtain in turn. I ended my remarks about Poland with the claim that she had never been given the opportunity to make use of the right of self-determination. The same applied to Hungary, where the uprising of the people was bloodily suppressed by Soviet tanks. Finally I referred to the question of incorporating the Baltic States into Russia. In conclusion I told Kozlov that Russia ought to withdraw her troops from these countries and permit them to hold free elections. To this Kozlov, passing over the case of Poland, Hungary and the Baltic States in total silence, stated that there are no Russian troops in Rumania, and that the population there had taken advantage of the right of self-determination but did not change the system of government, and that I was altogether in the wrong. To this I again stated that many reliable inhabitants of my state are of Rumanian origin and that they claim categorically that the present government in Rumania was not elected by the Rumanian people and I added : 'To be frank, Mr Kozlov, no one in America believes in what you have told me about Eastern and Central Europe. And I do not think it is the truth.' During all the conversation Kozlov was excited but he did not lose control of himself, which is more than I can say for Ambassador Menshikov, who went purple in the face and began interrupting the talk, repeating Kozlov's arguments in a loud voice. The epilogue to this meeting was the statement Kozlov gave the press that I am not an expert on international affairs, and that all the peoples behind the Iron Curtain have governments they themselves chose.'

Before the arrival of Khrushchev, scheduled for September 15, 1959, ACEN developed feverish activity. It was initiated by my letter published in the *New York Times* on August 6th, expatiating on the basic demands of ACEN towards public opinion and American policy. The letter expressed disbelief that his visit might bring any advantages to the United States but, as it was to occur, then the ideas of the Captive Nations week should be transformed into political action, primarily reminding the Soviet visitor very firmly of the as yet unsettled matter of the restoration of freedom and independence to the nine enslaved nations. It should be made plain to him that only by enabling these nations to establish governments and institutions of their own choice would one of the main causes of international tension be removed. This same subject, supplemented by comment on the moral disarmament of the American peoples, was developed by me in a syndicated interview by the journalist Milt Freudenheim, published first in the *Chicago Daily News* on August 5th, and also at press conferences in Washington, Chicago and New York. The reporter of a Washington paper, having pessimistically stated that the émigrés he met at this press conference were condemned to exile for ever, ended on a quite unexpected note of optimism : 'They seemed doomed to exile, though who can be sure? Not many years ago a small, enthusiastic man plodded round Washington trying to get people to read long, badly-typed denunciations of the Japanese. His name was Syngman Rhee.'

In a similar way I spoke on the subject of Khrushchev's visit as chairman of ACEN at a meeting in Freedom House in New York on September 10th, then with Senator Douglas and Congressman Pucinski at a meeting of several thousands in Chicago on September 13th, and at an equally large meeting in Carnegie Hall, New York, on September 20th. At the last, when I stressed the right of the nations incorporated forcibly into Soviet Russia—primarily the Ukrainians—to genuinely independent existence, I was unexpectedly interrupted by a storm of applause. One of the organizers of the meeting explained the cause of this reaction. 'There are about 2,000 Ukranians in the audience, who marched here in a procession of protest. As a Pole, they gave you warmer applause than they would have given a Ukrainian speaking of the same thing.'

On the day of Khrushchev's arrival, September 15th, the ACEN members performed the ceremony of hauling up the flags of the nine nations on their building opposite the headquarters of the United Nations, while on the next day Vice-President Kovago and I formed part of a delegation led by Mrs Claire Luce Booth, former American ambassador in Rome, who handed to Sir Leslie Munro, appointed by the UN to watch over the Hungarian case, a report on the current situation in that country.

This ACEN activity was only part of the campaign which was started by the opponents of Khrushchev's visit. In Washington Senators Douglas, Dodd and Bridges, and Congressman Judd, formed a Committee for Freedom of all Peoples to arouse the vigilance of the American nation against the visit; similar efforts were made by the organization American Friends of Captive Nations under Christopher Emmett, and the Conference of Americans of Central and Eastern European Descent with Mgr Jonas Balkunas, a Lithuanian by origin, at its head. In the strictly Polish sector, the Polish-American Congress and the Polish Council of National Unity in the USA were also active.

In addition to this a number of Polish, Ukrainian and other ethnic group organizations, associations of ex-combatants and former political prisoners organized ceaseless picketing of Khrushchev. In this action a leading place was taken by a former prisoner of Auschwitz for many years, the Hungarian refugee, Dr Bela Fabian. After these preparations, wherever Khrushchev appeared, he was greeted by hostile crowds waving placards of the kind 'Khrushchev the hangman of the Ukraine.' 'Khrushchev, accomplice of the murderer Stalin.' Everywhere he stopped, and particularly the headquarters of the Soviet delegation to the United Nations on Park Avenue, looked like a besieged fortress, so many mounted and foot police surrounded it, not to mention the demonstrating crowd, between which and the police incidents sometimes occurred.

However, from the political point of view the most important was a visit by an ACEN delegation, consisting of the chairman, General Bela Kiraly and Ambassador Juraj Slavik, to the Department of State. This delegation put forward the need of bringing up the case of the nine nations in talks with Khrushchev in the way discussed for many years with the State Department, to which a reply was received that these were precisely the intentions of the American government.

After taking all these measures, it was possible to undertake observation of the course of Khrushchev's visit, in order to seize upon everything which might in any way, no matter how distant, be connected with Poland and the other countries behind the Iron Curtain, and which might also throw a certain light on the first person in the Kremlin as politician and man.

It started from an incident throwing a certain light on the tactics selected by Khrushchev for his American visit in relation to the problem of the Iron Curtain countries. It was an incident during the questions put to Khrushchev after a lunch and his speech of September 16th in the National Press Club in Washington, broadcast on TV throughout the country. The president of the club, William H. Lawrence read to Khrushchev the following question which had reached him from one of the guests in the hall : 'In your opening remarks, Mr Khrushchev, you spoke about avoiding outside interference in the affairs of other nations. How, then, do you justify Russian armed interference in Hungary?'

When this question had been translated into Russian for Khrushchev, he reddened like a beetroot, despite the fact that his interpreter, Oleg Troyanovsky, had chosen moderate terms, and burst out : 'The question of Hungary has stuck in some people's throats like a dead rat. He feels that it is unpleasant and yet he cannot spit it out. If there is a desire that our discussion take that turn, then of course we for our part could think of quite a few questions of a similar character.'

Another conflict on the same theme occurred the same afternoon during Khrushchev's visit to the Senate Foreign Relations committee. In reply to a greeting by the chairman, Senator Fulbright,

Khrushchev expressed his sorrow that Congress had appropriated funds for subversive activity in other countries, which did not serve the idea of peace. To this Fulbright stated in the first place that the reply gave him some difficulties, since the same words in the United States and in Russia had different meanings, after which he said with emphasis : 'We have not appropriated money to subvert freedom any place. On the contrary, all we have undertaken was to encourage and develop freedom. If you agree not to use force to make people accept your system. . . .'

Khrushchev angrily interrupted : 'When we arranged with President Eisenhower the exchange of visits, it was agreed that we would not discuss other countries. We have no authority from them to do so,' and when Fulbright referred to Korea, Tibet and Laos as examples which did not permit of any reliance on Soviet assurances of not interfering in the affairs of other countries, Khrushchev once again took refuge behind the alleged agreement with President Eisenhower and ironically advised Fulbright to apply in this matter to Peking.

Other controversies followed. On September 17th at a reception at the home of the former Governor of the State of New York, Averell Harriman, General David Sarnoff, president of the Radio Corporation of America, asked Khrushchev why the Russian government did not permit the broadcast of American radio and TV programmes to Russia, whereas in the United States no restrictions existed as to the broadcasting of such programmes from Russia to America. Encouraged by his host, General Sarnoff added with a smile that he had been born in Minsk. To this Khrushchev replied, 'No government can let another government deal with questions of educating its youth. We know the tastes of our people better than you do, even though you were born in Minsk.'

The same evening, at a dinner for Khrushchev at the Economic Club of New York, the publisher Gardner Cowles reminded Khrushchev of his words concerning the need of a better mutual acquaintance between the Soviet and American peoples and asked why in Russia freedom of information was forbidden, which serves precisely this aim. It was possible to notice at once that Khrushchev reddened and fell into a rage, although he stated comparatively calmly that according to the agreement with President Eisenhower neither side would interfere in the internal affairs of the other. At this moment a loud impatient cry was heard in the depths of the hall : 'Answer the question.'

Now Khrushchev burst out and shaking his fist he began to shout, 'I'm an old sparrow, so to say, and you cannot muddle me by your cries. You might not listen to me if you don't want to; but surely you must show enough hospitality not to interrupt. If there is no desire to listen to what I have to say, I can go. The question of what our public listens to or reads should be decided not by any outside government or any outside influence but by our own people and by its government. We jam the voice with which some of you want to speak to our people. If the voice with which you broadcast to our country will be a friendly voice, we shall not jam it. I think that should be clear.'

On September 19th, in San Francisco, at a dinner given for Khrushchev by the World Affairs Council of Los Angeles and the mayor of the city, Norris Poulson, came a still greater public scene, when Poulson reminded Khrushchev in his speech of his threat which had circled round the whole world, 'We shall bury you,' Khrushchev got angry and shaking his fist again, which seemed to be his favourite gesture, he threatened to break off his trip if he were the subject of such attacks. During his tirade he added : 'It is a question of war or peace between our countries, a question of life or death for the peoples. If you want war, we will give you war.'

This last threat made a startling impression on his audience. Brutal strength looked out from behind the jovial round face of this tubby little man. Sudden silence fell and a chill went through the hall, as though the phantom of death had flown by.

The meeting with the leaders of trade unions on September 20th in San Francisco changed into an uninterrupted course of incidents and insults. The president of the AFL-CIO, George Meany, had refused to take part, but seven presidents of individual trade unions attended who were also vice-presidents of AFL-CIO, including Walter P. Reuther, president of the United Automobile Workers. They asked Khrushchev a whole series of unpleasant questions, including those on the subject of the exploitation of workers in countries with communist governments, particularly East Germany. Reuther spoke on the basis of his own observations, since I myself heard him say a few years ago, 'I went with my brother to Russia in 1934 and spent eighteen months in a car factory in Gorki as an instructor. Later I travelled far and wide across Russia and I know what Communism is in practice.'

As these questions were asked, Khrushchev's face took on a purple hue, and when they finished, he started banging his fist on the table and hurling insults, such as 'You are hopelessly sick with capitalist fever.' The workingmen's leaders replied similarly, but the protocol cast a veil over this, stating merely 'a lively exchange across the table.'

When the president of the Oil, Chemical and Atomic Workers, O. A. Knight, raised the question of the right of self-determination of the peoples, Khrushchev was not pleased with the introduction of a new subject and shouted : 'I've never liked fleas when they jump all over.'

There was a fast two or three minute interchange across the table, the contents of which the protocol discreetly omitted, merely stating that 'at one point Khrushchev, talking to Joseph Curran, president of the National Maritime Union, exclaimed, 'How can you open your mouth like that and represent the workers? Do you want a discussion or is this a bazaar?' At this point Khrushchev became quite excited and pounded the table. The Russians accompanying Khrushchev were so upset that a violent dispute broke out about even such an innocent question as the translation of the English word 'fatigue'. When Reuther named the Soviet trade unions, of which he was himself a member at one time, 'a company union', a dispute again broke out, the contents of which the protocol did not describe, however. At Reuther's comment that whenever a sharp question was asked Khrushchev got angry, the latter reacted with an insult : 'And what you represent we call—capitalist lackeys.'

Next, Knight reverted to the right of self-determination for peoples and the quelling by force of the Hungarian insurrection, asking among other things why the Russians intervened in Hungary. Khrushchev then shouted : 'There was no interference. There was a counter-revolution, thugs and hooligans, who received arms from outside and took power in Budapest. And the government asked us for aid, and we gave it, and we're proud of it. We are proud of this feat ! There would be fascism there had we not done so.'

To this Reuther said, 'Was Nagy a fascist? I thought he was a communist?' Khrushchev : 'Don't mix good things with dirt.' Here the protocol notes 'exchanges across the table,' but no more, which enables us to suppose that uncensored expressions were heard.

Khrushchev : 'Have we exhausted the Hungarian question?'

James B. Carey, president of the International Union of Electrical, Radio and Machine workers : 'We have touched on it, we have certainly not exhausted it.'

Now Paul L. Phillips, president of the United Papermakers and Paperworkers, asked for the reason of the jamming of Radio Free Europe and the Voice of America. Looking angrily at Phillips, Khrushchev said : 'What do you prefer to have for dinner? What is your favourite dish?' Phillips : 'Probably roast beef.' Khrushchev : 'I, borsch. You continue to enjoy your roast beef and I borsch.'

Reuther, to Khrushchev: 'But you prescribe and insist on borsch for all.'

The crown of Khrushchev's visit was the talks with President Eisenhower at Camp David. They were confidential in nature and it was not until after some time that information reached ACEN from a reliable source that the case of the nine nations had been brought up among others in such a way that Khrushchev demanded recognition of the status quo in the Iron Curtain countries and that he met with a refusal. But, whereas he had already made this demand to Vice-President Nixon during the latter's stay in Moscow, and in a very brutal manner, he now did it in a calm and cautious way. It was not revealed which side first started discussion on the subject of the Iron Curtain peoples, but it is certain that the concentration of the talks on the Berlin question and summit conference pushed the question of the nine nations into the background.

From all these political talks, the figure of Khrushchev emerged as a politician gifted with much inborn intelligence and political talent above the average. Nothing in what he did or said was scholastic, but there was knowledge; preparation was lacking but instinct was there, dictating strokes and devices by which Khrushchev came in to counterattack, reaching for arms in ever new spheres and changing the course of the discussion. His interlocutors, with the exception of the workers' leaders, made with their polite remarks and cautious reactions to Khrushchev's threats the impression of tennis players sent to match a boxer. The elegant tennis player sets out to serve the ball, while the boxer jumps over the net and punches him on the nose. The peasant-like intelligence and shrewdness of Khrushchev, his earthly sayings and folk proverbs, a large sense of humour, though going hand in hand with vulgarity, a tendency to play the fool, and contempt for the traditional forms and customs of diplomacy, upsetting the balance of the professional diplomats, made him a dangerous opponent for those who entered into discussion with him. A belief in the future, arrogance, self-confidence and awareness of the strength he represented emanated from Khrushchev. A proof of this was his brutal openness and frankness, cynically not reckoning with the truth and frequently taking refuge in threats. He was primitive, raw, even coarse, and perhaps for this reason super-sensitive as to his own dignity and treatment by others, but at the same time he was interesting and impressive by his own kind of picturesqueness and originality, created by a mixture of virtues and vices, displayed cynically and without any embarrassment before the surprised Americans. But in the first place he aroused fright and alarm for the future by his behaviour and methods of a typical Russian bear, the frequent outbreaks of anger, the use of threats and brutal frankness which were undoubtedly mistakes from the point of view of Soviet policy. To his older sayings, which had already entered the political vocabulary : 'we shall bury you; your grandchildren will live in a communist system,' were added new threats which, linked with the awareness that this man who underwent frequent, uncontrolled outbursts might by his own decision unleash an atomic war, showed dramatically and warningly in what great and daily danger the world was living. This result cannot be regarded as a success either for Khrushchev or for Soviet policy. In summing up his stay in the United States, this must be inscribed to the minus side of communist strategy and tactics.

He came to the United States with his whole family, i.e. wife, two daughters, son and son-in-law. He brought them all out of domestic retreat and made them actors on the political stage, which freed the rest of us from the duty of discretion which ought to be maintained in relation to the private life of eminent people. By bringing his family, Khrushchev sought to bake two pies at one stove. One, political, stressing not only the equality of Russia and the United States but also of the two 'ruling families'. Khrushchev might rightly suppose that the prestige of the Soviet ruler would gain by this, when at a banquet at the White House the President of the United States would break bread on an equal footing not only with him but also with his family. The echo of this must flatter the national pride of the Russians. They would certainly say : 'Our Nikita is some guy !' The second pie—eternal gratitude of his whole family for this social promotion, and also the trip to America which : 'let Nikita shout what he likes at meetings, but speaking between ourselves, in the family, it is a legend and paradise on earth which is worth seeing.'

From the time of landing, against the background of the ceremonial welcome in Washington by the President and his wife, batteries of microphones, TV cameras, speeches, the diplomatic corps, crowds of dignitaries, rows of troops of the three armed services, and bands—in a word, the glitter and pomp proper to this kind of occasion—they looked exceedingly provincial, as if cut out roughly by an axe in clothes below the average level of Americans. The President looked embarrassed and did not demonstrate his broad smile known all over the world as he travelled along uncomfortably squeezed between the two massive figures of Mr and Mrs Khrushchev. Also during the welcoming ceremonies, as at all receptions and speeches during the whole trip, the family looked somewhat out of place, more exotic despite their European clothes than African chiefs in head-dresses and coloured robes.

The Americans looked at them with calm curiosity. So this is the Russian bear which wants to bury us? He looks like a decent fatty, particularly when he smiles. If they felt any hostile feelings, they did not betray them. On the contrary, Khrushchev encountered manifestations of that easy civility natural to Americans, which in any case the President and press appealed for. Incidents of aggressive behaviour from the Americans were rare, whereas the American ethnic groups and political emigrations from the countries of Eastern Europe caused the security authorities and police massed everywhere a great deal of trouble.

However, the mood began to change as the visit went on, when the average American had read something in the press about Khrushchev's statements and had seen on TV how he shook his fist, angry and dangerous. Towards the end of his stay a wave of dislike flowed across the country and those who had opposed the visit triumphed. This wave was also directed against one of his daughters, who looked fiercely at everyone and did not reply even to the most innocent of questions, evidently afraid that capitalist trickery was concealed behind it. However, Mrs Khrushchev was excluded on account of her very motherly look and calm behaviour, also the son Sergei, whose main passion was butterflies.

The second visit of Khrushchev to the United States, more exactly to New York, since this time his opportunities for travelling were restricted by the American government to Manhattan and the Soviet property in Glen Cove, Long Island, was preceded by the Paris squabbles, or the unsuccessful Summit conference, which was to start there on May 16, 1960. As his pre-condition, Khrushchev put forward the demand for an apology by President Eisenhower for sending a U-2 reconnaissance plane over Russia; the President refused and the Summit did not come off, except that Khrushchev, during the press conference, produced a whole series of methods of 'personal diplomacy' already known to the world : he banged his fist on the table, shook it above his head, called the reconnaissance flights 'criminal, piratical and cowardly', and compared the Pentagon generals to a cat which got into a pigeon house, or ate cream and was caught by the neck for doing so and well smacked. The hall reacted not only with applause, but first of all by whistling and shouts of protest, and from this an unpleasant spectacle emerged, such as the oldest representatives of the press did not recollect ever seeing before.

Before the conference in Paris, ACEN developed feverish activity.

Its delegation spent several days on Capitol Hill in Washington, seeking support of Congress for the demands already submitted to the State Department that the question of the nine enslaved nations also be brought upon the agenda of the Paris meeting. The initiative in this connection was taken upon himself by Congressman Zablocki, a member of the Foreign affairs committee of the House of Representatives, and the result of this was what was known as the 'Zablocki resolution' of May 2nd, supported from the start by some dozen Congressmen, including eight of Polish descent, and passed unanimously in the House by 250 votes and no opposition. It expressed the hope that in the approaching Summit conference, the United States would bring up the matter of restoring human rights and the basic freedoms to the captive nations. A project identical with that of Zablocki was introduced into the Senate by Senator Douglas; however, it encountered opposition from the chairman of the Foreign Relations committee, Senator Fulbright, who objected in principle to all types of resolution not being decrees or laws, but merely desiderata, and it did not come to voting there.

On the occasion of reaching agreement, as is the custom, between the attitude of the Foreign Affairs committee and that of the State Department, it was officially stated in a letter by the Department of April 19th, addressed to the chairman of the Foreign Affairs committee, Congressman Thomas E. Morgan, and signed by the Under-Secretary of State, William B. Macomber Jr. that: 'The Department believes that it is desirable to reaffirm our views on the situation in Eastern Europe to the Soviet leaders at every appropriate opportunity and, in consultation with their Western colleagues, US officials will be giving consideration to this question in connection with the summit conference ... it seems possible that an appropriate opportunity might arise for consideration of an issue such as Eastern Europe during discussion of the general problem of East-West relations.

'The Soviet Union, for its part, has consistently refused at past meetings of representatives of the Four Powers to enter upon any discussion of the situation in Eastern Europe as a basic international problem, the just solution of which would contribute immeasurably to the reduction of world tensions and to the establishment of a lasting peace.'

In other words, the State Department letter stated categorically that there had been efforts by the United States to start discussion on the situation of the nine countries, but unfortunately they had come to nothing in view of the uncompromising attitude of the Soviets.

Khrushchev's second visit confirmed yet again his unusual sensitivity to the question of Eastern Europe, the first symptoms of which appeared during the visit of Vice-President Nixon to Russia. My colleagues and I from ACEN presented this problem precisely on the day before the arrival of Khrushchev in an interview by the famous commentator Edward Murrow over the CBS TV network, which covers all America. Khrushchev arrived September 19th, on the Soviet ship *Baltika*, which was anchored in Brooklyn, from where he came by car to the headquarters of the Soviet delegation on Park Avenue, surrounded by a close police cordon, amidst cries of 'Murderer; Butcher of the Ukraine' uttered by groups of émigrés waiting along the route. He was accompanied by, or there arrived shortly after him, the heads of the communist governments of the nine Iron Curtain countries. Tito also appeared. A foretaste of what was soon to come was provided by Khrushchev's first speech in front of the forum of the General Assembly of the United Nations on September 23rd. In a long oration, amidst attacks on the Western powers, he demanded the complete and immediate liquidation of colonialism in any shape or form throughout the world, proposing the passing of an appropriate motion.

Something happened which gave the only occasion of its kind to the governments of the Western world to bring up the matter of the Soviet colonies in Eastern and Central Europe. ACEN at once started feverish activity, trying to convince competent American circles and Western delegations to the UN that the proper time had come for them to take advantage of the opening of the problem of foreign rule in other countries, performed, ironically enough, not by the West but by Khrushchev, and to execute a frontal attack, demanding officially and formally that Soviet rule in the nine countries should be considered. ACEN's foreign representations intervened in this sense in the ten capitals. The UN delegations received the ACEN pamphlet 'Some Facts on New Colonialism', setting forth the course of the Soviet seizure of power in the nine countries, while about a hundred telegrams were also sent to these delegations, demanding that a resolution should be adopted concerning the liquidation of colonialism also in Eastern and Central Europe; more important, members of ACEN intervened personally with about sixty delegations to UNO, including those from the newly-emergent African states. Some of the African delegates heard our expositions with wide-open eyes, like tales of the iron wolf. There were among them those who admitted with disarming sincerity : 'We have never heard of this and know now nothing about it,' and requested all sorts of documentary material. Unfortunately, the West did not manage this sort of counter-offensive, but merely applied half-measures and even these not in an organized way, but only improvised by individual delegations. They consisted entirely of rejecting Khrushchev's arguments in the discussion which developed, by indicating the Soviet domination in Eastern Europe but without drawing any definite conclusions and demands from this.

The first to do this was the head of the American delegation, James Wadsworth, who said on the same day : 'The Soviet Union ... demands immediate plenary consideration of the elimination of colonialism in the world. This is a strange demand indeed from a country whose imperialism has embraced more people, more territory and more oppression than anything else the twentieth century has ever seen.'

Next the Prime Minister of Canada, John Diefenbaker, speaking on September 26th, pointed to Soviet rule in the nine countries and in the Ukraine, while he was followed on October 5th by the Prime Minister of Australia, Robert Menzies, condemning Khrushchev's hypocrisy and calling the Soviet Union the greatest colonial power in existence. Others spoke in a similar way after them.

The outburst occurred on October 12th, when the Philippine senator, Lorenzo Sumulong, stepped up and said : 'The Soviet anti-colonial declaration should also cover the inalienable right to independence of the peoples of Eastern Europe and elsewhere, who are deprived of their political and civil rights, and have been swallowed up by the Soviet Union.'

Khrushchev fell into a rage and, having pulled off one of his shoes, began thumping the desk with it and by turn threatening the Philippine delegation, which was sitting some distance away. Loud insults fell from his mouth addressed to Senator Sumulong, including that of *kholuj*, translated inaccurately by the interpreter, who clearly wanted to soften down the term, as 'jerk'. Fortunately the communist leaders from behind the Iron Curtain did not follow his example and did not take off their shoes, which would have made the stifling atmosphere in the hall still more unbearable. They merely restricted themselves to banging their fists on the desks. Khrushchev, having later been given his turn on the platform, asked Senator Sumulong to visit the Soviet Union, and see how free its people are, to which the Filipino replied that if he accepted the invitation it would be in the hope that he would do better in Russia than others who had gone there.

This however was the prelude to an incident which occurred towards the end of the session, when the American Under-Secretary of State, Francis O. Wilcox, stated : 'Everyone here in this Assembly hall is fully aware of the sad fact that there are a number of states in Eastern Europe which do not have their complete independence.'

Khrushchev again took his shoe off and began banging it on the wooden surface. As in response to an order, all the Iron Curtain delegations began banging their fists on the desks and an indescribable din arose. At the same time, the Rumanian delegation, Mezincescu, demanded to speak regarding the question of the order of the agenda, and when he was given floor, he accused the president of the Assembly, the Irishman Frederick Boland, of partiality in this office, adding : 'I wish the Irish people and all the peoples of this Assembly enjoyed the freedom of the people of Rumania.'

Boland switched off Mezincescu's microphone and began banging the chairman's gavel on the table so hard that, at the moment when he announced the closure of the session on account of the disgraceful scene, the gavel broke from its handle and flew back over the chairman's head. The session ended amidst indescribable tumult and din.

XXXI

COMRADE WIESLAW[1] IN THE SHADE OF
THE STATUE OF LIBERTY

I was able to see Gomulka who came to the UN General Assembly soon after Khrushchev, and I had to notice he had not changed much since the time when I saw him in 1947 in the Sejm. Only the wrinkles on his face had deepened, and his skin become more waxen. But apart from this, the same baldness, eye-glasses and ascetic severity in his appearance. He was already the second generation of Gomulka's to land in the United States, but as far as can be understood, his parents—later a mining family in Pennsylvania —shed tears in the permanent émigré manner at the sight of the Statue of Liberty, whereas Wladyslaw Gomulka eyed it dryly, planning hostile speeches against a country which had been hospitable to his ancestors and to this day is the fatherland of his uncles and sisters.

Much water has flowed since those Warsaw events and many things have happened in the meantime and ... stopped. From Spring in October in Poland, October had come in Spring. The 'Wezyk movement' in literature had disappeared without trace, and no one was any longer bold enough to write any 'poems for adults'. The heavy hand of control had already shut the mouth of writers and the pencil of the censor was beginning to go mad as before on the columns of newspapers. Those who had returned Gomulka to power in October 1956 were today revisionists, who were being liquidated and replaced by the old Stalinist guard of the men of Natolin, ruling at the time when Gomulka was behind bars. The allegedly liquidated Secret Police was conspiring in the Ministry of Internal Affairs and slowly, though in hiding, was stretching its tentacles over the entire country. The régime was already neglecting the agreement made with the Church and kept on infringing it, arresting priests under various pretexts, intensifying an atheistic campaign and removing religion from schools. The emigration already knew of Cardinal Wyszynski's sermon to pilgrims at Czestochowa on August 17, 1959, containing the words : 'the pa-

[1] Wartime underground pseudonym of Gomulka.

tience of the Church faced with government chicanery is about to become exhausted' and also known was Gomulka's speech at the harvest festival on September 4th of the same year, attacking individual peasant farms and forecasting special laws which would force the peasants into collectivization. The autonomous workers' councils which after the October *coup* appeared in the factories like mushrooms after rain had disappeared, and in their place courts had been introduced for idle workers and private enterprise was hardly breathing under the pressure of new restrictions and increased taxation. Apathy and a feeling of hopelessness was again spreading in Poland. But although there was a marked change for the better between the previous Bierut period and the present one under Gomulka, yet the situation in Poland was steadily worsening. The only constant factor, the Ark of the Covenant between the old and new times, was the iron premier, 'Amputated Hand', Jozef Cyrankiewicz.

All these changes for the worse, well-known in the United States, brought much disappointment to the Americans. In the period preceding the October *coup*, American policy in relation to Poland had not differed in practice from the policy towards the remaining Iron Curtain countries, with only a few deviations, dictated by the facts that Poland was a war-time ally, whereas Hungary, Rumania and Bulgaria had belonged to the enemy camp, that Poland is the largest country in Eastern Europe, and that in the United States there lives the powerful Polonia of over six million persons. There also existed a certain difference of approach to the Yalta agreement. The basing on it of American policy towards Poland encountered much opposition in Congress on the part of those who, along with Polonia and the Polish political emigration, regarded Yalta as a serious error of American policy and as sanctioning of the fourth Partition of Poland; but taking Yalta as the basis for American policy towards the remaining Iron Curtain countries did not arouse reservations either in Congress or among the emigrations of these countries, who, when putting forward the demand for free elections, always referred to Yalta as a basis for this demand, which the Poles never did. Apart from these deviations, each of the American policies, including the policy of liberation, was considered to be the same towards Poland as, for instance, to Albania; though the latter paradoxically, not having common frontiers with Soviet Russia, seemed to give better chances of its peaceful realization.

After the October *coup*, a marked change occurred and American policy towards Poland underwent a turn in the direction of Gomulkaism, recognized as the Polish variation of Titoism. It was expressed in economic aid for Poland which in 1959 attained the sum of $650 million, of which $426,300,000 were in the form of agricultural products, the payment for which was to be returned in zloty, and these again were to be used in Poland. Hence there were many ideas as to how to make use of these large sums, frozen in Poland, and as the first was the project of Engineer Wladyslaw Biernacki, of building a hospital for children in Cracow. The law necessary for the use of American funds for this purpose was passed by the House of Representatives thanks to the efforts of Congressmen Zablocki and Machrowicz, and the way to this additional assistance was open.

Polonia and the emigration left no shadow of doubt that the support for the Polish variation of Titoism was not enough, and they would not be satisfied with any programme for Poland other than the restoration of full independence and a democratic system. However, the positive attitude towards economic aid, adopted by both sides after the October *coup*, accompanied as it was by constantly renewed demands for its further increase, played an important part in granting it.

'We should like to give Poland aid in kind and credits, and your attitude did not so much affect our decision as facilitate it,' I was told by a high official of the State Department, looked upon as Ambassador to Warsaw who, however, after obtaining a higher post stayed in Washington, 'but if Polonia along with you were to speak out against it, the granting of this aid would be unthinkable to us.'

Along with this government action, a wave of sympathy for Poland which arose after the Poznan revolt and the Polish October, resulted also in aid from private initiative. Its best example was the action of a lawyer in his thirties, John Richardson Jr., who despite the fact that he was the father of four children also adopted a teen-age girl refugee from Hungary. Richardson, overcome by the desire to do something for Poland, and having learned of the great shortage there of medicine, wrote about a hundred letters to pharmaceutical firms, with a request for gifts in kind, and was soon able to supply Polish hospitals free of charge with injections and medicine to the value of two and a half million dollars.

However, the situation in Poland which was deteriorating through the fault of the government began to act as a brake on the assistance, the first sign of which was the lessening in 1960 by a half of the credits demanded by the Warsaw régime for purchases in the United States, and this despite the fact that Poland's undertaking to repay in twenty years the claims of American citizens to an agreed ceiling of forty million dollars made the best possible impression in America.

A second American activity which developed after October on a quite wide scale was the so-called 'cultural exchange' between Poland and the United States. In its framework, mainly thanks to the financial aid of the two greatest Foundations—Ford and Rockefeller—thousands of books devoted to knowledge, also other scientific aids, were sent to Poland and hundreds of Polish scholars and specialists were able to come to the United States in order to complete their studies at American universities, in hospitals and various kinds of scientific institutions. American artists began appearing in Warsaw, while the United States was able to see excellent performances of the ballets 'Slask' and 'Mazowsze', and Polonia and the emigration saw Warsaw theatricals also. But in this sphere too the first signs appeared of worsening in the form of the demand by the Warsaw régime that it alone be responsible for the choice of people taking advantage of the cultural exchange, behind which was undoubtedly concealed the desire to give privileges to Communist party members. Because the United States cannot become a country to which only communists are to come, the further fate of cultural exchanges became dubious.

October also gave birth to a more advantageous atmosphere for the problem of the recognition by the United States of the Polish western frontier on the Oder and Neisse rivers. The struggle for it in the United States has been going on ever since it arose, and its end is not visible. The problem itself had already been discussed in the emigration in hundreds of publications, articles and memoranda, submitted to the White House, the State Department and Congress, by all émigré organizations without exception and the Polish-American Congress. Since the establishment of the Representation of the Polish Political Council in the United States, I myself had taken dozens of them to the State Department, and I also succeeded in publishing in the English-language newspapers a number of letters devoted to this matter, which is so well known that it relieves us from having to go over once again the arguments put forward by both sides concerned—Poland and Western Germany. An interesting episode in it was a sort of dramatic duel held in the House of Representatives between Congressman Machrowicz, who was an enthusiastic supporter of recognizing the frontier and was attacked directly on this account by the German press, with Congressman Reece of Tennessee, who was firmly against it. On August 15, 1957 and August 23, 1958 Congressman Machrowicz introduced into the Congressional record two long memoranda

opposing the arguments contained in the memoranda of Congressman Reece, also entered in the record. In this way, Congress was
made thoroughly familiar with this important and as yet unsolved
problem, as to which the official attitude of the United States
government is expressed in such a manner that the decision concerning the Polish western frontier may be reached, in accordance
with the protocol of the Potsdam conference in August 1945, not
until the final international conference settling in a peace treaty
all problems which the war created, including the partition of Germany.

This formal attitude however is supplemented and changed by
the reasoning I heard from competent lips : 'Soviet Russia has
three frontiers on the west. The first between East and West Germany, relatively easier than the others to move east, as it is artificial
and unjust, for it divides one and the same great nation into two. If
lasting and real peace is ever attained, it will have to disappear.
The second is the Oder-Neisse line. This, from your point of view
inviolable Polish-German frontier, is also the second defence line
of the Soviet territorial seizures, stronger than the first. Russia is
more master of this frontier than you are. After all, you are completely under Soviet domination and if Russia were to come to an
agreement with Germany regarding a change of this frontier, you
would have to agree to it. Russia is not the only defender of this
frontier, it is also the greatest threat to it. The third is the present
Polish-Soviet frontier, recognized by the West at Yalta and for us the
final one under present circumstances, although you regard it as unjust because of Wilno and Lwow.

'Under conditions such as these, why should we recognize Soviet
frontier No. 2? Why should we strengthen it by our recognition,
without any exchange or equivalent from Russia? If you were a
fully independent State, it would be recognized by us without consideration as to Germany, since it would push back Russia to your
frontiers with her in the east. But after all, you are not. So let
Russia offer something equally valuable in exchange, then we shall
recognize the western frontier. Let her agree, for instance, to the
unification of Germany, since this in addition would render harm-
less objections from Germany's side against this frontier, with which
we must also reckon. Remember that the question of recognizing
your frontier is primarily a problem between the United States and
Russia, not between the United States and Poland.'

This reasoning is on the whole in accordance with the political
equation which emerged in the United States after the October
coup. 'The chances of recognition are in inverse proportion to the

degree of dependence on Russia.' After the October *coup* it looked as if Poland had gained a certain degree of independence and the chances of recognition went up.

One element constantly working in Poland's favour is time, and the fact of holding the western territories, in accordance with the principle *beatus possidens*. Undoubtedly under their influence, although not exclusively, occurred the claim for the inviolability of the western frontier by General de Gaulle in March 1959, repeated by Premier Debré in a speech to the Chamber of Deputies in October that year, which did not go without echo in the United States. In any case, the reply of President Eisenhower went along this line when asked at a press conference on May 11, 1960, whether he intended to bring up the question of the German frontiers at the summit conference. The president stated : 'At this time we wouldn't raise it. As a matter of fact, they've been living with these boundaries for a long time and I would see at this moment no possibility of changing them except by methods that would be unacceptable, so it might be raised by someone but I have no plan to do it.'

Another important factor is the wide knowledge in the United States of the fact that the defence of the Oder-Neisse frontier is a national problem eliminated by Polonia and the emigration from the battle conducted against the communist system and that it unites all Poles without exception. This was expressed in a speech by Vice-President Nixon in October 1960 in Buffalo, where he said : 'All Poles in Poland as well as abroad are linked in their determination to defend the new western frontier. It is urgent therefore that the next administration formulate and carry out policies in such a way as to contribute to the maintenance of the hopes and to strengthening of the morale and vitality of the Polish people. The Oder-Neisse border between Poland and Germany is a fact of post-war history.'

Such an alarm was raised in Western Germany by these words of Nixon, for it was interpreted there as recognition, that the State Department found it necessary to calm down the German ally, and the spokesman of the Department, Lincoln White, stated that American policy as regards the frontiers had not undergone a change, in which there was a certain disavowal of Vice-President Nixon. At the same time he recalled the assurance of Chancellor Adenauer that he rejected the use of force to settle the problem of the frontiers, and added that Western Germany neither demanded nor obtained from NATO any promises of help in enforcing territorial demands, nor would Germany enforce them.

The Adenauer statement recalled by White made a good impression at the time in the United States and it weighed and continues to weigh unfavourably for Poland on the scales of the settlement of recognition of the frontiers, showing in the opinion of the Americans that Poland has nothing to fear and that in fact the possession by Poland of the western territories was strengthened by this statement, not weakened. Regardless of this moderation in external declarations, West Germany has for years been making efforts to obtain from the United States support for the change of the frontier to its advantage, possibly made in confidential form or even by a promise, at some unspecified time, of future support. This action, conducted with the help of their own embassy and millions of dollars put at the disposal of German propaganda, with a powerful lobby in Congress and wide support created by the millions of Americans of German origin in their own press and countless organizations, has not yet been crowned with success, owing to a large extent to the work of the Polish-American Congress and the Polish political emigration. And if this emigration is reproached that it has not been able by its influence to obtain recognition of the Oder-Neisse frontier by the United States Government, yet justice requires that it be admitted some merit for paralysing German efforts to find among the political emigration persons prepared to discuss the problem of the frontiers, which would imply that these frontiers are not final and their problem is still open. However, these efforts have come to nothing.

It is the same with the demand for the return of German assets frozen in the United States during the war, worth at present over half a milliard dollars. Here the action of the Polish-American Congress and Congressmen of Polish origin, led by Machrowicz, in demanding the use of these funds for compensation due to Poles from Germany, has prevented their being paid out.

However, a factor working against United States recognition of the frontiers is the growing economic and military power of West Germany, which makes it an increasingly valuable ally of the United States. The weight of this element may grow increasingly and in this way also Poland will pay for the fundamental error made years ago by Soviet policy. For it is only to the arming of Eastern Germany by Russia and her aggressive attitude in Europe that the world owes the rebirth of the West German army. Both in the United States and generally in the West, the idea of permanently disarming Germany was very popular, and had it not been for the Russian error, Germany would be disarmed till this day. But what was possible years ago without the agreement of Germany cannot today be done without her approval. Now it is not the wartime allies who decide the fate of the reborn German army, but a sovereign powerful Germany.

We came out in the United States against the rebuilding of this army, delivering memoranda and repeating at the end of each conference on this subject : 'The Poles do not want to be liberated from the communist yoke by a German army. If it ever crossed into Polish territory, Poland would take up arms against it, even if it wore American uniform and was under American command. For if this army ever found itself in the western territories, there is no power in the world which could force it to leave them. Under conditions such as these, the value of a German army allied to the United States would be counterbalanced by the hostility of the Polish army. So is it worthwhile to rely on a German amy?'

This was however a voice crying in the wilderness.

The relapse since the October *coup* weighed unfavourably on this matter as on the whole of Polish-American relations, and in particular the crowning of this reversal in the field of international politics, which was the arrival of Wladyslaw Gomulka at the session of the UN General Assembly in September 1960, in Khrushchev's suite and at his bidding, not on his own initiative or at the invitation of the American government. As news arrived from Poland of the deteriorating internal situation, there was a decrease in the liking which Gomulka had acquired for himself in the United States by the changes introduced after taking over power in 1956, both inside the country and in relation to the Soviets. The expulsion of Marshal Rokossovsky and several dozen Russian generals, the agreement restricting the freedom of movement of Soviet garrisons in Poland which, if it did not put an end at least set limits to the exploitations of Poland, and finally certain gestures by the régime's diplomacy in the Western world and minor attempts to stress tactics or views different from those of the Soviets—all this had been recognized in the United States as the start of Polish Titoism. In proportion as Gomulka's journeys to the Kremlin and Crimea grew more frequent and his statements more servile, revealing complete submission to Soviet strategy and policy, so the features of the Polish Tito began to fade. For although it had entered American heads that the father of Yugoslav Titoism is not the person who gave it its name, but geography, and that what is possible for Yugoslavia, which has no common frontier with Russia, is not possible for Poland, it was rightly felt that Gomulka had not utilized the margin of freedom he had acquired and that had he wanted to, he might without risk have permitted himself a larger dose of independence.

The Rapacki plan propagated by the régime did not improve the situation either. Each variation of it was regarded as a sheepskin under which was hiding the Soviet wolf, trying by all forces to obtain the removal of American troops from Germany, in order to make that country more susceptible to Soviet infiltration, subversion and all kinds of pressure. 'And once we begin to withdraw our troops from Europe,' says popular American opinion, 'they will not stop till they reach America. If that were to happen, it would perhaps be the first step towards neutralizing Europe and later its peaceful subjugation by the Soviets.'

Thus this visit by Gomulka along with Khrushchev and other heads of states of satellite governments, showing clearly the relation of subordinate to master, acted on the Americans like a bucket of cold water. And in addition Gomulka found himself in the company of the Hungarian Janos Kadar, again stressing by this the reversion from the negative line taken in 1956 towards Soviet armed intervention in Hungary. And whereas in March 1960 the Vice-Premier Piotr Jaroszewicz was received by President Eisenhower, which as a rule does not happen to visitors of secondary international rank, yet no steps were taken from the American side for such a meeting with Gomulka. He had to do with a brief visit to the Secretary of State, Herter, which came about almost casually, in an office in the UNO building, not with any ceremony in the State Department. And although the result of this meeting was the extension to Poland by the United States of customs privileges, this was only proof of American patience and optimism.

The last vestiges of illusion were dispelled by Gomulka's speech at the General Assembly. And although it must be supposed that further economic aid for Poland and cultural exchanges will go on as long as the conviction prevails that they serve the Polish people and not the régime, yet the hopes of a Polish Titoism, after his speech to the UN, fell to the lowest level since 1956. The speech was preceded by press information that Cardinal Wyszynski, under pressure of the régime and so as not to render difficult Gomulka's situation in New York, had withdrawn his pastoral letter, in which he had accused the government of an increase in its attacks on the Church, carried on with quite inhuman fanaticism. This news did not create a more favourable mood, but the speech was awaited with interest which afterwards changed into deep disappointment.

At the General Assembly on September 27th Gomulka, following blindly in the footsteps of Khrushchev, demanded 'in the

Author expressing thanks to President Lyndon B. Johnson for proclaiming August 1st, 1964 'Warsaw Uprising Day', during the ceremony at the White House. See *Epilogue*

Prime Minister of Canada Lester B. Pearson at the ceremony of unveiling a commemorative plaque honouring Canadian fliers who died flying support missions for the Polish wartime underground. From left to right: Zygmunt Jaworski, President of the Polish-Canadian Congress; Prime Minister Lester B. Pearson; Group Captain Stefan Sznuk, President of the Supreme Council of the Polish-Canadian Congress; the author. See *Epilogue*

name of the Polish people' complete disarmament, in agreement
with the Soviet proposal, which was equivalent to demanding one-
sided disarmament by the Western world; he supported the idea of
peaceful co-existence, of which he himself had said at a meeting in
Katowice on July 6, 1960, that its strategic aim was the victory of
Communism over capitalism; he demanded the admission to UNO
of communist China, the transfer of the UN headquarters to another
country, and the dismissal of the Secretary-General, Hammarskjöld;
he accused the United States of perpetuating the cold war; and in
the Congo dispute he came out on the side of Lumumba, who was
supported by the Soviet Union. In fact his speech was a copy of
Khrushchev's tirades.

The ambassador of Nationalist China, Dr Tingfu Tsiang, at once
rose to answer : he is one of the most convincing, calm speakers I
ever heard. Then as at a command, all the delegates of the communist bloc, including Gomulka, rose and quit the hall. Dr Tsiang
stated that the Chinese people, like the Polish nation, are fighting
for the same cause and with the same enemy, and success on one
front makes the fight easier on another. In this respect, Gomulka was
evading the truth when he spoke in the name of the Polish people.

Observing the worsening American-Polish relations, and wishing to add my support to aid for Poland despite all, I published a
letter in the *Chicago Tribune* on January 11, 1960, in which I
endeavoured to prove that dissatisfaction with Gomulka's policy
ought not to affect unfavourably economic and cultural aid for
Poland, nor the cause of recognizing the Oder-Neisse frontier, since
all this serves the Polish people but not the communist régime.

After Gomulka's speech in UNO 'in the name of the Polish people',
I stated in a letter published in the *Evening Star* in Washington,
that he did not represent the genuine aims and feelings of the Polish
people, who by their enthusiastic welcome of Vice-President Nixon
in Warsaw had clearly shown that they were on the side of American democracy in its fight with Soviet Communism and that in
the victory of the United States they see their own victory and
liberation from the yoke of Communism. I added :

'In only one respect was Mr Gomulka in full agreement with
the feelings of the Polish people in the homeland and abroad. It
was when he spoke about the fears raised in Poland by the rebirth
of the German army in connection with the German revisionist
claims aimed at the Polish western territories. The recognition of
the Polish western frontiers along the Oder-Neisse line by the United
States might dispel these fears and such action is more than ever
necessary.'

K

XXXII

'LE ROI EST MORT. VIVE LE ROI!'

On September 30, 1960, the huge hall of the Sherman Hotel in Chicago was full to the brim by 9 a.m., at which time the opening of the Fifth Convention of the Polish-American Congress was scheduled. Over 3,000 delegates and guests early occupied places in the hall and balconies. A mood of excitement and tension prevailed in the hall, which a few minutes after 9 a.m. exploded in a storm of applause as a tall, slightly bent man entered and with hand outstretched approached the KPA president Rozmarek.

The applause and shouts continued unabated when the newcomer greeted the leaders of KPA and when, turning to the hall, he raised both hands in a gesture known to all the world.

The ovation was broken off by the striking of the gavel and the voice of Rozmarek greeting the guest. He ended his short speech with the words: 'Ladies and gentlemen! I have the honour to introduce to you the President of the United States, Dwight D. Eisenhower, who will say a few words ...'

Sitting among the members of the board I listened to the President's speech, feeling distinctly the thread of melancholy which went through his words. For this commander-in-chief in World War II was today bidding farewell to a part of the nation represented by a few thousand delegates staring at him as at a picture, with affection and sorrow, since they were aware of the fact that they would certainly not hear him again in this role. They did not begrudge him applause, and the enthusiasm emanating from the audience was reflected in the emotion on the face and in the voice of the President, who spoke of the eternal attachment of the Poles to freedom, which made them a model for the whole world, of the initiative of President Wilson which aided Poland regain her independence, and of the enthusiastic welcome given by the people of Warsaw in August 1959 to Vice-President Nixon, which meant that the Poles, like the Americans, believe in freedom.

But one passage in the speech specially attracted my notice. It was devoted to the policy of liberation and defined the present attitude of the President to this, his own creation. The President said : 'In 1952 I promised the American people that whatever I could do by peaceful means would be done, in order that those people who are held in bondage by a tyrannical dictatorship might finally have the right to determine their own fates by their own free votes.

'This is still a tenet in the faith of every right-thinking American. It is as yet unachieved, but this does not mean that anyone must give up hope.'

This was the swan song with which the doctrine of liberation was bidden farewell by its creator.

When the President ended, Rozmarek took his turn and, thanking him warmly for coming and speaking, he intoned in a strong tenor : 'May he live a hundred years.' The few thousand present at once caught the tune and the song shook the walls of the hall. The face of the President took on a look of surprise and he leaned to Rozmarek, asking him what the song meant. When it was explained to him the hall again saw the famous smile, this time mixed with emotion, and both hands again raised up.

When the song was ended, the President quit the convention amidst cheering, shaking hands right and left, and the hall buzzed like a hive. Everyone was commenting to his neighbour of the first notable fact in the history of Polonia, the presence of the President at the Polonia convention and his words, and no one paid attention to the gavel of the chairman. I was commenting on the speech to Karol Wagner, director of Radio Free Europe, when I heard the voice of my neighbour, the president of KPA from Baltimore, Szymon Jarosinski, calling me to order.

'Take the stand, please. President Rozmarek is asking you to speak.'

I hastened in the direction of the rostrum, very startled. I was prepared to speak, but had not expected to be called upon at this early stage. However, having mobilized on the way all my senses, in a half-hour speech I started by conveying greetings from ACEN to the convention, and then ran over the events in Poland since the previous convention in Philadelphia in May 1956, i.e. the revolt in Poznan in June 1956, the manifestation at Jasna Gora in August 1956, the October overthrow which was a spark which fell on Hungarian fuel, evaluating it as a defeat of the Soviets felt behind the Iron Curtain at a time when on this side of the Curtain they had achieved a number of successes, of which the last was the communist domination of Cuba. In turn I came to characterizing the relapse since the October *coup* and the arrival of Gomulka in the

United States in Khrushchev's suite, also his speech at the United Nations, evaluating it as in the letter of October 10, 1960, in the *Evening Star*. I terminated my speech with a prediction regarding the future : 'What can we do under these conditions for Poland? Certain hopes are emerging in connection with the growth of the importance and role of the UN. Sooner or later, by the aid of this institution, the remains of colonial rule by the Western states in Africa and Asia will be liquidated, and Soviet Russia will remain the last and greatest colonial empire in the world. Then it will be increasingly difficult for Khruschev to state that the nine countries behind the Iron Curtain voluntarily, of their own free will, have chosen a communist system for themselves. Then Soviet rule in these countries, which are colonies of Russia, will come beneath the pillory of the public opinion of the whole world in a more glaring light than at present. Without waiting for that, however, it is necessary already now to demand that the United Nations pass a resolution, demanding from the Soviets the withdrawal of Russian troops from the countries of Eastern Europe and enabling them in this way to hold free elections under international control. This would be the first step on the way to Poland's regaining independence, with a western frontier on the Oder and Neisse rivers.

'In conclusion, I should like to glance at the situation of Poland within the framework of the millennium, the celebration of the thousandth anniversary of the existence of the Polish state. This historical perspective authorizes us to take the optimistic view that what enemies have not been able to do for a thousand years, cannot be done by the Soviet Union now. For the systems and doctrines such as Communism pass and are gone, and the Polish nation is eternal.'

After me spoke Fr. Jan Malinowski, in the name of Polonia in Argentina, and then the speeches went on in their ordinary way under the chairmanship of the highly respected and widely loved Judge Tadeusz Adesko. In the course of a two-day discussion devoted primarily to the affairs of Polonia and then to international and internal American matters, there was no lack of warm moments. These included a lively exchange of views on the subjects of the departures of leaders of Polonia on visits to Poland. Those who opposed the trips, with Rozmarek, Edward Kozmor and Congressman Roman Pucinski in the forefront, had behind them a decided majority of the delegates; and when Adela Lagodzinska, chairwoman of the Polish Women's Alliance of America, asked Rozmarek to go with her to Poland, his reply, 'I will go, but not until it is genuinely free and independent,' was enthusiastically applauded.

The result of the two-day session was a number of resolutions defining the views of the convention on various political problems. The most important called upon the American people to mobilize all moral and material forces for the fight against communist imperialism and demanded that the United States government should reply to the programme of the conquest of the whole world by Communism with a programme for the rule of freedom and democracy in the whole world, not excluding the Soviet Union and communist China, and this on the basis of the right of self-determination of all peoples and by the use as instrument of UNO. The resolutions demanded the refusal to recognize the *status quo* in the countries behind the Iron Curtain and the submission of their case to the forum of UNO, and its inclusion in the agenda of all international conferences in which the Soviets took part, in order to achieve the withdrawal of Russian troops from these countries, which would enable free elections to be held in them under the control of UNO. A separate resolution demanded that the United States government bring the Katyn case before UNO, and another welcomed the co-operation of the nine emigrations of Eastern Europe in the framework of the ACEN.

The resolutions devoted to the situation in Poland, after stressing that Polonia associated itself with the homeland in celebrating the 550th anniversary of the Battle at Grunwald and the centenary of the birth of Ignacy Paderewski, also, after condemning the symptoms of a relapse since the October *coup,* stated that the Polish nation was still under the rule of governments forced on it by Russia, that Gomulka's coming to power had not changed this basic truth in any respect, in view of which the need still existed for the representation of the Polish nation by Polonia. This need dictated the establishing in 1944 of the Polish-American Congress, and justified its further existence and activities. They warned against communist infiltration and contacts with the régime's diplomatic outposts in the United States, also against trips to Poland by those who occupy high or leading positions in Polonia. They spoke out for cultural exchanges and economic aid by the United States for Poland as long as evidence exists that this serves the interests of the Polish people. Finally, resolutions demanded that the United States recognize the frontier on the Oder and Neisse and laid down Poland's rights against Russia to the eastern territories, the towns of Lwow and Wilno, and the 1939 frontier.

In the intervals between the deliberations, taking advantage of the fine weather, I went for a walk with Karol Wagner and Stanislaw Smialowski, former worker in the Warsaw insurgent broadcasting station 'Lightning Flash', along the inland American sea, Lake Michigan.

After returning to the convention, there was a continuation of the incessant hand-shaking with new acquaintances, and chance conversations. I met the 1905 revolutionary Izydor Brudzinski who came from Los Angeles. He had fascinated me and Captain Dziob a year ago in Lenart's restaurant with a tale of the armed attacks against the Tsar's gendarmes in Minsk Mazowiecki, prison and flight to America. There too was that other fighter of those years, Franciszek Gregorek, an old acquaintance from Baltimore. I was invited by Jarosinski, the president of the KPA from that city, to a frugal reception with delegates from the state of Maryland. With a glass in one hand and a sandwich in the other, I sat down by Gregorek and reminiscences started. He was a member of the fighting organization in Czestochowa, so as a former pupil of that town I helped him to recall forgotten names, and he therefore chatted as if to one of his own and the intervention of lady delegates was necessary to separate us.

The evening of the first day of the convention I called in at its office, in which, as always, ruled the chief of staff, Captain Dziob. I met a friend from Washington, Burke, Mr and Mrs Trawinski from Chicago, Kwik from Bridgeport, and a Home Army couple from Warsaw, Wlodzimierz Molarow and his wife, who lost a son in the Insurrection. They were sitting with paper cups in their hands full of a liquid which did not resemble water either by sight or taste, and were resting after the labours of the day, some speaking of former services in the 'Sokols' and then in General Haller's Army, others of adventures in the underground movement. The 1960 convention did not differ in any respect from the usual cross-section of the greater Polonia congresses: the revolutionaries of 1905, Haller soldiers of World War I, Polish-American veterans from World War II, soldiers of the Polish Armed Forces in the West, and the Home Army. The men of 1905 had in their time met those of 1863, and those of 1863 those of 1831, so it was possible to stretch into the past an unbroken thread of the fight for Poland to Kosciuszko and Pulaski. In Poland, it was picked up by the people of Poznan in June 1956 and it is being spun now by hands invisible and unknown to anyone.

On the second day of the convention in the afternoon the hall was again crammed to the edges for the same reason as the first morning, since they were also expecting an eminent guest. The difference was however apparent in the preparations to receive him. Whereas before the appearance of President Eisenhower all kinds of precautions had been taken in the hall, always accompanying the heads of states on their public appearances, which included among others the stationing of agents of the Secret Service in the balcony above the head of the President and shutting all doors into the hall just before his arrival, now the waiting, excited crowd was grouped in the huge lobby in front of the convention hall and in the aisles between the rows of seats. Sitting on an elevation, I first heard cries and applause coming from the lobby and presently a stream of people flooded the hall, boiling round a tall, young, faultlessly dressed man with thick dark hair brushed to the side, moving with a smile on his face with strong jaws in the direction of the platform. Immediately behind him I saw the familiar face of Mieczyslaw Cieplinski. The hall rose to its feet and a stormy ovation ensued. The young man, passing us, shook hands with a strong, energetic grasp which, it occurred to me, must also be very worn from that. He shortly reached the rostrum, not alone like President Eisenhower, but surrounded by a close circle of feverish and smiling, mostly young faces, among which women were not lacking. The young man smiled to the hall, which was applauding madly. And again, as on the previous day, three strokes of the gavel were heard and when silence descended, the penetrating voice of the President, Rozmarek: 'Ladies and gentlemen delegates! I have the honour to introduce to you the Democratic candidate for the Presidency, John Fitzgerald Kennedy, who will address you.'

Loud applause was again heard, over which dominated single voices shouting 'Long live President Kennedy!' In this manner the impatient had already made their choice several weeks before schedule. When the ovation went on excessively the young man standing on the platform raised his hand in a gesture known all over the world as a request for silence, and began his speech.

Senator Kennedy belonged to those members of Congress who were interested more than others in the cause of Poland and the remaining countries of Eastern Europe. I had observed from close by his fight in the Capitol to amend the decree passed in October 1951 on the initiative of Congressman Laurie C. Battle of Alabama and hence known as the 'Battle Act', forbidding on principle government aid to countries under Soviet rule. To get round this Act and aid Poland, the late Secretary of State Dulles had taken refuge in the use of the Export-Import Bank, to which were transferred funds at the disposal of the President so that the Bank could give Poland loans to their value. Apart from this Dulles had had to take refuge in the contortionist interpretation that Poland is neither under Soviet rule nor controlled by it, which was mocked by opponents of aid and considered by its supporters, including Senator Kennedy, as an erroneous approach, since it was too far divergent from reality. In order to clarify the situation and simplify it, Senator Kennedy introduced an amendment to the 'Battle Act' aimed at accepting the principle laid down in his speech in the Senate on August 21, 1957, that nations 'in neither the completely friendly nor completely dominated categories' should obtain various kinds of aid as long as the President believed that this was in the interests of the security of the United States. His bill, introduced in the Senate in 1958, was rejected by forty-three votes against forty-two mainly thanks to the opposition of Senators Knowland and Bridges. Renewed a year later, it passed the Senate on September 12, 1959. An identical bill, introduced in the House by Congressman Zablocki, was stalled through lack of government support in the Foreign Affairs committee.

Senator Kennedy stated his credo most fully in the matter of Eastern Europe in a speech made in Milwaukee at a Pulaski banquet on October 17, 1959, in which, having referred to his stay in Poland in August 1955 and his pilgrimage to Jasna Gora, where he saw a cross belonging to Kazimierz Pulaski, he said among other things :

> How can we help these liberty-loving peoples regain their liberty without subjecting them to even more cruel repressions—or subjecting the world to an even more disastrous war? Freedom behind the Iron Curtain and world peace are actually inextricably linked. Poland has now attained at least a measure of national independence and at least a relaxation of communist rule.
>
> If the present emphasis on a thaw in the cold war should end and tensions rise again, the present good relations between Poland and the United States would undoubtedly cease, the growing contacts between the Polish people and the West would be cut off, and the present degree of freedom of speech and religion in Poland would prove to be short-lived. On the other hand, if a real thaw develops and Soviet-American relations improve, the prospects for the continuation and perhaps the expansion of this limited degree of Polish freedom are good. So, in a real sense, the condition for Polish freedom—the condition for the freedom of the still captive peoples—is peace.
>
> If our policy can finally begin to recognize that there are varying shades and degrees within the communist world, then and only then can we take the initiative away from the Soviets in Eastern Europe. In Poland—and in other cracks that appear in the Iron Curtain—we can then begin to work gradually, carefully and peacefully to promote closer relationships and nourish the seeds of liberty. Expanded trade between Poland and the United States, increased travel and tourism by Americans in Poland, the use of our capital

and technology for Polish industry and housing projects, expanded
student and teacher exchanges and more people-to-people contacts
—all of these could play important parts in such a policy—in addition to the usual diplomatic and information projects.

All of this will require patience, imagination and strength on the
part of our own government. It will require that we do everything
we can to make it harder for them to revert to the tactics, the
tensions and the terrors of Stalin's cold war. To reach these ends there
are no magic policies of liberation—there is only hard work—but
that hard work can and must be done.

In a speech made at the International Institute, in Gary, Ind., on
February 4, 1960, speaking in similar tones, Senator Kennedy made
a sharp criticism of the policy of liberation : 'But in the face of
rising hopes and growing expectations—in the face of an increasing
opportunity to crack the monolithic unity of the communist world
—the United States has adopted a policy which was futile from
its very beginning—a policy of empty slogans and impractical for-
mulas, a policy which we never intended to carry out—to which
we never gave one iota of tangible support—and a policy whose
very adoption, unfortunately, deprived us of any hope for formulating real alternatives for Eastern Europe, for formulating policies
of real action—policies of real hope.'

In a statement made just before the KPA convention on the occasion of Pulaski day, Senator Kennedy defined more closely what he
had in mind, speaking of diplomatic actions. Stating the need for
a definition to the world by the future President of the policy aimed
at assisting Poland and other nations to regain freedom, he said :
'Our delegates at the United Nations should have permanent instructions to press for the restoration of free elections wherever
communist imperialism has denied them.'

In the same way Senator Kennedy spoke out in the course of
several talks which I was able to have with him during my many
years' wanderings around the Capitol. In one of them on February
3, 1958, which took place together with the late Ambassador Jozef
Lipski, after discussing current problems, he finally asked a question of a somewhat personal nature : 'Do you gentlemen know
my brother-in-law, Stas Radziwill?' The 's' at the end of the first
name did not sound as soft as in the mouth of a person from Warsaw, and had a rather sharp borderlands accent, but was far from
the hard 's' with which the Anglo-Saxons replace this softened
consonant. The Ambassador knew the person to whom the question referred, and entered into a lively chat on his subject, to which
I added some information about my meetings in the underground,

L

in the home of the Speaker of the Sejm, Rataj, and in the European Hotel, with the father, Prince Janusz. After finding this link between the two worlds—American and Polish—the mood of the talk got noticably warmer and took on friendly human accents. Ambassador Lipski and I came away from it with the impression of deep interest in Polish matters on the part of the young politician who visited Poland not only in 1955 but also in 1939. So he saw it as independent still.

A certain personal pleasure connected with Senator Kennedy was caused by a photograph brought me once by a colleague in ACEN, the trade-union leader Michalak, with the recommendation to look at it closely. In it I saw Senator Kennedy surrounded by an ACEN delegation, in which I did not take part, although one member was Michalak. I returned the photograph saying that in view of the well-known habit of American politicians to be photographed with delegates, I did not see anything much in it. To this Michalak said: 'But look closely at what is lying on the table.'

I looked again and felt the agreeable influx of blood to the heart familiar to all authors. On the table in front of Senator Kennedy was lying *Fighting Warsaw*, the English edition of *In the Name of the Republic*.

The speech of the Democratic candidate for President was listened to by the whole audience in silence and with attention betraying much interest. After all, a man was speaking who within a few weeks might become President of the United States. It was broken only by outbursts of applause, when some stronger phrase or conclusion was heard. The Senator did not read his speech as on other occasions when I heard him, nor did he use any notes, but spoke impromptu, very lively, very fluently and with conviction, in a way which the Americans call 'off the cuff'. Not until he was reaching the end did he bring out of his pocket a small piece of paper and amidst the redoubled attention of a few thousand listeners, he read from it the programme of his policy in the question of Poland and Eastern Europe, contained in seven paragraphs :

1. Use American economic strength to promote peaceful change behind the Iron Curtain whenever this would help wean the so-called captive nations away from their masters.
2. Never, at any summit meeting or in any treaty deliberation recognize Soviet domination of Eastern Europe. Poland's claim to independence and liberty is not based on sentiment or politics but is deeply rooted in history, culture and law.
3. Strengthen the economic and cultural ties between Poland and the United States by expanding reciprocal trade, tourism and in-

formation services. The investment of American capital and technology in Poland should be encouraged.

4. Increase the exchange of students, teachers and technicians to give more Poles an opportunity to see the blessings of liberty and give Americans an opportunity to assist the Poles in building an independent economy.

5. Strive to restore the traditional identification of Poland and Eastern Europe with the European community. Poland through the centuries has belonged to the European tradition of freedom and national independence.

6. Eliminate Poland's very real fears of the West and of Germany, in particular by making plain American intention that disputes between East and West can be settled by peaceful negotiations. Never again will Eastern European nations be violently stripped of their territories and resources.

7. Make use of American funds frozen in Poland to build a national library, a housing district, new schools and to reconstruct the Warsaw castle.

On ending his speech which was followed by a noisy ovation, Senator Kennedy quietened the hall with a gesture and added : 'And now I will introduce to you my brother-in-law, Stanislaw Radziwill, who will say a few words.'

A young man stepped on to the platform and began to speak in Polish. I stared at his features, seeking a likeness between father and son, and found it,

The culminating point of the appearance of the presidential candidate at the convention was the programme he announced. At first sight it was possible to see the difference between it and the Republican policy of liberation. The latter proclaimed the liberation of the countries of Eastern Europe by the use from outside by the United States and the Western world of all peaceful means, i.e. they envisaged the initiative as coming from without, while the countries behind the Iron Curtain were given a more passive role; Senator Kennedy on the other hand envisaged only American aid for the gradual self-liberation of these countries, and thus expected the initiative to come from them and gave them an active and main role, leaving the United States in an auxiliary role.

Less than four months later, gazing at Senator Kennedy when he was standing on a platform on the steps of the Capitol as he took the oath on the constitution as President of the United States, I thought : the policy of this country towards Poland and Eastern Europe is going together with this man into a new path. Will it really prove new and what will come out of it?

One passage of Kennedy's inaugural speech had a universal application, and thus included the countries of Eastern Europe : 'Let every nation know, whether it wishes us well or ill, that we shall pay any price, bear any burden, meet any hardship, support any friend, oppose any foe to assure the survival and success of liberty.'

After the ceremony of taking the oath, the traditional parade moved off in a snow-storm, watched by the hundreds of thousands of Eskimos into which the population of Washington had changed, lining Pennsylvania Avenue. And as the parade was filling the main streets of Washington with the noise of bands and the stamp of marching thousands, a solitary car was driving through the deep snows of Pennsylvania, going to a distant farm near Gettysburg. It was President Eisenhower, making way for his successor, going to his quiet asylum, to live out there the rest of his life in well-earned peace. 'Le roi est mort, vive le roi !'

Ten days later President Kennedy made his first State of the Union message before the joint houses of Congress, in which one passage was in complete accord with the programme announced at the KPA convention and was a forecast of its realization :

> While our attention is centred on the development of the non-communist world, we must never forget our hopes for the ultimate freedom and welfare of the East European people. In order to be prepared to help re-establishing historic ties of friendship, I am asking the Congress for increased discretion to use economic tools in this area whenever this is found to be clearly in the national interest.
>
> This will require amendment of the Mutual Defence Assistance Control Act along the lines I proposed as a member of the Senate and upon which the Senate voted last summer. Meanwhile, I hope to explore with the Polish government the possibility of using our frozen Polish funds on projects of peace that will demonstrate our abiding friendship and interest in the people of Poland.

It was necessary to adopt an attitude towards this first offer made by the President in an official capacity, so as chairman of the Polish delegation to ACEN I wrote a letter to the press which obtained a good reception, since during the week it was printed in the *New York Times, Washington Post, Washington Evening Star, Chicago Daily Tribune* and *Christian Science Monitor*. It ran : 'We welcome with hope and gratitude the promise made by the President in his State of the Union message of further economic aid to Poland and of using American funds frozen in Poland on projects of peace. If the funds are used to build hospitals, veterans' homes, orphanages, schools, libraries, etc., this will benefit the Polish people and not the Communist régime.'

In both speeches the President stressed all the dangers of the period in which the United States and the world were : these were his words :

> I speak today in an hour of national peril and national opportunity. Before my term has ended, we shall have to test anew whether a nation organized and governed such as ours can endure. The outcome is by no means certain. The answers are by no means clear. All of us together—this Administration, this Congress, this nation— must forge those answers.
>
> Each day the crises multiply. Each day their solution grows more difficult. Each day we draw nearer the hour of maximum danger, as weapons spread and hostile forces grow stronger. Time has not been our friend. We must never be lulled into believing that either power [Soviet Union and communist China] has yielded to its ambitions for world domination—ambitions which they forcefully reiterated only a short time ago. The tide is unfavourable. The news will be worse before it is better. And while hoping and working for the best, we should prepare ourselves now for the worst.

Having heard these passages of both speeches, I sighed with relief. The new President had at any rate full awareness of the fact that the United States and the Western world had already entered the Third World War, conducted admittedly by other arms than all those preceding it, but for life and death all the same. And even though atomic bombs do not burst in this war, yet, in the sphere in which the fight is going on, they are playing no less a role by their very existence and number than by their explosions.

Also the new President saw clearly where to seek for the main elements in deciding this war that was in progress :

> In your hands, my fellow citizens, more than mine will rest the final success or failure of our course. In the final analysis, the hopes of all mankind rest, most of all, upon the pride and perseverance of fellow-citizens of this great republic.
>
> Can we forge against these enemies a grand and global alliance, north and south, east and west, that can assure a more fruitful life for all mankind? Will you join that historic effort?

The fate of the whole world and Poland will depend on the reply which the 180-million American nation gives to this dramatic question.

EPILOGUE

Many things have changed in the world since the memorable November day in 1947 on which Zosia and I set foot on American soil.

We left Poland at a time when the United States was at the height of its military power, with which Russia could not match her strength. The United States had the monopoly of the atom bomb and, on that basis, would have been able to exert pressure upon Russia in order to force her to leave Poland and the other countries behind the Iron Curtain. Now, that monopoly is a thing of the past, because not only Russia but also Britain, France, and Red China have the atom bomb or the hydrogen bomb, while West Germany has it in a well advanced laboratory stage. As the production of the atom bomb becomes cheaper and simpler, it won't be long before Monaco and Andorra can boast of it.

At the time Zosia and I, in disguise, went aboard the Swedish ship that took us away from Poland, Czechoslovakia was half-free, China was under the control of the Nationalist Government of Chiang Kai-shek, no one even thought of the Korean war and the partition of Indochina, and Cuba had a government which was hostile to Communism and which recognized the Polish exile government in London. On the other hand, during that same period of time, Tito was a protegé of the Kremlin and Yugoslavia a loyal member of the 'great family of the socialist nations'. Now Czechoslovakia is a satellite; mainland China has a communist system more ruthless than the Russian; part of Indochina had been set aside as a communist North Vietnam, posing a threat to the rest of South-east Asia, while Cuba is ruled by communist fanatics. Yugoslavia had become a hotbed of a pestilence called Titoism, and her present attitude towards Russia is that of total independence. While in the past, with the exception of Ethiopia, Liberia, and the South African Union, there had been no states in Africa enjoying full independence, nowadays I spend long hours over Africa's modern map learning the names of its new mushrooming states.

In the period 1939-60, the Western powers had granted full independence to forty-one colonies of a total area of 9,995,258 square miles and a population of 801,535,000, and the process of granting independence is still going on. However, in the same period of time the communist empire had expanded its rule to include fifteen new countries occupying a total area of 6,979,140 square miles and a population of 765,007,000.

At the time we left Poland, Stalin was the absolute ruler in the Kremlin and his servile agent Bierut was his counterpart in Poland. Today, Brezhnev and Kosygin are rulers of a different type in that they take account of the Politburo and the Central Committee. Following the Polish 'October revolution' and the Hungarian November revolt, the Kremlin's rule over Poland and other satellites had become weaker than in Stalin's day. It rests upon different premises, not exclusively upon terror and decree. In the old days, Communism used to be a homogeneous doctrine based upon Marx's and Lenin's digma. Today, not only is it contaminated with the heresy of 'Titoism' but it is suffering from such ailments as revisionism, liberalism, opportunism, dogmatism, sectarianism, and orthodoxy, to say nothing of various milder 'colds', such as the thaw and deviations to right or left. It was no one but Khrushchev who, in a speech delivered in June 1960, called for a revision of Lenin's teachings formulated decades ago, because they take no account of the historical changes the world has gone through. What Khrushchev had really thought of Stalin's doctrine is best illustrated by the removal of Stalin's body from the mausoleum in the Red Square in Moscow. Khrushchev abandoned the theory of the inevitability of an armed show-down with the capitalist world and replaced it with the concept of a show-down accomplished by all possible means short of total war. The Soviet theoreticians of Communism are much quieter now in their talk about the inevitability of wars among the 'imperialist' states, as the latter have been living together in peace for a number of years. No longer are they said to be in need of new territorial conquests which would open up for them new sources of raw materials and new outlets for their goods. The reason is that these capitalistic states have done just the opposite by granting freedom to their colonies. And no word is being said any longer about the self-destructive tendencies inherent in capitalism because it had been alive, undergoing transformations, and has been flourishing, as for example in the European Common Market. Finally, no one harps any more on the theories of the rich getting richer and the poor becoming ever poorer in the capitalist states, because the prosperity of the workers in those countries has no match anywhere else in the world and has been steadily growing.

While Eugene Warga, the noted Soviet economist, had fallen into disfavour back in 1949 for stating that the American system would not waste away, the year 1960 saw him restored to grace. Now another Soviet economist, Professor Lieberman, openly speaks in favour of an economy based upon the law of supply and demand as well as upon the element of profit.

Russian living standards have risen considerably. In 1960 the Soviet chargé d'affaires in Bonn, Andrew Timoshenko, went so far as to deliver a lecture at the Polytechnic School in Munich dealing with the 'Soviet millionaires'. Timoshenko stated that in 1940 there were two millionaires in his country; in 1954, 980; and in 1960, 2,000, including 780 multi-millionaires. That last category is made up of the Soviet aristocracy, notably artists, actors, writers, poets, Red Army marshals, big industry executives, and—one jockey. Marshal Konev, being a member of the social élite, owns a palace at the Crimea, a villa near Moscow, a stud farm and a private racing stable. This is not bad at all for a 'workers' and peasants' state'. These examples could easily be multiplied. In short, one can observe a retreat from the Marxist-Leninist doctrine in all important sectors of the ideological front as well as a process one might term the 'modernization of Communism'. As the case of Professor Lieberman and the Soviet millionaires show, there may even be some indication that the Capitalist cancer has been eating away the living substance of Communism.

While in 1947 the peoples of Soviet Russia, held in blind submission by Stalin's iron hand, had shown no sign of independent thought, in recent years a beginning of a ferment has become manifest in the cultural field. Boris Pasternak's name symbolizes that ferment. As elsewhere in the world, so in Russia, among the leaders of that ferment are university students who display a soundly sceptical attitude toward Marxism-Leninism, a tendency towards heresy, as well as an indomitable curiosity about all things Western.

For their part the capitalist countries, too, have undergone changes such as the establishment of a welfare state in Britain, and a similar movement just starting in the United States, which finds its expression in the growing political and economic power of the labour unions, in continuously rising wages, new means of combating chronic unemployment, the ever broadening scope and increasing rate of old age and medical assistance, and finally in a vigorous campaign against the abuses of capitalism. A recent example of the last was the case of the nine high executives of electric

firms who received jail sentences for conspiracy with intent to over-
charge the public. According to Adolf Berle, noted author and former Assistant Secretary of State, five hundred major corporations,
all registered members of the New York Stock Exchange, representing two-thirds of American industry, are no longer owned by five
hundred families but by twelve and a half million shareholders.

So much for the New York Stock Exchange. One should bear in
mind that there are more stock exchanges in the United States.
The war on poverty advocated by President Johnson, and his idea
of building the 'Great Society' point in the same direction.

These examples are indicative of the changes taking place within capitalism; taken together, they are part of the process of uni-
versalization and democratization of capitalism. Accompanying all
this is the revolutionary development of technology, epitomized by
the electronic computer, automation, and man's entry into
space.

These developments of the past seventeen years merely confirm
the old truth that nothing in this world is permanent, and that
everything, including communism and capitalism, is subject to
changes which are brought about not only by wars and revolutions,
but also by evolutionary processes. How will all this end, is a question
so difficult that Hamlet's 'to be or not to be?' is an easy one by comparison. There is no single answer to it. Instead of one, there are
several answers which seem to solve only preliminary issues. One
of these answers is the proposition that while the continuing armaments race, by the nature of things, contains the germ of an atomic
conflict, the changes taking place within the communist as well as
within the capitalist systems are working in the opposite direction
by reducing the differences between them.

In this world picture communist China constitutes a special element. From obedient fosterling of Soviet Russia Red China is changing before our eyes into a giant who has already become independent of Soviet aid and who intends to take first place within
the communist camp. The ironclad rule of life, in which force is the
chief regulator of relations between states, will inevitably push
Soviet Russia down to second place. The fact that the two countries
have the same political system does not rule out conflicting interests, nor does it protect them against armed conflict. In the past,
absolute monarchies waged wars against one another whenever state
or national interests made it necessary, even though their political
systems were identical. Common nationality, especially when it
has a chauvinistic tinge, constitutes a stronger bond than a common political creed. A subscriber to this opinion is President de

*L

Gaulle, who sees in the Soviet Union first of all Russia, which is eternal, and only then a state ruled by a communist system, which is transitory. Soviet-Yugoslav relations provide the best evidence that the same truth is adhered to in all communist systems. If Yugoslavia had a common frontier with Russia, Titoism would have met the same fate as did the Hungarian revolution, which was led, after all, by a communist, Imre Nagy, who paid for it with his head. Today, the world is witnessing an ideological duel between Peking and the Kremlin, a difference in strategy and tactics between the two, a rivalry in Africa and South America, and an altogether amazing clash over tiny Albania. Things have gone so far that the Albanian dictator, who enjoys Red China's mighty protection, has found some of his own subjects guilty of spying for—Russia.

However, the most serious conflict within the communist family is looming elsewhere. It is developing along the Sino-Russian frontier, several thousand miles long, where peoples of the yellow race live under Russian rule. One may surmise without sliding into sheer fantasy that the day will come when the slogan 'Asia for the Asians' will be revived and over-populated China will lay claim to its yellow-skinned kinsmen living across the border in sparsely populated Russian territory. Russia, as the weaker party, will then have to fall back.

God alone knows how the problem of China will affect the process in which the Soviet Union and the United States are the principals. Logically it should bring the Soviet Union closer to the Western world. However, very few historical processes develop logically. By taking over first place in the communist world, the orthodox Chinese, who in principle continue to profess the theory of the inevitability of war with the capitalist world, may even force Russia to wage a hydrogen bomb war against the West, much though Russia would wish to avoid it. We shudder at such a possibility and so I prefer to conclude these risky speculations, even though they may be justified to some extent by the present realities.

A number of revolutionary changes have also occurred among the people who appear in the pages of this book. When I see the bearded face of Fidel Castro delivering a speech from the balcony of the presidential palace in Havana, I am reminded of the former dictator Batista, as he talked to me in the same palace in 1956 about a Cuban national hero who was of Polish descent. He was General Roloff-Mialowski. It would have never occurred to me in those days that the members of the Turkish Parliament—Bozbag, Aktas, and Mrs Tlabar, all three of whom looked after me in Turkey, would be imprisoned on an isolated island, following a military coup, and that minister Zorlu would be hanged. Nor could I have had the slightest presentiment that the vivacious and exuberant Mayor of Manila, whom friends saw as future president of the Philippines, would die suddenly of apoplexy.

Gone from this world also is Pope John XXIII, a true genius who had taken upon himself the form of a parish priest. By convening the Vatican Council for the task of modernizing the doctrine, rites, and organization of the Church, he had ushered it into the nuclear age. His work has been taken over by Pope Paul VI, who was a secretary at the office of the Apostolic Nuncio in Warsaw in the early years following World War I. In October 1963 His Holiness received my wife and myself in audience, during which he spoke a few sentences in Polish, expressing regret that he could no longer speak the language as well as in his Warsaw days.

But the severest blow came with the assassination of President Kennedy. The entire world, friends and foes alike, have endured this blow. So have the Polish people in Poland and in exile. In Warsaw, thousands of people stood for hours in long lines in front of the American Embassy in order to sign a memorial book. The Embassy employees had to help with the flowers that were being placed around Kennedy's statue, which had been hurriedly brought in by a Polish sculptor. Poles living in exile joined the American people in their mourning. They also expressed their sympathy to the president's widow and her small children, who received thousands of letters from Poland.

When Kennedy was laid to rest at the National Cemetery in Arlington, he took with him into the grave the hopes of the Polish people, which were so closely connected with his interest in Poland and his friendly feelings for her.

Likewise, it is hard to pass over in silence the change that has occurred lately in the Kremlin. Nikita Khrushchev, who during his visit in the United States impressed nearly everybody with his fighting spirit and the picturesque personality on which I have dwelt in this book, disappeared from the Kremlin swiftly and without much ado. Fate seems to be terribly unjust, indeed, if we consider that the very features in Khrushchev's behaviour which had been lauded in the past have now been recognized as the reason for his sudden ousting. It turned out that Khrushchev, an enemy of the cult of the individual so far as Stalin was concerned, was after all, not so resolutely opposed to it when his own person was involved. It has now been revealed that Khrushchev, a supporter of collective party rule, had in fact established a personal, arbitrary rule. People were told that he had given precedence to family

(Adzhubey) over party ties. In other words, he was found guilty of nepotism. Finally, it was said that his shoe-pounding performance at the United Nations was not done to produce a calculated effect but simply evidence of his vulgarity. Khrushchev has been replaced by Brezhnev and Kosygin—people without colour and of lesser calibre. Nevertheless, a step has been taken towards the democratization of the party leadership and also away from the Stalinism to which Khrushchev had been gradually reverting.

Noteworthy changes have also occurred recently on the American judicial scene. In Chapter XXIV I deplored the fact that the rulings of the US Supreme Court had been so liberal that they deprived of practical meaning the Smith Act of 1940, directed against subversive activities of the Communist Party, as well as the Internal Security Act of 1950 under which members of the Communist Party must register.

Since then, on June 6, 1961, the Supreme Court has announced new rulings which recognize active membership in an organization seeking to overthrow the government of the United States (in practice this means membership of the American Communist Party) as a punishable offence. As regards the Internal Security Act, the Supreme Court also upheld the duty to register, reversing its own earlier decision and decisions of subordinate courts, under which that duty had been suspended for the past eleven years. In both cases the ruling was based upon a majority opinion of five to four.

However, when it comes to combating communist subversive activity, such gains meant little or nothing in the face of the setbacks which resulted from the unsuccessful, ill-conceived, and amateurishly executed invasion of Cuba in 1961, and the consolidation there of communist rule, achieved with the help of thousands of Soviet advisers, technicians, and massive deliveries of Russian arms. Ninety miles from the American shore, a base had been established from which Communism might spread its tentacles all over the Western Hemisphere; and Uncle Sam, who with a single blow could crush Castro and the latter's cohorts, had been watching it helplessly, restrained from taking proper steps by his own exaggerated respect for the law and for international agreements. A victorious show-down with Khrushchev in 1962 over the Russian rockets has not changed that situation essentially. American national pride and prestige suffered a severe blow. Nothing can repair the damage short of pulling out the thorn that has been stuck in the body of the American continent. The only consolation is that again one can hear the shots fired by Free Cuban guerillas in the same mountains in which Castro had once fought Batista's forces. Perhaps from here the liberation of the unhappy island will come eventually.

What a paradox, that the United States, which does not dare to start armed intervention right on its own border in order to quell the communist contagion in Cuba, has for the same purpose intervened with arms, and justly so, in an area situated thousands of miles away in distant Vietnam, where more and more American blood is shed in the struggle against communist guerillas.

In effect the United States is at war with North Vietnam, though a war has never been formally declared. Nevertheless, scores of thousands of American officers and men have been taking part in it. One might call it a pocket-size Korean war. Yet it carries in itself the germ of a conflict that could engulf not only all Asia, but the entire world. This is how the spark, merely smouldering below the surface at the time of my visit to South Vietnam in 1959, has burst into flames which it is becoming difficult to extinguish.

All these changes merely confirm the truth that the world is moving forward—or backward, depending on the standpoint of the observer. In any event, the world is in constant motion which is gaining momentum. That motion looks more and more like a world revolution. But Karl Marx is not the father of that revolution, nor is Russia its mother. It stems from a swelling tide of rebellion against slavery, violence, poverty, backwardness, and ignorance. The most exciting question is, who will be able to direct the tide. So far, the tide has directed the swimmer.

As far as Poland is concerned, the period 1961-64 has brought about further deterioration of its internal situation both economic and political. Apart from economic stagnation evidenced by considerable unemployment, high prices, and periodical crises on the consumer goods market, further curtailment of freedom has become apparent in areas such as culture, literature and the press. In other words there has been further retreat from the October revolution. It had compelled thirty-four leading Polish writers and scholars to send a memorandum to Premier Cyrankiewicz, which was significant both in its contents and its brevity, because, in just two sentences, it contained criticism as well as a programme for improvement :

> Restrictions in allocations of paper for printing books and periodicals, as well as tightening of press censorship, are creating a situation which is endangering the development of Polish national culture.
>   The undersigned, recognizing that the existence of public opinion, the right to criticize, the freedom of discussion and access to reliable information are necessary factors to progress, and being motivated

by civic concern, demand that Polish cultural policy be changed to conform to the spirit of the rights guaranteed by the Polish Constitution and to the national good.

The reprisals applied against some of those who signed the memorandum brought about a wave of protest from literary, scientific and political organizations all over the world, and also caused repercussions in the United States Congress.

The period 1961-64 was also marked by further increase in the role and prominence of the Security Police, secretly operated by the Ministry of the Interior. Supported by PAX, an organization of the so-called 'régime Catholics', the Security Police was primarily concerned with the persecution of the Catholic Church and the harassment of Cardinal Stefan Wyszynski. On the occasion of the fifteenth anniversary of the Declaration of Human Rights, I published a letter in the issues of December 12, 1963, of the *New York Times* and the *New York Herald-Tribune* and also in the *Washington Post* of December 20th, in which I stated :

> Priests are arrested, seminaries closed, monks and nuns expelled from convents, organized pilgrimages are banned, wayside chapels and crosses removed, parents who baptize their children fired from government jobs, exorbitant taxes are levied on churches, etc. There are instances where church equipment, such as portable organs and vestments, is sold at auctions by tax collectors.

This has resulted, on the one hand, in the ever decreasing freedom of action of the Church and of Cardinal Wyszynski and, on the other, in their growing popularity and influence upon the Polish people.

So much for the situation in Poland. As far as Polish political exiles are concerned, they have continued, without change, their activitiy begun in 1945. Several anniversaries observed in 1964 stirred up in them deep emotions and sad memories. The historical dates included : the twenty-fifth anniversary of the outbreak of World War II; the twentieth anniversary of the battles of Monte Cassino, Falaise, and Arnhem; and the twentieth anniversary of the Warsaw Uprising—the most dramatic of them all. These anniversaries brought about a sort of retrospective national soul-searching which led to the following conclusion : the war was inescapable but the Warsaw Uprising could have been avoided, if the Polish people had known that it could not improve Poland's bad political situation in the international arena. Spectacular celebrations commemorating the Warsaw Uprising were held throughout the world—except in Poland, where the communist régime banned them in an

effort to belittle the importance of the Uprising, because it recalled too vividly the conduct of the Soviet Army, which, after
having reached the suburbs of Warsaw, purposely halted its march
and did not come to the aid of the people of Warsaw.

What vivid echoes the Warsaw Uprising still produces the world
over may be seen in the fact that President Lyndon B. Johnson
issued a proclamation declaring August 1, 1964, 'The Warsaw Uprising Day', in which he stated :

> I invite the people of the United States to observe this day with
> appropriate ceremonies and activities, and I urge them to mark this
> event as an exceptional demonstration of man's courage and devotion.

The signing of the proclamation on July 31, 1964, which actually
marked the beginning of the celebrations in the Western world,
took place in the Rose Garden in the White House, in the presence
of more than one hundred former soldiers of the Polish Home Army,
headed by General Tadeusz Bor-Komorowski, former commander-
in-chief of the Warsaw Uprising, leaders of the seven million strong
American Polonia, and Karol Rozmarek, president of the Polish-
American Congress. Thanking President Johnson for issuing the
proclamation, I said :

> Important as this Proclamation is to the seven million of Ameri-
> cans of Polish descent living throughout this land, it is of even greater
> importance to the thirty-one million Poles living in Poland today. To
> them it is a most welcome assurance that they have the continued
> love and sympathy of the great American nation and of its great
> President.

In conclusion of the festivities marking this anniversary, a commemorative plaque was unveiled on December 12th in Ottawa,
near the tomb of the Unknown Soldier. The plaque was donated
by former soldiers of the Polish Home Army now living in Canada,
to honour twenty-six Canadian airmen killed over Poland while
dropping supplies for the Polish underground fighters. Fifteen of
those airmen had been shot down over Warsaw during the Uprising. The ceremony in Ottawa was attended by the Prime Minister,
Lester Pearson, members of the Canadian government and Parliament, and representatives of the Canadian Army. Present also were
the families of some of the airmen, and about a score of delegations
from the Canadian Polonia, carrying wreaths and banners. In reply
to my address, in which I officially turned the plaque over to the
Canadian people, Prime Minister Pearson said, concluding his
speech :

Shortly after the war, I visited torn and stricken Poland with a United Nations Relief Mission. I shall never forget the haunting scene of carnage and destruction in Warsaw.

I remember on that visit when we were across the Vistula at a small town not far from Warsaw, one of the members of the Polish government of that day saying 'this was the spot, where the fate of Warsaw was decided'. Because that was the spot where the Russian orders were given not to go forward at that time.

I saw also the emergence of the Polish city of Wroclaw from the ruins and rubble of Breslau.

Poland was—and is— a tragic victim of the great war, and the cold war which followed. But once again, it will be—as it has been before —POLONIA RESTITUTA.

INDEX

Abel, Col. Rudolf Ivanowich, 225
ACEN — News, 106
Acheson, Dean, 197
Achilles, 246, 253
Adampol, 178
Adams, Sherman, 122
Adenauer, Conrad, 204, 285, 286
Adesco, Tadeusz, 292
Adzhubey, Alexei, 308
AFL–CIO, 105, 249, 271
Africa, 106, 132, 163, 216, 302, 306
Aktas, Basri, 176, 190, 306
Albania, 47, 103, 230, 232, 247, 252, 281, 306
Aldunate, Roberto L., 134
Alsace and Lorraine, 191
Alsoph, Joseph, 13, 211
Amau Eiji, 166
American Committee for Investigating the Katyn Murder, 78
American Friends of Captive Nations, 268
Ancona, 34, 108
Anders, Wladyslaw, 30, 98, 107, 109, 172
Andorra, 302
Ankara, 176, 177, 178, 204
Antonov, Gen. Alexey, 140
Aramburu, Gen., 133
Arciszewski, Tomasz, 23
Arechaga, Jimenez de, 133
Argentina, 133, 134, 292
Argun, Dielaver, 176
Arlington, 60, 205, 307
Armenia, 247, 252
Armistice Commission in Korea, 89
Arnhem, 310
Assembly of Captive European Nations (ACEN), 103, 104, 105, 106, 120, 122, 131, 133, 134, 135, 138, 156, 159,

160, 162, 164, 165, 169, 170, 173, 174, 182, 183, 191, 192, 194, 195, 199, 203, 204, 246, 247, 248, 249, 258, 265, 266, 267, 268, 269, 273, 275, 277, 291, 293, 298, 300.
Associated Press, 201
Association of Active Struggle, 62
Association of Polish Armed Forces in America, 63
Association of Patriot Priests, 73
Association of Polish Ex-Combatants, 265
Athayade, Astrogesilo de, 132
Athens, 179
Atlantic Charter, 200, 230
Atlantic City, 101
Auschwitz, 103, 268
Australia, 105, 165, 173
Austria, 198, 199, 204
Ayub Khan, Mohammed, 176, 186
Azerbaijan, 247

Babel, 20, 103, 158
Baggio, Sebastian, 134
Baginski, Kazimierz, 17, 24, 25, 26, 32, 33
Baig, M. S. A., 175, 176
Balkunas, Jonas, 268
Baltic Countries, 252, 267
Baltika, 277
Baltimore, 291, 294
Banerjee, Pratap Kunar, 175
Bang-Jensen, Povl, 162
Barros, Pimentel de, 132
Bastille, 38
Batista, Fulgencio, 135, 136, 137, 306, 309
Batory, Stefan, 157
Battle Act, 295, 296
Battle, Laurie C., 295

313